A Political Space

Globalization and Community

Dennis R. Judd, Series Editor

A Political Space

Reading the Global through Clayoquot Sound

Warren Magnusson and Karena Shaw, Editors

Globalization and Community / Volume 11
University of Minnesota Press
Minneapolis • London

Visit the companion Web site for this book at http://web.uvic.ca/clayoquot

Published by the University of Minnesota Press
111 Third Avenue South, Suite 290
Minneapolis, MN 55401-2520
http://www.upress.umn.edu

Library of Congress Cataloging-in-Publication Data

A political space : reading the global through Clayoquot Sound / Warren Magnusson
and Karena Shaw, editors.
    p.   cm. — (Globalization and community ; v. 11)
    Includes bibliographical references and index.
    ISBN 0-8166-4039-4 (HC) — ISBN 0-8166-4040-8 (PB)
    1. Clayoquot Sound Region (B.C.)—Politics and government.   2. Politics,
Practical—Case studies.   3. Environmental policy—British Columbia—
Clayoquot Sound Region.   4. Environmental policy—Case studies.
I. Magnusson, Warren, 1947–   II. Shaw, Karena.   III. Series.
JS1734.C53 P65 2002
320.9711'2—dc21

          2002008344

Contents

Preface

This book invites the reader to explore contemporary politics through a particular site. That site, Clayoquot Sound, appears to be at the *periphery* of contemporary power and authority and thus to be *marginal* to the study of politics. We argue that this appearance is an effect of particular assumptions, assumptions that need to be challenged. Clayoquot (pronounced *Clák-wot*) is more usefully interpreted or "read" as a *center* of interaction among the movements, powers, and authorities that produce the world in which we live. By reading the global *through* Clayoquot—that is, by exploring Clayoquot Sound as a microcosm of global politics—we hope to disrupt the assumptions that constrain our political imagination.

At Clayoquot, we can observe a number of increasingly familiar—but still inadequately analyzed—phenomena: among other things, the shift from an industrial to a postindustrial economy, the rise of environmentalism as a new form of political consciousness, the emergence of postcolonial challenges to existing authority, the development of transnational political movements, the articulation of new forms of science, the recognition of hybrid identities, and the proliferation of new institutions and practices of political negotiation. There are not many sites where these phenomena appear so clearly or in such interesting relations. Moreover, Clayoquot is a particularly interesting example of the disruption of the routines, practices, and assumptions that bind politics to the modern territorial state. When we attempt to understand Clayoquot, it is difficult to pretend that politics is everywhere and always what we have imagined it to be. The same might be said of other places, but we think that Clayoquot is a useful point of entry for those who wish to understand the patterns of contemporary politics.

Some readers will pick up this book because they are interested in

Clayoquot Sound or in the environmental struggles that Clayoquot has come to symbolize. After all, Clayoquot was an important moment in the development of the international campaign against logging in the world's temperate rainforests; for a long time it was the international campaign's poster child. We have tried (within the book itself and on the Clayoquot Project Web site) to cater to the needs of readers who are specifically interested in Clayoquot or in environmental campaigning. What motivates this book, however, is the belief that Clayoquot is much more than *that*, much more than a site of environmental campaigning (however photogenic). The more research we have done, the more interesting Clayoquot has become to us as a place where *other* aspects of contemporary politics—be they gender relations or urban-development conflicts or struggles over the nature of community—come into focus. We want to encourage readers to think about Clayoquot as a site where they can explore features of politics that are characteristic of almost any neighborhood in the world, whether as "near" as the Microsoft headquarters in Redmond, Washington, or the skid row of Vancouver's Downtown Eastside, or as "distant" as the office towers of Hong Kong or the villages of the Philippines.

We are advocating a particular method of inquiry, a method that privileges the site itself rather than the interpretive frame that we bring to it. Clayoquot Sound is our exemplary site. Everyone is now obsessed with reading or interpreting the newly "globalized" world order. We think that many of the extant readings are based on fundamental misunderstandings. Such misunderstandings are almost inevitable if we go from Washington or New York *down* to the local level or *out* to the wild and distant frontier. The political geography that we carry with us, a geography that flows from dreams of imperial domination, always misleads us. In resisting that geography here, we have not freed ourselves from our own delusions; nor could we do so. We have not developed a radically new analysis of global/local or local/global politics. On the other hand, we do believe that the method we have adopted—to read the global *through* the local—is an appropriate one. How else can we hope to loosen the grip of those *political* assumptions that bind us to dreams of empire and obscure other human possibilities?

Obviously, we hope that readers will learn from and be challenged by this book. On the other hand, we may also succeed in a different way if readers are encouraged to go from this book to the Clayoquot Project Web site (web.uvic.ca/clayoquot), there to take up the challenge of reading contemporary politics through Clayoquot and through other sites beyond it, in their own way. Royalties from this book will be used to maintain the site. The site contains a range of useful resources, such as the following:

The Clayoquot Documents: A three-volume set of documents (approximately eight hundred pages) from the Clayoquot conflicts, including public reports, journalistic commentaries, partisan propaganda, economic analyses, maps, statistics, and much else. (The documents are cited by reference number—e.g., CD II/E/6—in this book. A full list of the documents and an explanation of the referencing system for them are provided in the "Research Guide" at the end of this book.) Virtually all the primary material that our contributors have drawn upon is in *The Clayoquot Documents*. The documents can be accessed in full text form, enabling readers to explore, extend, or challenge the interpretations of events developed in the chapters that follow—or, indeed, to develop analyses of events at Clayoquot in relation to other sites, questions, or concerns.

Web Resource Guide: An annotated list of Web resources useful for researching events in Clayoquot Sound, exploring subsequent developments, and examining the contexts within which Clayoquot might be considered. There are resources on indigenous politics in Canada, ongoing forestry disputes, the activities of environmental groups, the development of tourist economies in British Columbia, and so on. A partial list of these Web sites (current at the date of publication) is given in the "Research Guide." Other Web addresses are cited in the references to the Introduction and in Karena Shaw's essay.

Additional resources: A range of other resources for conducting research into Clayoquot Sound, including the proceedings of the workshop from which this book emerged, an extensive "time line" of events at Clayoquot, and an index to *The Clayoquot Archive*, a large research collection now on deposit with the Clayoquot Biosphere Trust.

We encourage our readers to go from Clayoquot to other rich or unusual sites with different circumstances, sites from which we might engage in a global conversation.

Acknowledgments

The Clayoquot Project was seeded by funding from Research Grant No. 410-94-0575 from the Social Sciences and Humanities Research Council of Canada (SSHRC). We are grateful to the SSHRC for its contribution not only to this project, but to other research in the humanities and social sciences in Canada. In recent years, SSHRC has been virtually the only source of funding for Canadian researchers in these fields. Faced with repeated cuts to its budget and ongoing pressures to divert its limited resources into projects with an immediate payoff, the SSHRC has continued to provide some funding for basic research in the humanities and social sciences. Without this support, it is difficult to see how independent academic work in these fields could continue.

For the International Workshop on the Politics of Clayoquot Sound, we received vital support from the International Development Research Centre, the International Institute for Sustainable Development, the Canadian Forestry Service, the Foundation for Ecology and Development, the Canadian Centre for Foreign Policy Development, the Committee on Alternatives for British Columbia, and Lighthawk Air Services. We are grateful to all of these agencies, which supported our work without strings and in a spirit of intellectual openness.

The people who attended the workshop (some of whom have written for this volume) all made substantial contributions to our endeavors. Our thanks go to Laurie Adkin, Charles Agobia, Barbara Arneil, Graham Ashford, E. Richard Atleo, Marlene Atleo, Jan Bate, Tzeporah Berman, Kevin Brown, William K. Carroll, Ben Cashore, William Chaloupka, Solomon Chrom, Juliet Craig, Radhika Desai, Hamar Foster, Maureen Fraser, Fred Gale, Jack Gillie, Joanna Gislason, Robert Hackett, Donna Haraway, Christopher Hatch,

George Hoberg, Lillian Howard, Bill Irving, Anita Krajnc, Thom Kuehls, Valerie Langer, Matthew Lucas, Timothy W. Luke, Karen Mahon, Mary Martin, Martha McMahon, Ross McMillan, R. Michael M'Gonigle, Ashis Nandy, Uma Nandy, Clive Pemberton, Harry Post, Jeremy Rayner, Andrew Ross, Catriona Sandilands, Paul Senez, Gary Shaw, Dhirubhai Sheth, Peter Stephenson, Tom Stere, Duncan Taylor, Christopher Tollefson, James Tully, Nancy Turner, R. B. J. Walker, Adam Wellstead, Geoff Whitehall, R. Jeremy Wilson, and Sharon Zukin.

The then-president of the University of Victoria, Dr. David Strong, the then-associate vice-president for research, Dr. Alex McAuley, and the then (and still!) Dean of Social Science, Dr. John Schofield, were all supportive. The Eco-Research Chair, Dr. R. Michael M'Gonigle, provided us with important material assistance, as did Dr. R. B. J. Walker, coeditor of the journal *Alternatives: Global, Local, Political.* The university archivist, Jane Turner, provided useful guidance in the development of *The Clayoquot Archive.* Many people loaned or donated materials to the archive, or offered assistance in locating materials. We are especially grateful to Joan DuBlanco, Barry Campbell, Maureen Fraser, Ross McMillan, Nancy Turner, and Lorna Walsh, as well as to the Association of BC Professional Foresters, the BC Securities Commission, the Clayoquot Biosphere Project, the Clayoquot Sound Central Region Board, the Clayoquot Sound Scientific Panel, Cortex Consultants, the District of Tofino, the Forest Alliance of BC, Friends of Clayoquot Sound, Greenpeace Canada, International Forest Products, the Long Beach Model Forest Society, MacMillan Bloedel, the Ministry of Aboriginal Affairs, the Ministry of Forests, the Office of the Ombudsman, Parks Canada, the Sierra Club of Western Canada, the Sierra Legal Defence Fund, and the Western Canada Wilderness Committee.

We had invaluable assistance from Valerie Langer, who was principally responsible for fund-raising, did much of the groundwork for both the archive and the workshop, and made crucial contributions to the structure and substance of the project, as well as to our understanding of events at Clayoquot. Andrew Ross created the Clayoquot DataBase, collected most of the material for the Clayoquot Archive, and sustained the project office during the summers of 1996 and 1997. We are especially indebted to him and Valerie. Kevin Brown and Ian Matthews provided additional assistance during the 1996–97 academic year. Tami Jones and Kevin Brown helped with the physical arrangements for the workshop, assisted by Geoff Whitehall, Juliet Craig, and Andrew Ross. Since 1999, we have had further assistance from Delacey Tedesco, Cathy Rhodes, John Twomey, and Matthew Jackson. We are truly grateful for their support—and for the funding that has made it possible to pay these students at some fraction of their real worth to the project.

We have had much assistance from people in the Clayoquot region. We are especially grateful to the Nuu-chah-nulth people, who have shown great patience (as always) with incomers to their land. It is an honor to be touched by their generosity and wisdom. Many other people in Tofino and Ucluelet have also been helpful and supportive. If we do not name individuals here, it is for fear of some unintentional omission, and not for want of remembering people's kindness. The Clayoquot region has often been vexed by outsiders who claim to know what they cannot know. We are grateful to all those who have helped us to proceed to better understandings. It is a tribute to the people of the region that there is such openness to academic inquiry and such willingness to share knowledge.

Royalties from this book will go toward maintaining the Clayoquot Web site and *The Clayoquot Archive*. We hope that these research resources will be useful to people in the region, as well as to scholars more generally.

Warren Magnusson and Karena Shaw
Victoria B.C., Canada, and Keele, England, June 2001

Introduction

The Puzzle of the Political

Warren Magnusson

If ours is a time of "globalization," then the politics of Clayoquot Sound is paradigmatic. It is not really that the politics of Clayoquot (or other such places) involves a movement from the local to the global, or even the other way around, despite what so many contemporary commentators suggest. Rather, the politics of places such as Clayoquot puts traditional distinctions between local and global, small and large, domestic and international—and much else—into serious question. If Clayoquot is paradigmatic, it is because the *puzzle* of politics is especially apparent there. What forms does politics take? How are we to relate to it? In Clayoquot, the appropriate responses to such questions are unclear, and the answers we get from the conventions of political science are not very helpful.

This book is an experiment in political analysis, not least because it is suspicious of the traditional assumption that the containment strategies of modern politics are inevitable and necessary. The state as we know it is an obvious form of containment, in that it separates the politics of one country from the politics of another, but also in the sense that it confines politics to the business of government and puts other kinds of business—economic, social, cultural, environmental, scientific, spiritual, familial, personal—on the other side of a bar. We know, of course, that we cannot really separate one aspect of life from another, nor can we treat countries as if they were completely independent of one another. In a way, we always knew this, but now we are reminded of it every day, when we go on the Internet or turn on the television news. China may be separate from the United States, but it is part of the same global economy, shares the same global environment, and participates in much of the same mass-mediated culture. We certainly can go looking for politics in the corridors of power in Washington and Beijing—

many have done so, and their reports are interesting—but, if we keep look-ing for politics in the places where it used to be, we may soon discover that the world has passed us by. In retrospect, much of the politics of the great capitals of the nineteenth century seems of little interest, since it turned round and round in circles. By contrast, things were happening on the streets and in obscure meetings in out-of-the-way places that gave birth to the movements that have since changed the face of the world: movements against slavery and for the rights of women, nationalist and socialist move-ments, religious revivals, and so on.

The contributors to this book are not all political theorists, and even the political theorists have other academic interests. Nevertheless, the book centers on the puzzle of the political, more than on Clayoquot per se or the issues that have arisen there. This may not always be apparent to the read-er, for we take Clayoquot very seriously as a site of investigation. Readers who simply want to understand the story of a particular environmental conflict, or to learn more about the contemporary struggles of indigenous peoples, or to get a sense of what might be done to resolve conflicts over clearcut logging, community economic development, and globalized tour-ism will find most of the chapters helpful. Political theorists may find it hardest to see that this book is for them. Few disciplines are as hidebound as political theory, tied as it is to a few dozen classics and a handful of ques-tions that have been posed over and over again. To the extent that political theorists have admitted anything new to their deliberations, they have been forced to do so by the attention given elsewhere to various linguistic, cultural, and psychoanalytic thinkers. Foucault, Derrida, and Deleuze, like Freud and Marx before them, have thrown new problems at political theo-rists. So too have the thinkers associated with major social movements, such as feminism and environmentalism. All this is enriching, but the ex-tent to which political theory still consists of meditations on *texts*—even if they are the texts of Jacques Derrida or Judith Butler, rather than Plato or John Locke—is remarkable. In this book, we seek to do political theory in a different way, by beginning from a *site* rather than a text.

No doubt the distinction between sites and texts is problematic. As Derrida would remind us, a site such as Clayoquot can only become intelli-gible textually. We "write" Clayoquot in various ways (as the contributors to this book do). Out of these writings, "Clayoquot" appears, and we think upon it as an object for understanding. In a sense, there is no Clayoquot outside the textual productions of "Clayoquot": every time we seek to bring the ur-Clayoquot (the Kantian thing-in-itself) into view, we produce yet another text that works along with other texts to form our understanding.

Videos and photographs, even the sights and smells of direct experience, are immediately textualized as we circulate them among ourselves as representations of the "real" Clayoquot. The first human inhabitants of the region represented it to themselves in stories that convey the mystery and history of the place. Others have done the same more recently. "Il n'y a pas hors-texte," as Derrida famously said. We do not wish to argue against that conclusion. On the other hand, we are of the view that political theory has been too much obsessed with texts of a particular kind, ones that might be lined up on people's shelves with *The Republic, Leviathan,* and *Das Kapital.* Much can be learned from the study of such texts, but a discipline that gives itself over to their study is in danger of neglecting other sorts of sites.

The point about Clayoquot is not that it is unique. There are many other sites from which we could have begun this inquiry: Clayoquot Sound just happens to be near where we live, on Canada's Vancouver Island.[1] Clayoquot Sound is of special interest to us (and to a number of our contributors), because we have a personal history with it. But that is not the main reason why we have chosen it as a point of entry into the most difficult problems of contemporary political theory. In a way, it is the ordinariness of the site that makes it special. Clayoquot is not the sort of place where important things are supposed to happen. For one thing, it is in Canada, and Canada (as the English would put it) is as boring as Belgium (which is to say as boring as any country in the world, except perhaps for Switzerland). Worse, it is a *small* place in Canada, well away even from the cities that Canadians think are big, such as Vancouver or Toronto (which, in any case, are second-rate places from a certain perspective).[2] Clayoquot is just a tiny speck out there, not at the center of the world, like Washington or New York or Paris. It cannot have determinative power; it is governed, not governing, with respect to the main things that determine people's future. At least that is the way it is supposed to be, if things work the way that we normally imagine. Political theory, in its conventional mode, is a way of worrying about power in its normal forms. So, Clayoquot is outside its purview, except as one of innumerable places at the extreme edges of power. And yet—and we all know this too—the actual plays of power are different from the ones that we have in mind when we do political theory. Things never seem to work the way our models tell us. One of the reasons for this (we want to suggest) is that little places like Clayoquot burst out of their containers and impose themselves on the world. If we are to understand the politics of the twenty-first century, and particularly if we are to come to terms with the *neglected* issues in political theory, we are well advised to begin from places like Clayoquot, rather than from places like Washington or Beijing.

But why should we not begin from a site of violence *over there*, rather than from a peaceful place *near here* like Clayoquot? Wouldn't that allow us to get at more profound issues? Of course, some of the folks at Clayoquot would be surprised to have their place described as "peaceful," because it has been riven by internal conflict for much of the past decade. Nonetheless, the conflict at Clayoquot has been remarkably peaceful by global standards: no deaths, not even any serious injuries. Insofar as Clayoquot has been a site of global struggle—as it has—that struggle has been peaceful. So, shouldn't we have chosen a gorier place, with bodies in the streets? Isn't that what is paradigmatic about the nascent politics of the twenty-first century? The violence? The *horror*, as Joseph Conrad put it? Let's hope not. In any case, we know quite a lot about the things that lead to murderous violence. In fact, conventional political theory is centrally concerned with the ways and means of restraining such violence. That is what the state is about, according to Hobbes, Weber, and many others. Politics, on the other hand, is about more than that. To contain or control violence may be a major political objective, but politics always transcends violence: it generates meanings and establishes forms of life. If we want to understand the new forms and possibilities of politics, we need to raise our eyes above the immediate deployments of violence and counterviolence and look *also* at other things that are happening. To say that Clayoquot has been relatively peaceful is not to say that it has been free from human exploitation, environmental degradation, or genocidal colonization: on the contrary. Indeed, it is a place where the softer violences of modern life play themselves out in ways familiar to anyone anywhere in the world. What is paradigmatic about Clayoquot is that it has *not* been swept into a maelstrom of murderous violence. Whatever we may suppose from watching CNN, the majority of people in the world live in places where they can go to market without much fear that they are going to be gunned down on the way. That is the kind of place Clayoquot is too. It is of particular interest analytically, not because of its violence or lack of violence, but because of the way that local and global politics have become manifest there.

In focusing on Clayoquot we refuse the temptation to search in some foreign place for an exotic "other" to use as a caution or to pose as an example for our own people. Instead, we stay "here" where we are. By being so resolutely local, we are plunged like Alice through the rabbit's hole, and come out "there" in the world at large. One could find similar pathways elsewhere, but in few places is the documentation so rich and interesting. Part of the beauty of Clayoquot as a focus for analysis is that is has been so profusely textualized, as the reader will discover on the Web site that serves as a companion to this book. Thanks partly to this profuse documentation, and partly to the ways in which Clayoquot claimed a space for itself in global politics, the relations—and hence the political possibilities—that are implicit in most sites are made especially visible at Clayoquot. We take advantage of this by inviting readers into this little world, and asking them to think the political *through* it. If we are right about the problem that we face—namely, that we are all accustomed to looking for politics in *central* places and framing our thoughts in terms of the *central* issues defined by previous theorists—then this book will only work as a collaborative effort. The collaboration between editors and contributors has, of course, been important, but more important by far is the prospective collaboration between writers and readers. Together, we have to work out the politics of Clayoquot and other such localities, in order to work out the politics of the world. If readers can see the method in our madness, they may find ways of reading the political that are much more productive than any we have imagined ourselves.

Karena Shaw and I began our collaboration in 1995. This book is only one aspect of an open-ended project. Over a four-year period, we assembled a documentary "archive" of materials about the recent politics of the region. That collection *(The Clayoquot Archive)* is now in the care of the Clayoquot Biosphere Trust in Tofino, British Columbia. From that archive, we drew a selection of key documents that we organized into a two-volume set that we prepared for the International Workshop on the Politics of Clayoquot Sound in May 1997. That workshop drew together community activists, interested scholars from around British Columbia, and a number of international guests, some of whom have contributed to this book. *The Clayoquot Documents,* prepared for the workshop, are now also on-line at web.uvic.ca/clayoquot, along with a third volume that covers 1997–2000. The *Proceedings* of the workshop are also on-line at the same site, together with other relevant materials, including maps and statistics. Readers can follow the links from our site to the sites of the many other organizations that have been involved in the controversies over Clayoquot, and that have offered their own analyses of the place. (Some of these sites offer magnificent photographs, which may convey better than we can why this place has stirred so many people.) The essays that form the central portion of this book were *not* written for the workshop. They were drafted afterwards by workshop participants who had been particularly stimulated by what they had seen and heard. The site we are examining has continued to evolve, and we have tried to take account of that evolution throughout. Nevertheless, we are acutely conscious of the fact that the site we are examining is bound to be different when you, the reader, see these words from what it is now when we, the editors and contributors, write them. For that reason, among others, we urge all readers to use this book in conjunction with the Web site.

Discovering Politics through a Site

As R. B. J. Walker suggests in his essay, the location of Clayoquot (or of any other place) remains a mystery even if we manage to locate it on a map.[3] Indeed, map readings stand in an odd relation to the cultural understandings that we use to locate places. Clayoquot is in the area Americans know as the Pacific Northwest, which means that it is on the eastern shore of the Pacific Ocean. It is a remote, northern settlement, well south of London, England, and on about the same latitude as Paris. It is part of a wilderness settled five to ten thousand years ago, and now dotted here and there with hotels, campgrounds, and high-end resorts. It is largely undeveloped, although it is part of what the United Nations describes as the world's most developed country (as measured by the Human Development Index). To tourists it may seem like a "white" place, although it is home to the Nuu-chah-nulth people, and its shores are dotted with the remnants of Japanese fishing settlements. It is an intensely local community, in which commercial production has been oriented toward the global market for more than two hundred years. (See Timothy Luke's account of this in this volume.) It is a small place in British Columbia, a Canadian province, and yet the politics of land use there has been played out in Frankfurt, Germany, San Francisco, California, and many other places across the Atlantic and the Pacific. To "map" Clayoquot realistically—that is, to specify a location for it that is politically meaningful and to relate the different scales of Clayoquot politics to one another—actually means to discard the image of mapping altogether. The only realistic map of Clayoquot is the sort of account that we attempt to give here, which is not a map at all.

Part of the difficulty that geographers are now having is that maps are largely dysfunctional as means of understanding spatiotemporal relations. Spatiotemporality can only be understood in four-dimensions (if then), and four-dimensional space defies static two-dimensional mapping. The geographers' problem is akin to the economists'. The latter would like to represent the world through mathematically defined exchange relations. Unfortunately for the economists (but fortunately for us humans), the relations that actually determine the way we live transcend exchange relations. In any case, the determinate relations are nonlinear, and rarely susceptible to predictive modeling. Economists try to persuade us to forget everything but the few facts that they wish us to consider, and go on to present accounts of the global economy that bear about as much relation to reality as the imaginings of the fourteenth-century cartographers, who had to fill in bits of the world that were beyond the range of contemporary sailors. We will not be bullied into accepting such pseudoscience. Nor, indeed, will we be bullied into accepting any of the other alternatives on offer, be it the reduction of psychology to an endless series of speculations on the work of Jacques Lacan or the inflation of psephology into a discipline that can pass for political science. Instead, we are starting from the assumption that Clayoquot *cannot* be located—except within social sciences and political theories (the former always being implicitly the latter) that beg the most important questions. We do not pretend to have been able to free ourselves from our own preconceptions, but we have tried to structure this book as an ongoing invitation to exploration and critique, rather than as a definitive account. Whatever the intellectual merits of this approach, it poses a narrative problem: if we want to insist that it is impossible to place Clayoquot on a map or to understand Clayoquot in the conventional terms of social science or political theory, but nevertheless we want to invite readers to *start from here* in rethinking the politics of the present, how are we to initiate the discussion without structuring it restrictively?

Among environmentalists or "green" political thinkers more generally, there is a temptation to think of Clayoquot—and of places like it—in narrowly environmentalist terms. We think that this is a grave distortion—as harmful to green politics as it is to political understanding. Clayoquot is a site where one could examine any or all of the following phenomena:

- the globalization of political struggle through the mass media, cultural exchanges, and international trade relations
- the shift from an industrial to a postindustrial economy dependent on information technology and oriented toward the consumption of signs
- ethnonationalist resistance to the homogenizing impact of the capitalist economy and Western culture
- the global challenge to patriarchal gender relations, as well as to the norms of sexual and personal identity
- the rise of indigenous peoples as credible claimants to sovereignty under international law
- the threat of environmental calamity and the concomitant rise of a globalized environmental movement

- the ongoing critique of state institutions for their political (especially their democratic) inadequacy
- the problematization of science as a contested and highly politicized way of knowing the world

No doubt it was the issue of forestry that brought Clayoquot to the attention of many people outside the region.[4] But, within that issue were all the matters just listed.

If Clayoquot has any presence at all in global political memory, it is as a place where the struggle against clearcut logging in "old-growth" temperate rainforests reached a certain pitch. The environmentalist blockades and mass arrests of 1993 attracted television cameras and made news stories not only in Canada, but also in the United States, Europe, and other places. (See Karena Shaw in this volume for a fuller account.) It was in this context that Clayoquot suddenly "went global," in the sense that it grabbed the attention of the global media, at least momentarily (Magnusson 1999). The effect was impressive enough, from an environmentalist perspective, to make Clayoquot a suitable launching point for a broader international campaign to save the world's temperate rainforests.[5] The environmentalists had only recently decided that the best way of describing the coastal forests of British Columbia, southern Alaska, Washington, Oregon, and northern California was to say that they were part of a vast ancient rainforest, which had already been largely devastated in its southern reaches.[6] If one puts this rainforest onto a map—as Ecotrust, the American environmental organization did—one could see that Clayoquot Sound was almost at the midpoint of this forest, at a place where it seemed logical to the draw the line and say, "No pasarán!"[7] This forest, the environmentalists said, was the largest of its kind, the greatest example of a type of ecosystem that was always extremely rare (M'Gonigle and Parfitt 1994). There were sister forests on the coasts of Chile and New Zealand and there had once been such forests on the Atlantic coast of the British Isles and even on the eastern edge of the Black Sea. But all these forests were threatened, just like the better-known and more extensive *tropical* rainforests. From an environmentalist perspective, Clayoquot was thus at the political center of the ancient forest, at the front line (to change the image) of what remained to be preserved, and an important node of activity in a broader struggle against inadequately regulated industrial forestry.

Clayoquot "went global" in a way that no previous struggle over forestry in British Columbia had—and in a way that no struggle over forestry in the United States has ever done. This was not just a matter of gaining temporary media attention. What might elsewhere or previously have been framed as an issue of government regulation—should the authorities in British Columbia permit this logging or not?—was reframed *politically* as a question that corporate consumers had to resolve.[8] Corporate consumers in the United States, Germany, Britain, Japan, and elsewhere were targeted by environmentalist campaigners as the determinative authorities, and it was assumed that the "publics" to which these authorities responded were the end-consumers of wood products in Europe, Asia, and North America.[9] If one could stimulate the environmental sensitivities of the end-consumers, one could generate anxiety among corporate consumers about possible adverse publicity, and get them to put pressure on the logging companies to "come to the table." Coming to the table ultimately meant working out understandings with the environmentalists, understandings that might well be at odds with the desires of the government. This, indeed, has been the drift of events at Clayoquot since 1994, and it has provided a template for action in the coastal forests of British Columbia more generally. (Karena Shaw discusses this further in her essay.) The political practices developed at Clayoquot through the international "markets campaign" were by no means entirely original. There have been similar campaigns around the production of Nike shoes, the marketing of furs and whale meat, the proliferation of fast-food outlets, the use of child labor, and so on (Klein 2000). Nevertheless, Clayoquot stands out as an important instance of a type of political campaigning that is sure to become more and more common: campaigning *within the global market.*

There was another Clayoquot that sat uneasily with the Clayoquot of the ancient forest. This was the Clayoquot of the Nuu-chah-nulth, the region's first people.[10] (See Umeek's commentary in this volume.) If environmentalists have succeeded in making their presence felt globally in the past three decades, so too have the world's indigenous peoples. The indigenous peoples of Canada, Australia, New Zealand, and Scandinavia have been particularly important in providing leadership within the broader community of indigenous peoples, who number about 300 million worldwide. Indeed, it was at Port Alberni—within Nuu-chah-nulth territory, not far from Clayoquot Sound—that the World Council of Indigenous Peoples was established in 1974 (Manuel and Posluns 1974; McFarlane 1993).[11] Because the Nuu-chah-nulth people had settled the Clayoquot region thousands of years ago, the environmentalist tendency to represent the area as "wilderness" and frame the issue of logging in terms of "wilderness preservation" was often offensive from a Nuu-chah-nulth perspective. In different ways, Umeek of Ahousaht (E. Richard Atleo), Thom Kuehls, and Gary Shaw in this volume all draw our attention to the ways in which the struggles of the Nuu-chah-nulth people to advance themselves on their own territory have shaped a situation that might otherwise have been conceived in crudely environmentalist terms. In large part, the struggles at Clayoquot have been Nuu-chah-nulth struggles for self-determination, overlaid with issues that the environmentalists and their opponents in the logging industry have raised. Even under Canadian law, the Nuu-chah-nulth have rights that trump those of the logging companies, the provincial authorities, and the marketers of ecotourism.[12] In relation to international law and global public opinion, the Nuu-chah-nulth position may be even stronger. Thus, it is no exaggeration to say that Clayoquot represents one of the great, unresolved issues of our time: how are the rights of indigenous people to be properly recognized in a context of globalized economics, contending sovereignties, and cultural hybridity?

It is worth noting that proper recognition of indigenous peoples is probably impossible within the framework of the state system, as normally conceived. Not to put too fine a point on it: the United States of America would have to be dissolved if the rights of indigenous peoples were to be given proper effect. This is only one aspect of what is at stake. One is tempted to say that justice will not be done, because too many people have too much to lose. Be that as it may, the morally powerful claim for indigenous rights has already begun to eat at the structure of state sovereignty, and no more evidently than in British Columbia. Unlike most of North America, but like Australia, British Columbia was a place "settled" under the British Crown without cover of treaty (Tennant 1990; Fisher 1992; Barman 1996; Asch 1998).[13] Thus, there can be no pretense that the original inhabitants of the province gave away their land or sold it to the incomers. On any of the familiar principles of property, British Columbia belongs rightfully to the descendants of its original inhabitants. This is, to say the least, an unsettling idea from an incomer's perspective. It sets conceptions of property, as well as sovereignty, in motion. One of the interesting features of the Canadian/BC/Clayoquot situation has been that the motion has not been toward simple denial. There have, of course, been those who have attempted to move in that direction, but so far the more powerful movement has been toward a new framework of accommodation, one that bends concepts of sovereignty and property to provide more room for indigenous peoples.[14] What has happened in the Clayoquot region is an example of this.

A third Clayoquot has also gained attention, at least in the Canadian media. This is the new Clayoquot of ecotourism, which Timothy W. Luke and Catriona Sandilands discuss in their essays. Tourism has already displaced forestry and fishing as the region's main industry.[15] Obviously, the main thing the region has to offer is its "natural wilderness": the sea and the mountains, beaches and wildlife, hiking trails and campsites, surfing and whale watching, cozy meals in chi-chi restaurants with the waves pounding below on the rocky shore. Industrial forestry and industrial fish farming (or aquaculture, as it is called) pose the most obvious threats to the tourist idyll. If ecotourism is the obvious niche for Clayoquot in the new global economy, the region's prosperity seems to depend on lining business up with the environmentalist cause (and also with the cause of indigenous rights: aboriginal artifacts and aboriginal experience both sell). But such an alignment puts indigenous leaders and environmentalists into an awkward relation with people whose status and livelihood is bound up with the old extractive economy. The shift from industrialism to postindustrialism also changes the character of the labor market to the disadvantage of many men, and this puts traditional gender relations under strain. Fears associated with these changes resonate with the sense that outside forces (sometimes represented by incoming people) are overwhelming "the community" that was there before. So, difficult changes are afoot in Clayoquot, changes akin to the ones affecting many, if not most, other communities. Those changes would have generated much internal tension whether or not there had been controversies over the environment or indigenous rights. The fact that the latter controversies gained international attention and that they have unfolded within political spaces that stretch far beyond the region (as it is understood locally) have at times made the transition exceptionally difficult.

There was and is a fourth Clayoquot: the Clayoquot of the state. Although we have emphasized the ways in which the politics of Clayoquot have burst the bounds of the state—by going global, shifting into the domain of the market, raising issues of recognition that cannot be resolved within the existing state system—we have not meant to deny that the state's presence is important. On the contrary, the story of Clayoquot is partly one of state action to regain control of a situation that keeps spinning out of control. In Clayoquot, the relevant state is Canadian, but many, if not most, of the important powers are provincial, not federal.[16] As Karena Shaw explains in her essay, the BC authorities were involved in a number of efforts to take control of the situation in Clayoquot before it exploded on them in 1993.[17] There were also efforts on the part of the municipal authorities and various local interest groups to develop a consensus solution to the region's land-use problems. The indigenous authorities and the federal government were also drawn in, once the difficulties in the region reached a certain peak. Since 1994, there have been continuous efforts to develop a new framework of local authority that would allow for resolution of outstanding issues and reestablish the authority of the state as a whole. It may appear, at first sight, that the ongoing reconfiguration of local authority is simply a response to the crisis of 1993, when there was a campaign of mass civil disobedience. In fact, the crisis of local authority was already apparent in the early 1980s, and it has not yet been resolved (despite publicity to the contrary). The most effective forms of authority are at one remove from traditional institutions—itself a sign of strain. Clayoquot has been a veritable proving ground for all the latest techniques of governing through consensus, contract, and partnership. These techniques bend the state out of its traditional shape, even as they reinstall it as a frame for authoritative action.

It was in the context of state intervention that a fifth Clayoquot became particularly apparent: the Clayoquot of scientific representation. The British Columbia government set up a Scientific Panel (which is the focus of much of Gary C. Shaw's attention in his essay).[18] That Panel was to generate a frame of scientific truth, within which disputes about Clayoquot could be resolved. Almost immediately, however, the question "Whose science?" was raised: The science of the Nuu-chah-nulth, derived from their observations, oral histories, practices of medicine, gathering of food, and other activities? Or the science of those local environmentalists who had made a particular study of the region? Or the science of the corporations, universities, and government departments that made Clayoquot only a small part of their purview? The methodological differences between these forms of science were substantial, and those differences reflected sharply different understandings of what constituted a "truth." Thus, the effort to arbitrate matters scientifically actually exposed the fact that there is less of a consensus about the nature of science than many people like to pretend. As in disputes about genetically modified foods, the proliferation of scientific and pseudoscientific claims tended to provoke people to make claims of scientific authority on the basis of their positions in the world. This just deepened the authority crisis of science itself. One of the unusual features of the Clayoquot situation has been the effort to reestablish scientific authority by inserting it within a dialogue that affirms the possibility of legitimate epistemological difference. The Clayoquot of scientific representation is thus a site in which the politics of science is particularly apparent.

The Clayoquot of scientific representation, the Clayoquot of the state, the Clayoquot of ecotourism, the Clayoquot of indigenous peoples, and the Clayoquot of the ancient forest are all important. So too are other Clayoquots, such as the Clayoquot of the local community or the Clayoquot of resource extraction. How do these different Clayoquots relate to one another? How, in fact, is any particular representation of the place produced politically? And how is one representation or another made to dominate the place? Isn't this what politics is about: producing the representations that force us to understand a situation as this or that? This is what we have to consider.

Explorations and Investigations

We begin this book with Karena Shaw's "Encountering Clayoquot, Reading the Political." Her intent in this essay is to lead readers through the recent events at Clayoquot, helping to orient them in relation to the analyses that follow. Her account emphasizes both her perceptions as someone who returns regularly to the region and her concerns and sensitivities as a political theorist. As she indicates, it may be well to compare her account with others available on our Web site and in *The Clayoquot Documents*: the complexity of events at Clayoquot means that no one account does justice to the whole story.

The first two analytic chapters are by well-known American theorists of environmental politics: William Chaloupka and Timothy W. Luke. Chaloupka and Luke both pose the problem of Clayoquot as one of politics, and frame that problem in quite general terms. Chaloupka focuses on *strategy,* and in particular on the way that strategy works to narrow the gap between ethical absolutes and political opportunities. As he notes, Clayoquot is a place that invites ethical absolutes: We must protect the ancient forest from the depredations of the loggers! We must recover our homeland! We must defend our community! We must save our livelihoods! What Chaloupka notices is the way that the leading environmental activists at Clayoquot managed to move away from their own absolutes toward an effective political strategy. He draws some broader lessons from this experience about the way green politics—and politics in general—has to be practiced if it is to generate positive change. Luke's analysis is complementary, in that it sets out the political economy of Clayoquot Sound in a way that clarifies the region's position within the new world order: he explains the dangers, difficulties, and political opportunities. Luke puts particular emphasis on the shift from "extractive" to "attractive" models of development, and shows how the environmentalist protests against logging in Clayoquot have worked as "envirotisements" (or ecological advertising) to attract tourists and tourist/retirement development to the region. This shift involves hardships for some and opportunities for others. Luke, like Chaloupka, ends on a note of cautious optimism, and that optimism is keyed to a recognition that communities such as Clayoquot can and do respond *strategically* to the dangers and opportunities of global change. In the first commentary, I take up the problem of contextualizing strategic action: is it to be within the "urban global" or within the old frameworks of state sovereignty? I suggest that sovereignty is a dubious frame.

R. Michael M'Gonigle is also suspicious of the sovereign state, although his reasoning is different. M'Gonigle has been a prominent environmental activist and scholar in British Columbia for two decades, and a strong advocate of the need to rebalance central with local authority, and in the process to transform both. He emphasizes the need for *structural change* to deal with the issues that Luke and Chaloupka discuss. He situates the controversy in and around Clayoquot within the context of other struggles over natural resource extraction in British Columbia, and suggests how people in the province (and elsewhere) could move strategically toward greater control over their local economies (and hence over their lives). Catriona Sandilands approaches the issues more skeptically. As another person who is in a sense "local" but not "native," Sandilands is struck by the way that the Clayoquot region is being reconstructed as a simulacrum of "nature" for the benefit of tourists and retirees. For her, this is deeply troubling. Like Luke and Chaloupka, she nevertheless senses something positive about the way that the region has been politicized. There has been an unsettling of positions, a move toward *dialogue*, an implicit recognition of *hybridity* and *multiplicity* as inevitable and positive features of the politics of Clayoquot. In the second commentary, Sharon Zukin (a prominent urban sociologist) extends the analysis that Sandilands offers, by drawing attention to the way in which the multiple "cultures of nature" in urban localities like hers (New York City) intersect with and in various ways overdetermine the ones that appear at Clayoquot. This brings us back to the issues that Luke posed.

In the next essay, Thom Kuehls focuses on another aspect of the global situation: the ongoing presence of indigenous peoples. Kuehls is fascinated by the implications of the Nuu-chah-nulth's 1984 declaration that Meares Island (in the center of Clayoquot Sound) was henceforth to be considered a "tribal park." He uses that declaration as a key to understanding the assumptions that underpin nonaboriginal declarations of sovereignty. Those assumptions clearly make it difficult for the Nuu-chah-nulth to assert their rights and interests effectively within a discourse of sovereignty. In the third commentary, Umeek of Ahousaht (E. Richard Atleo), himself a Nuu-chah-nulth hereditary chief, pushes Kuehls's analysis further. Umeek's perspective is, of course, global, in that it is rooted in a response to the effects of European and Euro-American colonialism. On the other hand, his understanding is also local, in that it grows out of the understandings of his own people. He challenges us to think of Clayoquot in an entirely different way. Gary C. Shaw takes up a similar theme, but he focuses especially on the report of the Clayoquot Sound Scientific Panel, which purported to put "normal science" (in Thomas Kuhn's sense) into a new relation with local and aboriginal science. Shaw emphasizes the politics of claims to *scientific authority*, and draws attention to *colonizing* practices that have been *gendered* in particular ways. As he notes, the Nuu-chah-nulth have been gravely disadvantaged by those practices, but the issues raised at Clayoquot are of much wider import.

In the penultimate essay, the prominent international relations theorist R. B. J. Walker brings us back to the problem that motivates this book as a whole: the *ontology of the political*. Most analyses of Clayoquot (and other political sites), he suggests, presuppose the answers that they are purporting to seek. We have ready-made categories that tell us what is "there" in places such as Clayoquot, and then we fit the "facts" into the boxes. Walker's plea is, in effect, for a reading of Clayoquot that loosens the hold of these ready-made categories and enables us to think the political more openly. In the Conclusion, we take up that theme.

Notes

1. Nearness is relative, of course. Vancouver Island is quite large: just over thirteen thousand square miles (bigger than Belgium or Maryland and Delaware; three or four times the size of Cyprus or Puerto Rico). A range of mountains runs up the center of the island and divides the stormier and wetter west from the drier and milder east. Clayoquot Sound is a large bay, about a third of the way up the west coast. Victoria, the provincial capital, is about a four-hour drive to the southeast. (This is where the University of Victoria is located.) The total population of the island is more than seven hundred thousand, but fewer than five thousand live in and around Clayoquot Sound. In fact, the entire west coast of the island is sparsely populated. Almost half of the island's population is in greater Victoria, and most of the rest live in a string of settlements along the east coast, facing the mainland rather than the open Pacific.

2. To be precise about the population figures: According to the 1996 Canadian Census, there were 4,243 people living in and around Clayoquot Sound then, including 1,170 in Tofino, 1,658 in Ucluelet, and 1,083 in the various Indian reserves. There has been significant population growth in the region in recent years, but Tofino (site of most of the expansion) still had only 1,479 people in 1999.

It may be worth reminding readers that Vancouver—the third-largest city in Canada (after Toronto and Montreal) and the second-largest in the Pacific Northwest (after Seattle, but ahead of Portland)—is *not* on Vancouver Island, but on the mainland, just north of the U.S. border. About half of British Columbia's four million people live in greater Vancouver. Clayoquot Sound is relatively accessible to Vancouver by ferry and road—about a five-hour trip.

3. That said, we have included a few maps of the area following this Introduction. These maps were the ones used by proponents of the Clayoquot Biosphere Reserve, which Karena Shaw discusses in her essay. As such, the maps were intended to "locate" Clayoquot for the purpose of designating it as a special place under the United Nations' "Man and the Biosphere" program. There are many other ways in which the region has been mapped. To get a sense of the way the area appears to the provincial government, see www.bcstats.gov.bc.ca/data/pop/maps/RegDist/RD23.pdf or www.bcstats.gov.bc.ca/data/pop/maps/rdea/rdea23mp.PDF. One can pick out administrative boundaries and discern settlement patterns on these maps, but one must go to a different government site (www.for.gov.bc.ca/het/Clayquot/T-toc.htm) to understand how the area has been divided up for purposes of forestry. Environmentalists see the region in a different way, one that emphasizes its connections with the larger temperate rain forest on the west coast of North America—and draws attention to the threats implicit in ongoing logging. But neither the environmentalists nor the government are able to represent the area in a way that seems adequate to the Nuu-chah-nulth, for whom it is part of their national territory. See Black (1999), as well as note 10.

4. Forestry is a huge industry in British Columbia, and forestry practices have long been controversial. The best account is in Wilson (1998). See also Drushka, Nixon, and Travers (1993), Marchak (1983, 1995), M'Gonigle and Parfitt (1994), Barnes and Hayter (1997), Tollefson (1998), Marchak, Aylcock, and Herbert (1999), Hayter (2000), and Cashore, Hoberg, Howlett, Rayner, and Wilson (2000). See www.for.gov.bc.ca/hfp/forsite/jtfacts/index.htm for the BC government's summary of the industry.

5. The Coastal Rainforest Coalition (www.coastalrainforest.org) is now the coordinating international organization for the BC campaign. The Rainforest Action Network (www.ran.org), Greenpeace (www.greenpeace.org/~forests/), and the Natural Resources Defense Council (www.nrdc.org) are its sponsors. In British Columbia itself, the Western Canada Wilderness Committee (www.wildernesscommittee.org), Greenpeace Canada (www.greenpeacecanada.org), and the Sierra Club of British Columbia (www.sierraclub.ca/bc) have been prominent in the campaign. Smaller organizations such as the Forest Action Network (www.fanweb.org) and the Raincoast Conservation Society (www.raincoast.org) have also been important in the Great Bear Rainforest campaign (described in Karena Shaw's essay in this volume). The key Clayoquot-focused organization is the Friends of Clayoquot Sound (www.ancientrainforest.org). Relevant maps, photographs, and campaign accounts are available on the Web sites noted. A good place to begin surfing is at the Coastal Rainforest Coalition site, where there are links to many of the other organizations.

6. "According to William Dietrich, the term 'ancient forest' was coined in 1988 by executives of the Oregon Natural Resources Council, a regional group that has played a key role in monitoring timber sales and national forest plans. They dispensed with 'old growth' as too jargony and 'primeval forest' as rather dark and obscure; 'ancient forest,' in contrast, stressed a long-standing, preexistent nature that fascinated people and convinced them to protect it. The term has stuck and has provided a resonant metaphor for efforts to save old-growth forests of the Pacific Northwest" (James D. Proctor, "Whose Nature? The Contested Moral Terrain of Ancient Forests," citing Dietrich [1992]; in Cronon [1996, 278]).

7. See www.ecotrust.org and www.inforain.org. Compare Ecotrust Canada and

Gill (1997). Folk singer Bob Bossin adapted the slogan "No pasarán" from the Republicans who defended Madrid against the fascists during the Spanish civil war of the 1930s. He used it in a song he wrote about one of the first major struggles over forestry in Clayoquot: "Sulphur Passage" (1988). The song was featured in a widely distributed video.

    8. As I note in the first commentary in this volume, the BC authorities have certain advantages, in comparison with their counterparts in Washington and Oregon. Whereas most of the timber-producing land in the United States has been privatized, in Canada most of that land remains in public hands. Except in the territories of the far north (which do not yet have provincial status), the land belongs to the provincial, rather than the federal, government (and so *federal* forestry regulations are not the main issue: the provinces are the key regulators). This is the situation in British Columbia. Logging companies are normally granted exclusive rights in particular areas, on condition that they pay royalties (called "stumpage fees") to the province in its guise as the ultimate landowner. (The most important form of forest tenure is the Tree Farm Licence [TFL]. During the period we are discussing, there were two Tree Farm Licences in the Clayoquot region, one belonging to MacMillan Bloedel [since taken over by Weyerhauser] and the other to Interfor.) The province also determines the annual allowable cut—which might as accurately be described as the annual required cut—and sets other conditions relating to the construction of logging roads, protection of wildlife, and so on. Often the licensee is required to maintain local processing facilities. Thus, the province is able to use its ownership of the land as a way of preventing the logging companies from exporting all the processing jobs elsewhere. American competitors of the BC companies have complained that the BC government effectively subsidizes logging (and restrains open competition) by adjusting stumpage fees and other regulations to ensure that the BC companies retain a comparative advantage in the American market. On this and other issues, see the references in note 4.

    9. See Doyle, Elliott, and Tindall (1997) and Bernstein and Cashore (2000). Compare Magnusson (2000).

    10. There are fifteen remaining Nuu-chah-nulth tribes, one of whom (the Makah) is located in the United States. Nuu-chah-nulth territory extends along the west coast of Vancouver Island from the Brooks Peninsula in the north (past Kyuquot) to Sheringham Point in the south (past Port Renfrew) and then across the Strait of Juan de Fuca to Cape Flattery on the northwest coast of the Olympic Peninsula of Washington state. (For the geographic distribution of the Nuu-chah-nulth tribes, see the Web site of the Nuu-chah-nulth Tribal Council at www.nuuchahnulth.org. The council was formed in 1973. It does not represent the Makah, nor does it represent the Ditidaht in the current BC treaty process [www.bctreaty.net/].) Neither the British nor the Canadian governments signed treaties with the Nuu-chah-nulth, but between 1882 and 1889 the Canadian government established 164 small Indian reserves on Nuu-chah-nulth territory (www.aaf.gov.bc.ca/aaf/nations/nuuchah/nuuchah.htm). The reserves average about thirty hectares. Forty of these reserves, totaling 1,132 hectares, belong to the Ahousaht, Hesquiaht, and Tla-o-qui-aht, the three tribes whose ancestral lands are in the Clayoquot watershed. According to Canada's 1996 census, there were 1,083 people living on these reserves in 1996 (http://www.statcan.ca/english/census96/list.htm). More of the Nuu-chah-nulth live off reserve than on. There are differing estimates of the total Nuu-chah-nulth population, but the figure

is probably less than ten thousand, even including the Makah. The Makah signed a series of treaties with the United States, beginning in 1815. The 1855 treaty (http://digital.library.okstate.edu/kappler/treaties/mak0682.htm) provided for the Makah Indian Reservation (pop. 1,214 in 1990), near the northwest corner of the continental United States.

11. Port Alberni (www.city.port-alberni.bc.ca) is a small city (pop. 19,334) at the head of Barkley Sound, south of Clayoquot. It is in effect the "county town" of the Alberni-Clayoquot Regional District (pop. 33,284). (The population figures given here are for 1999. See www.bcstats.gov.bc.ca/data/pop/pop/mun9699e.htm and www.bcstats.gov.bc.ca/data/pop/pop/rdea/rdea23.PDF.)

12. The legal situation is complex. The key Canadian court decisions are on-line at www.bloorstreet.com/300block/ablawleg.htm and library.usask.ca/native/cnlch.html (the latter for the law prior to 1978). On the current treaty process, see www.bctreaty.net/.

13. For contrasting histories of aboriginal–Canadian relations, see the Web sites of the Canadian Department of Indian and Northern Affairs (www.inac.gc.ca/pubs/information/treaty.html), the BC Ministry of Aboriginal Affairs (www.aaf.gov.bc.ca/aaf/history/history.htm), the Assembly of First Nations (www.afn.ca/About%20AFN/history_of_the_afn.htm), the Union of BC Indian Chiefs (www.ubcic.bc.ca/landquestion.htm), and the Nuu-chah-nulth Tribal Council (www.nuuchahnulth.org).

14. Of course, there is no guarantee that the movement will continue in the same direction. The new Liberal government of British Columbia, elected on May 16, 2001, is thought to be unsympathetic to the claims of First Nations. (The Liberal Party denies this: see www.bcliberals.com/Campaign_2001/Platform.shtml.) The BC Liberals (no relation to the federal party of the same name) won a huge victory in the election, taking 56 percent of the popular vote and all but two seats in the legislature. (The left-of-center New Democratic Party [NDP] had been in power for ten years.) The BC Liberals, like the federal Alliance (a right-wing party that has, for the moment, displaced the Conservatives as the official opposition in Ottawa) opposed the only treaty recently negotiated with BC Natives, that with Nisga'a people in northwestern British Columbia. Now in government, they have scheduled a referendum to establish new principles for negotiation. Natives have denounced the referendum, and urged people to boycott it.

15. See www.bcstats.gov.bc.ca/data/bus_stat/tourism/trr_an97.pdf for information on the growth of tourism in the region. Also see the Web sites of the Tofino–Long Beach Chamber of Commerce (www.island.net/~tofino/) and the Pacific Rim Tourist Association (www.alberni.net/~pacrimtourist/). Information at www.bcstats.gov.bc.ca/pubs/bcbi/bcbi9905.pdf indicates that tourism is catching up to forestry, in terms of its contribution to the BC economy.

16. The province generally has jurisdiction over lands and forests, whereas the federal government controls coastal fisheries. "Indians and Indian Lands" are under federal jurisdiction, but most of the land that could be used to settle outstanding native claims belongs to the province; therefore, as a practical matter, the province is involved in aboriginal affairs.

17. As Wilson (1998) explains, efforts of this sort were not confined to the Clayoquot area. One thrust of the BC government under the NDP (1991–2001) was to

develop negotiated solutions to forestry and wilderness issues, solutions that would be acceptable to all "stakeholders." The results were mixed. See Gawthrop (1996) and Harcourt and Skene (1996) on the NDP's first term in office. Carty (1996) offers more academic commentary.

18. See Scientific Panel for Sustainable Forestry Practices in Clayoquot Sound (1994a, 1994b, 1995a, 1995b, 1995c).

Works Cited

Asch, Michael, ed. 1998. *Aboriginal and Treaty Rights in Canada.* Vancouver: University of British Columbia Press.

Barman, Jean. 1996. *The West beyond the West: A History of British Columbia.* Toronto: University of Toronto Press.

Barnes, Trevor J., and Roger Hayter, eds. 1997. *Troubles in the Rainforest: British Columbia's Forest Economy in Transition.* Victoria, B.C.: Western Geographical Press.

Bernstein, Steven, and Benjamin Cashore. 2000. "Globalization, Four Paths of Internationalization and Domestic Policy Change: The Case of Eco-Forestry in British Columbia, Canada." *Canadian Journal of Political Science* 33:1 (March): 67–99.

Black, Martha, ed. 1999. *Out of the Mist: Treasures of the Nuu-chah-nulth Chiefs.* Victoria, B.C.: Royal British Columbia Museum.

Carty, R. K., ed. 1996. *Politics, Policy, and Government in British Columbia.* Vancouver: University of British Columbia Press.

Cashore, Benjamin, George Hoberg, Michael Howlett, Jeremy Rayner, and Jeremy Wilson. 2000. *In Search of Sustainability: British Columbia Forest Policy in the 1990s.* Vancouver: University of British Columbia Press.

Cronon, William, ed. 1996. *Uncommon Ground: Rethinking the Human Place in Nature.* New York: W. W. Norton.

Dietrich, William. 1992. *The Final Forest: The Battle for the Last Great Trees of the Pacific Northwest.* New York: Simon and Schuster.

Doyle, Aaron, Brian Elliott, and David Tindall. 1997. "Framing the Forests: Corporations, the B.C. Forest Alliance, and the Media." In *Organizing Dissent: Contermporary Social Movements in Theory and Practice,* ed. William K. Carroll, 2d ed. Toronto: Garamond Press. 240–68.

Drushka, Ken, Bob Nixon, and Ray Travers, eds. 1993. *Touch Wood: BC Forests at the Crossroads.* Madeira Park, B.C.: Harbour Publishers.

Ecotrust Canada and Ian Gill. 1997. *Seeing the Ocean through the Trees: A Conservation-Based Development Strategy for Clayoquot Sound.* Vancouver: Ecotrust Canada.

Fisher, Robin. 1992. *Contact and Conflict: Indian-European Relations in British Columbia, 1774–1898.* Vancouver: University of British Columbia Press.

Gawthrop, Daniel. 1996. *Highwire Act: Power, Pragmatism, and the Harcourt Legacy.* Vancouver: New Star Books.

Harcourt, Michael, and Wayne Skene. 1996. *Mike Harcourt: A Measure of Defiance.* Vancouver: Douglas & McIntyre.

Hayter, Roger. 2000. *Flexible Crossroads: The Restructuring of British Columbia's Forest Economy.* Vancouver: University of British Columbia Press.

Klein, Naomi. 2000. *No Logo: Taking Aim at the Brand Bullies.* Toronto: Alfred A. Knopf Canada.

Magnusson, Warren. 1999. "State Sovereignty, Localism, and Globalism." In *Canadian Politics*, ed. James P. Bickerton and Alain-G. Gagnon, 3d ed. Peterborough, Ontario: Broadview Press. 57–78.

———. 2000. "The Globalization of Political Space: Reflections on Clayoquot Sound," in *Prospects for Development in the Asia-Pacific Area*, ed. Robert E. Bedeski and John A. Schofield. Canadian Western Geographical Series, vol. 37. Victoria, B.C.: Western Geographical Press. 79–95.

Manuel, George, and Michael Posluns. 1974. *The Fourth World: An Indian Reality*. Don Mills, Ontario: Collier-Macmillan Canada.

Marchak, M. Patricia. 1983. *Green Gold: The Forest Industry in British Columbia*. Vancouver: University of British Columbia Press.

———. 1995. *Logging the Globe*. Montreal and Kingston: McGill-Queen's University Press.

Marchak, M. Patricia, Scott L. Aylcock, and Deborah M. Herbert. 1999. *Falldown: Forest Policy in British Columbia*. Vancouver: David Suzuki Foundation and Ecotrust Canada.

McFarlane, Peter. 1993. *Brotherhood to Nationhood: George Manuel and the Making of the Modern Indian Movement*. Toronto: Between the Lines.

M'Gonigle, R. Michael, and Ben Parfitt. 1994. *Forestopia: A Practical Guide to a New Forest Economy*. Madeira Park, B.C.: Harbour Press.

Scientific Panel for Sustainable Forestry Practices in Clayoquot Sound. 1994a. *Report of the Scientific Panel for Sustainable Forest Practices in Clayoquot Sound*. Report 1 of 5. Victoria, B.C.: Cortex Consultants.

———. 1994b. *Progress Report 2: Review of Current Forest Practice Standards in Clayoquot Sound*. Report 2 of 5. Victoria, B.C.: Cortex Consultants.

———. 1995a. *First Nations' Perspectives Relating to Forest Practices Standards in Clayoquot Sound*. Report 3 of 5. Victoria, B.C.: Cortex Consultants.

———. 1995b. *Sustainable Ecosystem Management in Clayquot Sound: Planning and Practices*. Report 5 of 5. Victoria, B.C.: Cortex Consultants.

———. 1995c. *A Vision and Its Context: Global Context of Forest Practices in Clayquot Sound*. Report 4 of 5. Victoria, B.C.: Cortex Consultants.

Tennant, Paul. 1990. *Aboriginal Peoples and Politics: The Indian Land Question in British Columbia, 1849–1989*. Vancouver: University of British Columbia Press.

Tollefson, Chris, ed. 1998. *The Wealth of the Forests: Markets, Regulation, and Sustainable Forestry*. Vancouver: University of British Columbia Press.

Wilson, R. Jeremy. 1998. *Talk and Log: Wilderness Politics in British Columbia*. Vancouver: University of British Columbia Press.

Mapping Clayoquot Sound

There are various ways of locating or "mapping" Clayoquot Sound. The following maps are the ones that were included in the 1999 proposal to establish a Clayoquot Sound Biosphere Reserve.

Readers unfamiliar with the area should note the size and location of Vancouver Island, as indicated in Figure 1. The only well-settled part of the island is on the east coast: from Victoria, past Nanaimo, to a point about midway along the coast. Vancouver and Seattle are on the mainland, just to the east of the area in the inset. The Biosphere Zones in Figure 2 were designated as such by the proponents of the Biosphere Reserve. The Zones are keyed to the Protected Areas that are marked in Figure 3. The Principal Settlements noted in Figure 4 are all quite small: Tofino and Ucluelet are the largest, and neither of them has a population of more than two thousand. The various native villages—that is, the ones other than Bamfield and Hot Springs Cove—are much smaller. Generally, the areas that have been in dispute with respect to logging are the ones outside the "Core Protected" Zones noted in Figure 2.

For other sorts of maps, including ones that show the location of Indian reserves, the boundaries of Tree Farm Licences, and so on, visit the Web Sites noted in our Research Guide. See the Introduction, notes 3, 7, and 10, for further guidance.

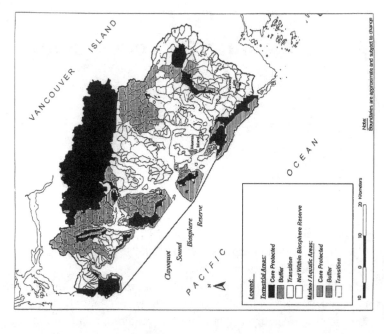

Figure 2. Clayoquot Sound biosphere zones

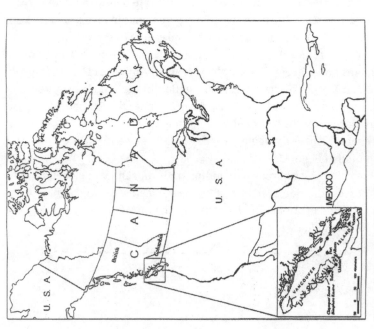

Figure 1. Location of the Clayoquot Sound Biosphere
Reserve

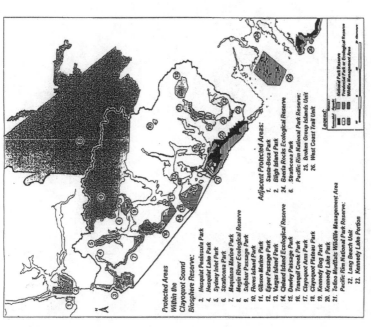

Figure 3. Protected areas in and around the Clayoquot Sound Biosphere Reserve

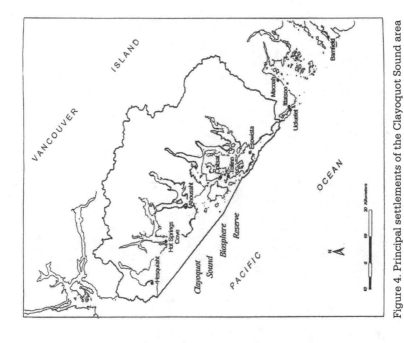

Figure 4. Principal settlements of the Clayoquot Sound area

Encountering Clayoquot,
Reading the Political

Karena Shaw

I first arrived in Tofino—the main non-Native village in Clayoquot Sound—for a three-week visit on December 20, 1988. Just getting to Clayoquot Sound was a striking experience: a two-hour ferry ride from Vancouver to Vancouver Island, then a three-hour drive over rugged mountains, with not so much as a house or gas station for the last hour or so. At the end of the road was Tofino: a sleepy, rain-drenched hamlet. I knew little about the politics or history of British Columbia, even less about the precise region I was visiting.[1] I was an American university student on holiday. Nevertheless, I was soon drawn into the politics of the place.

My first encounters were highly encouraging. They made me think of Tocqueville's descriptions of democracy in early republican New England (Tocqueville 1990, 62–83, 248–53): here in Clayoquot was civic engagement of a kind that I had not encountered while growing up in California's Central Valley. I went to a meeting sponsored by the Tofino–Long Beach Chamber of Commerce. It was part of the local community's response to a bitter conflict that past summer over road building and future logging plans in Sulphur Passage, a pristine area in the heart of the Sound.[2] That conflict had not been the first: there had been an even more dramatic controversy over logging on Meares Island in 1984.[3] The village looks out on Meares, where a lovely sugarloaf-shaped mountain seems to rise up from the sea itself. The village's water is piped over from Meares, so the question of logging there is especially sensitive. In any case, things had evolved to the point at which people were assembling to hear two reports on the region's future: one from Ric Careless (CD II/B/1)[4] and the other from Robert Prescott-Allen. The reports were impressive: Careless explored the region's potential as a tourist destination, and Prescott-Allen described how the principles and practices of sustainable development, expressed in the United Nations' recently published World Commission on Environment and Development Report (Brundtland and the World Commission on Environment and Development 1987), could be applied within the region. What impressed me most were the responses of the audience. Although there was some suspicion about the proposals, participants engaged in a vibrant and engaged conversation about the way a sustainable development planning process might work in Tofino. There was certainly no consensus about priorities—some emphasized the need to limit the clearcut logging of the region, others expressed concerns about the overexpansion of tourism, still others talked about alternative forms of economic development, justice for Native peoples, and so on—but the spirit of the meeting suggested that here was a community with an engaged, proactive vision of its own future.

This impression was reinforced, in my own mind, by the community's response to an oil spill that began washing ashore on New Year's Eve. Within twelve hours the village had mobilized: groups patrolled the miles and miles of beaches after each high tide, collecting bag upon bag of thick, corrosive, tarlike oil; a command center kept track of where oil was washing up, directed people to remote beaches, and organized the pickup of collected oil; local businesses and individuals donated food and organized a "soup kitchen" for volunteers; others set up a facility for cleaning and rehabilitating oil-soaked birds, seeking advice on how to proceed by telephone. The tiny, remote community came to life and seemed to move with one purpose and enormous effectiveness. The number of people participating was very high. Other things in the village came to a halt as everyone focused on removing the oil as quickly as possible: with each high tide the ocean delivered more oil, in smaller chunks more and more difficult to collect. It was not until many days later that the provincial government made an appearance— a few folks in helicopters surveying the scene—and longer still before any government-organized help arrived. Volunteers, however, streamed into the area from Vancouver, Victoria, and beyond to pick up the slack as the locals began to fade from exhaustion.

As I observed these events, it seemed to me that the situation in Clayoquot Sound was both extraordinary and important. The community was seeking to challenge a narrative about its future that seemed inevitable to most observers and many participants: that the Sound would be clearcut logged by large multinational logging corporations (as much of the rest of Vancouver Island had been); that the profits from this logging would flow to the urban headquarters of these corporations; and that the local inhabitants—Nuu-chah-nulth and non-Natives—would be left to carry on with their local affairs, coping with whatever impacts (positive or negative) the logging had on their livelihoods. This was, after all, the story of British Columbia, and indeed of much of Canada. Given this, images of David and Goliath—or even Don Quixote?—came to mind.

However, the vision and ambition of the community—the energy, commitment, experience, and resources of the people involved—suggested to me that if any community could achieve what they sought, this one should. After all, the region had a lot going for it: a relatively small population, great natural resources, well-established institutions of liberal democracy, and a favored geographic location in relation to both Canada and the United States. If such a community were unable to seize some control over its future, this would be deeply troubling.

I left Clayoquot Sound inspired and intrigued by the place, its peoples, and the challenges they faced. My curiosity brought me back soon after, and since then I have been coming and going from there, alternately living amid its complexities and observing it from far away. It has never ceased to be an engaging, intriguing, and deeply challenging place. The attraction is not difficult to explain: it is a place of spectacular beauty, and my response to it mirrors not only that of most who visit the region, but that of many who have, over the years, arrived for a visit only to stay for a year, a decade, or a lifetime. I was, however, also drawn by the challenge it posed to me as a student and teacher of politics. My observation of and participation in events there has continually reminded me of the complexity, richness, and *difficulty* of effectively thinking and acting politically. Time and again, Clayoquot, more than anything in my formal studies, made me realize the limitations of how we understand—and teach—politics today.

Although the task the peoples of Clayoquot had chosen was monumental, it also seemed relatively straightforward: to disrupt the inevitability of the narrative that threatened the place they held dear, to assert some control in relation to the landscape surrounding the community, as well as the local economy. What surprised me most about events that followed was not their success—although that in itself was impressive—but two other things: what their success required, and what it revealed. In order to disrupt the narrative about the future of Clayoquot Sound, a whole assumed terrain of politics had to be called into question: the issue was not just whether or how logging should occur, but who should decide. Based on what authority? Democratic? If so, expressing whose will? The local people's? (Which ones?) Provincial voters'? International consumers'? Perhaps it should be decided on scientific authority? But whose science would be used? Interpreted or practiced by whom? These questions provoked others: Who did "own" Clayoquot? What was Clayoquot "for"? Should it be put to the "use" of local people? Should its wealth fill provincial coffers? Shareholders' pockets? Nuu-chah-nulth economies? Ecotourist operators' accounts? Or, indeed, should it be left "pristine," and removed from human economies?

All of these are intensely political—as well as historical, moral, economic, administrative, and ecological—questions. They generated debates not only in Clayoquot Sound, but, as events proceeded, across Canada (CD III/B/4, CD III/C/3, CD III/C/8, CD III/C/11, CD III/D/5–6); in shareholder meetings in the United States, the United Kingdom, Germany, and Japan (CD IV/9, CD VI/7, CD VI/18); in town councils and the European Parliament (CD V/A/8); in courtrooms and international media (CD III/D/1–3, CD II/E/11, CD III/D/8).[5] I would never have predicted the scale, complexity, and intensity of conflicts that lay ahead of the region as I observed members of the community debating possible sustainable developing strategies and picking up oil off beaches in 1988. Nor, I think, did anyone else: ultimately, the disruption of the narrative future of Clayoquot Sound involved not only those in the region, but people at diverse sites around the world.

Some believe the problems I heard about in that meeting in 1988 and that came to a head in 1993 have finally been resolved, thanks to a 1999 memorandum of understanding (MOU) between the main contending parties and the agreement that led to the area's designation as a United Nations' Biosphere Reserve in the spring of 2000. The truth is that the most difficult issues in Clayoquot are still unresolved, or have simply been displaced onto other areas.

This has been manifest most obviously in the struggle to create new and possibly different futures in the Sound, a struggle that has proven extremely difficult: slow, uncertain, intensely and sometimes bitterly contested, and exhausting. There is a constant, weary struggle to keep things from slipping "backwards" into familiar narratives, and a much more tenuous and difficult-to-grasp sense of what the alternative might be. Both parts of this equation—the disruption of familiar assumptions and terrains of politics and the struggle to articulate different futures from those we have inherited—pose crucial challenges to all who are interested in politics, whether as students and teachers of politics, as activists, or as citizens. It is in this sense that I see Clayoquot as a microcosm of politics: the particularities of Clayoquot may be unique, but the underlying tensions—the questions and problems at stake there—are not.

That said, there is no way of analyzing these underlying tensions without engaging with the particularities. In this essay, I will introduce readers to events in the region, and to some of these particularities, in much the same way that I was introduced: as an outsider coming from a foreign country. My account should be checked against other histories of the struggles in and over Clayoquot; some of these histories (most of which are brief and quite readable) are on-line in *The Clayoquot Documents.*

My account proceeds in three parts. The first focuses on the period from 1988 to 1993, when Clayoquot Sound was forced into the public eye, and struggles focused primarily on framing the future of Clayoquot as a political issue. This was a period when, even as the provincial government attempted to contain the conflicts through "sustainable development" processes, the conflicts kept exceeding its efforts. It culminated with the mass protests of the summer of 1993: the period when the region was most prominently in the glare of international media attention. The second section covers the period from 1994 to 1997, which was inaugurated by two new provincial government containment strategies that had the effect of shifting the locus of political conflict out of the public eye. Rather than a time of dramatic protests and arrests, this was a period of the micropolitics of committee meetings about scientific epistemology, management plans, and techniques of implementation, on the one hand, and international markets campaigns, showdowns at shareholder meetings, and secret negotiations, on the other. The third section brings events up to date, exploring the developments that enabled the designation of the region as a United Nations Biosphere Reserve in 2000, and suggesting that the issues at stake in Clayoquot were re-posed, rather than resolved, by the Biosphere Reserve designation. Rather than a resolution, the designation suggests yet another refiguring of the terrain of politics in Clayoquot Sound.

Politicizations: First Nations, Sustainable Development, and Community Conflict

My second visit to Tofino, in January 1991, introduced me to a much more complicated political landscape than I had first encountered. I quickly realized that my earlier sense of a unified community with shared aspirations was only partly accurate. Although there was a shared desire among the local communities for more control over their futures, there were significantly different visions of both what this meant and what it should lead to. During the period leading up to 1993, much of the local political terrain was absorbed by competing efforts to frame what kind of a problem was manifest at Clayoquot, and thus what kind of solution should be applied. Perhaps the most prominent struggle was between local environmentalists, who insisted that clearcut logging was the problem and wished to preserve intact ecosystems, and the provincial government, which believed that environmental protests were the problem and wished to preserve an economy dependent on resource extraction. However, as we will see, this was only the most obvious, and by no means the most important, struggle over how the issues should be framed, however much it functioned to conceal the much more complex struggles at the local level.

I arrived amid the threat of a boycott against most Tofino businesses organized by the local Nuu-chah-nulth First Nations. For some time, the Nuu-chah-nulth had been running a former residential school site—located on a small beach near town, and bordered by two tourist resorts—as a modest tourist hostel.[6] They had decided to petition the federal government to change the site's official designation to "reserve land," which would give them jurisdiction to develop it into a tourist resort.[7] They had an offer of partnership from the Best Western resort chain, and were hoping to develop an attractive resort that would bring much-needed income and employment to the region's Native peoples. When they requested a letter of support for their application from the Tofino village council, a number of local businesspeople organized a petition of opposition. Their stated concerns were that the development was inappropriate to the site, and that having a "reserve" on the beach would make the beach less attractive to tourists. The Nuu-chah-nulth challenged this position, accusing them of racism and of a desire to eliminate competition for their own businesses. The village council was swayed by the business opposition, though, and refused a letter of support (Harper n.d., 88). The Nuu-chah-nulth responded with the threat to boycott all local businesses. As plans for the boycott proceeded, charges of racism flew fast and furious. The local environmental group, the Friends of Clayoquot Sound, organized "antiracism workshops."[8] Non-Native residents argued among themselves about how to respond, with some organizing a counterpetition and others rallying in support of the first petition.

In the years I had been away, the level of politicization and engagement of the region's First Nations had dramatically increased, and this in turn had fundamentally altered the character of regional politics. The change was the result of a number of events. One was the continuing fallout from the first antilogging blockade in the region, in 1984 at Meares Island, where Tofino residents and members of the Clayoquot/Tla-o-qui-aht[9] band of the Nuu-chah-nulth had combined their efforts to prevent logging on the island. The blockade had been temporarily resolved when the Tla-o-qui-aht declared Meares Island a "tribal park" (CD II/A/1) and, in support of this declaration, applied for and received an injunction to halt logging on the island until their outstanding land claims were resolved (CD II/A/2; CD II/D/5). The injunction had given the residents of Tofino some breathing room: their viewscape and the watershed that provided their drinking water would not be logged in the short run.

For the Nuu-chah-nulth, however, this was but the beginning of a long and expensive legal struggle to establish their title to Meares Island. Although some Tofino residents made efforts to raise funds to support this legal action, the brunt of it was (and is) borne by the Nuu-chah-nulth. Simultaneously, a number of other developments significantly raised the profile of Native politics in Canada, including the 1990 confrontation at Oka between Mohawk warriors and the Quebec police (York and Pindera 1991), which spawned sympathetic information blockades in Tofino and elsewhere across Canada (Harper n.d., 88). In addition, a range of legal decisions in British Columbia and elsewhere in Canada effectively strengthened the legal status of Native land claims.[10] These high-profile events combined with the success of the injunction preventing logging on Meares Island to encourage Nuu-chah-nulth leaders to be more assertive in relation to local political issues. However, their experience of being left holding the bag in the Meares case had also made them cautious in their support of environmentalists. It seemed that although the Nuu-chah-nulth might contribute to environmental struggles in the Sound, the consequences of their contributions would fall largely on their own communities. This caution turned to suspicion when local environmentalists were unable get the Tofino village council to support the Nuu-chah-nulth's application for a tourist resort. As they attempted to gain more self-sufficiency and continue their legal struggles, the Nuu-chah-nulth not only received little support, they were prevented from participating in the emerging tourist economy by the very people who were benefiting from the Nuu-chah-nulth's efforts to protect Meares Island. The acrimony that accompanied the boycott made it clear that, although there was considerable support for Native rights among the non-Native population of Tofino, this support did not extend to a majority of the local electorate. The effect of this was the exposure both of important political divides within the non-Native communities of Tofino and of divides between Native and non-Native political interests.

As the Nuu-chah-nulth boycott moved from planning to reality, other tensions began to surface, particularly in relation to the now-ongoing sustainable development processes. The meeting I had observed in 1988 had borne fruit. Following it, the community had put together its own Steering Committee on Sustainable Development, composed of local representatives: a village alderman; a logger; a fisheries technician; the owners of a construction business, a tourist business, a fish processing plant, and a marine supply business; and a member of the Chamber of Commerce. Its work had proceeded apace: community meetings solicited residents' views on past, present, and possible future economic development for the region

(CD II/E/10). The level of engagement and agreement was very high. However, once burned by their experience in the earlier Meares Island planning process—in which long hours of work to produce community-approved plans for the future of the island had resulted in the logging company (MacMillan Bloedel) walking away from the table and the provincial government completely ignoring the planning team's recommendations (CD II/A/2)—the Steering Committee feared its efforts would be in vain unless it could solicit government sanction for and participation in the process. This led it to approach the government in August 1989 with a report on the Committee's work to date and a request for government support for a more extensive sustainable development process (CD II/C/1). Some residents would later argue that this relinquishing of local authority was a significant strategic error, as it formally extended the conflict beyond the locale of Tofino.

The provincial government agreed to support such a project, but also asserted control over it, significantly expanding both the representation on the negotiating team and the terms of reference for the process. Although still organized on a consensus model, the new process (called the Clayoquot Sound Sustainable Development Task Force) was based on sectoral representation and included representatives from a much broader regional and resource perspective. The new process included three representatives from Tofino, but also representatives from Port Alberni, Ucluelet, and the Alberni-Clayoquot Regional District,[11] from the two logging companies with interests in Clayoquot (Fletcher Challenge, Canada and MacMillan Bloedel), from the IWA,[12] Ministries of Environment and Regional Development, and the Nuu-chah-nulth Tribal Council. Not surprisingly, the broader representation introduced new levels of difficulty into the process.

In particular, the new Task Force quickly ground to a halt over the contentious issue of whether and where logging should be allowed to proceed while the Task Force's work was ongoing. Environmentalists became concerned that the process had been turned into a "talk and log" process—a way to keep environmentalists and local residents busy while logging proceeded apace. They sought a good-faith commitment from logging and government interests to at least reduce, if not halt, logging while the process continued. They argued that the government should encourage diversification of the economy by providing job retraining for any loggers whose jobs might be affected by a reduction in logging. However, with other members of the process firmly committed to representing the interests of their sector, no one had any impetus to give ground on the issue, and the process quickly stalled (CD II/D/4; CD II/D/5). The response of the government was to reorganize the process for a second time into the Clayoquot Sound Sustainable Development Strategy Steering Committee (CSSDSSC), implementing some changes in the structure and terms of reference, expanding the representation on the board yet again, and, more important, relieving the committee of the responsibility for deciding on short-term logging plans. These decisions it referred to the BC Cabinet in hopes that relieving the committee of this responsibility would enable it to focus on longer-term issues.

The new CSSDSSC cautiously began work, and everyone anxiously awaited the Cabinet's decision on short-term logging, believing that it would be the crucial indication of whether the government would support any changes to "business as usual." The caution was also an effect of the toll these processes were beginning to take on the lives of those involved. The Task Force had dragged on for six months, and some local participants were beginning to resent the impact the endless meetings had on their lives, not least as the representatives of some sectors were paid employees of the industries whose interests were at stake, whereas locals were generally participating while also trying to maintain their businesses, families, employment, and so on. When the Cabinet's decision on interim logging came down, the environmentalists felt their fears were confirmed: the rate of cut in the region showed little change, and the Cabinet sanctioned logging in a watershed that the environmentalists considered pristine (CD II/E/2). In the end, the two environment representatives chose to withdraw from the process in protest (CD II/E/3). One of the tourism representatives, concerned about the apparent failure of the government to commit to a diversification of the economy of the region, also resigned (CD II/E/4). The government announced that despite the rupture of the consensus-based process, it would continue without the participation of those sectors whose representatives had resigned. The environmentalists geared up to do everything they could to discredit the process: the truce was over and the battle over logging, on hold since 1988, began anew.

Signs of the battle quickly appeared. Soon after the provincial government's decision to permit new logging, and in the same week as the Nuu-chah-nulth boycott of Tofino businesses began, a logging bridge was burned beyond repair in an act of sabotage. MacMillan Bloedel responded by driving logging machinery into Tofino in the early hours one morning and loading it onto a barge to be transported to the logging site. With the reporter from the local paper snapping photos, the barge began its journey across the harbor only to hit a rock and dump its cargo overboard (Harper, n.d., 96). Environmentalists were gleeful, but the anger and frustration in the air was palpable. Not only was the town of Tofino internally divided, but the

Nuu-chah-nulth communities were still angry at Tofino's refusal to support their economic diversification efforts, and both Ucluelet and Port Alberni— the two closest non-Native towns—rallied in support of the logging industry and rained criticism on the "cappuccino-sucking urban environmentalists" who had "invaded" Tofino. Over the next few months, the environmentalists turned their attention to plans for direct action and the building of international coalitions to support their efforts. Meanwhile, the CSSDSSC continued and the Nuu-chah-nulth boycott, though eventually resolved (ibid., 108), left lasting resentment and suspicion in the communities. Rising tensions were reflected in acts of vandalism, shouting matches in parking lots, and a sense of anxiety as people further committed to hardened positions (ibid., 89, 96, 105–6).

I got a rather different perspective on what was at stake in conflicts over the Sound when, toward the end of the summer of 1991, I volunteered to help a well-known local whale researcher, Dr. James Darling, with a new project he was undertaking. He had been commissioned by the Hesquiaht, the Nuu-chah-nulth band whose territory covers the northernmost reaches of the Sound, to do an inventory of the condition of all of the resources they had traditionally harvested from their territory. This project involved first combing through oral histories that had been collected from Hesquiaht elders by anthropologists in the 1950s, looking for references to resources they had traditionally harvested from their environment, and where and how the resources were collected. We then mapped the locations of all of these resources, and headed out to locate them and evaluate their current condition.

It was a fascinating project. The first thing that struck me was the sheer number of species the Hesquiaht had used from their environments. Whereas their forests were now being devastated (the Hesquiaht's territory has been heavily impacted by clearcut logging) for two or three species of tree, in the past they had harvested dozens of different species from the forests, many more from the marine environments (Turner and Efrat 1982). In addition to the obvious ones—salmon, herring, seal, shellfish—were many others, including grasses, herbs, seaweed, cedar bark, berries of all kinds, sea creatures I had never heard of, and whales.

The precision, specificity, and accuracy of the information we were working from was amazing. In some cases, a particular species would be harvested during only one week of the year, with its condition being carefully monitored to determine the precise timing. In other cases, a resource would only be located in one specific and remote place that could only be reached with difficulty and might only be visited once a year—hence the necessity of knowing precisely when the resource would be ready for harvest. Some of the resources were quite easy to locate and verify, but on many days we would set out on what appeared to be a wild-goose chase. One day we were in search of high-bush cranberries (a plant none of us had ever positively identified before). In pouring rain, we followed what seemed to be impossibly vague instructions: walk up a riverbed for about fifteen minutes, then turn left and walk through the forest for another ten minutes and there we would find the patch of high-bush cranberries that the Hesquiaht harvested once a year. Walking up the river in the pouring rain was no easy task, and walking through the forest was nearly impossible. We were convinced we were about to become hopelessly lost (we were without our Hesquiaht guide that day), but it was beautiful and remote and we had the feeling of being the first to see each change in the light and scenery, so we continued. We reached where we thought we were supposed to be, laughing at the impossibility of finding our way back, let alone anything resembling a cranberry bush. And there we spotted what was clearly a patch of high-bush cranberries, perfectly matching our guidebook description. We shook our heads in amazement, convinced the plants must be everywhere and now we would be able to identify them on our way back to the boat. But we did not see another one in the rest of our week of tramping up and down rivers. Again and again the information contained in the reports would be astonishingly accurate, leading us to species and regions we had not known existed.

I had to leave long before the study was completed, but I had gained a very different view of the "wilderness" of Clayoquot Sound, and a deep respect for the way that it was known, cultivated, and supported by the Nuu-chah-nulth. The experience also affected Darling, who went on to join with other locals to form a new organization, the Clayoquot Biosphere Project (CBP), a project in part geared toward developing scientifically rigorous data similar to and compatible with the traditional knowledge of the Nuu-chah-nulth (Greer 1997, 23–24).

By the time I returned to Clayoquot Sound in the summer of 1992, the Clayoquot Biosphere Project was hard at work. Its formal mission was to be a nonprofit research and education organization, committed to pursuing and facilitating research into intact temperate rainforest ecosystems. The creation of the organization was partly motivated by the belief that to the extent that decisions about the future of the region were being made on scientific grounds, they were being made in the absence of adequate scientific data about the precise ecosystems affected. The existing scientific data often consisted either of studies done on other kinds of forest ecosystems or of short-term studies, as opposed to the kind of long-term, precise data that emerge from careful observation across seasons and years, such as the traditional knowledge of the Nuu-chah-nulth. The CBP was also, however, motivated by a desire to develop community-based research that engaged and was responsible to local communities. Its aspiration was to create a research center similar to the one at Woods Hole, Massachusetts (Ecotrust Canada and Gill 1997, 76), one that would not only bring world-class researchers to the area, but would provide education, training, and opportunities for local researchers, especially First Nations, and would contribute to the diversification of the local economy by guaranteeing its status as a prime destination for major research projects on intact temperate rainforest ecosystems. It was also hoped that the government might hesitate before granting a logging permit for an area that was involved in an extensive research project that could not be replicated elsewhere.

The Clayoquot Biosphere Project was only one example of an explosion of political activities as all participants in the Clayoquot struggles sought to establish claims to what mattered most about the region. Various environmental organizations were by then conducting a range of campaigns. The Friends of Clayoquot Sound rallied local support for direct action, and lobbied international environmental organizations to take up the cause of temperate rainforest protection. The Western Canada Wilderness Committee (www.wildernesscommittee.org) began building a trail into a pristine area to encourage visitors to view the threatened ecosystem for themselves. Ecotrust (www.ecotrust.org) brought international journalists to the region, encouraging them to compare the struggles in the region with struggles to preserve tropical rainforests in Central and South America in hopes of shaming the BC government into better forestry practices (CD II/E/11, CD III/D/5–6). All sought to focus a maximum of national and international media attention on the region. Reporters and film crews working in German or Japanese became a not-uncommon sight. In response, logging companies joined together to form a new public-relations organization—the Forest Alliance (www.forest.org)—and the government of British Columbia dramatically expanded its international public-relations work on forestry issues (Doyle, Elliott, and Tindall 1997).[13] In Ucluelet, an industry-sponsored community-based "Share" group, on the model of the Wise Use movement in the United States, gained strength, expressing concern about the future of logging jobs and local economies and rallying support for logging interests at a community level (CD II/D/2, CD V/11). The CSSDSSC, meanwhile, rambled on toward its conclusion.

All of this happened in the context of massive transformations in the local economies. Each year, commensurate with the media attention focused on the region, tourism grew by leaps and bounds.[14] New hotels, restaurants, cafés, bed-and-breakfasts, whale-watching and nature tour companies appeared, seemingly overnight. Local "information centers" attempted to educate tourists either to the viability or to the tragedy of clearcut logging in Clayoquot Sound. This changing local economy had the effect of disrupting the daily lives and patterns of residents who had lived in Tofino for generations: complaints abounded about long lines at the grocery store, nowhere to park, crowded beaches, local hangouts overrun by strangers, and the frantic pace of life as everyone (else) struggled to cash in on the new economy. Fear of the alternative—being squeezed out by the new economy as house prices and property taxes skyrocketed, rental housing became unavailable as every extra room was converted to a bed-and-breakfast, or the town simply became unlivable—also haunted conversations. Often the blame for these changes—and the resulting alienation of the community—was laid at the feet of the environmentalists who seemed intent on directing endless attention to the region. Many people wondered if their contributions to struggles to halt clearcut logging would have the effect of saving the region from one evil only to have it overrun and destroyed by another.

The summer came to a close with the Friends of Clayoquot Sound blockading a logging road, shadowed by an increasingly aggressive contingent of pro-logging "Share" supporters. Interactions between the two groups were heated. The blockade resulted in sixty-five arrests (CD V.2, 370), and the Friends of Clayoquot Sound promised that this was only the beginning. They were right, as it turned out.

When I returned for the summer of 1993, it was to swirling discontent. Environmentalists were vowing that it would be the summer of a thousand arrests, though no one—not even them—was sure this was anything more than brave talk. There were enough indications to create a stir, though: the international efforts of the FOCS were beginning to pay off, with the creation of a new globally oriented network for the conservation of Clayoquot Sound and with increasing interest in Clayoquot by some heavyweight international environmental organizations such as Greenpeace (CD III/A/1; CD III/C/2; CD III/C/11, V.1, 252). The European Rainforest Movement had presented a letter endorsed by twenty environmental organizations to the Canadian embassy stating that it would be advising consumers not to purchase wood products from Clayoquot Sound (CD V.2, 371). Preparations for blockades and posturing for media attention reached a fever pitch, with the planned "kickoff" on July 1: Canada Day. There was a collective holding of breath, with the government and the logging industry hoping the environmentalists were bluffing, and the environmentalists hoping they were not.

The events of the previous several months had ratcheted up the conflict considerably. In the previous fall, the CSSDSSC had come to its final awkward conclusion: after a failure to reach consensus, it forwarded a few "majority options," strongly criticized not only by some of its members—especially representatives of mining and tourism interests—but by many other parties as well (CD II/E/12; CD V.2, 371). The matter was turned over to the provincial government. The government had changed in the fall of 1991, when the social-democratic New Democratic Party (NDP), out of office since 1975, had returned to power. The NDP had support from the forestry workers' unions, but also from aboriginals and environmentalists. It had promised to bring an end to the "War in the Woods," and had to this point seemed open to environmentalists' concerns. Early in its tenure, the new government had announced a plan to commence a series of extensive roundtable discussions—the Commission on Resources and Environment (CORE)—across Vancouver Island (although excluding Clayoquot Sound, because of the ongoing CSSDSSC) on the development of future land-use plans, and committed itself to creating further protected areas (CD III/D/2; Wilson 1998). Both won praise from environmentalists.

The new year brought two developments that tempered such praise. First, the NDP purchased a large block of shares in MacMillan Bloedel, the logging company with the largest interest in Clayoquot Sound, thus becoming for a time the largest single known shareholder (CD III/C/8; CD V.2, 371). Second, in a dramatic announcement on a hill overlooking Clayoquot Sound, the government presented its "solution" to the Clayoquot problem: the Clayoquot Land Use Decision (CLUD) (British Columbia 1993; CD III/B/5). Billed as a "compromise solution," the decision predictably pleased virtually no one, though the logging companies and Share groups quickly rallied to support it. For the environmentalists, however, it became the lightning rod for their campaigns.

Although the decision increased the protected spaces in the Sound, much of the new protected area was either shoreline or bog forest, with many of the pristine watersheds, mountain viewscapes, and rare ecosystems left unprotected (Sierra Club of Western Canada 1993). Although some other parts of the Sound were designated "special management areas," there was no indication of the conditions under which they might, or might not, be logged. Worst of all for the government, the NDP's purchase of

MacMillan Bloedel shares gave the appearance of a conflict of interest, with the government having little motivation to protect the region (Seaton 1993). By now the profile of the region was such that environmentalists could easily make the argument that this treatment was not good enough for Clayoquot Sound: as the largest remaining relatively intact temperate rain-forest ecosystem on Vancouver Island, it was simply too special and too rare to risk its ecological integrity. This argument played very well, especially in Europe, where populations were not reliant on the forest industry for their economic well-being and where the idea of such wilderness is especially appealing.

Resistance to the CLUD was further strengthened by the response of the Nuu-chah-nulth, who complained that the government had once again made unilateral decisions about huge tracts of land that were subject to unresolved land claims without consulting them. Their complaints were later upheld by the ombudsman for British Columbia (McCallum 1993; CD III/C/9; CD V.2, 380), triggering a series of developments that would prove to be crucial.[15] The objections of the Nuu-chah-nulth were especially embarrassing to the NDP because they followed upon the NDP's commitment to commence a massive effort to negotiate modern treaties with the province's First Nations (CD V.2, 377), most of whom had never signed treaties and thus still had claims to most of the province's land base (Tennant 1990; Fisher 1992).[16] This combination of Nuu-chah-nulth and environmentalist criticism, combined with the appearance of a potential conflict of interest on the part of the provincial government, rendered the CLUD a huge liability, exacerbating the problem of Clayoquot Sound for the NDP. It was a liability not least among portions of the party's own membership: many longtime NDP supporters tore up their membership cards in protest over the decision. Despite an enormous public-relations campaign—including mailings in support of the decision to every house in British Columbia (CD III/B/5) and trips by government (including the premier) and industry spokespeople to Europe and the United States—the decision became the catalyst for the explosion of protest that characterized the summer of 1993.[17]

July 1 saw demonstrations against the CLUD at Canadian embassies and high commissions in England, Australia, Germany, Japan, and the United States. No logging roads in Clayoquot Sound were blockaded by environmentalists, however, as they faced a counterblockade organized by Share supporters hoping to keep them out of the woods. This standoff lasted a few days before the protesters were able to stage their first blockade, complete with a Canadian Member of Parliament (Svend Robinson) and a Member of the European Parliament (Paul Staes). Although there were no arrests

(Svend Robinson would be charged one year later and sentenced to fourteen days in jail) (CD V.2, 372), there was keen media coverage, much of it casting a skeptical eye on the number of blockaders and predicting a fizzle in environmentalist support. The next few days' blockades passed similarly, with crowds of between fifty and one hundred people and an average of eight to ten arrests each day. The blockades were very carefully choreographed; they were peaceful and well organized, designed to attract support rather than to actually prevent logging from happening. Each day the protesters would stand on the road in the predawn; forestry workers would arrive and the injunction ordering the protesters off the road would be read (CD III/C/1); those who did not wish to be arrested would move off the road and the Royal Canadian Mounted Police (RCMP) would arrest those who remained. The logging trucks would drive through and the event would be over for the day. This structure was in some contrast to earlier blockades, where smaller numbers of supporters had pulled stunts—locking their arms together with bike locks inside cement-filled barrels, suspending themselves on the end of logs carefully positioned to block the road such that if moved the protesters would be dropped into the river below, and so on— designed to slow down the loggers for much longer periods of time. But the strategy had changed: the emphasis now was on attracting the broadest possible support, and thus the blockades were as orderly, peaceful, and predictable as possible, encouraging even the timid to join the protest. Often the Share-organized counterprotests were much noisier, angrier, and more chaotic.

The strategy worked. Even as media attention began to fade, the number of protesters began to grow. The face of the protest began to change as the participants became more diverse in age, appearance, and occupation. Slowly, incredibly, day by day the momentum of the blockades built, defying the jaded eye of the skeptics. Each day, word of the number of arrests would fly from mouth to mouth over morning coffee in Tofino, and the feeling of amazement grew. Each evening, a few people would gather briefly at the Friends of Clayoquot Sound office to view the evening news and see what the world was watching.

Special "theme days" were organized: forestry workers, elders, farmers, deaf persons, women and children, clergy, and businesspeople each had their day of protest. Celebrities began to appear in Clayoquot, drawing yet more attention. Cover stories appeared in *Maclean's* (CD III/C/11), the *Globe and Mail* (CD III/B/4), the *San Francisco Chronicle* (CD III/C/7), and other international media.[18] In a carefully staged visit, Robert F. Kennedy Jr. and representatives from his organization, the Natural Resources Defense Council (www.nrdc.org), came to pledge support for the Nuu-chah-nulth in their struggles for justice. Kennedy was given an honorable welcome, carried ashore in a traditional carved canoe, given masks and artwork, and a new relationship was formally cemented. Well known for the assistance his organization had offered the James Bay Cree in their fight against the Great Whale Hydro project, his visit attracted significant media attention (CD III/D/8; CD III/C/11). On July 15, amid much fanfare, the rock band Midnight Oil arrived to give a free concert in support of the protesters. The Nuu-chah-nulth at the last minute requested that the concert not take place at the site of the protest, so the concert was moved to "the Black Hole," the large clear-cut that was the site of the protesters' "Peace Camp." A crowd of more than five thousand showed up, logging was stopped for the day, and the concert was broadcast live on MTV and its Canadian counterpart, MuchMusic. The international profile of Clayoquot Sound continued to grow.

As the arrest toll mounted daily, the momentum appeared unstoppable. For those who supported the protesters, it was an exhilarating time: surely now, finally, the government would see that it had to change its approach. Although most of the faces on the blockade and the vast majority of those arrested were strangers to Tofino residents, there was a strong core of support for the blockade in town. Local businesspeople quietly donated supplies to the Peace Camp, helped with logistics, and visited from time to time. When the camp was blown down by a large storm, many town residents opened their doors to shelter more than ninety protesters until the camp was rebuilt—no small feat for a town of only a thousand in the midst of its busy tourist season. The support for the protest was low-key, however, as the public face of the town was focused on accommodating the swarm of summer visitors.

The Peace Camp, located twenty-five minutes from town by car, developed into its own thriving community. Governed according to nonviolent, ecofeminist principles, the entire community met each evening to plan the next day's activities, still operating by consensus despite the large numbers of people involved. The camp was not without conflict, of course, but there was a genuinely engaged spirit as people arrived each day and were immediately granted a place in the self-government of the group. Many protesters later said that the experience of the camp had a much more lasting effect on them than the actual arrest experience (CD III/C/2–4; CD III/D/7; McLaren 1994). Often bombarded from the outside by angry pro-logging supporters, the camp banded together and maintained an energy of its own, silently supported by, but very separate from, the bustling tourist town of Tofino.

The protests had by now reached a scale where their daily nuances became news: charges for arrestees were changed from "civil" to "criminal" contempt of court; buses of "Victoria businesspeople supporting Clayoquot" en route to the blockade were themselves blockaded by logging trucks as they tried to drive through Port Alberni in the predawn; two separate "mass arrest" days resulted in 309 and 242 arrests, respectively, and successfully halted logging for one day each; the first arrestees were sentenced to what seemed to many to be excessively long jail terms; blockade leaders were arrested and charged with "aiding and abetting" criminal activity (they were quickly released, as the RCMP feared they would lose control over the protests without the leaders). The latter two events had particularly strong reverberations across Canada, as prominent lawyers, judges, and activists expressed concern about the apparent suppression of the democratic right of protest. This prompted debate about the appropriateness of civil disobedience and the treatment of the protesters (CD III/D/1–3). By the end of August, the arrest toll was more than eight hundred, and public opinion polls suggested strong opposition across British Columbia to logging Clayoquot Sound; nevertheless, the government remained silent. Environmental leaders began to express puzzlement about how the government could sustain its position under the weight of criticism it was receiving.

With fall approaching, the government's strategy emerged: with a two-pronged effort, it sought to pull the rug of legitimacy out from under the protesters' feet. First, it announced that the Nuu-chah-nulth would be one of the first First Nations to begin treaty negotiations with the provincial government. As part of this process—and partly as a way to mollify Nuu-chah-nulth leaders in the wake of the ombudsman's decision in their favor on their CLUD complaint—the government and the Nuu-chah-nulth negotiated an Interim Measures Agreement (IMA) that gave the Nuu-chah-nulth significant control over the management of resources in Clayoquot Sound during the treaty negotiation process (CD IV/3). By apparently transferring authority away from itself in this way, the government reorganized the strategic terrain for environmentalists. Now the environmentalists could not necessarily use the treatment of First Nations as a justification for their own activities, and they would potentially have to confront First Nations if the latter chose to approve logging plans in areas the protesters sought to protect. By apparently bringing the Nuu-chah-nulth "onside," the government sought both to increase its own legitimacy and to drive a wedge into the tenuous relationship between environmentalists and First Nations. It was a classic "divide-and-conquer" strategy, but its effects reverberated far beyond such strategic motives.

The second key element of the government strategy was the announcement of a "Scientific Panel for Clayoquot Sound" (CD III/C/14; CD III/C/15; CD IV/2). This panel, to be composed of "world-class" specialists, was to survey all available scientific information about the temperate rainforest ecosystems of Clayoquot Sound and come up with the most scientifically rigorous standards anywhere for environmentally sustainable logging in the Sound. In other words, scientific authority was being harnessed to stitch together the now yawning gap in political authority of the provincial government.

This two-pronged strategy—designed to give the provincial government some leverage to increase its international legitimacy, now badly damaged both by the summer of arrests and by the more sustained international campaigns—received significant attention from media, not least because the government promoted it heavily in an international media campaign. Environmental groups reacted very cautiously to both aspects, saying all would depend on the specific results each produced. Almost everyone else retreated, exhausted, to recover from a long, difficult summer. The exception was the Friends of Clayoquot Sound, who worked to create support networks for the hundreds of arrestees who continued to face trial.

Even as the protests wound down, and the new government strategy began to unfold, all parties seemed to pause and take stock of the situation. The environmentalists had succeeded beyond their hopes: the extent of support for a change of policy toward Clayoquot had been more loudly proclaimed than they had hoped. However, they had not achieved anything concrete: not one tree in Clayoquot Sound was protected from logging. A new strategy was necessary. The provincial government, bruised and battered, having repeatedly failed in its containment strategies, could only hope that its more recent efforts would be more effective. For the Nuu-chah-nulth, the situation looked brighter than ever before: their claims had at least been recognized; they had been given control over some resource management decision making in the short run, and would be one of the first Native groups to enter treaty negotiations with the provincial and federal governments. How this might translate into longer-term political gains remained uncertain, however. Local residents of Tofino and Ucluelet were perhaps the most stunned. In a few short years, their sleepy, resource-extraction-dependent communities had been transformed: not only splashed across media in faraway places, but increasingly invaded by visitors from those places. Some felt their livelihoods increasingly threatened, and others began to cash in on the new economy, but all shared a sense that their region's future had been taken out of their control, however much they disagreed about who was to blame. The early enthusiasm for a sustainable development process as a means of achieving local control and authority seemed very distant indeed.

Mediations: The Micropolitics of Scientific Authority, Community Control, and International Markets

Over the winter of 1993–94, the mass trials of protesters kept the Clayoquot spectacle in the public consciousness, even as it moved away from the Sound to the law courts in Victoria. With few precedents to guide them, judges were forced to tread new legal ground in dealing with the protesters. In order not to "clog" the courts, the decision was made to try the protesters in large groups. However, the logistics proved virtually impossible, with the result that many protesters and legal observers argued that some arrestees had been denied basic legal rights (CD III/D/1–3; CD III/D/7; MacIsaac and Champagne 1994). Sentences were drastically inconsistent. The courts were accused of pandering to the NDP, and the bad publicity for the provincial government continued. In a particularly ill-advised move, the Crown maintained aiding and abetting charges against Tzeporah Berman, one of the protest leaders, for more than a year, inciting outrage and inspiring a high-profile campaign against the government for suppressing democratic rights (CD III/C/10).[19]

In the early spring, a pro-logging demonstration at the legislature in Victoria reminded the province that the issues raised the previous summer remained unresolved. In what was billed as the largest political gathering ever at the legislature, fifteen to twenty thousand loggers, their families, and supporters descended on the capital in vehement opposition to the NDP's CORE process, which had just tabled a recommendation that the annual allowable cut of timber on Vancouver Island should be reduced (CD IV/6). Although the demonstration was not directly in response to Clayoquot, the choice of tactics was in part a response to the previous summer's protests, as were the anger and fear at the prospects for the logging industry in British Columbia. Although it lasted only one day, the demonstration was a stern reminder of the vise the NDP was in: many of those who had traveled to Victoria to display their displeasure with the government's policies had also voted for the NDP in the previous election.

Although these two events extended the memory of the previous summer's protests, by the spring of 1994 the political terrain of the struggle over Clayoquot Sound had fundamentally shifted. There would be no return to the mass protests of 1993. On the contrary, events early in 1994 signaled a very different character and locus for Clayoquot politics.

In the same month as the pro-logging demonstration, there was a less visible, but equally powerful, development in environmentalists' international campaigns, now coordinated by groups such as Greenpeace (www.greenpeace.org) and Rainforest Action Network (www.ran.org). Over the previous year, the international campaigns had become increasingly focused on pressuring companies that purchased large volumes of forest products to cancel contracts with the companies that harvested in Clayoquot Sound. The environmentalists claimed a significant victory when two large companies from the United Kingdom—Scott Paper and Kimberly-Clark—both canceled pulp contracts with MacMillan Bloedel after Greenpeace and other international environmental organizations threatened them with a consumer boycott. Although each of the contracts was for less than 2 percent of MacMillan Bloedel's total sales, the cancellations caused the companies considerable concern, as they feared a "snowball effect." Partly as a result of the cancellations, MacMillan Bloedel, the Nuu-chah-nulth, and Greenpeace began informal, private communications in search of common ground that might lead to a truce. These talks were secretive, but in the long run would have important implications for the way events unfolded in Clayoquot (CD IV/8).

Other key developments that spring involved the evolution of the two processes the provincial government had set in motion the previous fall: the Interim Measures Agreement with the Nuu-chah-nulth and the Scientific Panel. Soon after its creation, the Panel underwent a transformation that would have a profound impact on its work. Some of the new appointees to the panel joined forces with the Nuu-chah-nulth to insist—based on the newly negotiated Interim Measures Agreement—not only that Nuu-chah-nulth have representation on the Panel, but that their traditional knowledge systems be given equal weight with Western scientific findings in determining appropriate resource extraction techniques in Clayoquot Sound. Although not much was said about this development at the time, the potential impact began to emerge with the release of the first two of five Scientific Panel reports (Scientific Panel for Sustainable Forestry Practices in Clayoquot Sound 1994a, 1994b), in February and May of 1994, each of which strongly emphasized not only the contributions of the First Nations members to the structure, organization, and functioning of the Panel, but also the necessity of including First Nations' traditional knowledge in any future management of logging in Clayoquot Sound. Environmentalists—

realizing again how necessary it was that they improve their relations with the Nuu-chah-nulth—reacted cautiously to these developments and await-ed the remainder of the reports. The Panel continued its work, largely be-hind closed doors, throughout the summer.

The other process was the implementation of the Interim Measures Agreement. In early summer, the government and Nuu-chah-nulth an-nounced the mechanism through which the Nuu-chah-nulth would be able to oversee resource development while the treaty process was ongoing: the Central Region Board (www.island.net/~tofino/ncrb.htm). The Central Re-gion Board was to be composed of half Nuu-chah-nulth representatives and half non-Native representatives (CD VI/2). The Board would be able to approve or reject all resource-management decisions in the region, with a double majority required for any plan to proceed. Its mandate, however, was even broader than that:

> the mission of the CRB is to manage lands and resources in Clayo-quot Sound, prior to the conclusion of a treaty, in a manner that: provides opportunities for First Nations consistent with aboriginal resource uses and heritage, and considers options for treaty settle-ment; conserves resources in Clayoquot Sound and promotes re-source use that supports sustainability, economic diversification and ecological integrity; [and] encourages dialogue within and be-tween communities and reconciles diverse interests. (CD VI/2)

The new Board was greeted positively in the region, especially because all but one of the newly appointed non-Native Board members were local resi-dents. The apparent shift to more localized control over resource use and management was seen as a promising development. After the announce-ment, however, the Board slipped from view as the members began to meet, behind closed doors, to establish a working protocol and a strategy for tackling their broad mandate.

Simultaneously, the Nuu-chah-nulth and the provincial and federal governments embarked on the extended and complex process of negotiat-ing a modern-day treaty. It was in this forum—rather than in the shorter-term Interim Measures Agreement—that the Nuu-chah-nulth placed their hopes, and it was to consume enormous energy and resources over subse-quent years. Although open to the public, and holding great potential for shaping the future of Clayoquot Sound, these negotiations were not well at-tended by non-Native residents.

Although many crucial negotiations about the future of Clayoquot were under way, their venue had shifted: the logging road and the international media were no longer the primary battlegrounds. Rather, future possibilities and necessities were hammered out in meetings of the new Central Region Board and the Scientific Panel, treaty talks between the Nuu-chah-nulth and the provincial and federal governments, and private discussions between the Nuu-chah-nulth, MacMillan Bloedel, and the environmental groups. Most of this activity was distant from the public eye. Even the international campaigning (the environmentalists' markets campaign and industry and government public-relations campaigns) was increasingly happening as much behind closed doors—in shareholder meetings, private communications, and the like—as in public venues. Although there were still frequent newspaper advertisements and demonstrations at corporate headquarters, these usually took place far from Clayoquot Sound.

In the town of Tofino, it was tourism business as usual; the town was politically quiet, with many people still struggling to respond to the ongoing social and economic changes, or recovering from the long-term effects of their political activities. The future of the region was not at the forefront of people's minds—a relief to many. In nearby Ucluelet, the future was more on people's minds: with MacMillan Bloedel's logging operations in the region virtually at a standstill owing to the blockades and the Scientific Panel, many of its employees were temporarily—perhaps permanently—laid off. Individuals and families struggled to figure out what they would do next.

Although the demonstrations and arrests in 1993 were made in the name of democracy, the changes that resulted actually rendered processes in Clayoquot much less democratic. Meetings about the future of Clayoquot Sound took place behind closed doors, and the most important meetings—between the Nuu-chah-nulth, environmental groups, and MacMillan Bloedel, which led to the "truce" that enabled government-sponsored processes to function—excluded the elected government entirely. The government, it became increasingly clear, had little or no capacity to resolve the issues at stake in the crisis, in part because of its dependence on discourses of legitimacy over which it had little or no control. Thus, the actors with the capacity to bring "peace" to Clayoquot also had no democratic accountability reducible to modern theories of democracy. Clearly, this was a situation that exceeded any categorical assertion or theorization of sovereignty as well.

Further, as these processes continued, it became increasingly clear that the ecological future of the region would hinge in part on highly technical "scientific" decisions. These were decisions that no one, however, could pretend were anything other than political, thanks not least to the inclusion of traditional ecological knowledge in Scientific Panel recommendations, and to the institution responsible for implementing them, the

Central Region Board. The most political site in Clayoquot Sound became the struggle over the interpretation of Scientific Panel recommendations, as local organizations realized. The Clayoquot Biosphere Project responded by sponsoring a number of "Community Science Workshops" in an effort to engage locals and researchers in a critical dialogue about the implications of the Scientific Panel's recommendations. The FOCS also shifted its efforts to the micropolitics of scientific authority, in part by expanding its "Forest Watch" program, designed to ensure that actual logging practices matched the expectations set out in logging plans. The FOCS appeared before the Central Region Board each time logging plans were submitted, struggling to ensure that the Scientific Panel's recommendations were interpreted and enforced as rigorously as possible. Who would be hired to do pre-logging wildlife inventories? What methodologies would they use? Would they do time-depth research, or onetime scans? Would traditional ecological knowledge be incorporated? Would violations of logging plans be prosecuted? These were the key questions for the future of each of the watersheds—and, by extension, the future economy—of Clayoquot Sound. Ecotrust Canada responded by mapping the recommendations of the Panel using Geographical Information System (GIS) technology, again in an effort to assert a particular interpretation (Ecotrust Canada and Gill 1997, 36–55). Companies that wished to log in the region also jumped into the fray, submitting a variety of plans based on different interpretations of the Scientific Panel's recommendations to the Central Region Board. Meanwhile, the Board—the body formally responsible for interpreting the recommendations—struggled to formulate an approach that did justice to the complex interplay of interests and the interweaving of Native and non-Native scientific evidence. Discourses of democracy slipped further and further from the sites of politics as questions of interpretation, culture, time, economy, knowledge, value, and expertise assumed centrality.

As these processes trundled along, the region temporarily closed to logging. At the same time, the fishing industry began to come under strain from a variety of sources: not only were wild stocks in decline, but their status was further threatened by the failure of the United States and Canada to agree on how they should be managed.[20] In addition, the increasingly important fish-farming industry was criticized on environmental grounds, throwing provincial aquaculture policy into question (Ellis and David Suzuki Foundation 1996).[21] Although tourism continued to grow, it became clear that some kind of economic transition strategy was necessary. The region managed to band together to request such a strategy, but the resulting government-sponsored process revealed what everyone already knew: no one had a clue exactly how to proceed.

Clayoquot Sound was not much in the public eye between 1994 and 1997, but this was not because the difficulties that had earlier plagued the region had been resolved. On the contrary, in many ways the region was under greater pressure than ever. Its future, however, was being negotiated away from the glare of publicity, in highly technical and complex negotiations, usually behind the closed doors of committee meetings. The spaces and character of politics had changed drastically from the logging road conflicts of a few years earlier.

Resolutions and Nonsolutions: The Biosphere Reserve and Beyond

Over the next few years, the conflicts over the future of Clayoquot Sound slipped so far from public view that many Canadians were surprised when, on May 5, 2000, at a small ceremony in Pacific Rim National Park, Clayoquot Sound was officially declared a United Nations Biosphere Reserve. The next day's *Globe and Mail* contained a photo of Jean Chrétien (prime minister of Canada) and Ujjal Dosanjh (the new premier of British Columbia) unveiling a plaque commemorating the declaration. The headline of the accompanying article read: "Clayoquot Sound UN Dedication Ends Timber Battle." The article announced that "the designation marks an end to the so-called War in the Woods that flared in the summer of 1993 when more than 800 protesters were arrested in demonstrations against the two main logging companies in the area" (*Globe and Mail*, May 6, 2000, A2). Although it noted that the ceremony was boycotted by the Tla-o-qui-aht in protest of stalled treaty negotiations, and that "politicians and environmentalists concede that conflicts still plague the region," the overall tone was one of relieved celebration: the conflicts over the fate of Clayoquot Sound were essentially resolved. Or so we are supposed to believe.

One way of reading the ceremony is as a symbolic affirmation of Canadian sovereignty. The prime minister and the premier try to show the world that they are still in control, and that the settlement at Clayoquot stems from their authority. Ironically, they can only do so by invoking the authority of the United Nations. Moreover, those close to the situation would argue that the authority underpinning the apparent settlement does not belong to the Canadian state, but rather to the First Nations, the environmentalists, the Canadian division of Weyerhauser (the huge American logging company), and local communities. Weyerhauser had bought out

MacMillan Bloedel, the corporate icon of BC forestry, just after the latter company—the one that was blockaded in 1993, and that was always at the center of the disputes in Clayoquot—joined five major environmental groups and the Nuu-chah-nulth Tribal Council in a memorandum of understanding that was to govern future logging operations in the region. That memorandum of understanding, signed on June 16, 1999, was what gave substance to the Biosphere Reserve. Without it, the Reserve would not have been possible. Although neither the provincial nor the federal government had had much to do with the memorandum of understanding, they had promoted the Biosphere Reserve. That gave the premier and the prime minister the cover necessary for taking credit for "peace in the woods."

It is obvious why the governments concerned would want to associate themselves with the apparent settlement. Less obvious is why the non-governmental actors—so much at odds a few years earlier—could have come to an agreement. Had anything really been settled? And if not, why did the parties enter into an understanding that was so widely hailed as a settlement? Let's consider the second question first. The memorandum of understanding was the result of negotiations between environmental groups, the Nuu-chah-nulth, and MacMillan Bloedel. To understand how these negotiations could have succeeded, when so many earlier attempts failed, we need to consider the changing circumstances of each of the major actors.

The environmentalists were motivated by both their successes and their failures. The campaign in Clayoquot had ultimately been a "success" in that MacMillan Bloedel had wound down its operations in the Sound after 1993, and stopped logging there altogether in 1997. The company insisted, however, that the halt to logging was only temporary. Moreover, it continued its operations elsewhere in the province, in places that the environmentalists had more difficulty protecting. By making Clayoquot their "poster child," the environmentalists realized that they might only have transferred the basic problem of excessive and damaging clearcut logging to other parts of British Columbia. The problem that had brought them to the barricades had been addressed only superficially, as a conflict over the future of a particular area, rather than structurally, as a contest over the future of forestry in British Columbia. Would ecologically sustainable forestry become general, or would just a few "special" areas be saved from clearcut logging?

Environmental groups responded to their dilemma by linking their various campaigns with one another (using Clayoquot as a linchpin) and by intensifying their efforts to bring pressure on logging companies to develop more ecologically sustainable harvesting methods by politicizing their foreign markets, especially in the United States and Europe. This shift was expressed in the development of the Coastal Rainforest Coalition (http://www.coastalrainforest.org), composed of Greenpeace, Rainforest Action Network, and Natural Resources Defense Council. Initially formed in 1994 to focus and coordinate the groups' campaigns in Clayoquot, the coalition later expanded its focus to temperate rainforests all along the coast of British Columbia.

Initial efforts to expand the geographic scope of the campaign were not entirely successful. In the summer of 1997, Greenpeace initiated a direct-action campaign in the sparsely populated mid-coast region on the mainland of British Columbia (which they dubbed the "Great Bear Rainforest"), hoping it would snowball and attract people as the campaigns at Clayoquot had. Instead, it encountered significant resistance, initially from forestry workers, rapidly spreading to some local First Nations leaders, and eventually to the provincial premier, Glen Clark, who tagged Greenpeace supporters "enemies of British Columbia."[22] Rather than snowballing, the campaign struggled against intense criticism. The region was more remote and inaccessible than Clayoquot, and few people were willing to put their bodies on the line on its behalf. Without a local community to support the action, and in the face of widespread criticism, the environmentalists realized that the logistics of sustaining a direct-action campaign on the mid-coast were overwhelming. More important, they realized that public opinion in British Columbia was not yet sufficiently in favor of structural changes in the forestry industry to sustain their campaign. This drove home the extent to which public support of Clayoquot Sound was based in large part on its "special" status, and on trying to protect that region specifically, rather than on a broader commitment to restructuring the forest industry. Trying to achieve "special" status for the mid-coast region was going to be a limited, if necessary, tactic.

Rather than abandon direct-action strategies, or the tactic of creating name-recognition status for the "Great Bear Rainforest," the environmental groups shifted their attention to creating this status through direct-action campaigns elsewhere, particularly in England, Germany, and later the United States.[23] In this way, the direct-action campaign became increasingly closely linked with the markets campaign—in the long run, a more effective strategy. This strategy was twofold: mobilize consumer interest in the region enough to raise the specter of a consumer boycott of any company that purchased products from corporations that logged in the Great Bear Rainforest, then use this specter to encourage companies to cancel contracts with corporations that logged there and to purchase instead from companies that harvested in an ecologically sustainable manner and, preferably, not in old-growth rainforest. The environmental groups could thus simultaneously seek to protect regions of the Great Bear Rainforest and push companies toward more sustainable harvesting methods. Refusals to purchase products from the Great Bear Rainforest mounted. By December 1998, twenty-seven major companies, including Xerox, FedEx, Kinko's, 3M, and Bristol-Myers-Squibb, had committed to only purchasing sustainably harvested wood products.[24]

By December 1999, *Time* magazine called efforts to save the Great Bear Rainforest the best environmental news of the year. Although the region was still unprotected, *Time* was impressed with the progress made toward convincing companies not to buy wood that was from endangered forest types or was not sustainably harvested. In March 2000, environmentalists and logging companies signed a truce modeled on the memorandum of understanding at Clayoquot (Hamilton 2000). Environmentalists seemed to have achieved the upper hand. As Linda Coady, vice president of environmental enterprises for Weyerhauser's Coastal Group and chairwoman of the negotiating committee for logging companies involved in the mid-coast region, put it: "If we do not respond to these challenges, continued targeting of BC forest products in the international marketplace will lead to job loss, falling revenues for companies and government alike, community instability and lost opportunities for First Nations" (Lee 2000). The truce, in turn, led, on April 4, 2001, to a new agreement to protect the region, this one negotiated among environmentalists, First Nations, logging companies, unions, and coastal communities and, eventually, recognized by the provincial government. This agreement protected forty-two untouched rainforest valleys, and deferred logging in another seventy-seven valleys pending studies by a scientific panel on the model of the Scientific Panel for Clayoquot Sound. The agreement will cost five hundred jobs, but the government has committed some money for short-term mitigation. Most important, any logging done in the future will be ecosystem-based, with First Nations in control of it. The tactics developed through the Clayoquot struggles seemed to have paid off (Gill 2001).

In late 1997, the situation had looked rather different to environmentalists, who had suffered enough setbacks in the Great Bear Rainforest to give them pause. In order to capitalize on their early successes in the markets campaign, they needed to show a willingness to work with businesses to develop more sustainable harvesting practices. They needed to help show a way forward so that they did not become marginalized as preservationists with no concern for the economic and environmental well-being of the province. This danger was reflected in their sensitivity to opposition by First Nations leaders. Without the support of the indigenous peoples who claimed the land the environmentalists were defending, environmental groups were likely to encounter rocky ground both provincially and internationally. Having succeeded in getting the issues into the public eye, they now needed to start delivering solutions—or at least progress—in order to sustain and expand their campaigns. Their very strength and successes were forcing them into a less oppositional stance.

For forestry companies, the early successes of the environmentalist markets campaign posed a serious challenge. Despite the companies' efforts to simultaneously loosen provincial forestry regulations and hold them up as sufficient, they were going to be held to a higher standard of operation by the politics of the international marketplace. This was not, however, their only concern. By 1997, a long-predicted crisis in the BC forestry industry had begun to take hold (Marchak 1983, 1995; Drushka, Nixon, and Travers 1993; M'Gonigle and Parfitt 1994; Barnes and Hayter 1997; Tollefson 1998; Marchak, Aylcock, and Herbert 1999). The forest industry was facing a significant downturn. After years of high profits, MacMillan Bloedel recorded losses in 1997 of more than $350 million. The year 1998 was terrible for the industry, with job cuts, plummeting sales, and a number of mill closures; total industry losses for the year were more than $1.1 billion. In this climate, the challenges posed by environmentalists and, increasingly, by First Nations' land claims, which were gathering legal support, were even more potentially damaging to logging companies. With an eye to this emerging crisis, MacMillan Bloedel hired a new CEO, an American restructuring expert named Tom Stephens, and gave him the task of turning around the company's fortunes. His measures included trimming jobs, selling off parts of the company's diverse business interests, and introducing a comanagement system that gave unionized employees a say in how the company was run. He saw achieving peace with environmentalists as necessary for a turnaround. To this end, he met with environmentalists and announced that, over a five-year period, MacMillan Bloedel would shift from clearcut to variable-retention logging in old-growth forests. Environmental organizations responded with cautious approval.[25]

In 1997, MacMillan Bloedel wound down its operations in Clayoquot, citing the need to restructure to accommodate recommendations of the Scientific Panel. It worked out an arrangement to create a joint-venture company with the Nuu-chah-nulth, who were keen to pursue economic development opportunities but needed not only infrastructural and institutional support, but also access to the Tree Farm Licence owned by MacMillan Bloedel if they wished to get into the logging business. Thus MacMillan Bloedel and Ma-Mook Development Corporation (a Nuu-chah-nulth-owned economic development corporation) formed Iisaak Forest Resources Company, a joint-venture logging corporation, 51 percent owned by Ma-Mook and 49 percent by MacMillan Bloedel. Pending provincial approval, MacMillan Bloedel promised to hand over the Clayoquot portion of its Tree Farm Licence to the new corporation. In this way, MacMillan Bloedel kept one foot in Clayoquot Sound, which had by this point become much more important to it as a public-relations tool (in relation both to the European markets campaign and to BC's First Nations, who would presumably be controlling some of the future logging opportunities in the province) and as a potential site for developing alternative forestry methods, rather than as a profit-making enterprise. Instead of being the source of stinging attacks, Clayoquot now promised to be a site that could be pointed to as the pioneer of the future of forestry in British Columbia.

Thus, under environmentalist pressure and broader economic pressures, MacMillan Bloedel needed to make peace with environmentalists, and Clayoquot was the place to begin.[26] The most obvious sign of its success is that twenty-four hours after the MOU was signed, MacMillan Bloedel announced that it was being bought by Weyerhauser in a deal that was very profitable for its shareholders.

As the post-1993 developments—the Interim Measures Agreement, the Scientific Panel, and the opening up of treaty talks—suggested, the Nuu-chah-nulth had become central to negotiations over the future of Clayoquot. Their situation was further strengthened by provincial-level legal developments. In 1996, the Agreement-in-Principle was signed for the Nisga'a treaty, which would become the first modern treaty, indicating a potentially positive outcome for the restarted treaty talks. In 1997, as Umeek of Ahousaht (E. Richard Atleo) discusses in his essay in this volume, the Supreme Court of Canada made its decision on the Delgamuukw appeal, a decision that recognized that "aboriginal title" had legal standing. These events indicated the gradual strengthening of the legal situation of First Nations in British Columbia. The challenge faced by individual Nations, including the Nuu-chah-nulth, was how to convert this into desperately needed economic and institutional strength. For this, the Nuu-chah-nulth needed both MacMillan Bloedel and environmental groups. MacMillan Bloedel held title to the Tree Farm Licence for much of Clayoquot Sound, which meant that it had control over the most lucrative industry for the Nuu-chah-

nulth: logging. It also, of course, had the necessary equipment and expertise. The last thing the Nuu-chah-nulth wanted, however, was to be dependent on MacMillan Bloedel. Rather, they sought to develop their own capacities for economic development. For this, the environmentalists were
crucial, as they offered a counterbalance to MacMillan Bloedel's strength:
their work had opened up the possibility and incentive for a different kind
of logging, one that would be more sustainable, more easily managed by a
relatively small group such as the Nuu-chah-nulth, but still viable as an economic venture. By drawing on both the environmentalists and MacMillan
Bloedel, the Nuu-chah-nulth could potentially create space to articulate
their own vision of the future for Clayoquot Sound, one that included logging as part of their economic base, but at a pace and in a way that were
compatible with the Nuu-chah-nulth and somewhat under their control.
With the help of environmentalists, the Nuu-chah-nulth also hoped to pursue alternative economic development mechanisms. In this way, MacMillan
Bloedel and environmental groups together provided an important opportunity for the Nuu-chah-nulth: by balancing their expertise and resources,
the Nuu-chah-nulth could potentially access each of their strengths without
fearing that one side or the other would gain too much control over their activities. It was a fine line, but in many ways it offered rich possibilities.

Given these developments, achieving peace at Clayoquot seemed increasingly possible. Environmentalists needed to sustain legitimacy against
claims that their preservationist ethic was reinscribing colonial relations
with indigenous peoples and turning British Columbia into an economic
disaster; MacMillan Bloedel needed to sustain marketplace profile, particularly by claiming to be moving toward ecofriendly forestry; the Nuu-
chah-nulth needed to develop economic independence. The dynamics were
bigger than Clayoquot, but Clayoquot was the site where they were being
operationalized.

The memorandum of understanding came out of this situation. The
MOU is an agreement between Iisaak Forest Resources, the MacMillan
Bloedel/Nuu-chah-nulth joint-venture forestry company, and five environmental groups (Greenpeace International, Greenpeace Canada, Western
Canada Wilderness Committee, Natural Resources Defense Council, and
Rainforest Action Network). One environmental organization, the Friends
of Clayoquot Sound, participated in the negotiations around the MOU but
abstained from signing it. Although it supported the decision of the other
groups to sign the agreement, it felt that its role should be that of watchdog,
and that it could better fulfill that role by not signing.[27] The MOU sets out the
conditions for ongoing cooperation among the signatories.[28] It commits

Iisaak to operate according to the spirit, principles, and recommendations of the Clayoquot Sound Scientific Panel, with special attention to a range of concerns (biodiversity, water quality, etc.) and potential uses of the land (scientific research, ecotourism, traditional Nuu-chah-nulth uses, etc.). It also targets areas already impacted by logging as sites for ecologically sustainable commercial forestry, and spares pristine watersheds from logging. These areas are instead reserved for other uses, such as traditional cultural uses, sustainable harvesting of nontimber forest products, and ecotourism. Where logging does occur, the emphasis will be on production of ecologically sustainable volumes of wood, and priority will be placed on maintaining old-growth forest characteristics within harvest areas and nurturing second-growth stands into forests with old-growth characteristics.

If Iisaak sustains its commitments in these areas, the MOU commits environmental groups to support and endorse Iisaak as a model of ecologically sustainable forestry, to assist its institutional development (including research, financing, and capacity-building endeavors) and to actively assist it in developing and marketing its products, whether value-added forestry products, nontimber forest products, or ecotourism products. The MOU thus commits significant energy from environmental groups in directions that might seem out of character: raising funds for, assisting in, and promoting the products from logging in old-growth forests. This marks an important shift in both the self-understanding and the public face of some of these environmental organizations.

Although it is not legally binding, the MOU sets out rigorous conditions for cooperation among the parties. It also contains a compelling vision for the future of Clayoquot Sound: pristine areas will be protected from industrial forestry, but used to support the economic health of the region in other ways; a viable, locally controlled ecoforestry operation will produce value-added products and provide an economic base for local First Nations, and there will be a gradual diversification of the economy into nontimber resources. As a broadly agreed vision of the future of the region, it is striking, especially given the extent of past conflicts. However, as all parties to the MOU emphasized, it will not be easy to achieve.[29] Still, there was much celebration upon its signing. Some commentators noted that women had played an important role in the agreement (Bossin 1999). Linda Coady, who had been brought in to feminize MacMillan Bloedel's image (as Nancy Scott had recommended ten years earlier [CD II/C/2]), was the chief negotiator for the logging companies, and her environmentalist counterparts were all women. Only the First Nations had male spokespeople. Thus, the process itself, as well as the ultimate agreement, appeared to have been empowering for more than one marginalized group, and this empowerment had had a positive effect on the outcome.

Although not officially connected, the achievement of the MOU facilitated negotiations over the possibility of proposing Clayoquot Sound as a United Nations Biosphere Reserve. The suggestion to propose Clayoquot Sound as Biosphere Reserve had been made in 1991 by the Clayoquot Biosphere Project, and in 1993 by Stephen Owen in the CORE response to the Clayoquot Land Use Decision. Negotiations on the proposal did not get under way, however, until much later, when it was raised again in the context of the Central Region Board. Unlike the MOU, these negotiations were conducted openly: one condition for a Biosphere Reserve designation is that the application have virtually unanimous support from the region. Achieving this level of agreement over the future of Clayoquot posed a significant challenge, given the history of conflict in the region.

The process proceeded slowly, with public workshops and consultations, including both public input and individuals or groups meeting privately with the coordinator of the Biosphere Reserve Nomination Working Group. The minutes of workshops, discussion papers, and government pamphlets promoting the idea were widely circulated, and a consensus slowly developed that the proposal was a good idea.[30] Achievement of this consensus was facilitated by the fact that the designation actually changes very little: it does not transfer jurisdiction over land use to any body outside the region; it does not confer protection on any new parts of the region; in fact, it does not guarantee much of anything. It is effectively a recognition of land use and jurisdictional arrangements already in place. As an information sheet distributed by the Biosphere Reserve Nomination Working Group put it: "Biosphere Reserves are land or marine areas which are given international recognition within UNESCO's Man and the Biosphere Programme *for promoting and demonstrating a balanced relationship between people and nature.*" ("The Clayoquot Sound UNESCO Biosphere Reserve: Proposed Context, Vision and Objectives," July 22, 1998). Thus, in early discussions, much energy was spent convincing the parties that the designation would not prejudice treaty negotiations, prohibit logging, or enable foreign organizations (such as the United Nations) to dictate policy in the region:

> A Biosphere Reserve Designation for Clayoquot Sound will not add
> more bureaucracy, will not result in a new set of criteria related to
> resource management, and will not mean that external agencies

will dictate resource management within the area. This designation will, however, recognize important work on land and resource
management that is already underway in Clayoquot Sound.
(Clayoquot Sound Central Region Board information sheet:
www.island.net/~crb/RESERVE.html)

Evidently, the symbolism of the declaration was important to many
of the participants. As the Central Region Board put it:

The Central Region Board's interest in potential Biosphere Reserve status is based on its desire to raise the international profile
of Clayoquot Sound, to promote innovations in sustainable
ecosystem-based resource management and institutional frameworks, to integrate planning for marine and terrestrial ecosystems,
and to use Biosphere designation as a tool for seeking funds to assist with economic diversification and transition. (Ibid.)

This latter possibility became the real carrot for negotiators. Once both federal and provincial governments began to hint at the possibility of con-
tributing significant financial resources if the designation went through,
some who had been resistant or lukewarm began to warm to the idea of a
Biosphere Reserve designation (O'Neil 1996; Sinoski 1999). By January 1999
(when some of the details of the MOU were still at issue), there was enough
consensus to put the nomination forward to the United Nations. A little over
a year later, the premier and the prime minister were able to come for the
ceremonies that marked the inauguration of the reserve. Those ceremonies
were intended not only to demonstrate the authority of the governments,
but also to affirm that all the interested groups—not just the signatories to
the MOU—were parties to the settlement at Clayoquot.

In that light, the Tla-o-qui-aht boycott of the ceremony was more than
a little troubling. The issue of "native land claims" had not been settled in
Clayoquot or elsewhere in the province. In fact, the issue has become more
heated since the agreement in principle for the Nisga'a treaty was signed in
1996 and the Supreme Court's final Delgamuukw decision came down in
December 1997. The Nisga'a agreement was opposed by the main opposition parties federally and provincially. It went into effect in May 2000, but
it is still subject to a constitutional challenge supported by the provincial
Liberals, who won a massive majority in 2001 and now form the provincial government. Despite all the talk about new treaties between Canada/
British Columbia and the First Nations, the one for the Nisga'a is the sole
treaty to have been concluded after nine years of negotiations in the province (and that was under the older process, not the new one launched with

much fanfare by the BC Treaty Commission). A second treaty, for the Sechelt (a band whose lands are on the south coast of the mainland, just north of the city of Vancouver), seemed to be in the works at one point: an agreement in principle was reached in 1999. However, that agreement fell apart because of internal opposition: the Sechelt band is now set to take its case to court. Although the Nuu-chah-nulth themselves are still in treaty negotiations, they may well decide to follow the example of other First Nations, and pursue their case through the courts. Such a move may be inevitable, because the provincial Liberals are not likely to negotiate with the Nuu-chah-nulth on terms that the Nuu-chah-nulth would find acceptable.

The village councils in Tofino and Ucluelet were less than enthusiastic about the MOU. This reflects ongoing resentment against "outsiders" (environmentalists, logging company executives, government bureaucrats, First Nations leaders), who seem to be working out the future of the region over the heads or behind the backs of the "local communities." Of course, "local community" is a code word that disguises many exclusions; nevertheless, there is widespread popular feeling behind this term. When word leaked out that a tentative agreement had been reached between environmentalists, Natives, and some of the logging companies in relation to the Great Bear Rainforest, local leaders in that region reacted with outrage. The provincial government was also put out. They did not want to be left out of another MOU and have a settlement like the one at Clayoquot foisted on them. Given the desperate situation of the fishing industry in coastal British Columbia and the scant opportunities for tourism development in many places—not least because Clayoquot and a few other places have a comparative advantage in terms of name recognition, accessibility, and tourist facilities—the loss of opportunities in forestry is an extremely serious matter for small coastal communities.[31]

It is not as if the environmentalists have "won" in Clayoquot or elsewhere. Interfor, the second-largest logging company in Clayoquot (and a major player in the Great Bear Rainforest), remains active, and there have been continuing protests about its logging activities on the fringes of Pacific Rim National Park. Environmentalists have been gearing up to prevent Interfor from going into the "pristine" areas in Clayoquot, where it still has some logging rights. There is no guarantee that Interfor will stop logging or sell its interests in Clayoquot Sound to Iisaak, although the Great Bear Rainforest agreement contains a commitment from it to consider doing so. Thus, old-style clearcut logging is still very much an issue in Clayoquot, as elsewhere in British Columbia. Even the prospective agreements between the environmentalists, the First Nations, and the logging companies are extremely fragile, in that they are keyed into a regulatory regime that is susceptible, on the one hand, to corporate manipulation and, on the other, to the vagaries of consumer preference. Will there be steady consumer support for better logging practices in Germany and the United States? Will the environmentalists be able to monitor those practices effectively enough (and publicize their findings in face of corporate advertising campaigns) to keep the logging companies honest? Old-growth trees continue to fall at a high rate, if not in Clayoquot, then elsewhere in British Columbia, as well as throughout the world.

Locally, the settlement tends to obscure what has been happening in and around Clayoquot Sound. The shift to tourism and retirement living has been pronounced, and has accelerated since 1993. Traditional logging and fishing are becoming less and less important within the local economy. More and more people are making their living by serving "outsiders" who come for leisure activities. Is this what a "biosphere reserve" actually means? If so—as the essays by Sandilands and Luke suggest—the future for Clayoquot is not quite as rosy as some might imagine.

The disputes at Clayoquot were never simply about logging, or indeed about the environment, and could not be resolved by an agreement about logging or environmental preservation. Much else has always been at issue, including democratic process, local autonomy, dispute resolution, the nature and use of the law, the organization and purpose of economic activity, gender identity and gender equality, and relations between Natives and non-Natives. In many instances, underlying issues have been largely ignored. Problems of poverty and social exclusion have a particular impact on First Nations communities, which have long suffered the effects of colonialism. Domestic violence against women is an issue everywhere, including in places such as Clayoquot, where established ways of life have been seriously disrupted. The marginalization of people who are remote from the centers of urban authority intensifies alienation and resentment. Most of the benefits of restructuring go to the few, and many of the few come from away. Capitalism, colonialism, and patriarchy are still entrenched, and the human relation to the biosphere is still exploitative and irresponsible. Clayoquot remains deeply problematic. Its politics, however—both past and present—have much to teach us about strategies and structures through which these relationships are being reshaped.

Notes

1. Readers who wish to fill in the background that I then lacked might begin with Barman (1996). See also Fisher (1992) and Carty (1996).

2. The land at issue was and is public, as are most forested lands in British Columbia. However, logging companies had been granted Tree Farm Licences (TFLs)— in effect, timber rights—in the areas at issue. See the Introduction, note 4 for references on the BC forest industry.

3. The controversy had generated an influential picture book (George and Dorst 1985). A later book (Dorst and Young 1990) of this sort deals with the Sound as a whole. As I was to discover, controversies over logging have led to a series of such books, each publicizing the issues in a particular area: the Queen Charlotte Islands (Islands Protection Society 1984), the Stein Valley (M'Gonigle and Wickwire 1988), the Carmanah Valley (Dorst and Young 1990), and, most recently, the mid-coast, or "Great Bear Rainforest" (McAllister, Young, and McAllister 1997).

4. See the Research Guide at the end of this volume for an explanation of CD *[Clayoquot Documents]* referencing system.

5. The CD references here are examples of these debates, but they extend throughout the material collected in *The Clayoquot Documents.*

6. As was the case in other Commonwealth countries, for much of the twentieth century indigenous children across Canada were—often forcibly—removed from their homes and families and placed in residential schools, usually run by religious organizations. This practice was devastating to Native communities, who continue to struggle with its effects. See Miller (1996), Fournier and Crey (1997), Chrisjohn and Young (1997), and Milloy (1999). There were two residential schools in Clayoquot Sound.

7. What in the United States is called a "reservation" is called a "reserve" in Canada. A reserve is often very small, and the reserve lands belonging to a particular band are not necessarily contiguous.

8. The Friends of Clayoquot Sound (FOCS) is a small, grassroots environmental organization that was formed when Meares Island—at the heart of Clayoquot Sound—was threatened with clearcut logging. They were the guiding force for the struggle against clearcut logging in the Sound during the period covered in this book. For a description of the origin of the organization, see CD II/A/2. For more information on its current activities, see FOCS at www.ancientrainforest.org.

9. Clayoquot is the Anglicized spelling of Tla-o-qui-aht, which is how the band now refers to itself.

10. The key decisions are noted on the Web site of the BC Ministry of Aboriginal Affairs: www.aaf.gov.bc.ca/aaf/history/history.htm. There are links to most of these decisions, which may be read on-line.

11. In 1965, the province of British Columbia divided itself into "Regional Districts" (http://www.marh.gov.bc.ca/LGPOLICY/MAR/content.html). A Regional District is akin to an American county in that it provides for a variety of local services at a level above the local municipality. Because much of British Columbia is sparsely populated, there are no municipal governments in many areas. Port Alberni, Ucluelet, and Tofino are the only municipalities within the Alberni-Clayoquot Regional District. The rest of the territory is unincorporated, and to the extent that municipal services are provided, the Regional District takes direct responsibility for them. The Indian reserves are not within the Regional District's jurisdiction. Services may be provided by contract, however. See Bish (1999), for an account of BC local government.

12. Originally the International Woodworkers of America, now called the Industrial, Wood and Allied Workers of Canada. For many years, the IWA was the biggest and most powerful union in British Columbia. See its Web site (www.iwa.ca/).

13. The Forest Alliance assumed responsibilities that had earlier been handled by the Council of Forest Industries: www.cofi.org/ (Wilson 1998, 37).

14. See www.bcstats.gov.bc.ca/data/bus_stat/tourism/trr_an97.pdf for information on the growth of tourism in the region. Also see the Web sites of the Tofino–Long Beach Chamber of Commerce (www.island.net/~tofino/) and the Pacific Rim Tourist Association (www.alberni.net/~pacrimtourist/).

15. The ombudsman is an independent official who reports to the provincial legislature rather than to the cabinet and is empowered to inquire into, and report on, cases of administrative injustice.

16. The key agency now is the BC Treaty Commission, whose Web site is at www.bctreaty.net/.

17. For the protesters' own accounts, see Berman et al. 1994; MacIsaac and Champagne 1994; and McLaren 1994.

18. *Maclean's* describes itself as "Canada's National NewsMagazine." At the time, the *Globe and Mail* was Canada's only national newspaper.

19. In Canada, the prosecuting attorney is called "the Crown" or Crown Attorney. One also speaks of Crown lands, Crown corporations, rights of the Crown, and Crown prerogative. Sovereignty inheres in the Crown rather than in the people, and all acts of the state are done in the name of the Crown. Most of the land in British Columbia belongs to "the Crown in right of British Columbia," that is, to the province.

20. A controversial agreement was finally reached in 1999: see the description of the new Pacific Salmon Treaty at www.dfo-mpo.gc.ca/pst-tsp/index.htm. For an environmentalist critique of fisheries management, see www.davidsuzuki.org/salmonmain.htm. See www.bcstats.gov.bc.ca/data/bus_stat/BCfishsector2000.pdf for BC government data on the industry.

21. For the government's views, see the Web site of the British Columbia Commissioner for Aquaculture Development at www.dfo-mpo.gc.ca/ocad-bcda/. Industry accounts are available from the BC Salmon Farmers' Association (www.salmonfarmers.org/) and the BC Shellfish Growers' Association (www.island.net/~bcsga/). Critiques of the industry are on the Web sites of many of the environmental organizations. For the Nuu-chah-nulth view, see www.nuuchahnulth.org.

22. For news coverage of these activities, see Hunter 1997; Hume 1997; Pynn 1997; Mollard 1997; MacQueen 1997.

23. See, for example, "Greenpeace Widens War on B.C. Wood," 1998; Fong and McCabe 1998.

24. Kenna 1998; Coastal Rainforest Coalition 1998 (on CRC's Web site).

25. Clearcutting involves the removal of all trees within a harvest area. In variable-retention logging, small patches of forest cover are left undisturbed within a harvest area. See Rainforest Action Network's press release on the issue at www.ran.org/ran/info_center/press_release/bloedel.html.

26. As suggested earlier, the deal at Clayoquot would become a template for MacMillan Bloedel's negotiations in the Great Bear Rainforest.

27. The FOCS has fulfilled this role effectively. In 1998, for example, it re-

leased a report titled "Implementing the Scientific Panel: Three Years and Counting." Grounded in research from its Forest Watch program, the report developed a detailed critique of the Scientific Panel and the Forest Practices Code, as well as analyzing the implementation of the Scientific Panel's recommendations in Clayoquot Sound (the only systematic evaluation to date). The report focused on the implementation of the Panel's provisions for community involvement, adherence to inventory and monitoring provisions, the creation of an adaptive management strategy, and its potential for ecosystem-based logging. It argued that application of the Scientific Panel's recommendations had been woefully inadequate and offered its own suggestions. The report is reproduced on our Web site in volume 3 of *The Clayoquot Documents*.

28. The memorandum of understanding is reproduced in full on our Web site in volume 3 of *The Clayoquot Documents*.

29. Although MacMillan Bloedel held the largest TFL in Clayoquot Sound (now transferred to Iisaak), another company—International Forest Products (Interfor)—holds the rest and has been resistant to negotiating any similar deal with environmentalists, and continues to pursue industrial-style logging in the region. The Friends of Clayoquot Sound have blockaded the company on several recent occasions.

30. Many of these documents are available on our Web site in volume 3 of *The Clayoquot Documents*.

31. See the Web site of the Coastal Communities Network at www. coastalcommunity.bc.ca/.

Works Cited

Barman, Jean. 1996. *The West beyond the West: A History of British Columbia*. Vancouver: University of British Columbia Press.

Barnes, Trevor J., and Roger Hayter, eds. 1997. *Troubles in the Rainforest: British Columbia's Forest Economy in Transition*. Victoria, B.C.: Western Geographical Press.

Berman, Tzeporah, Gordon Brent Ingram, Maurice Gibbons, Ronald B. Hatch, Loÿs Maingon, and Christopher Hatch, eds. 1994. *Clayoquot and Dissent*. Vancouver: Ronsdale Press.

Bish, Robert L., and Eric G. Clemens. 1999. *Local Government in British Columbia*. 3d ed. Richmond, B.C.: Union of BC Municipalities.

Bossin, Bob. 1999. "Nature Made It, Women Saved It." *Homemaker's* (September): 54–70.

British Columbia. 1993. *Clayoquot Sound Land Use Decision: Background Report*. Victoria, B.C.: Government of British Columbia.

Brundtland, Gro Harlem, and the World Commission on Environment and Development. 1987. *Our Common Future*. Oxford: Oxford University Press.

Carty, R. K., ed. 1996. *Politics, Policy, and Government in British Columbia*. Vancouver: University of British Columbia Press.

CD [*The Clayoquot Documents*. 1997. Ed. Karena Shaw and Warren Magnusson. Clayoquot Project, University of Victoria.]

Chrisjohn, Roland D., and Sherri L. Young. 1997. *The Circle Game: Shadows and Substance in the Indian Residential School Experience in Canada*. With contributions by Michael Maraun. Penticton, B.C.: Theytus Books.

Coastal Rainforest Coalition. 1998. Press Release, December 17.

Dorst, Adrian, and Cameron Young. 1990. *Clayoquot: On the Wild Side.* Vancouver: Western Canada Wilderness Committee.

Doyle, Aaron, Brian Elliott, and David Tindall. 1997. "Framing the Forests: Corporations, the B.C. Forest Alliance, and the Media." In *Organizing Dissent: Contemporary Social Movements in Theory and Practice,* ed. William K. Carroll. 2d ed. Toronto: Garamond Press. 240–68.

Drushka, Ken, Bob Nixon, and Ray Travers, eds. 1993. *Touch Wood: BC Forests at the Crossroads.* Madeira Park, B.C.: Harbour Publishing Company.

Ecotrust Canada and Ian Gill. 1997. *Seeing the Ocean through the Trees: A Conservation-Based Development Strategy for Clayoquot Sound.* Vancouver: Ecotrust Canada.

Ellis, David W., and David Suzuki Foundation. 1996. *Net Loss: The Salmon Netcage Industry in British Columbia.* A report to the David Suzuki Foundation by David W. Ellis and Associates, with recommendations by the David Suzuki Foundation. Vancouver: David Suzuki Foundation.

Fisher, Robin. 1992. *Contact and Conflict: Indian-European Relations in British Columbia, 1774–1898.* Vancouver: University of British Columbia Press.

Fong, Petti, and Aileen McCabe. 1998. "Greenpeace Launches British Offensive against B.C. Logging." *Vancouver Sun,* March 3, A1.

Fournier, Suzanne, and Ernie Crey. 1997. *Stolen from Our Embrace: The Abduction of First Nations Children and the Restoration of Aboriginal Communities.* Vancouver: Douglas & McIntyre.

George, Paul, and Adrian Dorst. 1985. *Meares Island: Protecting a National Paradise.* Tofino, B.C.: Friends of Clayoquot Sound and Western Canada Wilderness Committee.

Gill, Ian. 2001. "The Deal—Only a Start." *Vancouver Sun,* April 10.

"Greenpeace Widens War on B.C. Wood." 1998. *Montreal Gazette,* March 28, A8.

Greer, David. 1997. "Being There." In Ecotrust Canada and Ian Gill, *Seeing the Ocean through the Trees: A Conservation-Based Development Strategy for Clayoquot Sound.* Vancouver: Ecotrust Canada. 23–24.

Hamilton, Gordon. 2000. "Coastal Loggers Seek Eco-truce." *Vancouver Sun,* March 16, D1.

Harper, Frank, ed. N.d. *News around Clayoquot Sound, 1990–1991: Being an Anthology of Some of the Best-Beloved Blasts from The Sound Newspaper.* Tofino: The Sound Newspaper Society.

Hume, Mark. 1997. "The Greenpeace Crusade." *Vancouver Sun,* June 28, C1.

Hunter, Justine. 1997. "Forest Protests Promised: Premier Glen Clark Says Greenpeace Campaigners Are Enemies of B.C." *Vancouver Sun,* April 22, B6.

Islands Protection Society. 1984. *Islands at the Edge: Preserving the Queen Charlotte Islands Wilderness.* Vancouver: Douglas & McIntyre.

Kenna, Kathleen. 1998. "Corporate Giants Boycott B.C. Rainforest Products." *Toronto Star,* April 2, A13.

Lee, King. 2000. "Activists and Loggers Close to Rainforest Truce." *Victoria Times-Colonist,* March 16, A1.

MacIsaac, Ron, and Anne Champagne, eds. 1994. *Clayoquot Mass Trials: Defending the Rainforest.* Foreward by Robert F. Kennedy Jr.; portraits of Clayoquot protectors by Andy Sinats. Philadelphia: New Society Publishers.

MacQueen, Ken. 1997. "Coastal Leaders Condemn Environmentalists." *Vancouver Sun,* September 19, B4.

Marchak, M. Patricia. 1983. *Green Gold: The Forest Industry in British Columbia.* Vancouver: University of British Columbia Press.

———. 1995. *Logging the Globe.* Montreal and Kingston: McGill-Queen's University Press.

Marchak, M. Patricia, Scott L. Aylcock, and Deborah M. Herbert. 1999. *Falldown: Forest Policy in British Columbia.* Vancouver: David Suzuki Foundation and Ecotrust Canada.

McAllister, Ian, Cameron Young, and Karen McAllister. 1997. *The Great Bear Rainforest: Canada's Forgotten Coast.* Madeira Park, B.C.: Harbour Publishing Company.

McCallum, Dulcie. 1993. *Public Report No. 31: Administrative Fairness of the Process Leading to the Clayoquot Sound Land Use Decision.* Victoria, B.C.: Queen's Printer.

McLaren, Jean. 1994. *Spirits Rising: The Story of the Clayoquot Peace Camp, 1993.* Gabriola Island, B.C.: Pacific Edge Publishing.

M'Gonigle, R. Michael, and Ben Parfitt. 1994. *Forestopia: A Practical Guide to a New Forest Economy.* Madeira Park, B.C.: Harbour Publishing Company.

M'Gonigle, R. Michael, and Wendy Wickwire. 1988. *Stein: The Way of the River.* Vancouver: Talonbooks.

Miller, J. R. 1996. *Shingwauk's Vision: A History of Native Residential Schools.* Toronto: University of Toronto Press.

Milloy, John S. 1999. *A National Crime: The Canadian Government and the Residential School System, 1879 to 1986.* Winnipeg: University of Manitoba Press.

Mollard, Pat. 1997. "Activists Disregard Real Central Coast Voices." *Vancouver Sun,* August 19, D2.

O'Neil, Peter. 1996. "Victoria Pushes Biosphere Status for Clayoquot Sound." *Vancouver Sun,* December 20, A1.

Pynn, Larry. 1997. "New European Boycott Urged over Clearcuts." *Vancouver Sun,* July 18, A1.

Scientific Panel for Sustainable Forestry Practices in Clayoquot Sound. 1994a. *Report of the Scientific Panel for Sustainable Forest Practices in Clayoquot Sound.* Report 1 of 5. Victoria, B.C.: Cortex Consultants.

———. 1994b. *Progress Report 2: Review of Current Forest Practice Standards in Clayoquot Sound.* Report 2 of 5. Victoria, B.C.: Cortex Consultants.

Seaton, Peter D. 1993. *Report of the Honourable Mr. Justice P. D. Seaton, Commissioner.* Vancouver: Law Courts.

Sierra Club of Western Canada. 1993. "Clayoquot Sound Information Sheet." Victoria, B.C.: Sierra Club of Western Canada.

Sinoski, Kelly. 1999. "Millions to Be Reserved for UN Bid on Clayoquot." *Vancouver Sun,* January 23, A3.

Tennant, Paul. 1990. *Aboriginal Peoples and Politics: The Indian Land Question in British Columbia, 1849–1989.* Vancouver: University of British Columbia Press.

Tocqueville, Alexis de. 1990. *Democracy in America.* Vol. 1. 1st ed.: 1835; first English edition: 1945. New York: Vintage Books.

Tollefson, Chris, ed. 1998. *The Wealth of the Forests: Markets, Regulation, and Sustainable Forestry.* Vancouver: University of British Columbia Press.

Turner, Nancy J., and Barbara S. Efrat. 1982. *Ethnobotany of the Hesquiat Indians of Vancouver Island.* Cultural Recovery Paper No. 2. Victoria, B.C.: British Columbia Provincial Museum.

Wilson, R. Jeremy. 1998. *Talk and Log: Wilderness Politics in British Columbia.* Vancouver: University of British Columbia Press.

York, Geoffrey, and Loreen Pindera. 1991. *People of the Pines: The Warriors and the Legacy of Oka.* Boston: Little, Brown.

There Must Be Some Way Out of Here

Strategy, Ethics, and Environmental Politics

William Chaloupka

During the summer of 1993, the struggle over Clayoquot Sound first came into focus on a day that attracted international attention and launched a remarkable summer of protest. The musical celebrities and political activists of Midnight Oil gave a concert that drew five thousand people to the remote protest site (Ingram 1994). It turned out to be one of only three days during that summer when logging stopped. It was also a day that focused attention on Clayoquot in a way that could not be easily forgotten or denied. MTV broadcast the concert, which was also covered by CNN. The struggle over the magnificent temperate rainforests of Clayoquot made its way into the pop music press (Garrett 1993), but also into national (Bohn 1993; Lee 1993a, 1993b, 1993c, 1993d) and international (Farnsworth 1993) newspapers.

After Midnight Oil had taken an airplane tour of the Sound, the group's political as well as musical leader, Peter Garrett, told a local activist, "you guys are going to win here. In Australia and Europe we're fighting to protect forests a tenth this size" (Kuehls 1997). This is not the sort of comment one would usually expect to be exchanged among environmental activists. The tall, outspoken Australian with the shaved head must have seemed an alien in more ways than one. More is at stake in his remark than simple optimism—although that optimism is also notable, in an environmental movement that has often traded on a talent for permanent pessimism.

Given the strong focus of their movement on an ethical base, most activists expect to fight for each tree according to some natural (hence, moral) economy of its worth. The whole point of the struggle is to save trees that compose a sacred, indispensable, and imperiled environment. Each tree, as a part of that composite forest, has a special moral worth. When Christopher

Stone wrote his famous essay (Stone 1974) linking environmental ethics and environmental law (in the United States), he did not ask "should *forests* have standing?" It was *trees,* and hence *each tree,* that deserved the moral treatment accorded a moral agent. Stone's essay has been enormously influential among environmental activists. It just makes sense, once Stone pointed it out, that trees should have rights, that someone should be able to sue on their behalf. Garrett's remark is at odds with such a conception, and it raised a question. Are trees part of the arena of struggle, or are they individual moral agents?

Wallace Stegner, the essayist and novelist whose works are among the most influential among environmentalists in the western United States, called the environment a geography of hope. To acknowledge that the landscape also forms the geography of a struggle over control is almost to prove oneself a hypocrite. Garrett may have intended to shock his listeners—and to teach them something about their struggle. His remark must have raised a few eyebrows. But even if the Clayoquot activists were surprised by Garrett's bluntness, there is plenty of evidence that these activists had figured out a strategic approach of considerable force.

Implicit in Garrett's statement is political advice of a high order. The goal of the Clayoquot struggle was to take permanent control over the forest's geography, to supplant the corporations and governments that thought they had that sovereign power. The more trees, the more opportunity to win before you are defeated. And such a victory would have enduring consequences that would extend to other forests and even other countries. In Garrett's remark, the forest begins to be remapped. If green activists can tolerate the ethical tension the remark contains without losing their aplomb, their movement—and the struggle over the forest, and the trees—would change.

In this essay, I raise the possibility that the strategic aspect of politics needs to be much more important in environmental social theory. The Clayoquot example is used to demonstrate that ethics alone does not a strategy make—and that this distinction must be reclaimed in environmental theory. My use of Clayoquot examples is frankly partial; I am well aware that many participants in that movement did not exhibit the strategic sophistication I am identifying with some of the movement's leaders. The strong ethical orientation of green theory is obviously essential to the movement's sense of conviction and, thus, to its endurance and success. There is ample evidence that many—probably most—Clayoquot participants were not strategists, but were moved by the moral impetus inscribed in a familiar combination of utopian idealism, nonviolent existence, and green conviction.

But politics is inevitably strategic, too. My argument holds implications for the field of contemporary political theory, as well as for the more pragmatic field of green politics. Drawing on Michel Foucault's argument about the affinity of politics and the strategic realm, I am raising the possibility of a combination of ethical and strategic considerations. Such a combination provides a test, both for normative political theories that privilege the role of values while trying to ignore the contingency of the political world and for greens who have tried to generate a unique new metaphysics of green science and morality. At the end of the essay, I venture some tentative speculations on what Foucault's argument might imply for green politics, a discussion that also reflects on the more general debate over Foucault's politics and theory.

Every movement based on civil disobedience (or other forms of ethical protest) must confront the gap between the moralism of protest's justifications and the strategies such protest usually must deploy when it interacts with the political world, which is contingent and multileveled. This is doubly a problem for environmentalists, who, after all, claim to act on behalf of nature itself. Strategy is a human affair; trees do not compromise, form coalitions, or decide on timing. When humans act on behalf of trees— even when they also claim that the trees should have independent moral standing—strategic issues pop up like mushrooms in a good season. This fact forms the basis of a criticism of Stone's "standing for trees" argument (Ferry 1995). That this argument has been assimilated to the critique of environmentalism may make it all the harder for greens to recognize the inevitability of strategic considerations. But that strategic realm persists, whether or not we regret it.

At first glance, the Clayoquot struggle may seem little more than a new front in the timber wars that have raged for years from San Francisco northward. There are significant bioregional similarities between Clayoquot and the U.S. Pacific Northwest. And the environmental movements of the two areas are obviously cooperative; some activists who were introduced to direct action at Clayoquot went on to fill leadership roles in the San Francisco–based operations of Greenpeace and the Rainforest Action Network. In turn, it was U.S. scientists and activists who first identified "old growth" as a potentially viable political issue, as well as a coherent, scientific conceptualization that informed subsequent struggles up and down the Pacific coast (Dietrich 1992).

But, despite considerable affinities, the politics of Clayoquot has emerged in a much different configuration than has politics in the U.S. Pacific Northwest. Although both U.S. and Canadian activists have engaged in ostensibly similar strategies and tactics in their efforts to save old-growth forests, there have been notable differences, in strategy but also in outcomes. U.S. Earth First! persisted in spiking trees (or talking about spiking them) long after the tactic had been turned into the rallying cry by their adversaries.[1] Judi Bari's assault on that hoary trope—and her insistence on trying to build coalitions with timber workers—split Earth First!, almost permanently damaging it (Zakin 1993, chap. 14).[2] In southern Oregon, younger Earth First!ers have sought to entirely stop logging with road blockades and civil disobedience, but with less success than has been experienced by the Friends of Clayoquot Sound.

The differences do not entirely reflect political differences in the two cultures. The Headwaters Alliance—the northern California group that continues Judi Bari's struggle—has drawn enormous support in its battle to save redwood groves, but still faces an ambiguous future, in part because of the relatively small size of the forest stands in question and the fact that the lands in question are privately owned.[3] All of the U.S. Pacific Northwest struggles have revolved around the spotted owl and its protection under the Endangered Species Act, interpreted by the courts since its passage in 1973 as broadly preventing development or resource extraction if the survival of a formally endangered species is at stake. Given the breadth of this statutory protection, U.S. environmentalists have relied heavily on this aspect of forest struggles (see Dietrich 1992, chap. 4).

The well-developed backlash against U.S. greens has featured ridicule of the Endangered Species Act, making species protection a key sign of reaction against leftism of any stripe (see Helvarg 1994). Even when the worst excesses of the rightist antienvironmental "wise-use" movement limited its appeal to the broader public, the pressure exerted on environmentalists produced an effect. Faced with vituperative opposition, greens too often have been accused of responding with a smug opportunism, trying to find the magic legal remedy that would stop the logging and development when they probably should have been developing broader coalitions and seeking to neutralize or take advantage of the worst of the criticisms directed toward them. Environmentalists typically respond that the biological situation is urgent, that even the spotted owl deserves our extraordinary diligence, and that errors of zealousness are, in any case, erring on the side of protecting the earth. Even if those arguments are persuasive, political questions persist; what coalitions can you form and whom can you convince?

The political diagnosis just summarized is both a call to take serious-ly the strategic realm and an example of the kind of argument that comprises strategic politics: open to reinterpretation, contingent on facts and circum-stances that may or may not be quantified, but still crucial to political deci-sion making. When we strategize, we bring the normative into contact with the pragmatic. Green strategy combines bioscience, land ethics, and moral vision, but also some sense of media manipulation, public opinion, legal underpinnings, and the rhythms and resistances of legislative culture. To do strategy is to perform a balancing act while still trying to press forward or to gracefully manage a retreat. Strategy is nearly the opposite of certainty or commitment, even if both of those attributes might have helped get the strategist into her current opportunity (or mess).

Everybody knows that strategy is at the center of politics, but this is often a matter of much consternation. Intellectuals, journalists, and citi-zens often insist that communal life should revolve around values and morality. They resist what everybody seems nonetheless to know: politics happens in a strategic field that somehow can elude those values. Or mock them. Because values seldom seem fully confirmed by political outcomes, strategies often get the blame. Perhaps because of the resistance to strategy, it is the core that keeps disappearing. Activists are bashful to acknowledge their strategic moves. Strategy functions as a sort of open secret. Although its importance is obvious, everybody also knows that policy goals and com-munity values should drive political outcomes.

But it is not hard to find the strategic quality of politics, if one looks for it. Perhaps the clearest map is drawn in Murray Edelman's *Constructing the Political Spectacle* (1988). Edelman shows how the seemingly stable terms of political debate are subject to reversal: what one observer calls "spin," another might call "intention" or "explanation." Some problems are *useful*—sometimes so useful that their solution is delayed. Given the diffi-culty of ascertaining "real" intentions of political actors and the enormous stakes of political struggle, the simple "public policy" model of politics fal-ters. The political space is more than simply an arena for prioritizing prob-lems and implementing solutions. To cite just one clue to this complexity, the act of choosing whether something is a "problem" or an opportunity for power is the first step that then makes a series of rhetorical moves possible.

Most of the corporate and public officials we see on television or in the newspapers struggle bravely to keep the simple public policy model intact. This "remedy focus" begins with citizen attitudes (perhaps led by the elite and expert analyses championed by Walter Lippmann), rhetorically linking attitudes to outcomes. Opinion is the motor that supposedly drives the

remedy-seeking enterprise. As sensible as this model is, it is also convenient. With a public opinion justification at hand, the powerful are ready to
fend off charges that some more problematic motive might have "caused"
a particular set of outcomes. But from some other perspective, this whole
causal chain (elites identify a problem, seek a solution and support for that
solution, then implement the solution) could appear quite problematic.
The identified "problem" might be contested; why was it chosen, rather
than something else? The preferred "solution" could likewise be ques-
tioned. Then, the implementation brings in yet more instabilities, as politics produces its familiar and often perverse "unintended side effects."

In most political histories, strategy disappears and intention rules.
After all, justifications play important roles in politics, straining to shape (or
spin) the economies of power that emerge from transforming events. The
justification is always already at hand, and is always less embarrassing, less
dangerous than the strategies that may actually have given shape to the
event in question. Telling the historical story, it seems most natural to explain events in terms of what the winners intended—what justifications
they offered and how those justifications cohere with cultural and institutional themes that prevail in any given era. In the long run, this is what
one "wins" in the political world: at least some prerogative over the stories
that follow.

Historians usually translate events into narratives in which values will
gain (or lose) their institutional form. Trends (acceptable models of social
determinism) emerge. Events give way to outcomes, which winners inevitably must defend as they attempt to institutionalize some advantage. The
messy, context-bound horizons in which events actually occur do not provide the kind of permanent, easily retold, and compelling basis that institutions require for stable functioning. The wild, accidental, or even dialectical
mechanisms that produce an outcome seldom serve institutional interests.
In the one area of politics that highlights the strategic—media coverage of
election campaigns—that focus is a matter of ongoing criticism (Jamieson
1992, chap. 8).

Outcomes alter the economies of power, and in that condition of flux
there are administrative structures to implement, rules to write, expectations to manage, and disputes to resolve. And, always, there is another
anticipated struggle on the horizon. Aiming toward that next sequence of
events, stories of moral conviction and inevitability and justification seem
more useful—and more compelling—than the war stories or reminiscences
that might actually contain the strategic moves that made earlier successes
possible, or caused a prior failure. In the United States, Earth Day trans-

formed environmentalism, motivating a flood of legislative victories. What good would it do to recall that this flood was made possible by random fortuities (the weakness of Nixon-led Republicans, the rapid generational turnover of Democratic membership in Congress, the hyperactivity prevailing at the end of the Vietnam War)? Instead, environmentalists recast the stories as triumphs of their intention; the Endangered Species Act is remade into an act of biocentric heroism involving "indicator species," rather than the rushed, hopeful, but not entirely informed event that it actually was.

Strategy can also disappear if one persistently assumes that the configuration of political struggle is already obvious. If we already know the shape and course of events and outcomes, there is no need for strategy. But this "knowledge" could be perilous. Michel Foucault thought it so dangerous, in fact, that he put strategy at a central place in his argument. The critique of power is not over when one denounces power, or identifies its oppressive consequences; "[i]n order to analyze or to criticize relations of power it is not a question of affecting them with a pejorative or laudatory qualification, massive, global, definitive, absolute, unilateral; it is not a question of saying that relations of power can do only one thing, which is that of constraining and compelling" (Foucault 1978b, quoted in Davidson 1997b, 4).

Foucault adamantly denied that one could dispense with strategy in the face of a struggle that was reduced to the simplicity that dogmatic radicals adopt: "[o]ne should not imagine either that one can escape from relations of power all at once, globally, massively, by a sort of radical rupture or by a flight without return." Politics is not defined by this binary, brutal fracture, but by "games of power that one must study in terms of tactics and strategy, in terms of order and of chance, in terms of stakes and objective" (ibid.).

Foucault has been much misread on this question of global critique. Some have suggested that this position makes politics impossible, or that it cedes too much to the established order. Such critics may simply have been too eager to assimilate Foucault to a critique of other postmodernists. Others may have been opportunistic. But Foucault's point is seriously made. To study "relations of power" is to do much more than to issue global pronouncements. At a distance, one would miss the specificity, contingency, conditions, and aims of political intervention. As Arnold Davidson has made clear in his discussion of the collected Foucault works now being published in French, Foucault was studying "unexpected" sources for his "notion of strategy, his analysis of relations of power as strategic games. . . . [W]e know, for example, that when he read the texts of the Black Panthers in 1968 he discovered that they develop a strategic analysis freed of the Marxist theory of society" (Davidson 1997a, 4, quoting Defert in Defert and Ewald 1994, 1:33). To study politics, at this date, is to study strategy.

The implications of Foucault's move are potentially enormous for how we understand the workings of power and politics. At stake is nothing less than the elementary configuration of intellectual criticism—and, perhaps, an alteration of politics itself, especially traditional left politics of objection. If Foucault is right, as I believe he is, the relegation of social theory to the role of values articulation and moralist complaint could and should be altered. The role of the intellectual must incorporate strategies as well as normative concerns. To have articulated the morality of a problem is only to have begun the analytic work. Foucault's argument for this position has been hugely controversial in contemporary political theory. It is my contention that it would be just as controversial—and just as important—were it to influence the somewhat more parochial area of environmental social theory.

Despite the enormous resistances arrayed against it, the strategic realm persists, especially when one pays attention to specific events. At the level of the event, strategic considerations are most visible. We see the role of pace, control, and the attempt to problematize "legitimate" authority. Protest politics seeks to reclaim the ability to control the pace and location of crucial events from the dominant government or industry players who like to assume that this prerogative is always rightly theirs. The action moves from the committee room to the logging road, and the protesters determine when the struggle begins and when it will intensify or subside. The protesters also try to determine how long the play will last, and who will see it. Protest creates new players to challenge the stability of the powerful (see Chaloupka 1993 and Sloterdijk 1987). When successful, the protester temporarily installs herself as the least likely manager, the most improbable master of events.

The history of civil disobedience is replete with examples of this relationship between strategy and moral protest. Martin Luther King Jr. got himself bailed out of the Birmingham jail for the most pragmatic and strategic of reasons, then covered that escape with words of transcendent moral purpose (King 1991), just before he took the greatest strategic risk of his career up to then: sending children into a massive and dangerous campaign of civil disobedience. This sequence of events would eventually be remembered as locating the moral core of the civil rights movement. Randall Robinson, building an antiapartheid movement out of nothing, brought celebrities, elite decision makers, and other potential allies to the lawn of the South African embassy in Washington at a stately but persistent pace that he orchestrated. And environmentalists at Clayoquot took it upon themselves to decide when logging would happen during the summer of 1993.

The intellectuals of the environmental movement have long thought that their appropriate role was to articulate a grand refusal on behalf of the earth. Anyone who strays too far from that kind of green theory comes in for criticism that has sometimes been ferocious (for example, see Snyder 1996; Sessions 1996; Worster 1997; Foreman 1996). It is not hard to imagine that Foucault would have had different advice for green intellectuals. Paul Veyne, a respected Foucault interpreter, recalls a conversation in which Foucault described a course he taught in 1979: "this course will not tell you what you should do or what you have to fight against, but it will give you a map; thus it will tell you: if you want to attack in such and such a direction, well, here there is a knot of resistance and there a possible passage" (Veyne 1997, 230). Such a map—a strategic analysis—was appropriate and necessary intellectual work, in Foucault's view, because he recognized that "there was a specificity to power relationships, a density, an inertia, a viscosity, a course of development and an inventiveness which belonged to these relationships and which it was necessary to analyze" (Foucault 1978a, 184).

Foucault intervenes, interrupting our expectation of what a politicized intellectual should do, and making the case against a vision of power relations that is too abstract, missing the complexity that comes with specificity. The grand gesture, wrapped in moral certainty, self-righteousness, and clarity of purpose, regrets and disguises strategy, or tries to forget it. For a moralist, the reasons for an act are all one needs to know. And to the extent that moral certainty elides political strategy, there is never any reason for a partial step when a larger step is imaginable. In the United States, the typical environmental response to logging disputes that cannot be resolved satisfactorily in court has been to attempt complete blockades and shutdowns, in a manner analogous to a hard picket line at a labor strike.

There are no doubt situations that merit such a response. The point is not that such a response is never warranted, but that a dangerous convergence presents itself when a movement that already abjures strategy begins making decisions that gloss over strategic considerations (perhaps because they contain evidence of "compromise," which is morally unacceptable). The decision to attempt an actual forest-closing blockade may well match the severity of emotions about logging with the seriousness of effects that logging has. There is a coherence, a consistency, and an integrity about that decision—at least, if one ignores the strategic realm that would reintroduce some consideration of what precisely will be gained or lost by such an effort.

On the other hand, the willingness of the Clayoquot protesters to engage in a primarily symbolic blockade (mostly letting the logging trucks go through) is itself evidence that some strategic operation was in play. Whether or not it was much talked about in the press—and it did not seem to have been, from the records I have studied—this decision functioned to reveal the presence of a strategic dimension. Again, this is not to say that the decision was necessarily warranted or not. The flow of events more or less takes control over that determination. Based on their relative level of success, the Clayoquot protesters can justify most all of their mostly moderate and modest approaches. My point is that the largely symbolic blockade marked the Clayoquot events as strategic.

The outcome of this strategic approach is in some ways easily measured. The protest remained viable longer because it was easier to draw new recruits to the protest lines. Eventually, there were more than 932 arrests over less than four months (MacIsaac and Champagne 1994, xi), including 309 arrests on August 9. Activists called this the largest single civil disobedience action in Canadian history (Berman 1995), although the basis for that claim remains unclear.[4] Because the physical danger of the protest was reduced somewhat, in that the day-to-day stakes were lower for the corporation, a greater diversity of protesters could participate, broadening the political appeal of the movement. An estimated nine thousand people participated in the Peace Camp (Friends of Clayoquot Sound 1993b, 1). Press accounts of the protests emphasized their deliberate, even polite qualities (Nichols 1993, 23).

Judicial proceedings against blockaders and organizers continued for nearly a year (Berman 1995). Most of the arrestees were charged with criminal contempt of court for defying an injunction banning demonstrations on work sites controlled by MacMillan Bloedel, the largest timber company operating in British Columbia (MacIsaac and Champagne 1994, xi). Considering that most arrests involved similar actions by the arrestees, it became an issue that fines ranged from $250 to $3,000 and sentences varied from suspended sentences to six months in prison. Three elderly women who became known as the "Clayoquot grandmothers" were sentenced to four months in jail, but other protesters, tried long after the camp closed, were only assessed small fines (Berman 1995).[5]

The protest took control over the "course of development" of events, because there was anticipation of what would happen next, over how much the protest could grow, and so on. Given that the legal context of forestry law and practice provided relatively few and unpromising judicial options (at least when compared to the U.S. context), a range of alternative political outcomes still existed, and extending the protest allowed a longer period in which possibilities could be explored. The relationship of the logging to Native peoples was different than it was in the United States, and the unfolding protest summer allowed protesters time to at least try to untangle that difficult question, rather than forcing it to an outcome that might have been unfortunate. As the Clayoquot movement continued its activism after the summer of 1993, it continued to deploy civil disobedience, explaining each action in terms of the current situation. And that situation, as Valerie Langer (1996b) explained, might involve efforts to alter laws and policies, as well as to simply block a road: "civil disobedience . . . will continue to be used as a tool within the democratic process to change laws and policies. The Clayoquot blockades were instrumental in changing both forest policy and law in BC."

To put this another way, a strategic approach does not stop at denunciation. To do so would assume that the only interesting question involving power is whether it is rightly or wrongly possessed. Foucault's approach presupposes that the power exercised on the body is conceived not as a property, but as a strategy—that its effects of domination are attributed not to "appropriation," but to dispositions, maneuvers, tactics, techniques, functionings; that one should decipher in it a network of relations, constantly in tension, in activity, rather than a privilege that one might possess; that one should take as its model a perpetual battle, rather than a contract regulating a transaction or the conquest of a territory. In short, this power is exercised rather than possessed; it is not the "privilege," acquired or preserved, of the dominant class, but the overall effect of its strategic positions—an effect that is manifested and sometimes extended by the position of those who are dominated (Foucault 1979, 26–27).

Foucault's emphasis on strategy seeks to reveal the way power itself has functioned. Timber companies cannot only be understood as possessing license to cut timber, for example. They are engaged in (more or less effective and thus challengeable) strategies of maintaining their power to continue their operations as they see fit. They wish to appear inevitable, and the notion that their prerogative is a question of property right abets this wish. Viewing that prerogative as an ongoing project opens the possibility that it could be altered, even blockaded.

Conversely, the moral power associated with protests against logging is not "possessed" or owned on the basis of righteous analysis. That authority has to be created in action. And whatever prerogative to control the pace of events is garnered through direct action has to be defended, lest it be appropriated by police forces that usually work to regain that control for themselves, acting in the name of the state on behalf of the corporate interests. Even the class dynamic mentioned by Foucault is not entirely one-sided in this case. The loggers and protesters probably shared a middle-class position more than they diverged, given the prevailing level of pay for loggers and the traditional middle-class basis of the environmental movement. Morality generates certainties; strategy generates the opposite, as privilege and control are continually renegotiated.

A strategist knows that protest actions might end up inadvertently benefiting their adversary, who is, after all, strategizing too. A protest too easily demonized could consolidate the dominant position of power, or discourage potential allies. But the point is that the strategist *knows* about this possibility, and thus enters it into the analysis. At the same time, the protesters also know that their cause is just. But a strategist does not *possess* that knowledge as a right, in quite the same way that a moralist might. Understanding how wrong it is to clearcut Clayoquot, for example, energizes, motivates, and brings together those who share that understanding. But the clarity in itself assures nothing.

When protesters talk to reporters, they are all values, justifications, and pious outrage. This is as it should be; not everyone knows their reasons as well as they do, and this is a way of reaching out. When they go back to camp, however, they talk little of those things, perhaps even instituting rituals so these lofty elements will not be entirely forgotten. In camp, there are strategic decisions to make, not to mention a thousand logistical details to be resolved. How fast to push? How much to demand? Which coalitions to nurture, and which to abandon? How to balance the need for international visibility with the sometimes conflicting need to build a local organization? Who cooks dinner, and who cleans up? What should we do about a disruptive camper? A strategist is unashamed to recognize that such questions lie at the very core of their activity. This is what "think globally, act locally" actually looks like, late at night before the next morning's dawn arrests.

By all accounts, the Clayoquot protesters were not terribly explicit about their strategizing, back in 1993 or since. Comments at the 1997 workshop that occasioned this book usually tended toward dismissal: "We didn't really know what we were doing," "We just tried to make the right choice," "We kept pursuing this issue because it was so important to us, not because we had really figured out how we were going to do it." The pace of events tends to compound this sense of ad hoc decision making; one activist said they felt, in 1993, as though they were compressing twenty years of organizing into one summer. Looking back, the Clayoquot activists tend to explain the "hobbled together" aspect of their approach in terms of naïveté, common sense, principles, and good fortune.

Activist Valerie Langer (1996a) expressed this ad hoc quality: "The advantage of being a non-hierarchical, radical, grassroots organization is that you do what you feel needs to be done as far as the locals see it. . . . We've negotiated, we've educated, we've toured media and politicians, lobbied and, when we felt it was necessary, we blockaded." Elsewhere, Langer demonstrated an awareness of the contingent quality any successful strategist of protest movement must understand: "There are some things one cannot predict nor manufacture. Nobody manufactured the Clayoquot movement; it developed in an incredible, bounding manner" (MacIsaac and Champagne 1994, 190).

One of the reasons strategy is so difficult for greens is that this aspect of politics resists what theorists call metanarratives—the most abstract stories of connection and cause that play a historical and cultural role increasingly scrutinized by contemporary theory. Political outcomes can turn on accident or on the ordinary contingency of events; what happens today is conditioned by what happened earlier, in ways no individual player can usually control. The Clayoquot activists benefited from this contingency. They could selectively pick precedents from greens in Europe and the United States. Their central tactic, civil disobedience, which had long since turned ambivalent in the United States, retained the power to gain attention in Canada, although the precise reasons for that remain somewhat unclear. The novelty and exotic quality of Canada for Europeans provided an audience and a source of support.

But contingency requires more than simple recognition. It also mandates a kind of double consciousness, in which one must function at two levels—the ethical and the strategic—at the same time. Langer displayed a facility with this double consciousness when she acknowledged the role of government misdeed in building the movement:

> With every tyrannical attempt to silence the movement, the government challenged what Canadians deeply believe to be their rights. . . . As a campaigner for Clayoquot Sound . . . , I couldn't help but feel that the government's heavy-handed approach to the Clayoquot arrestees and their harsh sentencing made for very good campaign material. As a citizen, . . . I have been greatly saddened by the mass trials. (Ibid., 190–91)

Managing that tension—operationalizing both dignity and competence—is at the heart of the strategic element of the Clayoquot protest. Conceptualizing that stance is a matter of values, but also of a posture toward politics that is not entirely encompassed by values.

In other respects, the Clayoquot activists surely were fortunate. Although the basic moves of green politics (for example, a focus on ancient forests) had been worked out elsewhere, Canadian forest protection laws lagged behind. Yvan Hardy, then assistant deputy minister in charge of the Canadian Forest Service, told the *Washington Post* that battles over BC forests were unheard of when he entered forestry in the 1960s and forest professionals "were the only ones there. . . . It was a world by itself; there were no pressures. . . . [Since then,] all of the rules have changed" (Schneider 1997). The terrible effects of Clayoquot clearcuts prove the truth of his admission. In the United States, where the struggle over the forests had started by the time timber companies implemented clearcutting, the forests were seldom cut so ruthlessly—and almost never were they cut to the highway, where they could be easily seen. U.S. greens had to fight for forest protection in courts and committee hearings (resorting to civil disobedience as a last resort); the Canadian situation was somewhat more open. That meant that terrible damage had already been done to the Sound's forests, but it also meant that the activists' story was simpler and more dramatic.

A strategist turns problem into advantage; the fact that the legal system offered little way for activists to express what they saw as the real issues became part of the justification and impetus for civil disobedience. Even the economic picture was favorable, in some ways, for the Clayoquot activists. Compared to other timber struggles, the number of jobs at stake for timber workers paled in relation to the scale of the logging, owing to dramatic automation that the timber unions had earlier accepted. The Clayoquot activists found themselves in a "jobs versus environment" struggle, to be sure, but there were so few jobs at stake, and so much forest. Even here, the activists had good fortune; the link between mechanization and job loss was much clearer in Canada than it has been elsewhere.[6] The Friends of Clayoquot Sound (FOCS) took good advantage of this opportunity, emphasizing this aspect of their struggle (Friends of Clayoquot Sound 1993a).

Knowing that theirs was a long-term struggle ("In Australia and Europe we're fighting to protect forests a tenth this size"), the Clayoquot activists must have known, even if they hid this knowledge, that there was time. Understanding that, they broadened their protest to include the users of products made from the Sound's timber. And these protests were not limited to ethical appeals to individual consumers. Understanding the corporate character of the struggle, they worked on corporate consumers who, if convinced, could put significant pressure on MacMillan Bloedel.

After a protest at its Manhattan headquarters, the *New York Times* went on record saying it would not do business with a company that broke environmental laws (Davey 1995). The *Times* subsequently canceled its contract (Hatch 1996), as did the *San Francisco Chronicle* (Davey 1995). London's Daily Express Newspapers agreed to find alternative sources of newsprint. Greenpeace Europe estimates that newspaper and magazine publishers have canceled more than US$8 million in contracts with MacMillan Bloedel, replacing their paper with products from "clearcut-free" suppliers (ibid.). In Japan, the Nippon Telephone and Telegraph company canceled its contract for telephone directory paper, and several U.S. magazines announced policies against using old-growth paper (Hatch 1996).

The Clayoquot activists seem to have understood that their dispute with MacMillan Bloedel involved more than denunciation. Strategic adversaries are linked in a contingent political setting; each informs the other. But this is not always obvious, when the tones of moralism grow ever louder. It is thus notable that FOCS seemed to understand this; "The Forest Alliance, Share the Clayoquot and Share Our Resources, the Forest Forever TV ads all challenged us to become more sophisticated in our campaigns to protect Clayoquot Sound" (Langer 1996a).

An important implication of Foucault's argument is that seemingly foundational political elements actually emerge from political activity. This marks the success of the protests, as their adversaries are forced to alter their position. But this is also the process by which the normative elements of the scene are redrawn or reconstituted as the struggle unfolds. As the devastated landscape of the Sound makes obvious, MacMillan Bloedel did not always find it necessary to acknowledge the environmental impact of its actions. Now it does: "Clayoquot Sound also has important natural attributes including habitat for shorebirds, extensive eelgrass beds and ecosystems supported by large tracts of contiguous original forest" (Forest Alliance of British Columbia 1997b). "Large scale clearcuts (common practice until recently) are banned entirely" (ibid., 1997a). "Clayoquot Sound's global significance is not in question" (ibid.).

FOCS's success cannot be disparaged as merely a matter of good fortune. An observer from the outside is struck by the Clayoquot activists' self-assurance and willingness to strategize. One of the activists even ventured to write that "[w]e're dedicated to changing metaphorical landscapes, not the ones we live on" (Langer 1996a), hardly a remark that would be made by an activist who was not comfortable, at some level, with a strategic perspective. Where did the guilt and rigidity that damages greens elsewhere go in Clayoquot? My informal discussions, at the 1997 workshop, made it clear that such internal struggles continue in Tofino, but that is neither surprising nor necessarily distressing. As a strategic, fluid, competent, and successful model, the Friends of Clayoquot Sound stands out.

There are important caveats to register. FOCS was not operating in a vacuum. There had been a "valley-by-valley" struggle in British Columbia, going back for at least a decade. The precedent existed for mass action on behalf of environmental preservation in the province. And several of the specific tactics implemented by FOCS already had been worked out, if on a smaller scale, in earlier Clayoquot actions and elsewhere. In addition, FOCS had several advantages that its U.S. counterparts did not have. British Columbia has a vital social-democratic heritage, including a lively politics on the left. FOCS could draw on a constituency familiar with protest politics on peace and feminist issues; Clayoquot was easily attached to a familiar agenda. But the FOCS action was notable in its scope, duration, and forcefulness—in ways not entirely discounted by the possibilities inherent in the political context.

The materials distributed by FOCS display predictable political positioning, but what is striking is the group's *deliberate* effort to build a coalition and broaden its appeal. In part, its success correlates with its ability to talk about strategies and successes in a way that is entirely disarming—confident, but not arrogant; strategic, but not opportunist; ethical, yet contingent. At the 1997 workshop, one of the activists responded to the "jobs versus the environment" conundrum by insisting that the 1993 protests still allowed the loggers through the blockade, except for three days. Another activist said, "Yes, but that was the image we wanted sent out—our bodies stopping their trucks." Image, power, and aftermath intertwine in that exchange in a way that tells me that these folk knew what they were doing in 1993, at a high level. Environmentalists need to be conversant in the terms of strategy and contingency.

This deliberate quality was visible during the 1993 events. Some of these moves are obvious, but the point is that they seem to have been taken particularly seriously by FOCS. In a video distributed by the group, the first on-camera supporters are a retired logger who changed sides (and was arrested at the road blockade) and a well-spoken retired couple who referred with obvious regret about having depleted all conventional opportunities to influence policy (Friends of Clayoquot Sound 1993a). The First Nations are presented in the video, with some acknowledgment of the difficulties of their political position. Later we meet more retirees and two fourteen-year-olds. Each of these interviews is deliberately chosen to expand the coalition. The approach is neither self-righteous nor morally pompous.

FOCS knows that it has a case to make and a movement to build. The transcendental reassurance often evident in green politics somehow seems (at least comparatively) suppressed in its self-representations. FOCS did not directly inherit John Muir's moralistic overconfidence, nor his followers' hubris. One is struck by its resolutely deliberate approach. The Canadian location of the Sound contributed other advantages. The "subject position" of Canadians is that of producers of goods consumed elsewhere, and this was always well understood by FOCS, which accordingly sought to reach out to international constituencies from a very early date (Kuehls 1997). In short, from a Canadian base, there could be no confusion about the international dimension of the issue; Canada cannot be confused with the universal in ways that the United States sometimes is.

Canada's communitarian ethos—a well-developed cultural position, at least in comparison with the United States—also helped. Although the 1993 protest camp was committed to consensus, pacifism, ecofeminism, and other values, it was also defined by many rules and limits (ibid.). Some topics were open to the endless discussion that marks nonhierarchical, consensus-based meetings anywhere. Participants describe long discussions over whether drums should be played to accompany the morning's protest, for example. But other topics (including elements of the basic strategy) were not endlessly reopened. Some issues were resolved at the level of principle, often identified as "ecofeminist principle": "openness, friendliness and respect for all living things, no verbal or physical violence or damage to property, no weapons, alcohol or drugs, an atmosphere of calm and dignity." These principles translated into "cardinal rules": equality, nonviolence, and decisions by consensus (MacIsaac and Champagne 1994, 56).

Compared to such operations elsewhere, consensus in this case clearly had more to do with commitment than gridlock. Perhaps most notably, camp leaders managed to defuse controversy over the practice of tree spiking, despite the public stance taken by one activist and despite the fact that spiking has long been decried by U.S. timber companies to vilify their green adversaries. In Clayoquot, camp leaders denounced the practice as "macho environmentalism" and were generally able to steer news coverage away from what seems to have become a nonissue there (Bell 1993). In short, there is much evidence of a strategic theme, in some ways a successful one, operating in the Clayoquot events. But there also are frustrations and limitations apparent in those events and their aftermath. Strategy happens in a field that is not determined by the resolve or ethics of participants, nor by the justice of their cause. There is always another side, also strategizing.

Strategy can solve problems, but usually such solutions are only temporary. An ethical commitment can endure, but events shaped by strategies move on. Despite successes for the Clayoquot activists, elsewhere in British Columbia—and for that matter throughout the Pacific Northwest—forest politics has not yet been transformed. Beyond the boundaries of Clayoquot, logging continues at a dramatic pace. In the United States, old-growth logging continues at such a level (and with such powerful advocates) that the usually cautious Sierra Club now advocates a "zero cut" option for governmental lands. Even after such major opinion leaders as the *New York Times* and the *Washington Post* have repeatedly editorialized against massive old-growth logging, the practice persists. The recent ban on subsidized construction of new logging roads on public lands in the United States leaves some ancient forests in the Pacific Northwest at risk. Protests against logging have continued in the United States, often featuring civil disobedience. Various protests in northern California were widely publicized in the late 1990s, but civil disobedience also continued in Idaho, Oregon, and elsewhere.

In short, what success the Clayoquot activists have achieved does not seem to have been successfully exported beyond the Sound, as a model that works in other locales. In a real sense, it is the logging that has been exported. BC forest activists appeal to a large, solid constituency, and battles persist in other valleys, in some cases by individuals and groups who protested at Clayoquot. Nonetheless, activists have not managed to incorporate most of organized labor into their coalition. In some ways, timber companies—which themselves are strategizing this situation—have confounded the relationship between greens and First Nations peoples. Whatever positive attributes can be identified in the FOCS approach are seriously diminished by these facts. In a sense, Clayoquot activism begins to look like the best example of a certain kind of green activism, but that "best" is not good enough.

It is at moments like this that theory becomes necessary in any effort to reflect on (and hopefully produce) other possibilities. Foucault at least suggested the possibility of a new kind of politics, even though his main project involved the role of intellectuals and the configuration of the central intellectual projects of our time. The elevation of the strategic (which much of this essay has considered) is an important piece of this new politics, but it is hardly the whole story. Foucault proposed a permanent alteration in the relation between ethics and strategy. These two realms have usually been understood as being in a relationship of irreconcilable tension; one implements strategy at the expense of one's ethical position. At the end of his life, Foucault was studying this relationship from the perspective of the ethical, finding in classical precedents an ethical approach that "cared for the self."

The problem with the ethical realm, in Foucault's argument, is that power now operates in a way that normalizes several of its important aspects, making coercion, discipline, and the control of bodies a matter of mundane, everyday routine. This transformation of power confounds ethics at the same time that it ruptures the way intellectuals and citizens know power. The importance of Foucault's recommendations for how intellectuals should investigate power (discussed earlier) are thus not simply recommendations about scholarly focus, but function as cues to new political possibilities.

It is beyond the scope of this essay to attempt an overview of this new politics, but some examples might be useful.[7] Recall Foucault's lecture hall admonition (quoted earlier) that instead of locating "what you have to fight against," he would identify "knot[s] of resistance [and] possible passage[s]" (Veyne 1997, 230). One application of this suggestion to green politics is obvious. Although much green theory seems to view resistance primarily as a confirmation of the cause's moral necessity, the question of a possible passage out of that knot of resistance has not been the subject of much green theorizing. Backlash and resentment against environmentalists have become a key feature of forest politics, both in the United States and in British Columbia. FOCS in some ways contested that resistance, sometimes successfully and sometimes not.

Another example, this one not related directly to Clayoquot, might clarify the point. From an ethical perspective, many greens have adopted or at least tolerated the animal rights perspective, though the presence of this perspective in the environmental movement has not been entirely without controversy (Knox 1993). The animal rights (or ethical treatment) issue is an important ethical issue, not unrelated to the "rights of trees" argument mentioned earlier. But, assessing the antigreen backlash, animal rights has an entirely different meaning. While environmentalists have happily studied the categories of anthropocentrism and biocentrism, their political adversaries have just as happily orchestrated a backlash (in the United States, often emphasizing opposition to the Endangered Species Act). In ethical terms, animal rights and ecosystem health can probably coexist in most philosophical arguments. But in strategic terms, the presence of the animal rights argument potentially blocks a political passage for greens.

It might be useful for activists and other serious greens to understand that the ethical positions they defend—positions that seem timeless when attached to such terms as *biocentric*—are in fact constituted in the process of political struggle. Perhaps the best example in the current case is the whole focus on ancient forests. The Clayoquot activists routinely compared the forest to a cathedral, evoking its spiritual dimension. But their reference is more precise than they know; like the cathedrals, the focus on old-growth timber and ancient forests (and even the term *ancient forests*) has been built. As concern about logging in the U.S. Pacific Northwest increased, scientists and activists defined old growth as a political issue, eventually discovering not only that the scientific arguments were convincing, but also that the term *ancient forests* appealed to a broad potential constituency (see Dietrich 1992, chap. 13). Knowing this should not diminish the importance of the forest, nor should it undermine green commitment to forest preservation. But, politically, activists might better understand their struggle if they appreciate that the process develops the terms of moral contestation, and is not simply driven by those terms. This should not be a matter of embarrassment or reluctance; it is at the core of what politics now does.

From an ethical perspective, acceptance of a protest movement in a larger coalition may not be a matter of much concern. At the extreme, following the lead long ago established by Marxist theorists, greens have been willing to oppose potential allies, the better to solidify their moral position. But the best protest strategists have dealt with this tension more creatively. Again, the U.S. civil rights movement provides a vivid example. At the same time that Martin Luther King Jr. was quite willing to make his potential Democrat allies uncomfortable, he also paid close attention to party leaders and hoped eagerly to personally influence such political figures as President John F. Kennedy. The passage out of a morally superior but politically marginal position requires more adroit thinking about strategic relations to power than many protest movements ordinarily have produced. In one crucial example, the role of greens in electoral politics has been poorly theorized—indeed, it is hardly a matter for serious environmental political theorists to consider.[8]

Clayoquot activists possess a political model that, when articulated, sometimes seems surprisingly conventional. Claiming a measure of success, Langer adopted language and models of causation not much distinguished from the mainstream: "the FOCS worked to change the world's attitudes to ancient temperate rainforests. That dedication seems to be coming to fruition with Clayoquot Sound having become a symbol worldwide for our fears for the wild and natural areas and our hopes for its continuation" (Langer 1996a). Dedication, changing attitudes, and becoming a symbol— these are markers of a fairly conventional politics. But the actual political scene does not necessarily change according to such a linear model (work hard, alter attitudes, and change will accrue). As Foucault argued and demonstrated, politics now changes in fits and starts of redefinitions, transformations, and habituations. This is anything but a linear process. Nor does it necessarily change according to the rules commonly spoken in the dominant culture.

What remains to be done is to articulate a different green politics, something that would alter the relationship between ethics and strategy while it also altered how the world worked. Heavy on utopianism and idealism, green approaches have not made as much progress in this regard as they might have. The ethical realm assumes a measure of marginalization that must be made problematic. There are openings, here and there, and I have tried to identify some of them in the Clayoquot struggle. My conclusion from this project must necessarily remain partial. Environmental theory has to change. As crucial as it has been in articulating a green ethics that contributes to green solidarity, the intellectual wing of environmental thought has yet to show a passage out of the tension intensified by that same ethical dimension.

Notes

1. "Tree spiking" refers to the practice of embedding foreign objects (usually metal or ceramic spikes) in standing trees in order to discourage logging on the assumption that sawmills will be reluctant to process logs that might injure sawyers or damage expensive equipment. In the United States, tree spiking became emblematic both of the seriousness of groups such as Earth First! and of the backlash against those groups.

2. Bari was a leader of the struggle to save redwood stands in northern California, and subsequently the leader of a group that tried to reorient Earth First! so that they could build coalitions with workers, including loggers. She is perhaps best known as the victim of a bomb blast, the origin of which has never been determined in the courts (see Zakin 1993, esp. chap. 14). Bari died from cancer in 1997.

3. Both Bari's role and the relevance of private ownership of the lands in question are covered in detail in Harris 1996.

4. Canada's long history of organized labor activism provides several examples that are seemingly "larger," including the Winnipeg general strike of 1919, the strike by the Common Front of Quebec Labour in 1972, and Operation Solidarity in British Columbia in 1983. In several of these and other instances, the strikes were illegal and involved arrests and imprisonments, which arguably fits them in the category of "civil disobedience." It could be that Berman and others who have used such terminology are thinking about environmental protest or about movements that announced their adherence to principled civil disobedience. Or it could be that this estimate demonstrates the long-standing tension between greens and labor, a tension that exists on both sides of the border. Even in terms of environmental protest, some First Nations actions have been large and sustained. My thanks to Warren Magnusson for helping to clarify these points.

5. One of the Clayoquot grandmothers, Betty Krawczyk, was again sentenced

to jail in September 2000, this time for defying a court order in relation to antilogging protests in the Elaho Valley of the Great Bear Rainforest. She was released in time to run in the provincial election as a candidate for the Green Party. She ran against the then premier, Ujjal Dosanjh, and finished third behind him and the victorious Patrick Wong of the BC Liberals.

6. In the United States, environmentalists have struggled to demonstrate that automation and corporate decisions have been a major reason for lost logging jobs, but in the Clayoquot setting at least, agreements by labor to accept job attrition in favor of higher salaries were formalized and seemed harder to ignore.

7. Karena Shaw's insightful comments informed this and the next several paragraphs on the question of the new politics implied by Foucault's arguments.

8. The Green Party did relatively well in the 2001 provincial election in British Columbia, capturing 12.4 percent of the vote. Adriane Carr, who came to prominence as an activist at Clayoquot, led the party into the election. (As noted, one of the "Clayoquot grandmothers" ran against the premier himself. A prominent member of the Friends of Clayoquot Sound contested the seat in the region itself.) None of the greens were elected. Critics voiced the same complaint that had been made during Ralph Nader's run for the U.S. presidency: namely, that the Green Party was drawing votes away from the more ecofriendly of the two major parties. However, in this instance, the combined vote of the Green Party and the NDP would still not have been sufficient to deprive the right-wing party of its success.

Works Cited

Bell, Stewart. 1993. "Eco-feminists Run 'Peace Camp' at Clayoquot Sound." *Vancouver Sun*, August 19, B1.

Berman, Tzeporah. 1995. "Standing for Our Lives: A Feminist Journey to Clayoquot Sound." Master of Environmental Studies thesis, York University. 98–106.

Berman, Tzeporah, Gordon Brent Ingram, Maurice Gibbons, and Ronald B. Hatch, eds. 1994. *Clayoquot and Dissent.* Vancouver: Ronsdale Press.

Bohn, Glenn. 1993. "Midnight Oil to Rock Loggers in Early Morning." *Vancouver Sun*, July 9, B2.

Chaloupka, William. 1993. "Suppose Kuwait's Main Product Was Broccoli? (The Street Demonstration in U.S. Politics)." In *Rhetorical Republic: Representing American Politics*, ed. Frederick M. Dolan and Thomas L. Dumm. Amherst: University of Massachusetts Press. 143–66.

Davey, Robert. 1995. "Rainforest Crunch: Drive to Save the Clayoquot Sound Rainforest in Vancouver Island, British Columbia." *E* 6: 19–21.

Davidson, Arnold I. 1997a. "Structures and Strategies of Discourse." In *Foucault and His Interlocutors*, ed. Arnold I. Davidson. Chicago: University of Chicago Press. 1–17.

———, ed. 1997b. *Foucault and His Interlocutors.* Chicago: University of Chicago Press.

Defert, Daniel, and François Ewald, eds. 1994. *Michel Foucault: Dits et Écrits, 1954–1988.* 4 vols. Paris: Gallimard.

Dietrich, William. 1992. *The Final Forest: The Battle for the Last Great Trees of the Pacific Northwest.* New York: Simon and Schuster.

Edelman, Murray. 1988. *Constructing the Political Spectacle.* Chicago: University of Chicago Press.

Farnsworth, Clyde H. 1993. "Tofino Journal: Two Towns Do Battle over Canada's Rain Forests." *New York Times,* November 13.

Ferry, Luc. 1995. *The New Ecological Order.* Chicago: University of Chicago Press.

Foreman, Dave. 1996. "Around the Campfire: All Kinds of Wilderness Foes." *Wild Earth* 6: 1–4.

Forest Alliance of British Columbia. 1997a. "Clayoquot Sound—Opinion and Response." Http://www.realm.ca/forest/readingroom/clayoquot/clayk.html, November 25.

———. 1997b. "MB and the Clayoquot Sound Compromise: Background, Impacts and the Future." Http://www.realm.ca/forest/readingroom/clayoquot/claym.html, November 25.

Foucault, Michel. 1978a. "Clarifications on the Question of Power." Trans. James Cascaito. In *Foucault Live: Interviews, 1966–84,* ed. Sylvère Lotringer. New York: Semiotext(e), 1989. 173–84.

———. 1978b. "La Philosophie analytique de la politique." Trans. Arnold Davidson. In *Dits et Écrits, 1954–1988,* ed. Daniel Defert and François Ewald. Paris: Gallimard, 1994. 3:540–41.

———. 1979. *Discipline and Punish: The Birth of the Prison.* Trans. Alan Sheridan. New York: Random House.

Friends of Clayoquot Sound. 1993a. "Friends of Clayoquot Sound." Video. Tofino, B.C.

———. 1993b. "750+ Arrested." *Newsletter* (fall): 1.

Garrett, Peter. 1993. "Dare to Be Aware: Who's Protecting Nature's Rights?" *Creem* (November/December): 1.

Harris, David. 1996. *The Last Stand: The War between Wall Street and Main Street over California's Ancient Redwoods.* San Francisco: Sierra Club Books.

Hatch, Christopher. 1996. "International Update." *The Friends of Clayoquot Sound* (newsletter) (fall/winter): 7.

Helvarg, David. 1994. *The War against the Greens: The "Wise Use" Movement, the New Right, and Anti-Environmental Violence.* San Francisco: Sierra Club Books.

Ingram, Gordon Brent. 1994. "The Ecology of a Conflict." In *Clayoquot and Dissent,* ed. Tzeporah Berman, Gordon Brent Ingram, Maurice Gibbons, and Ronald B. Hatch. Vancouver: Ronsdale Press. 9–71.

Jamieson, Kathleen Hall. 1992. *Dirty Politics: Deception, Distraction and Democracy.* New York: Oxford University Press.

King, Martin Luther, Jr. 1991. "Letter from the Birmingham City Jail." In *The Eyes on the Prize: Civil Rights Reader,* ed. Clayborne Carson, David J. Garrow, and Darlene Clark Hine. New York: Penguin. 153–59.

Knox, Margaret L. 1993. "The Rights Stuff: Animal Rights Incite a Riot of Emotions, but Are They Part of the Environmental Movement?" *Buzzworm* (May–June): 31–37.

Kuehls, Thom. 1997. Interview with the author, September 28.

Langer, Valerie. 1996a. "It Happened Suddenly (Over a Long Period of Time): A Clayoquot History." Posted to http://www.island.net/~focs/history.htm on April 15.

———. 1996b. "Supreme Court: The Big Law." *The Friends of Clayoquot Sound* (newsletter) (fall/winter): 8.

Lee, Robert Mason. 1993a. "Anti-Logging Rock Group Met by Hundreds Chanting." *Vancouver Sun,* July 15, A1–2.

————. 1993b. "Rock Concert to Cheer Black Hole Bunch." *Vancouver Sun,* July 14, B3.

————. 1993c. "Rockers Slam Scare Tactics." *Vancouver Sun,* July 13, B2.

————. 1993d. "Rocking Activists Cling to Hope Protests Can Flip Clayoquot Call." *Vancouver Sun,* July 16, A1.

MacIsaac, Ron, and Anne Champagne, eds. 1994. *Clayoquot Mass Trials: Defending the Rainforest.* Philadelphia: New Society Publishers.

Nichols, Mark. 1993. "The World Is Watching: Is Canada an Environmental Outlaw?" *Maclean's,* August 16, 23–24.

Schneider, Howard. 1997. "Economy, Ecology Lock Horns: Canada Redefines Relationship with the Land." *Washington Post,* October 27, A1.

Sessions, George. 1996. "Reinventing Nature? The End of Wilderness?" *Wild Earth* 6: 46–52.

Sloterdijk, Peter. 1987. *Critique of Cynical Reason.* Trans. Michael Eldred. Minneapolis: University of Minnesota Press.

Snyder, Gary. 1996. "Nature As Seen from Kitkitdizze Is No 'Social Construction.'" *Wild Earth* 6: 8–9.

Stone, Christopher D. 1974. *Should Trees Have Standing?: Toward Legal Rights for Natural Objects.* Los Aptos, Calif.: Kauffman.

Veyne, Paul. 1997. "The Final Foucault and His Ethics." Trans. Catherine Porter and Arnold I. Davidson. In *Foucault and His Interlocutors,* ed. Arnold I. Davidson. Chicago: University of Chicago Press. 225–33.

Worster, Donald. 1997. "The Wilderness of History." *Wild Earth* 7: 9–13.

Zakin, Susan. 1993. *Coyotes and Town Dogs: Earth First! and the Environmental Movement.* New York: Viking Press.

On the Political Economy of Clayoquot Sound

The Uneasy Transition from Extractive to Attractive Models of Development

Timothy W. Luke

In surveying the political economy of Vancouver Island, many of the current conflicts in global capitalism can be read from traces they leave in the lives of the particular individuals who live on Clayoquot Sound. During the 1970s, Maureen Fraser, a burned-out social worker from Ontario, came to the Sound on a trip to enjoy the newly created Pacific Rim National Park. Now one of Tofino's most famous environmental advocates as well as the town's highly respected baker, she remembers her first trip into town in search of a cinnamon bun: "I couldn't find one because there was no bakery in Tofino. Nothing. I looked around and thought, 'This town doesn't know what's hit it.' Pacific Rim National Park has just been created right next to it, and it had this amazing Sound, and it had almost no services. No bakery. No bookstore. No place to rent canoes or kayaks" (Priest 1997, 28). After traveling elsewhere in Central and South America, she returned to the Sound and started selling banana bread to support herself. Slowly, she built a bakery, and expanded it into a café. Attracted to Tofino by the beauty of the Sound, she helped build, in turn, new attractions for many others just like her.

Her move to Tofino was neither self-consciously political nor tied to anything other than economic needs she saw as unmet when she arrived in the Sound. Yet, it is clear that Maureen Fraser's story, in fact, is very political and fairly indicative of larger economic changes happening all over the world as struggles between labor and capital, communities and corporations, peripheries and centers shift both their focus and pitch. Although she was drawn to the Sound by its natural splendor, Maureen Fraser stayed to provide some urbane refinements for a new economy centered on attractive rather than extractive strategies for growth. What once was, as R. Michael M'Gonigle observes in his essay in this volume, a zone of brutal extractive destruction, where whales were harpooned and butchered for bone, oil, and meat, has now become a site of refined attraction, where whales are watched by ecotourists intent on making nature videos for the folks back home.

Conventional analyses of all rural areas as underdeveloped peripheries under the harsh domination of overdeveloped cores in faraway urban centers—as Clayoquot Sound has been under the control of timber, fishing, and mining interests—are perhaps not as useful as they once were (Innis 1956; Frank 1976; Wallerstein 1979). Where wilderness once was the standing reserve of raw materials out in the peripheries, pieces and parts of it increasingly are being reprocessed, as Catriona Sandilands argues in her essay in this volume, in simulacral cycles of valorization that preserve stands of materialized rawness as recentered chunks of the core. These changes drew Maureen Fraser to the Sound, led her to defend it as an environmentalist, gave her personal story this political history in defense of Nature on the Pacific Rim, but they also have reshaped Tofino's town site to serve others like her with bakeries, bookstores, and backwoods ecotours as they jointly struggle to stop the logging, mining, and fishing that once supported this little village. Much of what has hit Tofino, Ucluelet, and Clayoquot Sound is a shift from an extractive to an attractive model of development, which is, in turn, a response to other extensive changes in commodity production, urban growth, and the quality of life all over the world. This essay begins to explore these shifts as they manifest themselves in the life of Maureen Fraser and her many neighbors in Clayoquot Sound.

Centers, Peripheries, and Their Connections

The creative cycles of destructive exchange—both wanted and imposed—between economic centers and peripheries is rarely straightforward. Moreover, the operational connections binding the two zones, which either continuously affirm the centers and peripheries or constantly confound their operations and assumptions, are not obvious. Nonetheless, recent developments in Clayoquot Sound reveal an interesting shift from extractive raw materials production to attractive services provision as rural regions deindustrialize. Indeed, this illustrates how the contemporary world economy assembles itself every day out of a vast multilayered mosaic of localities, regions, and nations, all, as Adam Smith suggests, seeking "to truck, barter, exchange, and trade" with each other in many millions of marketplaces. From these transactions, the costs and benefits of economic exchange as well as the surpluses and scarcities in ecological equilibriums flow to and from each locality, almost always in unequal, unbalanced, and unjust ways. To survive, each and every community must find a niche in one or many of the commodity chains linking localities, regions, and nations to every other marketplace around the world, which the towns of Tofino and Ucluelet have done historically with their ties to logging, fishing, and mining.

A few communities, as Innis (1956) and Wallerstein (1979) assert, can specialize in high-order tertiary services, focused on adding value to information, knowledge, or intelligence about everything else. Quite a few more may specialize in midrange secondary manufacturing, centered on adding value to goods and services through manufacturing industries. Many, however, must specialize in lower-level primary extraction, based on taking raw resources from the earth in farming, mining, fishing, or timbering operations (Frank 1976). Yet, the contradictions of effort and reward in the world's general economic exchange, as well as the cross-pressures of cost and benefit in the planet's basic ecological equilibrium, frequently break loose first in regions rooted in primary extraction, as the ecological struggles over forestry practices in Clayoquot Sound illustrate.

As Storper and Walker observe, all economic development in contemporary capitalist societies is principally "the outcome of productive activities organized in the form of industries . . . carried out by individuals and private firms employing wage and salary workers, acting under the conditions of generalized market exchange and the spur of competition" (Storper and Walker 1989, 8). Competition, unequal exchange, and spatially disequilibriated growth produce uneven development across all regions and industrial decline within a particular region, because "each territorial economy has its characteristic specializations" (ibid., 9). The post-1945 economy of British Columbia, Vancouver Island, and Clayoquot Sound provides many vivid examples of these destructively constructive dynamics, because they are territorial spaces organized historically around extracting raw materials from Nature.

Spatial concentrations of industry, whether they are primary, secondary, or tertiary in nature, develop within any given territory as particular ensembles of production. British Columbia clearly has been shaped by the growth processes of extractive industry in the segments of primary product production. Dominant ensembles of production, which link back into centers of extractive industry such as those in Clayoquot Sound, exhibit common characteristics in their regional mode of production and spatial organization. As Storper and Walker claim, they "employ large numbers of workers, absorb large amounts of investment; have unusually high rates of growth of output and/or employment; have major propulsive effects on upstream sectors; produce capital goods with critical effects on the products and processes of other sectors or produce widely-used consumption goods" (ibid.).

As new industrial ensembles emerge, there are many associated changes across the affected regions that recontour the economic spaces and settled places of particular countries. These internally differentiated territorial economies become more varied in their output, income, employment, growth, and overall social development as they shape themselves around primary, secondary, or tertiary production. The increasing integration of British Columbia into the larger economy of the Pacific Rim—along with the growing presence of white-collar, informational sources of employment and risk-averse, technoscientific finance capital in the urbanized areas of the province—coupled with less costly primary product exports from abroad, is reconfiguring the growth equation in the older extractive industrial base of Vancouver Island. At the same time, what is center and/or periphery has become much less certain. The expansion, instability, and differentiation of capital are bringing more people with new attitudes about the environment out into the island's smallest communities. The economic instabilities in the dominant industrial ensembles worldwide—ensembles with firms in the province—favor new attractive types of industry over older extractive ones. And the struggles between labor and capital now are manifesting themselves in the specific environmental, regional, and cultural conflicts over what the economy and society of Clayoquot Sound should become in the near future. Creating a new growth center in Tofino/Ucluelet for outdoor leisure, recreational, and sport industries means downsizing, if not entirely eliminating, much of the traditional timber industry. The environmental battles over preserving the old-growth temperate rainforest with its many ecological values, for the most part, simply resonate these inchoate trends in the business expansion, profit instability, and industrial differentiation behind the region's capitalist mode of production.

Granting primacy to attractive industries over long-established, extractive industries in Clayoquot Sound has tested the concords of community between labor and capital, First Nations and other Canadians, locals and outsiders, tourist operators and timber workers. The consolidation of new industries anywhere always changes the local regime of accumulation and division of labor in ways that will help some as they harm others. Storper and Walker suggest: "new industries introduce dramatic changes in employment relations, occupational structure, and income shares; these new arrangements of production and distribution, in turn, alter the nature of inter-regional and international economic relations," and, in turn, new forms of "urbanization, daily life, and political culture arise in association with the restructured economies of capitalism" (ibid.).

As M'Gonigle asserts in this volume, the political economy of Clayoquot Sound reveals in fine relief the complex contours of commodification in the contemporary global marketplace in which individuals and societies, localities and nation-states, First Nations and provincial authorities, town merchants and transnational enterprises are all struggling to keep well-paying jobs, realize adequate profits, and conserve productive resources. Who gets which jobs, where profits flow, and which resources are conserved for how long are issues behind the struggle to control the natural environment around Clayoquot Sound. In this complex interplay of interests, there are many strategies, interpretations, and goals in the mix with different agendas, even though all concerned often wish to maintain familiar forms of employment, occupational specialization, and income distribution. Few of them are uncontested, and most of them are not complementary. As this essay illustrates, politics must mediate their contradictions, contain their conflicts, and resolve their differences in some mutually acceptable, albeit never entirely agreeable, fashion.

Extractive and Attractive Models of Growth

As Innis's classic studies of the fur trade show (1956), extractive development strategies are totally invested in the deep structures of provincial, national, and international capitalism for Canada. In order to settle the land, to extract its agricultural, aquatic, mineral, and timber resources, Canadians built an economy and society organized around the labor force, technological regime, legal order, and financial system needed to serve the ends of resource extraction. This agenda has been the raison d'être of British Columbia from its earliest days. Consequently, there is a thick protective belt of assumptions, alliances, and agreements between Victoria and Ottawa bureaucrats, Vancouver and Toronto capitalists, and Vancouver Island and Ontario labor unionists that have deflected or destroyed most efforts to rethink, much less reengineer, the prevailing modes of extractive production, consumption, circulation, and accumulation when it comes to the province's many farming, fishing, mining, and logging operations. This economic amalgam of high profits, good jobs, and stable markets makes it very difficult for any sort of community, environmental, or labor activist who is intent on challenging the practices or premises of extractive development. Nonetheless, environmental protests have made a difference in the way some people of the province now imagine their economic lives.

The European exploration and settlement of Clayoquot Sound began with Spanish, English, and Yankee seafaring traders in search of seal and sea otter pelts during the late eighteenth century. Catholic missionaries arrived on the west coast of Vancouver Island in the 1870s, and waves of prospectors, miners, and other fortune seekers started searching the lands around the Sound in the 1880s and 1890s. By 1888, Tofino had its first white settler, and it built a school, post office, and church all around 1900 (CD II/E/6, v.1, 103). From these early days, extractive economic enterprises provided much of the region's employment. Gold mining in the 1890s was joined by the Kennedy River cannery in 1892 and lumber mills at Ahousaht and on Meares Island. A pilchard fishing and processing industry boomed in the 1920s when the Pacific Ocean's Japanese Current moved up against Vancouver Island's shoreline, but major transportation infrastructure was not constructed until World War II (CD II/E/6, v.1, 105). The Royal Canadian Air Force built an air station at Long Beach between Tofino and Ucluelet during 1942, and roads were cut from Ucluelet to Tofino in order to supply the new military base (CD II/E/6, v.1, 95–100). A road to Port Alberni was constructed in 1958, but it was not paved until 1971 when the Pacific Rim National Park was opened (CD II/E/8, v.1, 125) by Ottawa.

Small steamship lines brought some visitors from Victoria and Vancouver to Clayoquot Sound before the turn of the century, but much of this early tourism travel tapered back considerably during the Great Depression in the 1930s (CD II/E/8, v.1, 127–28). Greater numbers of leisure seekers did not arrive until the 1960s, when easier access to the region's beaches and forests was made possible by the forestry roads leading back to Port Alberni. Even so, tourist infrastructure was minimal, and most visitors were serious campers who staked out temporary sites on the region's many beaches that lacked even the most primitive support facilities. Visitation levels did not rise dramatically until the 1970s after the single road out was paved and the Pacific Rim National Park was opened (CD II/E/8, v.1, 125). In 1980, Tourism British Columbia addressed the region's tourism and travel potential in its regional master plans, which led, in turn, to a number of major investments in Ucluelet and Tofino as Parks Canada—on the basis of national park traffic—claimed five hundred thousand visitors were drawn every year to the Clayoquot Sound attractions (CD II/E/8, v.1, 126).

Ironically, however, sustained serious tourism did not take off in and around Tofino until the environmental showdowns of the early 1980s over clearcut logging on Meares Island, even though traditional logging work continued in and around the protests. As the Clayoquot Sound Sustainable Development Strategy tourism sector study group concluded,

> Clayoquot Sound was relatively unexplored by tourists until the
> mid '80's when the Meares Island issue received national attention.
> By 1985–86 several enterprising tour operators started to provide

nature cruising packages to both Meares Island and Clayoquot Sound. With the expansion of the adventure market and whale watching, Clayoquot Sound has become a major adventure travel area for Western Canada and the Pacific Northwest. (CD II/E/8, v.1, 127)

For many of Tofino's 1,100 residents with long-standing ties to the timber industry, the environmental struggles have served, first, to condemn their historically accepted forms of extractive industrial work, and, second, to obstruct their ability to earn a secure, comfortable income. For those with more ecological agendas, the mass-media coverage of these struggles has worked, first, to secure protection of the region's natural assets, and, second, to publicize them to millions of potential visitors worldwide as the perfect destination for new ecotours. Such "free media" exposure has switched the region's economy off its traditional extractive track and down new tracks toward attractive models of economic growth. Yet, at the same time, these shifts also are reconfiguring the shape and substance of classic center/periphery relations in these economic spaces.

In Tofino, the work of Maureen Fraser, as one of the town's most famous environmental advocates and an accomplished baker/coffeehouse owner/businesswoman, typifies these tendencies. Coming to Clayoquot Sound in the 1970s, she was an outsider, a female, and a white-collar tourist. Otherwise unemployable, her newfound occupation as a baker was not regarded by many in Tofino and elsewhere in the Sound as a high-pay, high-stability, high-status job. Nonetheless, as a lifestyle refugee from "the big city back east," she also began slowly providing that mix of high-quality goods and services at her bakery/café that urban "nature experience" consumers prefer over what loggers or fishermen willingly accepted before she arrived: bad prepackaged sweet rolls and institutional coffee from the typical rural convenience market/gas station combo. The local market was shifting, and she provided what the new buyers in the changing market wanted. In turn, the natural beauty preserved by her ecological work continued to draw more and more of these new consumers into this changed market.

Attractive development strategies have been tied historically in Canada and elsewhere to more marginal locations where there is no other alternative to extractive or manufacturing industrial employment. Natural attractions, such as unspoiled land and water in relatively undisturbed ecosystems, can provide recreational, ecotourist, or research opportunities in special niche markets, if these attractions can be made alluring enough by aggressive mass-media promotions. Still, these jobs are typically held by low-wage, nonunion, nonwhite, or female workers. Employment is concentrated around services: nature tours, hunting trips, fishing boats, vacation hotels, curio shops, tourist restaurants, automobile services, summer home maintenance, resort entertainments. Such jobs are not core employment opportunities with high benefits, good pay, or social status. Instead, they are often regarded as peripheral jobs, because, first, there are no benefits, pay is poor, status is low, and, second, women, older people, students, or racial minorities mostly perform them.

Attractive development, then, rests on forms of labor that often were marginal in the older extractive economy. Women did such work, or, if not women, then nonwhite men, because it was lower status, paid less, and ran with the seasons. Attractive development work mostly is service work, helping other people do things they cannot, will not, or should not do for themselves. Other people in a consuming public from elsewhere must be attracted in high numbers at consistent volumes to keep such attractive development models rolling. Consequently, a vast culture industry must be constructed to generate the "attractiveness" of such attractions as well as to develop ever more satisfying products once the attracted arrive. Many places around the world are beautiful, peaceful, bountiful, so something must be done to convince patrons to choose this beauty, peace, bounty over others.

The Struggle over Sustainability and Survival

The bountiful resources of Vancouver Island sustained its First Nations inhabitants for many millennia before contact with European explorers. It was word of these natural riches, carried by Yankee, Russian, Spanish, and English seafarers, that brought permanent European settlements to Clayoquot Sound and the rest of Vancouver Island in the eighteenth and nineteenth centuries. Already captured in the machinations of world markets, these European settlers quickly determined that extractive enterprises, such as trapping, timbering, mining, fishing, and farming operations, were the quickest ways to gain a livelihood for themselves. In turn, much of the identity and solidarity of British Columbian society now rests on extractive industry: the social roles it creates, the comparatively rich wages it pays, the environmental side effects it produces, the capital profitabilities it attains, the communal purposes it defines, and the political agendas it requires. Any effort to curtail extractive industries or to supplant them with some alternative economic strategy questions more than economic formulas. Such campaigns challenge almost every dimension of British Columbia's culture, markets, politics, and society in ways that can threaten individuals and communities with extinction. The alliance of individuals and groups with their machines, markets, and meanings are inextricably entangled with extracting raw materials from the earth. Any environmentally driven intervention that aims to reduce or eliminate these extractive activities will be hotly contested.

For all of their good intentions, the environmentalists' actions are threatening the viability of both corporate profits and high-wage labor in the Clayoquot's extractive industries. Public opinion and government regulations are forcing the big firms behind the region's industrial forestry to rethink their modes of operation. Capital, however, cannot be reconfigured without, at the same time, reshaping the overall labor force as well as the labor performed by specific individual workers. These corporate moves plus the rise of ecotourism are pushing the region toward attractive models of development.

Industrial forestry practices in British Columbia have been evolving since the 1950s toward much more capital-intensive and far less labor-intensive modes of operation. Corporate concentration and technological rationalization in British Columbia's forest industries have led to increasing volumes of wood cut (32,000,000 M^3 in 1961 to 74,000,000 M^3 in 1991) and decreasing levels of employment (2 jobs per 1,000 M^3 cut in 1961 to .88 jobs per 1,000 M^3 cut in 1991) (CD, v.2, 330). In 1954, the top ten timber companies harvested 37 percent of the provincial harvest, but their share rose to 59 percent in 1975 and 69 percent in 1990 (CD, v.2, 331). At the same time, fewer people are now employed per 1,000 M^3 of lumber cut in British Columbia than in all other industrialized nations around the world (CD, v.2, 357). Moreover, the wealth produced by these workers remains caught in highly extractive relations of appropriation as 72 percent of the dollar turnover from forestry in the Alberni/Ucluelet region leaves the area (CD, v.2, 357).

Consequently, the concentration of industrial forestry capital in Vancouver Island's timber business is leading to less employment, greater yields, and higher levels of productivity. In 1954, nearly 1.6 million hectares of ancient rainforest remained intact on Vancouver Island, which probably was close to two-thirds of the original stand. By 1990, this preserve had fallen to only 828,000 hectares. It took almost one hundred years to cut the first third of the rainforest; but the second third was taken in only thirty-six years, and nearly 90 percent of the low-level rainforests were harvested through 1990 (CD, v.2, 333–34). Indeed, in 1990, 64 percent of Vancouver Island's temperate rainforest had been logged, leaving 33 percent of the stand to be logged and 3 percent in some sort of protected area (CD, v.2, 334). These remaining hectares of rainforest resources, then, are the focus of tremendous ecological and economic struggles as communities of loggers with five or six generations of timber history face the exhaustion of their resource base and the extinction of their shared economic ties to wood harvesting in this human generation. Today, the Port Alberni/Ucluelet region only has just over 3,500 employed directly in the forest industry, and another nine thousand jobs are tied indirectly to forestry-related business (CD, v.2, 357).

At cutting levels from the 1980s, Vancouver Island's rainforest will be gone by 2020–25 (CD, v.2, 334). And, as loggers go out into more remote regions and steeper slopes, already high levels of soil erosion, watershed degradation, and wildlife endangerment will increase. Only fifteen of Vancouver Island's 170 primary and secondary watersheds over 5,000 hectares were entirely pristine in the 1990s (CD, v.2, 357). Likewise, on Vancouver Island, 60 percent of all salmon streams had been damaged by logging, and 30 percent had suffered a total loss of salmon habitat (CD, v.2, 358). Although the state did put aside a large tract of land in the Pacific Rim National-al Park during the 1970s to preserve some of Vancouver Island's temperate rainforest (albeit in second-growth cover), an equally large area of land, or nearly 24,000 hectares, has been logged every year on the island since 1972 (CD, v.2, 358). In Clayoquot Sound, almost a quarter of its rainforest has been clearcut since the 1960s, but the forests around the Sound are among the largest remaining expanses of temperate rainforests in the world (CD, v.2, 358, 357).

The conflicted history dividing extractive from attractive interests in Clayoquot Sound over how to preserve the old-growth rainforest may only forge brittle new economic agendas as the extractors struggle to meet the environmental expectations of attractive interests or the attractors labor to attain employment levels once carried by extractive enterprises. A prefiguration of these unstable amalgams is contained in MacMillan Bloedel's "Clayoquot Sound Compromise" (CD III/C/11, v.1, 260), on the one hand, and the Clayoquot Sound Central Region Board's "Mission Statement," on the other hand (CD VI/2, v.2, 205). A more "attractive" extractive development model pledges to accept community involvement, environmental regulation, and government oversight in exchange for the continuing ability to extract resources, albeit in a somewhat more attractive fashion. Likewise, a more "extractive" attractive development model promises to balance new attractive businesses with existing extractive enterprises to sustain the economy and ecology in a comprehensive campaign of jobs protection, jobs creation, and jobs diversification. At the end of the day, however, these contradictory compromises are bringing more corelike qualities to this one-time periphery as more high-value-adding labor seeps into industrial forestry and more complex educational purposes are stressed in the region's service-based attractive industries.

Left to their own devices, many logging operations will cut all possible corners to boost profits, but ecologically sensible practices are among the first corners to be cut. These shortcuts are immediately obvious in every forest clearcut, degraded stream bed, or eroded hillside anywhere in Clayoquot Sound. The scope and depth of the extractive economy in British Columbia is such that such activities cannot be terminated, but these ecologically irrational practices can be modified. And, the Clayoquot Compromise, so widely touted by MacMillan Bloedel after years of environmental protests, illustrates how extractive practices can be made more attractive by casting logging as vital to the survival of Ucluelet and other communities: sustaining one hundred jobs locally and three hundred jobs elsewhere in the company, keeping a medium-size sawmill open for a year, and offering home builders wood for ten thousand homes (CD III/C/11, v.1, 259). At the same time, these workers and mills will produce wood in new ways, that is, using techniques that allegedly reduce logging by a third, double protected areas to conserve old growth, ban large clearcuts, use special low-impact cutting methods, end cutting near shorelines, involve more government advisers, and listen more to local communities (CD III/C/11, v.1, 259). Attractive extraction accepts world-class standards for sustainable forestry by complying more fully with provincial regulations, attending to local publics, and taking account of environmental impacts on wildlife, fish, water quality, slope stability, windfall, cultural values, recreation, and visual quality in viewscapes (CD III/C/11, v.1, 260). Logs are still extracted, but only in a manner that "seeks to balance commercial logging and forest renewal with other uses to achieve sustainable use of the region's resources for successive generations" (CD III/C/11, v.1, 260).

In the face of this sort of co-optational maneuvering, ecological and community activists can start to compromise. Listening to the perspectives of labor unions, First Nations, or company employees, in turn, moves attractive development interests with preservationist goals to make more economistic compromises with big businesses, local residents, or indigenous peoples. The Central Region Board (CRB) for Clayoquot Sound was chartered in March 1994 in an interim agreement between the First Nations communities and the provincial government as a quasi-public, quasi-private agency. Allegedly a mechanism to incorporate First Nations' aboriginal knowledge about caring for Nature into contemporary bureaucratic policies, the CRB is

to manage lands and resources, prior to the conclusion of a
treaty, in a manner that:

- provides opportunities for First Nations consistent with aboriginal resource uses and heritage, and considers options for
  treaty settlement
- conserves resources in Clayoquot Sound and promotes resource use that supports sustainability, economic diversification and ecological integrity
- encourages dialogue within and between communities and
  reconciles diverse interests. (CD VI/2, v.2, 205)

Even attractive development goals, then, can be co-opted by communal
consent, provincial design, and corporate planning to supplement, or even
replace, the essentially extractive project of promoting resource use if everyone involved concurs that this somehow also serves the undefined goals of
sustainability, economic diversification, and ecological integrity.

Attractive development of diversified tourist and craft occupations
often is made extractive by coupling it with expanded employment, economic growth, and streamlined accumulation. The 1994 Interim Measures
Agreement was extended in 1996 until 1999 and enhanced with renewed
commitments by MacMillan Bloedel and Central Region First Nations to
harvest forty thousand cubic meters of timber in 1997 and 1998 and assess
new value-adding forest manufacturing opportunities (CD VI/2, v.2, 211).
Thus, attractive development gains a rationalized extractive boost by turning
the CRB coalition of First Nations, community activist, big business, labor
union, and provincial government authorities to explore the economic
potential of "a variety of activities including forest industry opportunities,
forestry training, value-added forestry, stream rehabilitation, salmon en-
hancement, road reclamation, silviculture, recreation and trail construction,
tourism opportunities and joint venture partnerships" (CD VI/2, v.2, 212).

As M'Gonigle notes in his essay in this volume, extractive and attractive models of development are extremely dependent on forces, interests,
and markets far removed from their peripheral sites of production and consumption. Dependency on others, whether it is distant timber, mineral, or
aquaculture markets, or indefinite consumer yearnings for highly stylized
environmental experiences in pristine Nature, is an integral feature of both
modes of production. Because they produce well-defined commodities,
such as minerals, cut trees, fish, or agricultural produce, extractive workers
often believe that they are more autonomous and important in the provincial economy. Yet, the image-driven, knowledge-based, or service-intensive

coproduction of unique experiences in attractive industries, such as old-growth forest hikes, kayaking trips, whale watching, or fine resort dining, often results in more environmentally and economically sustainable forms of work. Although there are individual and collective trade-offs in making the transition from a Fordist industrial to a post-Fordist service economy, and some merit in attaining ecological stability in exchange for lessened security, lower pay, and little status, the many social conflicts now raging in Ucluelet and Tofino show that this strategy also is a very hard sell.

"Envirotising" for Economic Growth

Many contradictions in the contemporary modes of extractive and attractive development around Clayoquot Sound are reflected in the cultural, economic, and political conflicts between Ucluelet, whose 1,700 residents have depended on logging for jobs, and Tofino, whose 1,100 citizens tend to work in service jobs supporting the thousands of tourists who come to hike, kayak, surf, fish, or whale-watch in the area (CD III/C/11, v.1, 254–55). At the end of the day, the machinations of the Central Region Board are allowing for the possibility of high-technology, labor-intensive boutique forestry continuing into the near future, but the collective aspirations of many are refocusing on means for exploiting the Clayoquot Sound's environment with "informative, entertaining, and enjoyable" year-round whale watching/hot springs/fishing/kayaking/hunting/sailing/beachcombing trips "for the whole family" (Chinook Charters 1997, 2–3). Such work, these interests hope, will keep Clayoquot's communities alive, while snaring ecotourist dollars and loyalties as well as giving support "to whale and wildlife research in Clayoquot Sound" (ibid., 6).

The shift to attractive models of development clearly depends on focused and sustained campaigns of advertising, such as those used by Chinook Charters and others, in order to position the natural attractions behind the attractive industries in the most favorable possible light in world media markets. Hitherto wild attributes, natural settings, or primitive conditions, which extractive industries destroy through corporate programs for settlement, harvesting, or civilization, attractive industries must stabilize, preserve, or restore. In turn, these attractions must be continuously reprocessed in mass-media images in various sporting, naturalistic, leisure, or recreational product lines to build a sustainable, but also predictable and merchandisable, "carrying capacity" for the community to vend as jet boat rides, whale-watching trips, sunbathing sites, or windsurfing venues.

Some zones of attractive development, such as Atlantic City, New Jersey, the Queensland Coast in Australia, Las Vegas, Nevada, or the French

Riviera, make little pretense of selling wilderness experiences to guests as their visitors' bureaus sell gambling, high-rise beach hotels, urban nightlife, or expensive exclusivity to outsiders. Lower-end start-ups, however, in more remote, and still somewhat extractive industrial regions with aspirations for launching such attractive modes of development, such as the Four Corners area in the American Southwest, the Cairns/Fort Douglas region of Queensland, the South Island of New Zealand, South Africa's wildlife preserves, or the Clayoquot Sound region on Vancouver Island, often have little to sell beyond "wildlife," "the environment," or "wilderness." Consequently, anything and everything that they can use to mobilize attention for their attractions must be exploited as they construct carrying capacity, cultivate their product image, and capture market share.

Often the impact of these more localized promotional efforts pales, however, beside the well-organized publicity campaigns, which were both local and global, mounted by environmentalists intent on saving Clayoquot Sound. On one level, these exercises in public opinion formation were quite successful. National polls conducted in 1994 found that, after several years of environmental publicity about Vancouver Island, 44 percent were strongly opposed to clearcutting, 23 percent were moderately opposed, while 20 percent moderately supported, and only 5 percent strongly supported clearcutting (CD, v.2, 358). Likewise, only one in seven Canadians, or 14 percent, believed that clearcutting in Clayoquot Sound was correct, and 28 percent felt that a complete ban on logging there would be appropriate (CD, v.2, 358). Resistance against logging was widely publicized, and the antilogging position became thoroughly popularized. Not surprisingly, then, environmentally centered tourism expanded exponentially, as the Clayoquot Sound Sustainable Development Strategy Steering Committee discovered, once the Meares Island protests received global airplay in 1983–84 (CD II/E/8, v.1, 127).

Nonetheless, on a second level, these issue advertising efforts have become, quite ironically, the foundation of a green sales pitch about the Clayoquot Sound and its pristine allure. Valerie Langer's "campaign" slide show, the "Stump Tour," and numerous other videotapes, slide shows, and photo spreads circulated broadly around Canada (Edmonton, Winnipeg, Toronto, Ottawa, Halifax, etc.), the United States (Los Angeles, Denver, Seattle, New York, San Francisco, etc.), and the world (Paris, London, Vienna, Sydney, Brasília, etc.). And sustained lobbying, advertising, and civil disobedience campaigns were continued in defense of Clayoquot Sound in Tokyo, Vancouver, Amsterdam, Hamburg, and Washington, D.C., among other places (CD, v.2, 355). Such successes, in turn, forced various Canadian government agencies to spend more than $47 million to defend their environmental records with the forest industry's side of the story (CD, v.2, 359).

These efforts—both for and against logging—have become a fresh genre of ecological advertising for Clayoquot Sound, supercharging its attractive developmental aspirations by showing how clean and green this part of British Columbia still can be, if and only if people are willing to go to great lengths to defend it. Such "envirotisements" become essential ingredients in the attractive political economy of the region as they, first, tout its ecological allure, second, demonstrate its precious rarity with images of spirited local, national, and global defense, and third, invite all to join the struggle by experiencing its uniqueness firsthand in supporting its attractive industrial alternatives as part of their personal leisure spending cycles back into whale protection, nature preservation, or forest restoration.

Envirotisements, in other words, help to create and sustain the attractions' carrying capacity. Tourism already employs more people in British Columbia than any other industry (CD, v.2, 357), and more than five hundred thousand people visit the tiny towns around Clayoquot Sound every year (CD, v.2, 358). Tofino alone sees $15 million a year from tourism, and the First Nations' second-biggest employer (21 percent of their workforces) is now tourism (CD, v.2, 358). Every successful antilogging ad, therefore, becomes a dual-purpose device that might change public opinion, but that also motivates hundreds of thousands of individuals to come enjoy what has been preserved on a whale-watching trip or tremble before what is being destroyed during a visit to a clearcut. Either way, envirotisements power the region's new attractive mode of development by filling campgrounds, boosting fuel sales, selling out sea kayak trips, or lifting meals served in the Tofino-Ucluelet area.

Seaside Adventures of Tofino, for example, casts killer whales, bald eagles, scenic bays, hot springs, and zodiac boats as sites to see and adventures to have as you "get away from civilization and into the quiet inlets of the . . . West Coast" on "Rainforest Treks, Whale Watching, Clayoquot Cruises, Hot Springs, Fishing" (Seaside Adventures 1997, 1). "Education filled days" on the West Coast Experience bring you "the rainforest, its varied terrain, and bio-diversity (including second growth), an abandoned First Nations Village, intertidal organisms, wildlife, and five types of beaches" (ibid., 5). The whole economic point of Tofino and Ucluelet becomes providing "one of the safest, most exhilarating, and educational view points possible" (ibid., 3) to experience the thoroughly envirotised splendor of the Pacific Ocean and Vancouver Island's wild west coast. In French, German, Japanese, Korean, and Spanish, the envirotising attractive industries of Clayoquot Sound remind everyone, "Don't forget your camera and plenty of film" (Sea Trek 1997, 5).

Moreover, these envirotisements' normative content persists beyond their print, broadcast, or performance circulation in the reshaped expectations of tourists and natives alike. The carrying capacity of attractive industry depends on those scenic assets and ecosystemic services that comprise "the nature experience" in Clayoquot Sound. To maintain the province's biggest industry and employer—namely, tourism—the land/sky/seascapes expected by the tourist gaze must be continuously revalorized as the capital stock driving the attractive model of growth, without compromising the survival of its still lucrative timber industry. The Clayoquot Sound Land Use Decision, the Clayoquot Sound Sustainable Development Strategy Steering Committee, and the Central Region Board all represent well-intentioned efforts to balance all "ecosystems, resources and resource values" in an interconnected sustainable fashion by creating Biosphere Reserves along with world-class sustainable forestry (CD VI/11, v.2, 241). Because the logging cannot be halted totally or immediately, and because the ecotourists cannot be turned away effectively, all the concerned parties try to live up to the envirotisements' normative designs by organizing visual corridors along major roads and sea lanes that can buffer smaller, more concentrated timber-harvesting areas from the tourist gaze and thereby preserving scenic assets, ecosystemic services, and economic viability for all concerned.

Just as the global economy shapes the structures and agencies of international exchange to create "world cities" (Sassen 1991) or "global cores" (Wallerstein 1979) as its highest-wage, largest value-added, and greatest status centers, so too does it now seem able to recontour the developed modern countryside or extractive peripheral zones of classic Fordist industrialism as "world biosphere preserves" or "global wildernesses" in its redevelopment of old primary product producing areas into new tertiary product consumption zones. What was once valued as cubic meters of timber or pulpwood shipped around the world by efficient extractors now attains revalorization as the natural setting of wilderness experiences by leisure consumers brought in from all over the globe by the slick facilities, high-class services, and gorgeous envirotisements of artful attractors. In fact, a planned response for occupying these niches in the capitalist world-system—as its inner dynamics of expansion, instability, and differentiation create them—can become a self-sustaining program of uneven redevelopment in circuits of circulation between "postmodernizing" cities and countrysides. As Majestic Ocean Kayaking promises, to serve these markets, the value-adding emphasis at such postmodern rural sites is essentially educational ("Learn about the rich variety of seashore life along the Pacific Coast") and environmentally entertaining ("Our trips are fun, safe and educational, with a conscious respect for man's environmental impact on the land and the water") (Majestic Ocean Kayaking 1997, 2).

Uneven Redevelopment and Rural Postmodernity

This shift toward tourism, outdoor sports pursuits, and leisure home markets in the Clayoquot Sound's economy, even though it comes as a response to environmental protests and government regulations, also could be seen as an exercise in "uneven redevelopment" (Massey 1994, 109–12). This is a major part of what has hit Clayoquot Sound without, as Maureen Fraser states, its residents really "knowing it." Capital and labor are being pushed by government intervention, public pressure, and environmental analysis toward a fundamental restructuring of their industrial investments and workforce characteristics, changing how centers and peripheries look and work. The new emphasis on British Columbia's clean, green, big outdoors, which the tourism ministry's and environmental movement's envirotisements relentlessly tout, coupled with Nature-minded migrants from elsewhere in Canada and very active tourism entrepreneurs in Clayoquot Sound, all link up nicely with the province's new postextractive growth aspirations in high-tech industry, financial services, and world-class tourism. Many areas on Vancouver Island are experiencing an aggressive form of "uneven redevelopment," as once robust timber towns are being progressively either downsized or closed down in order to be reborn as low-wage, low-security, low-status tourism destinations for white-collar, urban visitors from outside who are all eager to experience renaturalized wild sites, sounds, and smells in their "natural" surroundings. Because it is cast as sustainable development, community planning, or ecological modernization, such uneven redevelopment is accepted as "progress," albeit often grudgingly, as the environmental battles over Clayoquot Sound illustrate.

These processes of attractive industrial development can just as easily be cast as another type of "postmodernization" (Zukin 1988) conducted out in a rural periphery instead of an urban core. In cities, this process sees urban elites responding to increasingly competitive global markets and mobile capital investment by redeveloping inner-city areas in a bid to sell "the quality of life" tied to enhanced cultural capital investment in malls, theme parks, museums, shopping centers, or watersides. As Featherstone notes, "this process entails the deindustrialization of inner city areas and docklands, which become gentrified by members of the new middle class and developed as sites of tourism and cultural consumption" (Featherstone 1991,

107). At the same time, such postmodernizing cities generate their own unique cultural self-consciousness through imaginary blends of leisure, consumption, and style in the planned renewal of their everyday life. Indeed, "postmodern cities have become centers of consumption, play and entertainment, saturated with signs and images to the extent that anything can become represented, thematized and made an object of interest, an object of the 'tourist gaze'" (ibid., 101).

One of the most salable signs sought by these new middle classes is Nature, and the "nature experience" simply extends the cultural thematic shared by "shopping centers, malls, museums, theme parks and tourist experiences in the contemporary city in which cultural disorder and stylistic eclecticism become common features of spaces" (ibid., 103) out into the contemporary countryside. The changing political economy of Clayoquot Sound directly parallels the deindustrialization of inner cities and urban docklands with the demise of extractive forestry, fishing, and mining in rural regions. Here and now is where and when Maureen Fraser and many more like her appear on the scene. As Tofino, Ucluelet, and the surrounding countryside are gradually becoming gentrified by members of the new middle class (either as temporary leisure-seeking visitors or as permanent new environment-defending residents) and redeveloped as simulacral sites (whether it is for ecotourism, the nature experience, or other sorts of cultural consumption), one finds the working classes, the poor, or the First Nations being made less welcome, especially if they cling to older extractive types of work that degrade the environment.

From one perspective, these postmodernizing strategies for uneven rural redevelopment may represent a positive shift toward environmental protection, because the old-growth temperate rainforest, fragile marine ecology, and endangered wildlife of the Clayoquot Sound are being protected from further excessive levels of extractive industrial forestry. These outcomes slowly are becoming entrenched in the public policy consensus, and those who have struggled for so long to realize them should be rightly satisfied by their hard-won success. Yet, at the same time, from another perspective, some of their success rests on much bigger changes occurring elsewhere whose effects are diffusing inexorably through the entire global economy. The natural environment of Clayoquot Sound can be preserved, but not purely as such for its own sake. Instead, it is being transformed via deindustrialization into a renaturalized rural postmodernity that coexists with postmodern cities whose residents have certain expectations about the places they visit or occupy.

This postmodernizing transition in the region's linkages with global commodity exchange also can be illustrated by a store in Ucluelet: The Crow's Nest. Billing itself as "Ucluelet's OLDEST STORE," this establishment was built in 1908, and "operated continuously as a general store until 1988" (The Crow's Nest 1997, 1) that largely sold finished and manufactured goods from elsewhere to extractive industrial workers drawn to Clayoquot Sound. To extract the bounties of Nature, tools and implements from the outside were needed to produce the raw materials and foodstuffs required by the world market from this area. A block up from the Government Wharf, right up Cedar Street from the RCMP office, next door to the post office, and just across Main Street from the bank, this general store was an integral link in the old extractive export economy.

Today, however, The Crow's Nest is only a door or two away from the Ucluelet Tourism Info Centre, and its own early history is a self-valorizing attraction: "original shelving and oiled fir floors are just part of the atmosphere of this beautiful old landmark building" (ibid.). As an authentic attractor of tourist interest, The Crow's Nest in turn serves as an economic linchpin in the area's new attractive service economy by vending crafts, curios, and contact to Ucluelet's upscale outside visitors. Indeed, tourist leaflets announce that "today this historic building is Ucluelet's largest gift store selling locally made crafts, pottery, sweat shirts, books, souvenirs, gifts and stationery, as well as offering a copy and fax service" (ibid.). The world economy still connects to Clayoquot Sound through the same mercantile site, but its goods and services are tied to very different global commodity chains that have changed significantly as, first, more people come to the Sound to whale-watch, surf, and buy locally made pottery, and then, second, fewer stay to cut trees, harpoon whales, and mine minerals. The history of other long-standing local businesses suggests the same general trends in the transition from extractive to attractive strategies for economic growth. The general store in the old periphery after deindustrialization can reappear as an outpost boutique for the postmodernized capitalist center.

Bits of Tofino and Ucluelet are still locked into the old economies of extractive production constructed in modern countrysides, but more and more of both towns, like The Crow's Nest, are being remade, as Lefebvre says of the contemporary city, into "consuming displays, displays of consuming, consuming of signs, signs of consuming" (Lefebvre 1971, 114). When refugees from such cities appear, they first identify unmet needs and then begin to satisfy them. Once a Maureen Fraser can complain, "No services. No bakery. No bookstore. No place to rent canoes," such postmodernizing transformations will begin. Kayaking shops, whale-watching businesses, outdoors outfitters, boutique bakeries, First Nations craft shops, resort hotels, mountain bike outlets, and exotic restaurants all fuse with the natural beauties of the Clayoquot Sound beyond Tofino and Ucluelet, in the same stylist eclecticism found in most postmodernizing cities where the new middle-class tourists visiting the Sound live year round, whether they are from Germany, Australia, England, Japan, or California.

This postmodernized restructuring of any rural region's economy around attractive developmental assets, particularly if the region still has viable connections to extractive industries, often represents a radical re-adjustment in both individual and collective identity. When this disruptive transition is associated with environmentalistic pressure tactics, as it is now across the Clayoquot region, tremendous resentments can be created. Workers who held or still hold comparatively high-paying and high-status positions in extractive industry see themselves paying for deindustrializing environmental reforms with their old or existing jobs. Whatever new jobs are made available in attractive industries rarely are as numerous, well paid, or high status as those tied to extractive industrial work. Historically, these sorts of service-sector jobs went to women, teenagers, First Nations workers, or older people. This psychocultural transition from logger, miner, or mill worker to hotel bartender, whale-watching guide, or ticket taker is a very uneasy economic and social process.

Moreover, it is made politically much worse by perceptions of class-based, region-driven, or lifestyle-centered divisions of interest over the environment. Many old-time locals in the Clayoquot Sound see the protection actions on behalf of the temperate rainforest as a response to the recreational needs of faraway urban communities, such as Victoria, Vancouver, or Seattle. In many of the recent conflicts over the old-growth forest, these people talk plainly and painfully about

> feeling victimized by a dominant, urban, white-collar sector of
> the population, reinforced by recent arrivals from "outside." Many
> people working in resource industries were the second and some-
> times third generations in their families to do so, and it was diffi-
> cult for them to sit idly by while people in distant urban communi-
> ties appeared bent on actions that would force rural workers to
> abandon long-held occupations with no realistic opportunity for
> alternatives. Resource-industry workers and rural communities
> were also becoming resentful that, in the name of global environ-
> mental and conservation values, they were being asked to sacrifice
> employment at the same time as urban communities appeared to
> make few sacrifices in the consumption of resources and pollution
> of the environment. (CD, v.2, 352–53)

The destruction of the global environment, then, is not necessarily abated by actions such as the Clayoquot Sound Land Use Decision; it simply shifts elsewhere in the world in order to shield sites, such as Clayoquot Sound, that are revalorized by deindustrialization as postmodernized nature preserves, recreational zones, or biosphere reserves. Meanwhile, vast quantities of wood, pulp, and mineral resources simply will be extracted elsewhere at newly industrialized sites in Chile, Indonesia, or Russia to keep Victoria, Vancouver, and Seattle supplied with lumber, paper, and metals.

Conclusion

This essay has positioned the ecological conflicts of the 1980s and 1990s in Clayoquot Sound against changes in the larger provincial, national, and international economy. In a world in which lower-wage, nonregulated markets in Asia, Africa, or Latin America can provide the wood and pulp needs of North America, the industrial forestry sector in British Columbia is living on borrowed time anyway. Environmentalists organizing against established clearcutting techniques simply provide final notice to an already ailing business. Those left in the lurch, as timber licenses and lumber yields are cut back, must find new sources of employment for their communities and families to survive.

Fortunately or unfortunately, depending usually on whether one lives in Tofino or Ucluelet, the new middle classes in postmodernizing cities and suburbs around the world want "the nature experiences" that Clayoquot Sound can provide. Although servicing these markets does not have the same occupational status or income as forestry did, it might pay the bills without excessively degrading the environment. Without better roads or air service, the demand for "seaside adventures" is likely to remain sustainable in the Sound, preserving its carrying capacity and maintaining a rough equilibrium of human use and natural renewal in its lands, skies, and waters.

The dangers of attractive industrial development—such as changing consumer tastes, a major recession, heavy traffic, rising land prices, or ineffective publicity efforts—can trip up the slow and steady progress being made by the Clayoquot communities toward more sustainable forms of economic life. Likewise, the cultural conflicts unintentionally caused by active envirotising among the region's inhabitants could spark more nasty skirmishes between longtime residents and recent arrivals, First Nations and other Canadian peoples, white-collar visitors and blue-collar lumberjacks, ecological fundamentalists and corporate pragmatists, or nature purists and machine users on the beaches, out in the woods, or in town.

The strategies of attractive industrial development provide the means for coping with many threats to Clayoquot Sound's ecological integrity, but they also can cause new miseries as those who once imagined themselves masters of the woods are reduced to serving as the supporting cast for others' enjoyment of a simulacral Nature. Nonetheless, the demise of classical forms of extractive industrial ensembles in the Sound illustrates how other acceptable paths for sustainable economic and social development can be blazed out of rural deindustrialization with the right combination of local initiative, national backing, and global traffic.

Works Cited

CD [*The Clayoquot Documents*. 1997. Ed. Karena Shaw and Warren Magnusson. Clayoquot Project, University of Victoria.]

Chinook Charters. 1997. "Whale Watching." Tofino, B.C. 1–6.

Crow's Nest, The. 1997. "Visit Ucluelet's Oldest Store." Ucluelet, B.C. 1–2.

Featherstone, Mike. 1991. *Consumer Culture and Postmodernism*. London: Sage.

Frank, André Gunder. 1976. *On Capitalist Underdevelopment*. Oxford: Oxford University Press.

Innis, Harold. 1956. *The Fur Trade in Canada: An Introduction to Canadian Economic History*. Toronto: University of Toronto Press.

Lefebrve, Henri. 1971. *Everyday Life in the Modern World*. New York: HarperCollins.

Majestic Ocean Kayaking. 1997. "West Coast Wilderness Adventures." Ucluelet, B.C. 1–6.

Massey, Doreen. 1994. *Space, Place, and Gender*. Minneapolis: University of Minnesota Press.

Priest, Alicia. 1997. "Gentle Crusader." *Amicus Journal* 19:3: 27–30.

Sassen, Saskia. 1991. *The Global City: New York, London, Tokyo*. Princeton, N.J.: Princeton University Press.

Seaside Adventures. 1997. "Seaside Adventures." Tofino, B.C. 1–6.

Sea Trek. 1997. "Explore Tofino: Cruise the Wildlife Zone." Tofino, B.C. 1–6.

Storper, Michael, and Richard Walker. 1989. *The Capitalist Imperative: Territory, Technology, and Industrial Growth*. Oxford: Blackwell.

Wallerstein, Immanuel. 1979. *The World Capitalist Economy*. Cambridge: Cambridge University Press.

Zukin, Sharon. 1988. *Loft Living*. London: Hutchinson/Radius.

Commentary

On the Universal and the Particular

Sovereignty and the Urban Global

Warren Magnusson

Chaloupka and Luke both discuss the particularities of Clayoquot in relation to certain universals: in Chaloupka's case, the particularities of strategic
calculation in relation to the universals of environmentalist ethics, and, in
Luke's case, the particularities of the Clayoquot region in relation to the universals of a postindustrial global economy. In this commentary, I want to
draw attention to other aspects of the problematic relation between the particular and the universal. I will focus especially on two things: the question
of sovereignty as it relates to Canada in general and to the government of
British Columbia in particular, and the question of the urban global, as it relates to Clayoquot in particular and to the problem of the political in general.

Delusions of Sovereignty

For Canadians, the difference between Canada and the United States or
Canada and Europe is a matter of obsessive concern, for Europe and the
United States are the lodestars of the Canadian imagination, places that
count in a way that Canada does not. For anyone else, the difference is of
little interest, but I want to suggest that it may be helpful to think about the
particularities of a place such as Canada to get some critical perspective on
such universalist doctrines as sovereignty.

The United States and Europe are, in many respects, worlds unto
themselves. As such, they are more like empires than states, if by "states" we
mean political entities situated in a world made up of other, similar entities
with comparable power. The old European empires were not just that, but
also states, in the sense that they were enmeshed in a European state system. Now that the European state system has folded in on itself, and Europe
as a whole has been reduced to subordinate status in relation to the United

States, Europeans are faced with a peculiar identity crisis. Is Europe to reform itself into a new empire, to rival the American, or is it to become something else altogether, within the context of a new world order? The United States offers a certain model of sovereignty, in the sense that it really does seem to be a world unto itself, capable of ordering things as it wishes, with little reference to the rest of the world. But, of course, to the extent that the United States really is like that (and it is a bit of an exaggeration to suggest that it is), it is not really a sovereign *state*, because it exists without rivals, on its own, rather like the Chinese empire of old. If there are entities anywhere that correspond to the model of sovereign statehood—that is, of autonomy within a rivalrous universe of equals—they are not to be found in the United States or in the European Union, which have unique constitutions and unique positions in the world. Neither American nor European states relate to one another as purely autonomous entities, and neither the United States nor the European Union relates to the rest of the world as one sovereign among many.

Is Canada a better model of sovereign statehood, then? On the one hand, it is a "middle power" of sufficient size and economic weight to have been included in the G7, the club of advanced industrial countries. It is also a reasonably prominent actor in various international forums, including NATO, the Organization of American States (OAS), the Asia Pacific Economic Conference (APEC), the World Trade Organization (WTO), and the United Nations. On the other hand, it is certainly not of imperial stature: there are many other countries in the world of similar "rank." Thus, if there is any place where sovereignty should appear on the conventional model, it should be in Canada. That is not what we see when we look at the events in and about Clayoquot, however.

Let us first consider the "domestic" aspect of sovereignty, for this is what makes the image of the unified state (and hence the sovereign international actor) intelligible. The model is derived from the image of the monarch, and by extension from the image of the unitary state, such as Britain or France. But, of course, Britain and France are now enmeshed in the institutions of the European Union, as well as in domestic processes of decentralization. Canada presents an image of sovereignty that is not unitary—the country is federal, like the United States and Australia—but nonetheless contains important vestiges of monarchy. This is not just a matter of the continuing presence of the British Crown. More importantly, the federal prime minister and the provincial premiers command unified governments on the British model. Backed by disciplined political parties, they control the relevant legislatures or parliaments and can do more or less what they will through the various instrumentalities of government at their level. There is a constitutional division of powers, a bill of rights, and an independent judiciary that enforces the limits implicit in these measures and in the rule of law itself, but there is not the limiting fragmentation of authority with which Americans are familiar at both the state and federal levels. Within their respective jurisdictions, the federal prime minister and the provincial premier hold (or seem to hold) sovereign-like authority.

If we look at the Clayoquot example, however, it becomes clear that sovereign authority is not quite what it is cracked up to be. The provincial government had (or seemed to have) plenary authority with respect to forestry in Clayoquot. Not only did it have the undoubted right to regulate the forestry industry and thus to determine how many trees were to be cut, when, where, and how, but it also *owned* the relevant land. Unlike American state governments, Canadian provincial governments have retained ownership of most of the important forest lands, and they just sell rights to cut trees. The lands at issue in Clayoquot were covered by Tree Farm Licences issued by the provincial government, licences that could be modified by provincial legislation or, if necessary, expropriated (with compensation to the companies concerned). Given its double authority, as both landowner and sovereign government, it is not surprising that the BC government expected its 1993 Clayoquot Land Use Decision to be respected as the final resolution of the conflict. The government soon discovered, however, that it had no sovereignty in the relevant sense. It could not simply dictate the solution. Not only did the environmentalists mount blockades, but they did an end run around the government by appealing to global public opinion and lobbying consumers—both corporate consumers and end-consumers—in the United States, Europe, and Asia. The government was forced into a lobbying campaign of its own, a campaign in which it appeared not as a sovereign authority but as one group among others appealing for the support of opinion makers, consumers, investors, and others. In effect, the environmentalists (and to a lesser extent other actors) succeeded in redefining the relevant political space, from the space of provincial sovereignty to the space of global public opinion. In the latter space, the trappings of sovereignty confer no particular advantage, and are sometimes a burden.

The Nuu-chah-nulth challenge to the provincial government was just as profound, and it also depended to some extent on global public opinion. In this case, however, the sovereignty pretensions of the provincial government were confronted more directly, because the Nuu-chah-nulth had claims that predated Crown sovereignty and Crown ownership. If the Nuu-chah-nulth are (as everyone admits) the aboriginal inhabitants of

Clayoquot, then Clayoquot belongs to them, in the most profound way. We might use various terms to describe the right that the Nuu-chah-nulth have in relation to their own territory, and we might draw various implications from the terms that we use. However we look at it, it seems clear that the rights of the Nuu-chah-nulth are aboriginal: they do not derive from the British Crown, or from Canada or British Columbia in right of the Crown. Whatever rights the Nuu-chah-nulth have, they are prior to the Canadian state and prior to the province of British Columbia. Assertions of sovereignty on the part of the provincial government come up against this fact, a fact widely (if only implicitly) recognized in Canada and abroad.

The environmentalist ethic to which Chaloupka refers is only one among a number of universalist doctrines that have been invoked locally to resist assertions of sovereignty. There is, of course, the purported right of civil disobedience to which the blockaders appealed when they were brought before the courts in British Columbia. There are also the rights of aboriginal ownership and aboriginal self-government to which the Nuu-chah-nulth appealed. (Europeans seem not to notice that the claims of the Basques, the Welsh, the Catalans, and others are claims of aboriginal peoples, with much the same force and logic as the claims of the Mohawks and the Nuu-chah-nulth.) But, the list does not end there. The Share protesters, who opposed the blockaders, and demanded their own rights to the forests, were appealing to an implicit right to a livelihood: a right widely recognized, but not well enforced. Also, such communities as Tofino, Ucluelet, and Port Alberni were appealing to rights of local self-government. Those and other putative rights were framed in relation to a universalist ethic of democracy. People on all sides of the disputes in Clayoquot—not a few of whom had grown up in the United States—expressed strong resentment against the provincial government for presuming to exercise sovereignty in a situation in which it had (from their point of view) no right to do so. Right or not, the province soon found that it lacked the power. When a "settlement" of sorts was worked out in 1999, the provincial government was not even a party.

If we re-pose the question of Canadian sovereignty in this light, it becomes clear that the power of the Canadian state in relation to other states is not really the issue. The Clayoquot region, the province of British Columbia, and the kingdom of Canada are all embedded within global relations that make assertions of state sovereignty extraordinarily difficult. It is true that Canada has to "sleep with the elephant" (in Pierre Trudeau's famous phrase), but it is not the power of the U.S. government that is the issue so much as the presence of socioeconomic, cultural, and *political* relations (such as the ones that bind people to the principles and practices of liberal democracy on the one hand, and to the capitalist economy, on the other) that establish "global" conditions of political possibility.

The Urban Global

One of the issues we have to confront is the nature of the global.[1] It is not clear, for instance, whether the global in "global public opinion" refers to the whole world or (more likely) the part of the world that has been dominant globally for the past few hundred years. Nor is it clear whether the global refers to anything more than what is constituted by global market relations: the global economy, commodified global culture, and the political opinions that fit with those relations. A certain economism creeps into most accounts of globalization. One way of resisting that economism is to re-pose the issue in terms of the predominance of urbanism as a way of life.[2]

An intriguing feature of the conflicts at Clayoquot was that, although they were presented as conflicts over logging in "the wilderness," they were actually fought out by people who lived modern urban lives. It was not just that people came from cities far away to protest, or that folks all over the place could follow the struggle on their television sets, or even that many of the key battles were fought out in boardrooms in Vancouver, San Francisco, and New York. The "locals," the people from Ucluelet and Tofino and Ahousaht, were also urban people, if not wholly, then certainly in major respects. No doubt there was a time, not too long ago, when Clayoquot was remote, and most people there had only sporadic contact with the outside world. That has certainly not been the case for the last three decades. You can check your stocks or watch CNN in Tofino, just as you can anywhere else. Moreover, as Luke emphasizes, it is a place that is now organized as a convenient retreat for people from nearby, or even quite distant, cities. It is not a long drive from Vancouver or Victoria, or even from Seattle. People in a hurry can get there by air. During the blockades, people from the nearby cities came to the Peace Camp for the day. This is quite a common feature of "wilderness" struggles in British Columbia or other parts of the Pacific Northwest.

So, does it help to understand Clayoquot as a remote place, rather than as an outlying part of the local megalopolis? The Sea-Van region encompasses Puget Sound and the Georgia Basin, extending from Olympia (the Washington state capital) in the south to Campbell River (on the east coast of Vancouver Island) in the north. Clayoquot is, from one perspective, just an ex-urban or suburban outlier of this large urban region. (Home to one team each in the NFL, NHL, NBA, and MLB: major league, eh?) Offensive as this representation is to most people who live in Clayoquot, it nonethe-less captures an aspect of their reality. People there do not live in a world that is apart from the city. They live in a world where urbanism as a way of life is gradually engulfing everyone.

To recognize this is to see that economy, culture, and politics are as-pects of a way of life that has particular features and an immensely long his-tory, stretching back about ten thousand years. Capitalism, liberal democ-racy, and the so-called state system are all relatively recent phenomena within urbanism as a way of life. They are part of an ensemble of move-ments that we associate with modernity. These movements are not inno-cent of politics. Nor is urbanism as a way of life innocent. On the contrary, that way of life and those movements are all constituted politically as well as culturally, economically, or socially. The political is not something con-tained within states. It helps to constitute both the states themselves and the environment (in all senses of that word: socioeconomic, cultural, physi-cal) within which those states exist. The constitutiveness of the political—that is, of the more or less conscious effort of humans to use their own pow-ers to control the conditions of their lives—is often missed, because of the social-scientific tendency to naturalize what humans do (that is, to treat what happens as a more or less inevitable consequence of innate or other-wise predetermined tendencies in human beings). To call attention to the fact that our way of life has been (and continues to be) constituted *politi-cally* is to raise the possibility that we could live differently. But, if we recog-nize that the politics of the present greatly exceeds what is contained in and between states, then we can see that the *space of the political* is quite differ-ent from what we have usually imagined it to be. It is the space of the *urban* global, not just of the global economy or the state system or even of a glob-alized Western culture.

If the space of the political is the space of "urbanism as a way of life," then the politics of Clayoquot is a struggle over land, and we can put it on the same register as a battle over a new high-rise, a toxic-waste dump, or a "homeland" for the Kosovars. Note the extent of that register. Note also that the "far end" of the register was evident at Clayoquot, in that the Nuu-chah-nulth were raising questions about a national homeland for themselves. The politics of Clayoquot makes explicit what is only implicit in most North American land-use struggles: namely, that rights to the land, as between aboriginal inhabitants, more recent settlers, and people brought to the continent in involuntary servitude, have never been settled. Tocqueville knew this, and worried about it: his successors often forget. The high fences on the southern American border and the patrol boats off the Canadian west coast—where there have been much-publicized landings of "illegal Chinese migrants"—are signs of ongoing anxiety: What right do the descendants of earlier migrants have to keep out the present-day counterparts of their own ancestors? In a sense, then, the whole register of issues related to land rights is always present in urban struggles. Moreover, those struggles are always about who can call the place home, how they are to relate to the nature of the place, what kind of economy they are to have, how they are to connect with the rest of the world, and so on. State institutions are designed to keep such struggles within very narrow limits, but there is no guarantee that the strictures will be effective. Clayoquot is one place where the strictures were broken. Bosnia was another. The effort to "fix" Bosnia by reimposing state structures (in the form of new "statelets") proved to be disastrous: it made the situation worse (Campbell 1998). If the story of Clayoquot is more hopeful, that is not because Canadians are more peaceful folk than Bosnians, but because the state in Clayoquot "bent" sufficiently. People interested in Clayoquot were able to move from one political space to another, arguing their cases in different ways and appealing to different authorities. They were not confined within spaces where tensions could only be resolved by explosions of violence.

This is not to say that the politics of the urban global is benign, or that the proliferation of political spaces is the sole answer to violence. Things are not so simple. The point is that the state and the system of states are particular configurations of authority, configurations that have been constituted politically and that are contested politically on a day-to-day basis. Although they are intended to "contain" politics, they do not do so effectively. This is no bad thing, despite what analysts of the former Yugoslavia or sub-Saharan Africa may say. The descent into extreme violence is a terrible thing, and state formation is no doubt one way of arresting such a downward movement. On the other hand, state formation is just as often the cause of extreme violence. An overarching secular state is often seen as the only solution to the problems produced by efforts to create states of a sort that many people do not want. We should be skeptical about a political logic that suggests that the only solution to a problem is to re-pose the problem on a different scale or in a different form. Overarching secular states may be as stiffly contested as other sorts of states. The same may be true of current schemes to make capitalist globalization into a legal order. The order on offer is a replica of what exists on a lower scale in America and Europe, and the hope seems to be that it will not be as vigorously contested globally as it has been nationally. That seems doubtful, and it is no bad thing.

To see Clayoquot as a site of struggle within an "urban global" is to problematize its ostensible remoteness and smallness. All sites of political struggle are local, and each site is connected to the others in complicated ways. The space of politics is not confined to the space of the state. The putative hierarchies within state, culture, society, and economy are all unstable; one hierarchy trumps another, only to be trumped in turn; networks of power cut across the hierarchies; one regime bleeds into the next; movements resist the exercise of power, only to become centers of power in turn. One cannot say, a priori, that Clayoquot is small and far from the centers of power, whereas Washington is big and at the very center of things. More often than not, the center is a point of immobility, a point at which "action" in nearly impossible because the claim to centrality generates so many conflicting pressures. Actual change occurs otherwise, in spaces that people create for the purpose. The Clayoquots of the world are often the *major* sites from which changes are generated. We may be able to grasp this if we recognize that the world is a global city in which no one neighborhood is necessarily more important than the others.

Notes

1. My observations on this subject flow from an article (Magnusson 1994) I adapted as a chapter in Magnusson 1996. I have developed these ideas in other ways in contributions to various edited volumes: see Caulfield and Peake (1996, 324–47), Ericson and Stehr (2000, 80–104), and Isin (2000, 289–306). Isin's book offers an especially useful overview of the subject of the urban global.

2. This phrase was introduced by Louis Wirth (1938).

Works Cited

Campbell, David. 1998. *National Deconstruction: Violence, Identities, and Justice in Bosnia.* Minneapolis: University of Minnesota Press.

Caulfield, Jon, and Linda Peake, eds. 1996. *City Lives and City Forms: Critical Research and Canadian Urbanism.* Toronto: University of Toronto Press.

Ericson, Richard V., and Nico Stehr, eds. 2000. *Governing Modern Societies.* Toronto: University of Toronto Press.

Isin, Engin, ed. 2000. *Democracy, Citizenship, and the Global City.* London: Routledge.

Magnusson, Warren. 1994. "Social Movements and the Global City." *Millennium: Journal of International Studies* 23:3 (winter): 621–45.

———. 1996. *The Search for Political Space: Globalization, Social Movements, and the Urban Political Experience.* Toronto: University of Toronto Press.

Wirth, Louis. 1938. "Urbanism as a Way of Life." *American Journal of Sociology* 44: 1–24.

Somewhere between Center and Territory

Exploring a Nodal Site in the Struggle against Vertical Authority and Horizontal Flows

R. Michael M'Gonigle

> The philosophers have only interpreted the world, in various
> ways; the point is to change it.
>
> **Karl Marx**

When I was a teenager, my father and I used to go fishing a lot, weekends usually, exploring different rivers, lakes, and inlets of southern and central British Columbia. On one trip, in the mid-1960s, we were trolling for salmon off Vancouver Island, well north of Clayoquot Sound. As we puttered along in our small rented boat, a large ship appeared on the horizon, looming ever larger as it approached us. It was an unusual vessel for, as it approached, we could see that it was towing something very big. Soon we found ourselves face-to-face with a whaling ship returning home to the last commercial whaling station on Canada's west coast. It was towing a large cluster of sperm whales, recently killed in the North Pacific. To us both, the sight was profoundly disturbing, so much so that we gave up our own quest at harvesting the bounty of the local inlet, and put in to the dock— right next to the station's flensing deck. By now, of course, the whales were being hauled up. One at a time, a heavy hook was sunk into each whale's flesh and, as it was pulled in, several people sliced away on each side, winching off long fat strips of whale meat from the bloody and fast diminishing carcass. The sound of pulling, tearing, and ripping was more than either of us could bear. We left quickly, but the sights, and the sounds, linger in the memory still.

Two decades later, my own young family and I were living in the province's interior. We had returned home to British Columbia after many years living in the United States, where, not coincidentally, I had been working on international environmental issues including whaling (and finishing my graduate work). On one visit home during that period, I was car-camping and, accidentally happened upon a river valley near Vancouver that I had never heard of, but that had somehow avoided the logging road and the chain saw, and was still "undeveloped." Within a year, my new work involved a local wilderness campaign to "save the Stein." One day, a Native friend and I were driving up Fraser Canyon on our way back from Vancouver to Lytton, the town near the mouth of the Stein. This was, and is, a busy highway, not the least reason being that it is in the middle of major forestry operations. As one particularly heavy truck bore down on us, my friend looked up and watched wistfully as a full deck of freshly cut, old-growth Douglas fir logs swooshed by. "There goes some more of our friends," she said softly, with a pain in her voice that was eerily familiar.

In such situations, it is easy to "understand the world," and to judge it. In British Columbia, commercial whaling is now a thing of the past. The whaling station at Coal Harbour is closed, and a global commercial moratorium is in place. But the struggle to get a global commercial moratorium on the industry was achieved only after many of the world's populations of large whales had been reduced to near extinction (M'Gonigle 1980). Meanwhile, despite decades of growing controversy, the destruction of rare forest ecosystems continues in every corner of the planet today and is, in fact, a mainstay of many economies. In British Columbia, official government policy is explicitly based on the liquidation of the province's remaining old-growth forests as the foundation for provincial economic growth. The result has been a huge economic and social dependency on the destruction of forest ecosystems that are literally thousands of years old, that are, in the words of conservation biologist Reed Noss, the oldest living things on the planet.

For many of us, academics and activists alike, it is important to try to understand this world and, more important still, to try to change it. Since my first brush with the Stein in 1980, my own work has been in this provincial movement, first, as a campaigner for wilderness preservation (M'Gonigle and Wickwire 1988) and, second, as an advocate for a restructured forest industry (M'Gonigle and Parfitt 1994). Clayoquot Sound has been a lead focus for this movement but, despite its prominence today, it has been only one place among many. Although it is informative to assess the specifics of the Clayoquot Sound controversy, it is also useful to approach that controversy from the perspective of the larger provincial movement to which Clayoquot Sound has made a singular contribution.

This, at least, is the experience that I bring. It is the experience of a movement that, however haphazardly, is trying to bridge many gaps that seem so frustratingly unbridgeable—gaps between theory and practice, between environment and economy, between local and global. So great are these voids, and especially that between theory and practice, that the field most appropriate for making the bridge—ecological political economy— remains both seriously underdeveloped within the academic world and virtually inaccessible within the environmental movement. Instead, critical ecological thinking remains on the fringes, marginalized in the corridors of power, even in British Columbia, where an avowedly social-democratic government held the reins for almost a decade. The politics of Clayoquot Sound is an excellent manifestation of this seeming contradiction.

An Ironic Litany of Last Places Left

For years, no one outside Tofino talked much about Clayoquot Sound. In the late 1960s, when numerous people began to take the long drive over that twisty gravel road to the pounding surf of the open Pacific, it was to go to Long Beach, and then maybe into town (Tofino or Ucluelet) to get supplies. Few people went to visit Clayoquot Sound. Tourists were interested in the new national park (Pacific Rim) that runs between the two towns. The attractions were surfing and hanging out on the beaches that were occupied in those days by dozens of hippie driftwood shacks. Ocean kayaking did not even exist, and Gore-Tex was not even a gleam in anyone's eye. Even when logging in the area emerged as an issue, it was not Clayoquot Sound, but Meares Island that was in the news.

Like so many other wilderness controversies that emerged in British Columbia in the 1980s, Clayoquot Sound began as a local issue that got a lot of support from a trickle of new arrivals. Many of the hippies on the beach—some of them Canadians, many of them American war resisters— stayed on, as they did in other places in British Columbia, such as the Queen Charlotte Islands, the Kootenays, the Gulf Islands, and the Bulkley River Valley. Intent on turning their backs on a power politics running amok in Vietnam and Chicago, and getting "back to the land," many of these people brought a new sensibility to numerous local places, and a new politics to British Columbia. As they looked around, they saw a swath of clearcuts ranging over the landscape in the wake of the marauding forest industry. The number of valleys that still worked in anything like the "natural" manner was fast diminishing. For those who had sought a spiritual refuge in the wilder world, there was no place to hide. In Gary Snyder's memorable phrase at the time, "We're all on the front lines now."

The protest to stop logging on Meares Island followed a pattern that was soon to be familiar. Environmental activists (some from the Sound, some from Vancouver and Victoria) and First Nations worked together to articulate the critical significance of noneconomic concerns such as clean water, habitat for wildlife, an aesthetic environment, and traditional land rights. The opposition to these concerns was local, particularly affected forest workers, but also involved powerful nonlocal economic powers such as MacMillan Bloedel, the International Woodworkers of America (IWA), and the Ministry of Forests. Throughout the 1980s and into the 1990s, the goal of the provincial government was to contain these local resistances. The technique for doing so involved the creation of a series of planning processes, processes that were all founded on several unchallengeable and very problematic premises. As multi-stakeholder processes, the idea was not to create a cooperative vision of transformation but to hammer out some trade-offs and compromise. Opponents of industrial forestry development were allowed only a very subsidiary position in the planning process among many other interests, muting the potential impact of their vision. Similarly, the terms of reference were never to consider whether to log or not, but just when and where logging would take place. Anxious to avoid economic impacts, the government gave no serious consideration to reductions in the level of cut. Getting the cut out was the unassailable need. Meanwhile, those opposed to that premise had the burden of proof in every way—proving that clearcutting did not "mimic natural disturbances," proving that the planning system did not work or was not fair, proving that there was an alternative. In the process, environmental proponents found themselves needing to demonstrate that there could be new sources of employment. This invariably meant embracing a tourism strategy.

Above all, the basic assumption guiding these processes was that the provincial government must maintain unfettered, final decision-making authority over the outcome of any negotiations. The Sound and the Stein and the Stikine and the Slocan were, after all, Crown lands and provincial (not local) resources. As is the history of environmental decision making throughout the world, impact assessment and planning processes were treated as just a prelude, possibly a source of new information for the government to consider as it deemed fit when it made "its" decision. To those opposed to development, these processes offered some hope that maybe there would be a substantive change, but, in large measure, everyone saw them as a procedural opportunity to stall logging while they built more popular support for their cause. The dramatic aspect of the Meares Island court case of 1985 was that the two Nuu-chah-nulth bands actually obtained a substantive outcome: a temporary injunction that blocked logging.

At one level, what is at stake here is not difficult to understand: the province and the region need wood to fuel the forestry economy. But this situation characterizes renewable resource industries worldwide because of a simple fact: at the very time when the corporatist economic and political system has achieved global hegemony, it has begun to encounter natural limits that result from its own success. The stage for conflict is thus clear. With the high growth rates of the 1950s and 1960s, industrial corporations, organized labor, and public bureaucracies became attached to the unfettered flow of resources from local ecosystems such as Clayoquot Sound. Meanwhile, with growth rates compounding, pressures continuously mounted on the resource base, exhausting one ecosystem and then moving to the next as a target for development. The myriad resistances that began to emerge in the 1970s and 1980s in British Columbia were a response to this universal phenomenon, as people began to see their environment flowing away, and to become committed to protecting the few "last places left." In response, governments that were already concerned about how to deal with the fast diminishing resource base—with the impact of what in British Columbia is called "falldown"—became alarmed about this rising opposition that promised to move the falldown forward. Anxious to keep the wheels of the economy turning, planners strongly opposed a further diminution in the resource base to accommodate disruptive environmentalists, and worried about the higher costs associated with trying to gain access to more remote and less desirable forests and fish stocks. Forestalling these trends has been a major motivation for the free-trade regimes that seek to guarantee unconstrained access to the exploitation of the planet's remaining sources of wealth by limiting the ability of anyone to block such access on nontariff (i.e., regulatory) grounds.

Caught in this tension between insatiable global consumptive systems and deteriorating local productive places, Clayoquot Sound encapsulates the ecological problematic. This is a new problematic in theory as well as in practice. As Edward Soja (1989) has demonstrated, social theory has historically emphasized the temporal, that is, the historical, axis as determinative of human relations to the detriment of the spatial. In contrast, understanding how our institutions fit within the spatial dimension (or don't) is the signal characteristic of an ecological political economy. That such new thinking is happening now is, of course, not surprising given present trajectories. Any attempt to situate social systems within an ecological framework must be attentive to the historical dangers of such "natural" approaches (from social Darwinism to eugenics). Still, many of the problems of twentieth-century ideologies—from liberal individualism to communist statism—have stemmed in turn from their lack of recognition of the reverse—that is, of the socially constitutive character of natural and communal spatial contexts. By drawing on the experiences of Clayoquot Sound, and of other wild places in British Columbia, one can begin to appreciate the process of social self-constitution, and to envision the foundation for a new "constitution" for the future. This is, indeed, the task of ecological political economy: "to achieve a consciously self-regulating society in the face of the ecological abyss, to climb off the roller-coaster of run-away social evolution and actively take responsibility for social organization into our own hands" (Atkinson 1991, 180).

The Flow Economy, and Beyond

In light of the headlines of the 1990s, it is difficult to believe that, for the small handful of environmental activists who were active in British Columbia in the 1970s, the forest industry was not yet seen as a problem. In those days, public enemy number one was the province's energy producer, BC Hydro. The forest industry was the prime economic generator for the province back then, but there were still woods to be had. The biggest threats in those years came from the new dams that the power utility was planning or constructing on the Columbia and Peace Rivers (e.g., WAC Bennett, Revelstoke, Site C), and even from plans for coal-fired thermal plants (e.g., Hat Creek). Cheap energy was the province's competitive advantage to attract energy gluttons such as pulp mills. "Build it and they will come" was the philosophy that worked. Today, BC Hydro is almost invisible as an environmental target. The major reason is that the utility changed as a result of these protracted conflicts. Instead of seeking ever more supplies of power, the utility's strategy has shifted to becoming more efficient with the supplies that it already has. Conservation has replaced production as the source of investment. The adoption of a "demand management" approach is also central to any solution to forest industry conflicts today.

In the 1970s, more and more forested regions of the province began to run low of new areas to log. When I first happened on the Stein Valley northeast of Vancouver in 1980, for example, it was the last large unlogged watershed within one hundred miles of that city. Every other low-elevation valley had been roaded and cut to varying degrees. Any trip to Clayoquot Sound today demonstrates this same pattern. Driving into Port Alberni, one passes through Cathedral Grove, a small postage stamp of a park where a few relics of an ancient Douglas fir forest still stand. All around that grove are clearcut hillsides. This contrast with the denuded "working forest" is almost as dramatic for the tourist as are the beleaguered giants on show in the natural museum. Driving farther on, one passes through the infamous Black Hole where the landscape has been shaved from valley bottom to mountaintop, and burned. Once at the coast, one enters Pacific Rim National Park. As one follows the coast road along the ocean to Tofino, one can see that the band of old-growth forest is again very narrow, hugging the seashore in a pattern that has led locals to call this "leave strip park."

These patterns are global ones driven by international market demands. Although the forest industry in British Columbia is more than one hundred years old, the level of liquidation has increased dramatically over recent decades. Beginning in the mid-1940s, planning was intended to maintain the sustainability of the resource, and calculations were made of the "long run sustained yield." But these calculations were ignored as the actual level of cut went up year after year. Beyond the obvious pursuit of profits, the process was driven by international pressures that require any successful competitor to become ever more "productive," that is, to produce each unit of output ever more cheaply. In British Columbia, this is done by cutting more and more wood each year with the same, or shrinking, labor force. Thus are both corporate and organized labor caught in a perceived law of economic life, as is the provincial government, which benefits from the revenues generated by a competitive industry. Indeed, as one study concluded, the revenue outputs of the forest are allocated to these three interests in the following proportions: labor, 67 percent; business, 10 percent; and government, 6 percent (Schwindt and Heaps 1996).

At stake, therefore, is not big, bad business versus good, old labor, with a neutral government standing by. It is the whole system—and the dynamics that drive it. And the future is thought to mirror the past. For example, after the NDP came to power in 1991, a new round of planning processes was instituted to avoid the valley-by-valley conflicts over logging, by establishing a network of new protected areas. But these stakeholder exercises were beset with the same unassailable assumptions as in the past, and were thus oriented to ensuring that valuable, old-growth forests were excluded from protection as much as possible, with new parks skewed to high alpine "rock and ice." On Vancouver Island (where Clayoquot Sound is located), despite a target of 13 percent protection of the land base, less than 7 percent of the region's old-growth forests were so designated. Meanwhile, a Forest Practices Code was introduced to make industrial forestry more environmentally benign on the rest of the land base where logging continues. Yet, here too, a 6 percent ceiling was put on the allowable impacts that any new standards could have on the cut level. These limits, and the predictable reluctance to implement those provisions that might even affect this level fiber flow, has led to the code's inevitable failure (M'Gonigle 1999). As a result, rather than these processes leading to conflict resolution, they have been roundly condemned (Greenpeace 1997).

Critical explanations of the nature of wealth creation under capitalism have historically concentrated on the social sources of value, in particular, on the exploitation of labor (through the appropriation of surplus value). More recently, the alienation of consumers has also been brought into the equation. An ecological analysis builds on this social critique by pointing to the inevitable social and natural erosion associated with providing the economic flows necessary to support overbuilt institutions of all types. Large-scale institutions can, of course, be sustained by such flows over long periods of time, but they can only be so when they have a proportionally larger territorial base from which to draw. In other words, the sustainability of our modern institutions decreases with increases in scale; present growth inevitably creates the conditions for future decline. This is the ecological contradiction faced by industrial logging in Clayoquot Sound.

The advent of the field of ecological economics in the 1970s provided an important explanation of this contradiction by showing how material production is inherently an entropic process. Situating his analysis in the field of thermodynamics, the early leader of this new field, Nicholas Georgescu-Roegen, noted that "matter-energy enters the economic process in a state of *low entropy* (i.e., energy that is available to do work) and comes out of it in a state of *high energy* (i.e., waste energy)" (1973, 39). Any economy dependent on continuous flows of material or energy (throughput) is therefore inherently running contrary to the laws of the physical world—its very functioning is running it down. By drawing attention to the thermodynamic costs inflicted on the natural world by any economic system based on high levels of continuous production, ecological economics points to the inevitable need to reorganize the factors of production on some form of steady-state basis.

A number of unsettling implications follow from this analysis. For one thing, the economist's fascination with the benefits of substitution does not fare well unless the substituted good also embodies *less* entropy-generating activity. Substituting old-growth timbers with beams made of wood chips and glue may solve one problem, and cause a huge raft of others in the process. More broadly, from an ecological viewpoint, it is not capitalism per se that is the problem, but any form of high throughput economy. With their highly centralized modes of social organization, reworking the world to maintain a disconnected flow to the center is what the economism of *both capitalism and socialism* have been about. Productionism per se is the problem—and the high-energy/high-capital/resource-intensive industrial processes that make this productionism so productive.

This situation poses intellectual and strategic problems. In Clayoquot Sound, maintaining high levels of cut—what might be called linear through-put or flow—was all important for the government to maintain its tax base, as it was for MacMillan Bloedel to keep its shareholders happy and for the IWA to maintain its wage level. But, from an ecological viewpoint, the key to the problem of economic sustainability is to shift away from these linear flows by creating new, alternative structures that demand less throughput. The objective is necessarily to create economies and institutions that are more efficient, less consumptive, and more durable. This is not the incremental, reformist path of sustainable development, but the radical, reconstructive path of developing sustainability:

> To sustain our social organization, which is addicted to this linear growth, the volume economy achieves its wealth by sapping communities and environments of theirs. The value economy, in contrast, assumes that ecological and community processes are circular. That is, to be sustainable, these processes must maintain themselves, living on the stock of natural and social capital with which they have been endowed, so that they can return long-term stability to the forest and long-term value to the local community. (M'Gonigle and Parfitt 1994, 54)

Because a conservationist ethic to do "more with less" has to pervade all activities, these are precisely the sorts of proposals that environmentalists promote for Clayoquot Sound—preserving large areas intact where no economic flows are extracted, dramatically reducing the overall level of the cut, diversifying the economy into nonconsumptive uses of the environment (e.g., ecotourism), and developing new forest industries (in local woodlots, community-forestry initiatives, and value-added secondary manufacturing). But this low-throughput prescription challenges the prevailing institutions, the modus operandi of which is exactly the opposite. Instead of a transformative ecological strategy, the most recent stage for land-use planning for Vancouver Island is oriented to turning almost the whole forest land base outside the 13 percent protected areas into fiber farms. This is the goal of the controversial "Vancouver Island Resource Targets" plan completed in 2000 under the Ministry of Forests where some 30 percent of the land base is to be irrevocably zoned for intensive production (including accelerated old-growth liquidation) and another 30 percent for business-as-usual industrial forestry.

In contrast, the great innovation of the Clayoquot Sound Scientific Panel was to point forestry planning in the opposite direction by suggesting the need to limit economic activity to what was contained within the limits of ecosystem carrying capacity. This approach—widely known as "ecosystem-based management" (Grumbine 1994)—takes as its starting point the need both to maintain ecosystem integrity (its "composition, structure, and function") and to constrain human activity within that context. Simple enough in concept, and reasonable enough in intent, its implications are to replace an economically driven level of cut (and industry) by one that carefully draws what physical surplus the forest can yield without unsettling its ecological integrity. The issue thus becomes not so much *forest* management as it is *forestry* management: controlling human activities and impacts within the limits of ecosystem sustainability, rather than attempting to contain the consequences of this activity once the damage is done. And, necessarily, the new focus of such management is on sustaining the local community, equitably defined, not feeding the consumptive demands of distant powers.

This is the essential economic challenge of Clayoquot Sound, the shift from a linear centrist economy to a circular territorial one, and it is a prescription that applies very broadly. Despite its ruralness, Clayoquot Sound is sometimes characterized as a center of urban conflict. (See Magnusson's commentary in this volume.) The forest companies that work there are based in Vancouver, and they send their products and profits to Toronto and Los Angeles. The Ministry of Forests that regulates these companies is situated in Victoria, and the environmental activists pitch their messages to New York and Hamburg through a media that is overwhelmingly controlled by urban businesses. All these processes that control the future of the Sound are linear ones of extraction and dissemination. In contrast, the path for *urban* sustainability is the same as for rural, a circular path that lies not in ever more gasoline and wood and food and cash coming in from afar, and more CO_2 and garbage and effluent going out. Instead, a sustainable future entails these centers being progressively cut off from the ability to exploit remote resource regions at will. Were this to happen, greater reliance would necessarily be placed on the city's own circular processes—resource efficiency, materials recycling, industrial ecology, demand management, and so on. In the process, the city would demand less from Clayoquot Sound. Indeed, a shift to limited-input circularity applies to a vast range of sectors, from organic agriculture to preventive health, from energy conservation to participatory governance. It is central to the prescriptions inherent in an ecological political economy.

The challenges posed here are enormous, implying a basic socio-cultural reinvention. Indeed, to be pro-wilderness is not to be naively anti-production. One should not minimize the very real destruction of ecological values associated with industrial logging, especially compared with ecotourism. To equate in any substantive way wilderness tourism with logging as a part of the global capitalist economy is, on ecological grounds, simply inaccurate. Indeed, the major environmental problem associated with ecotourism is the high level of energy resources associated with getting the tourist to Clayoquot Sound, not the tourist's impact once there. Moreover, attempting to stop the destruction of functioning nature is so enormously difficult *in practice* that quibbling over the activists' imperfections *in theory* can easily become self-indulgent and counterproductive. Even though many forest workers share the desire for a different mode of production, many continue to embrace the high-flow ethic that is inherent to the multinational forest industry. It is not easy when it is that industry, and that workforce, that must be phased out not just in Clayoquot Sound, but everywhere.

Steadying an Unsteady State

If an ecological (or, what I would call a territorialist) analysis illuminates the problematic nature of the productivist flow economy, so too is a territorial critique of the centralist state uniquely informative. This is especially so to the extent to which the issue of ecological sustainability is a constitutional one that concerns the structures of economy and politics by which we self-constitute as a social and cultural collective. A territorial approach poses a particular challenge for a left that remains dangerously entranced by a false belief in the possibilities of state control and management. Historically, critical theorists have demonstrated how the activist state has, at best, worked to ameliorate some of the most egregious effects of private economic power (for example, through social welfare or environmental legislation) without challenging the overall momentum of its growth. A territorial perspective adds new depth to this critique by reconsidering the state's past and future character in light of the limits of centralism in all its forms.

Economically, we have characterized local places such as Clayoquot Sound as sources of raw material for the central flow economy. Politically, a parallel characterization applies to these places within the state system. In the face of continued demands for their resources, they have long been denied the political power to resist this exploitation, and have encountered huge obstacles in trying to create anything new that might be taken as precedent applicable more broadly. Historically, political theorists have sought to restrain the excesses of centralized public power primarily by dividing it *vertically* between centralized hierarchies (Montesquieu's three branches of legislative/executive/judicial authority) without a comparable awareness that the nature of hierarchical power requires that it be distributed *horizontally* by retaining certain powers at the local level. Despite the philosophical reference to popular sovereignty and the existence of federal systems and local governments, in practice, private and public power has freely accrued within centralized institutions that exercise control over large landmasses. Indeed, the history of the state has been about the gradual displacement of local sovereignty—local customs, local economies, local common property regimes—with new arrangements controlled from the top by a resource- and money-hungry state. From fourteenth-century enclosure legislation in England, to the seventeenth-century rage for beaver hats in colonial France, to twentieth-century "stakeholder" processes in Clayoquot Sound, antiterritorial impulses dominate state action. The motto of the state is clear: Enclose territory; secure the flow; control the community.

The operation of these impulses is nowhere more apparent than in the response to Native claims to authority over traditional lands. This movement is predicated on the very thing that centralist powers cannot tolerate: the recognition of an other territorially based source of legitimacy different from that of the centralist state. The history of land-claims settlements in Canada has foundered on just this point—on the bottom-line objective that First Nations (such as the Nuu-chah-nulth) must relinquish their claim to title in exchange for a grant of limited powers and limited territory from the Crown. For example, the official bargaining stance in land-claims negotiations of the British Columbia government is set by a land-selection model whereby First Nations will not be granted ownership over any more than 5 percent of their traditional territory. In the process, the transformative potential of Native title as an instrument to foster more self-sustaining regional territories for Native and non-Native alike within a reoriented ecological state is not understood, let alone given a moment's consideration.

This has long been a problem in Clayoquot Sound. For example, in March 1994, the provincial government and the Nuu-chah-nulth Tribal Council announced the conclusion of an Interim Measures Agreement (IMA) pending the completion of full treaty talks. This announcement was marred by an immediate disagreement over who had final decision-making authority: the First Nations' chiefs believing that the agreement gave them a formal veto, the provincial premier insisting that the Crown retained the final word. After so many weeks of intense negotiations, and a ceremonial announcement, the discovery of this fundamental disagreement would have been laughable if its import were not so significant.

In subsequent years, the Crown has sought to keep the Clayoquot virus from spreading, for example, by insisting that the ecological forestry advocated by the Scientific Panel did not apply to similar forest types elsewhere on the BC coast. The potential of innovative authorities such as the Clayoquot Sound Central Region Board (created under the IMA after the 1993 protests) was continuously constrained by government agencies concerned about the potential loss of control should the Board be successful. My own proposal that the Board be entitled to a first claim on all stumpage payments from forest licensees (in priority to the provincial government) was dismissed by a senior government official as potentially the most dangerous precedent he had seen in his public career. It was only the high international profile of the Clayoquot issue, combined with the sophisticated level of local organization, that was able to achieve specific innovations such as the Central Region Board, the reduction in cut levels, the rise in ecotourism alternatives, and so on. More generally, a deep antipathy continues against any form of public participation and environmental regulation that might seriously restrict natural resource development, and thus reduce economic flows to the center.

While social movements and academic theorists embrace new participatory approaches to environmental management (such as comanagement) and common property approaches for renewable resource ownership, governments of all political stripes resist such structural innovations. For example, mainstream social democrats remain psychologically attached to economic productivism and philosophically attached to instrumental state/Crown management. They are positively repelled by communitarian alternatives. The British Columbia NDP government's Forest Practices Code is a good example of the naive optimism that corporate economics can somehow be made environmentally acceptable, and that this can be achieved through sophisticated public interventionism like the staggeringly bureaucratic, 1,800-page code. Many people were surprised when then premier Glen Clark denounced Greenpeace activists as "enemies of the people" after they denounced the Code. They should not have been, for the Greenpeace critique went to the heart of the NDP's belief that it could "manage" from the top. In the case of more geographically localized social movements such as the Friends of Clayoquot Sound, or the activists in the Slocan Valley who seek greater local power to initiate a program of ecosystem-based transition, the NDP's reaction was intensely negative, bringing in the police to enforce continued forest liquidation. For the state-centralist social democrats, their antipathy to preservationist groups is heightened by their equally strong commitment to the forests as Crown, not community, resources.

Why the legitimacy of the state is now in question is, despite two decades of neoconservative assault, not understood. Yet, when the experience of Clayoquot Sound is understood through the lens of ecological political economy, one can begin to envision not only why the state must be deconstructed, but how a postmodern state might be constructed in its place. The key to such a state is that it would recognize, facilitate, and protect both the diverse experiences of ecological/territorial integrity and the community powers to maintain it. In light of the current problematic of sustainability, this is the basis for the state's claim to ecological legitimacy.

In a recent study, a group of us proposed such a solution to BC's forest controversies by allowing local communities to opt into a process of ecosystem-based economic transition (Burda et al. 1997). For those that do, the forest surrounding that community would be moved into a special trust status to be comanaged with the province according to ecosystem- and community-based principles. Beyond the specifics of the proposal is the fact that the very existence of such a tangible new arrangement would create the political space for all interests at the local level—from the logger to the environmentalist to the Native person to the small businessman—to begin to discuss, and create, their common future. New local tenures, new local businesses, and a new stewardship in relation to local forests all would become possible. Although the eventual outcome would be transformative in the approach to the forest land base, the transformation would only occur as communities look at their futures, and decide to take the plunge. Indeed, if the government passed our proposed Community Forest Trust Act tomorrow, nothing would change—until a community put up its collective hand and said, "Me first." The proposal does not merely tinker with the status quo, nor does it pose a radical change overnight. Instead, it proposes a radical change, but it proposes getting there incrementally. This is just the sort of instrument policy makers need. Instead, under the political compulsion to preserve centralism intact, instruments to provide the space in which to create alternatives are not permitted.

The Dialectic of Sustainability

The struggles in Clayoquot Sound can thus be seen as a manifestation of two opposing tendencies that exist as a dialectical tension in human relations: the tension between central and territorial forms of social organization.

Centrism is manifest in hierarchical organizations built around the imperatives of concentrated power and the exploitation of nonlocal resources, or
flows of energy. In contrast, territorial forms of social organization are those
that are rooted in forms of social power that are dispersed and on the
ground, and can be maintained by local resources. Although a perfectly territorial society (i.e., locally self-sufficient, nonhierarchical, ecologically stable) may never have existed in the past, neither could a completely centralist society ever be created and sustained. Instead, the significance of the
tension between center and territory is in the never-resolving dialectic itself.

In the pursuit of social sustainability—whether for Clayoquot Sound,
British Columbia, or the planet—one must learn how, on the one hand, the
universal tendencies to center power are held in check by territorial institutions and, on the other hand, how centralist institutions might be reconfigured to enforce, rather than erode, territorialist values at all levels. As André
Gunder Frank argues, the system of economic transfer and accumulation
that has been of so much concern to students of modern capitalism is not
specific to capitalism but is, in fact, millennia old (Gills and Frank 1991).
Public discourse must venture beyond accepted boundaries set by the market and the state to consider the costs of centrist growth itself. An awareness of the center–territory dialectic thus takes political ecology outside the
state-centric and still-productivist focus of both market and traditional left
analyses. It is to the generalized *dynamics* of these modes of organizing
power that a territorialist analysis looks, rather than at simply the specific
structures in which these dynamics may be embedded (including capitalism, the state, cities) at any time and place. In addition, as a prescriptive approach, traditional approaches to development take centrism as the model.
In contrast, a territorialist political ecology points to the reverse: to the critical importance of maintaining, indeed strengthening, territorial forces as
the counterbalance to centrist power and growth that alone can bring social and ecological sustainability.

In addition to a concern for the horizontal flows of resources from
local places to centralized institutions, a territorial analysis points to the
vertical nature of these flows—from grounded communities up into hierarchies of corporate or bureaucratic or urban power. As we have seen, in
practical terms, the complex social dynamic that drives the development
of Clayoquot Sound embodies a basic contradiction: the rise of central
power is, and always has been, sustained by the territorial structures that
precede that rise, and it cannot survive without them. Yet, driven to grow,
centralist institutions consume the very territorial processes on which
they depend. In doing so, they await their own demise. This is the story of

countless civilizations past that have risen only to fall. And today, this is the character of the center-driven, entropy-creating consumer society spreading out into every Clayoquot Sound on the globe.

Today, the dominance of centrist forms of power is almost complete. The experience of globalization is a profoundly centrist experience—center power seeking unconstrained access to the most remote sources of potential sustenance—and it defines our experience in a totalistic way. To speak of Clayoquot Sound as an urban issue makes sense in this spatial context—controlled from the city over the region, driven by consumerist multinationals and their associated bureaucracies. Ironically, the recognition of the historical prevalence of this centrist power constrains future possibilities, relegating to the romantic fringes the thought that somehow a territorially defined reality can be reconstituted or, more accurately, constituted anew in the face of the existing trajectory. And yet, if the centrist structure is constructed against the "laws of nature," then there is no alternative but to understand and confront this contradiction, and then to create the impossible.

Conclusion

With so much at stake, it is easy to appreciate why the conflict at Clayoquot Sound, or other similar conflicts to date, remains unsolvable. The problems are structural in nature, and the solutions are transformative in design. To speak of solutions is, of course, problematic insofar as one attempts to lay out some fixed utopian outcome. And yet, to the extent one begins to identify the nature and limits of the centrist forces in which we are enmeshed, the direction for change becomes clearer. Ours is a constitutional crisis, in the largest sense of the word, and to begin to resolve it we must invigorate (and, where we can, reinvigorate) territorial forces at all levels. We can do so not with a program here, and a policy there, but by changing the *dynamics* of our whole social evolution. Many specific strategies for doing this exist: community-based economic development, communitarian devolution of state authority, balanced urban and regional planning, forest tenure and land reform, social movement activism, and so on. In all of these approaches, there is a common need, not to replace, but to rebalance, the relations between center and territory. Only then might we change the world and create a new synthesis to take us respectfully, and with justice, into the ecological age.

Works Cited

Atkinson, Adrian. 1991. *Principles of Political Ecology.* London: Bellhaven.
British Columbia. 1995. *Forest Practices Code.* Victoria, B.C.: Ministry of Forests.

Burda, Cheri, Deborah Curran, Fred Gale, and Michael M'Gonigle. 1997. *Forests in Trust: Reforming British Columbia's Tenure System for Ecosystem and Community Health.* Report Series 97-2, Eco-Research Chair of Environmental Law and Policy, University of Victoria.

Georgescu-Roegen, Nicholas. 1973. "The Entropy Law and the Economic Problem." In *Toward a Steady-State Economy,* ed. Herman Daly. San Francisco: W. H. Freeman. 37–49.

Gills, Barry K., and André Gunder Frank. 1991. "5000 Years of World System History: The Cumulation of Accumulation." In *Core/Periphery Relations in Pre-Capitalist Worlds,* ed. Christopher Chase-Dunn and Thomas D. Hall. Boulder, Colo.: Westview Press. 67–112.

Greenpeace. 1997. *Broken Promises: The Truth about What's Happening to British Columbia's Forests.* Vancouver: Greenpeace.

Grumbine, R. E. 1994. "What Is Ecosystem Management?" *Conservation Biology* 8: 27.

M'Gonigle, R. Michael. 1980. "The Economizing of Ecology: Why Big, Rare Whales Still Die." *Ecology Law Quarterly* 9:1: 119–237.

———. 1999. "The Political Ecology of Biodiversity: A View from the Western Woods." In *Biodiversity in Canada: Ecology, Ideas, and Action,* ed. Stephen Bocking. Peterborough, Ontario: Broadview Press. 391–414.

M'Gonigle, R. Michael, and Ben Parfitt. 1994. *Forestopia: A Practical Guide to a New Forest Economy.* Madeira Park, B.C.: Harbour Press.

M'Gonigle, R. Michael, and Wendy Wickwire. 1988. *Stein: The Way of the River.* Vancouver: Talonbooks.

Schwindt, Richard, and Terry Heaps. 1996. *Cutting Up the Money Tree: Distributing the Wealth from British Columbia's Forests.* Vancouver: David Suzuki Foundation.

Soja, Edward. 1989. *Postmodern Geographies: The Reassertion of Space in Critical Social Theory.* London: Verso.

Between the Local and the Global

Clayoquot Sound and Simulacral Politics

Catriona Sandilands

Introduction: Snapshots from an Ecotone

Snapshot 1 (1972). I am standing with my mother on the government wharf in Port Alberni, waiting for my father's ship to dock. I am eight years old; my father is hydrographer-in-charge on board the *William J. Stewart,* and he is coming home after an extended survey trip of the BC coast. The smell of the pulp mill is everywhere, and I want to go swimming.

Snapshot 2 (1979). My "kissing cousin" Paul and I are on the rocks at Long Beach. He is wearing a leather jacket; I am wearing (and have worn for days) the blue Queens University sweatshirt he brought me. We have been "secretly" flirting since he arrived; my parents pretend not to notice. He is showing me the tidal pools; he is going to become a biologist.

Snapshot 3 (1990). My parents are on the "gangway" of the *Canadian Princess,* moored in (actually, built into) Ucluelet harbor. The trip was a retirement present for my father; the *Princess* was, until 1975, the *William J. Stewart.* Dad wasn't too unhappy when they decommissioned her, because he always found the cabins too short. I wonder if they still are.

Snapshot 4 (1993). I am standing on the Kennedy River Bridge; it is very early in the morning, and in the half-light the people and banners look like they are floating in a gray, foggy stew. The loggers haven't arrived yet; the people who are going to be arrested are claiming their spaces in the middle of the road. I can't really make out the trees, but when finally I can I am tempted to get arrested myself.

I am neither local nor "come-from-away" to the west coast of Vancouver Island; born in Victoria, I have visited Clayoquot Sound and its surrounding communities many times over the course of my life, and have witnessed its changes with a variety of conflicting sensibilities. Despite the fact that I now live in Toronto, I cannot take up the position of foreign correspondent; despite the fact that I have known Clayoquot since my childhood, I cannot claim to be a longtime resident. I have many relationships to this place, and memory makes it impossible to write as if I did not; at the same time, I have only one relationship to this place, a visitor always.

In writing this essay, I find my voice in the space between these positions. Between everyday work and special vacation, between the mundane and the spectacular, between the home and the away, I see that the reality of this place is also in this realm of conflict between local and global. Clayoquot Sound is made real through its existence as a local community; it is also made real through its existence as a global tourist destination. It is not only the "locals" who produce the meanings of the place, as the place exists in a variety of different maps of meaning simultaneously; its existence is as much a part of the glossy realms of mass representation as it is of the day-to-day productive lives of the residents of Tofino, Ucluelet, Port Alberni, Ahousaht, Opitsaht, and Hesquiaht.

Krall (1994) calls such places "ecotones"; the borderlands between distinct ecological regions are teeming with the overlapping life of both. Clayoquot Sound is an ecotone of the local and the global; it contains a rich and varied local culture at the same time as it embodies the complexities of a thoroughly globalized tourist—and political—gaze. Its existence can be reduced to neither; its specificity is as a highly visible and conflictual location of both. And so is mine: I am a child of the same late-capitalist border-confused contradictions that have produced Clayoquot Sound as an ecotone.[1]

This essay is thus a particularly situated view of the social and ecological landscape of Clayoquot Sound. It is about a nagging suspicion that I have had for a number of years: that the struggle to "save" the landscape is not so much about freeing the resident ecological and social communities to negotiate multiple possible futures and identities as it is about imposing a particular view of the landscape on precisely these communities. At the very least, local negotiations are shaped by their insertion into a global marketplace of images; more likely, the appearance of specific positions as if they were uniquely local hides the fact that this very specificity is a requirement of the global marketplace. And worst: the act of preservation to maintain a particular aesthetic-ecological sensibility is as much a gesture of inserting Clayoquot Sound into global capitalism as is clearcut logging for the eventual purpose of creating telephone directories.

The problem is not only that this is the case, although it remains important to describe just how this capitalist aesthetic insertion works. Given their prolonged politicization in and reflection on Clayoquot Sound, local residents and workers and international visitors and activists alike seem quite aware that tourist-friendly preservation is a strategic act, a partly instrumental representation of the landscape designed to achieve particular ends; I applaud this self-consciousness.[2] The problem is rather that this representation comes disguised as a liberation; one set of capitalist-embedded (consumer) constructions of nature gets to pass as a freeing of the landscape where another, less romantic (productive) aesthetic is demonized as if it were the only representative of multinational capitalism around. The problem is, then, that the tourist aesthetic appears innocent, and that this innocence passes in many circles as ecocentrism or as environmentalist political success, as a genuinely long-term and sustainable solution for Clayoquot. Rendered innocent, Clayoquot's "success" becomes a foundation-less model to which other communities aspire.

From where I stand, somewhere between here and there, I find this simulacrum of sustainability more than somewhat distressing. The "nature" of Clayoquot Sound is thoroughly immersed in the image exchange that often passes for environmental (more accurately, wilderness preservationist) politics in North America. In addition, the human communities interacting with—and partially constituted by—this nature risk sacrificing precious and fragile moments of local conversation to the deity of the desirable commodity. At the same time as I fervently hope that the landscape of Clayoquot is not torn apart by clearcut logging, I also hope that it is not kept cryogenically frozen as an artifact of a particular kind of global nature aesthetic. To foster the diversity and richness of the ecotone, a conversation about the future of Clayoquot requires that a variety of local and global human–nature interactions be fostered.

This essay is thus a space-clearing gesture. Its intent is to highlight some of the "erased" dimensions of Clayoquot politics—the constructive and constrictive logic of ecotourism, the hyperreality of much of what is called nature in global capitalism—not so much to solve the many contradictions, but rather to offer a conversational space that does not *immediately* equate environmentalism with an entrepreneurial tourist economic vision. Clayoquot Sound contains both a history and a potential of democratic conversations among communities over desires for sustainable human–nonhuman relations. In order to follow the potential, the invisibility of tourism as an active and desiring gaze on nature does nothing to facilitate this conversation, and needs to be made visible so that it can be challenged.

Globalization, Tourism, and Simulation

The grand narrative of social and ecological life in late capitalism into which Clayoquot and I both fall concerns the ways in which local natures such as the Clayoquot old-growth forests appear and are constructed in the context of globalizing capitalist relations of production and exchange. In particular, although the production and exchange of material commodities—lumber, pulp, perfectly straight trees for Buddhist temples—is a crucial relation that ties Clayoquot to a global capitalist economy, it is also in the globalizing realm of the image and the spectacle that struggles for the meaning and future of the region are negotiated.

Globalization is not a new phenomenon; one can, for example, speak of British colonialism as a strongly globalizing venture, and can thus understand the global division of labor that partitions the world into North and South, center and periphery, staple-producing and cosmopolitan regions as a relationship with a long (and sordid) history. But, as Scott Lash and John Urry note, "with postmodernity it is the global networks of communication and information that are crucial" (Lash and Urry 1994, 306). Although the extension of commodity relations into more and more spheres of social and natural life is thus grounded in a historical process of capitalist accumulation, the organization of the world according to specifically capitalist *cultural* forms is a more recent question. According to Lash and Urry, this organization has a number of defining features and impacts: among them, that

> the symbolic forms transmitted by the technical media of mass
> communication are central to contemporary cultural forms; that
> these developments greatly expand ideological scope since they
> enable symbolic forms to be transmitted to extended audiences
> dispersed in time and space; . . . and most importantly of all they
> produce images and less in the way of ideas, images that are diverse, pluralistic, and which overload the viewer. (Ibid., 307)

Arjun Appadurai notes that there are two key processes involved in cultural globalization: mediation and migration (Appadurai 1996, 3). Individually and together, these two constitutive features of modernity (or postmodernity, depending on one's point of view) have a tremendous, if uneven, impact on the work of the imagination, on the creation of "imagined worlds, the multiple worlds constituted by the historically situated imaginations of persons and groups spread across the globe" (Lash and Urry 1994, 307). It is important to understand these processes as situated in a distinctly capitalist version of globalization; at the same time, it is important *not* to consider them in terms of a center/periphery model, in which certain dominant Western cultural forms are carried on the backs of electronic signals and world travelers to the outer reaches of the globe. Of electronic media, for example, Appadurai writes: "always carrying the sense of distance between the viewer and the event, these media nevertheless compel the transformation of everyday discourse. At the same time, they are resources for experiments with self-making in all sorts of societies, with all sorts of persons" (Appadurai 1996, 3).

Understood as constituted in specific relations of production and exchange, media and migration are thus highly influential but nondetermining processes that compel a rearticulation of local identities with global cultural forms. Cultural flows are not only from North to South, as obviously demonstrated in the (voluntary and forced) migration of persons to Europe and North America. The flows are also not only about the (re)constitution of a dominant position; media images, for example, "may be used for oppositional movements, such as with regard to environmental issues" (Lash and Urry 1994, 307). But these cultural flows are, at some point, also inescapable. As Appadurai writes,

> few persons in the world today do not have a friend, relative, or
> coworker who is not on the road to somewhere else or already
> coming back home, bearing stories and possibilities. In this sense,
> both persons and images often meet unpredictably, outside the
> certainties of home and the *cordon sanitaire* of local and national
> media effects. This mobile and unforeseeable relationship be-
> tween mass-mediated events and migratory audiences defines the
> core of the link between globalization and the modern. (Appadurai
> 1996, 4)

Tourism is among the most significant practices to embody and constitute these global cultural flows. Unlike radio, film, television, emigration and immigration, tourism knows almost no national boundaries, regulations, or restrictions (the Internet has yet to be proven to be as significant). At one level, tourism actively participates in the homogenization of global culture. As Daniel Boorstin (1992) and John Urry (1990) note, the creation of tourist enclaves (such as Club Med) in "host" countries insulates the visitor from the experience of cultural difference by creating an artificial bubble of home around the holiday experience. Food is prepared in a way that the visitor already understands; cultural events are staged and watered down in order to conform to specific (Euro-Western) expectations. Although the tourist may have arrived in search of an exotic experience, the world of resorts, hotels, and bus tours is actually a realm of "pseudo-events," illusions born from the desires of the tourist public and industry. The tourist desires the comforts of home, and receives them in a safe and familiar package, albeit with gloriously exotic wrapping paper.

At the same time as tourism both demands and creates a certain uniformity of experience, however, there is a more "cosmopolitan" understanding of global travel that emphasizes (however inflatedly) its distinctiveness from overtly artificial, Disneyesque practices. To put it baldly, the cosmopolitan traveler's view of her distinctiveness relies on a sense of her desire for difference, or, as Lash and Urry put it, "an openness to other peoples and cultures and a willingness/ability to appreciate some elements of the language/culture of the place that is being visited" (Lash and Urry 1994, 309). In this view, the point of travel is not to be surrounded by familiar foods, smells, sounds, and sights, but to experience difference for its own sake; the point is not to be safe, but "to take risks by virtue of moving outside the tourist environmental bubble" (ibid.). Thus, in this view, the destination becomes desirable because of its ability to show its difference from home, rather than because of its ability to provide the tourist with all of the comforts of a well-equipped resort hotel.

But the difference between tourism and cosmopolitanism is neither as qualitative nor as large as cosmopolitans may think. First and foremost, both travel practices assume that "one has the right to travel and to consume at least initially all environments" (ibid.). Although it is clear that certain kinds of tourists travel in search of (apparently) authentic experiences of other cultures and natures, there is even in a cosmopolitan view the sense that the traveler has the *right* to view, experience, and otherwise consume the destination. That travel is constituted as a right rather than a privilege has everything to do with the status of the destination as a site for commodity production; tourism is a globalizing pattern of consumption that is entirely consistent with a neoliberal emphasis on trade unfettered by local or national interests. Indeed, especially in contexts where the invitation of foreign currency has (through various modes of subtle and not so subtle coercion) surpassed the invitation of foreign aid, tourism appears—

unlike some modes of resource extraction, for example—to be *in* the local or national interest. Tourism appears as if it is a "win-win" practice: in exchange for a few currency-bearing visitors, the host locale can keep its cultural and natural specificity, at the very least because tourists can be contained relatively easily within their enclaves, but more commonly precisely because it is this very specificity that makes the host locale a desirable destination.

There is, of course, a catch. Tourists (however cosmopolitan) and tourist providers actively participate in the insertion of the host locale into a global tourist economy. Insofar as the locale visited is consumed by the tourist—in other words, insofar as the place becomes a destination—it participates in global cultural production as an active object of tourist construction. The cosmopolitan, however much she seeks the exotic, still demands that the host locale be consumable in a manner that conforms to tourist expectations of some kind. Perhaps more crucially, the distinction between cosmopolitan and noncosmopolitan tourism is not between authentic and artificial experience, but between *types of commodities*. Where, in one kind of tourist experience, the traveler seeks the safety of the same, in another, she seeks the thrill of difference. And in between these two poles lies the vast majority of tourist experiences in late capitalism: the place must be unique and exciting enough to go there, but sufficiently within the visitor's preexisting frame of reference to be understandable and consumable.

Tourism thus plays a game of seduction between the familiar and the exotic; the local(e) appears in the global gaze as an invitation written in the language of the visitor, in the language of the global cultural flows of which tourism is a part. Brochures, travel guides, photographs, documentary films, slide shows, coffee-table books: these image-texts form the cultural field on which the local(e) must play and in which it must distinguish itself. To become a destination, a place must resonate with these images, must create and represent itself as an exotic and desirable (and generally well-adjectived) noun in a global lexicon of well-known consuming verbs. The global produces the local as a commodity; the local selects and organizes its specificity according to the modes of representation most likely to distinguish it in global cultural flows.[3]

I would not (and will not) argue that the local place becomes, in this process, *entirely* an artifact of a globalized tourist image and desire, but it remains vital to consider that tourism is neither a practice of neutral observation nor an artificial coating on the surface of a deeper reality. The orientation of tourist experience to the global exchange of *images* is especially significant. On one level, the destination must orient its representational practices to a global cultural marketplace that demands of each location a specificity coded in terms of marketable spectacle (Urry 1990). On another level, the destination must perform this spectacle for tourists, in order for the experience to live up to the representation. To the extent that this performance is marked as the reality of the local-as-destination, it becomes *hyperreal*, more real than reality, a constructive fiction of the tourist gaze that appears as if it were a genuine representation of the place itself— indeed, the *most* genuine representation—while other cultural productions come to be viewed as artificial, inauthentic, unnatural, tainted.

To go one step further: in Jean Baudrillard's (1983) language, the destination is not only a simulation but a *simulacrum*. A simulation is a copy of something real; a simulacrum is a copy of a copy that successfully poses as real and that masks the basic absence of any originary reality. In tourism, the destination is modeled on a vision of reality that never really existed except in the minds and desires of tourists and promoters. The simulacral destination is not only a fake but, in its ability to pass as reality, covers up the fundamental absence of reality behind it. Again in Baudrillard's terms, the global exchange of images—simulacra—not only increasingly orders the world, but increasingly replaces the real world with a copy of a reality that never existed, and *this copy is the only real available to us.* The lines between real and imaginary, natural and artificial, implode; in its "seeming" real we give to the simulacrum its legitimacy, its sense of unartificiality, even though its distinctiveness is only as an element *internal* to the process of replication and simulation. The world is "a hyper-real henceforth sheltered from the imaginary, and from any distinction between the real and the imaginary, leaving room only for the orbital recurrence of models and the simulated generation of difference" (ibid., 4).

To return abruptly to Clayoquot Sound, I wish to argue that the insertion of the place into global tourist cultural flows—indeed, the creation of the place *by* global tourist cultural flows—has rendered it simulacral. Although I do not follow Baudrillard into the argument that the whole world is already a simulacrum—totalized, finished, emptied of the real—and thus leave space for the possibility of a certain unhyperreality interrupting the multiplication and global flow of simulacra, one element of his argument bears special mention in the context of Clayoquot Sound: nature. Far from nature being the site from which simulation begins but at which it also ends, nature has become—especially in its creation as spectacular destination— precisely the simulacrum that hides the possibility of a nontotalized (and potentially democratic) reality in Clayoquot Sound.

Tourism, Wilderness Preservation, and Simulacral Natures

In his controversial essay "The Trouble with Wilderness," William Cronon (1995) argues that wilderness is profoundly unnatural.[4] "Far from being the one place on earth that stands apart from humanity, it is quite profoundly a human creation—indeed, the creation of very particular human cultures at very particular moments in human history" (ibid., 69). Although the term has been symbolically loaded at least since early Christianity, the idea that wilderness is sacred, sublime, and somewhere one might want to *visit* is a much more recent product of a largely Western, urban/industrial view of the world. In its current form as object of preservationist environmental concern, it is also the product (both conceptually and physically) of tourism. Thus, as Williams (1980) also notes, this nature is not only historically and culturally but also *class*-specific; it is an image in a bourgeois, urban mirror that universalizes, essentializes, and imprisons.

Cronon notes that the nineteenth century saw an important transition between notions of wilderness as "sublime" (terrible, awesome) and more pastoral views in which nature—while still romanticized—was considerably less daunting. In part, this transition occurred as a result of the opening of wilderness to a specifically tourist practice and sensibility; "as more and more tourists sought out the wilderness as a spectacle to be looked at for its great beauty, the sublime in effect became domesticated" (Cronon 1995, 75). The infrastructure of railways, lodges, and outfitted excursions into parks and reserves effectively transformed the experience of terror and anxiety at being lost in the wild into a sort of spectator sport. Patricia Jasen (1995) adds another important dimension to this transition: with the late-nineteenth-century development of tourism as an industry oriented to the production and exchange of spectacle, it became increasingly the case that nature was marketed and consumed as photographic image and travelogue itinerary item. By and large, tourists had a strong image of wilderness long before they visited it; in order for nature to become and remain a site for visitation, it not only had to come complete with at least some of the comforts of home, but it had to live up to the image that was already present in minds of (largely urban, bourgeois) tourists. Thus, even in the nineteenth century, wilderness was simulacral; it was partitioned, enhanced, provisioned, and created according to ideas of nature that were generated in the tourist industry.

As Cronon and Alexander Wilson (1991) both note, a significant element in this spectacular-simulacral wilderness was and is that it should be uninhabited. Cronon writes that the movement to create national parks and wilderness reserves forced (and continues to force) aboriginal peoples from lands they call(ed) home: "they were forced to go elsewhere, with the result that tourists could safely enjoy the illusion that they were seeing their nation in its pristine, original state, in the new morning of God's own creation" (Cronon 1995, 79).[5] Wilson expands on this theme, noting that the aesthetic of the pristine was and is an active intervention into nature that, especially with the advent of automobile-based tourism, insists on a strategy of "control [over] virtually everything within the field of vision" (Wilson 1991, 36). In particular, this aesthetic demands—based on its central ideal of untouched wilderness—that there be a complete separation of productive from consumptive landscapes. Thus, not only are aboriginal peoples removed and erased from wilderness in particular, but consumption is the only activity allowed presence.

Wilderness tourism relies on the illusion that it is not an economic practice, that the facilities supporting it are not productive and historically specific interventions into the landscape, that the act of constructing and presenting nature is not a creative and selective act but simply a revelation of what is "naturally" there. Wilderness itself relies on the active subtraction of humans from nature; it is a concept of nature that insists on the careful policing of the boundary between human and nonhuman, and on the equally careful policing of human activity to allow only certain kinds of (consuming) relationships to exist. For the illusion of wilderness to work, however, this policing must be completely invisible. This "romantic ideology," writes Cronon, "leaves precisely nowhere for human beings actually to make a living off the land" (Cronon 1995, 80) (except as tourist operators); human productive activity is, by its definition, evidence of the destruction of nature, and only by instituting a regime of consumption is nature said to be preserved. Thus, as tourist simulacrum, wilderness is produced according to a particular logic by which its constructedness is simultaneously enforced and erased; the active management of nature is both crucial to the maintenance of a particular aesthetic and prohibited from entry into view. Similarly, the act of consumption necessitates considerable intervention into pristine areas, but the activity of consumption is separated from the economic realm of its generation and maintenance.

Following Baudrillard, Thomas Birch thus argues that "wilderness reservations are not intended or tolerated as places where nature is allowed to get out of control, even though a degree of aberrant behavior is permitted" (Birch 1995, 142–43). Instead, wilderness areas are—literally— "lockups" for the wild (Birch separates wilderness as construction from wildness as potential), by which Western imperialist culture institutes its desire for absolute mastery over nature. In its guise as spectacle, as destination, nature becomes a resource to feed consumer culture; in this guise, it is tamed, domesticated, rendered a harmless and innocent product to be exchanged alongside other signs in the global marketplace. As a simulacrum, as a nature that never existed but that now defines the essence of nature to which all other natures are compared (and found wanting), it creates its own consumer demand. As Birch argues, however, it is the illusion of the naturalness and *reality* of this nature that allows the simulacrum to mask the absence of a real nature behind it:

> In order to do the job of preserving its reality principle, and in spite of its need to simulate or define the other [nature] according to its own models, the imperium must leave at least enough otherness intact to *maintain the glance of the other.* . . . The other must be able to cast its glance at the imperial enterprise to preserve the meaning of that enterprise, to legitimate its purpose of bringing law and order to wild chaos. . . . There must remain at least some vestiges of wildness to be kept at bay. (Ibid., 151; emphasis in original)

To restate Birch's case in a somewhat different language: there must be enough nature in the simulacrum of wilderness to preserve the logical illusion by which it is natural; the slave must actively participate in the constitution of the identity of the master. It is here that one must emphasize the difference between the simulacrum of wilderness and the simulacrum of, say, Disneyland. As Baudrillard notes in *America*, it is the act of leaving Disneyland to reenter so-called reality that marks—to the extent that we follow the path of belief from fantasy to real—our complicity with simulacral logic: the Anaheim street outside Disneyland is as imbricated in the order of simulacra as the Main Street inside. For nature, our belief in the reality of a wilderness outside its construction marks our complicity in the illusion; in a world where, as Bill McKibben (1989) has written, nature (in the sense of untouched, pure, and pristine nature) is already dead, our actions *as if it were not* only perpetuate the mirror-play by which humanless, consumptive, colonized and colonialist, *constructed* wilderness is the foundationless exemplar for all nature.

In the terms cast by contemporary tourism, it is the image of nature's not-quite-deadness that serves as its chief insertion into the circulation of commodified images and, notably, as its chief value in (some) preservationist discourse. Wilderness—discovered, invaded, sanitized, and *then* preserved via incarceration—is a destination because it is not everywhere, because it is not a landscape where people (visibly) work and live in their mundane and familiar ways, because it is not part of the everyday experience of (most) tourists. It is the unique and the marvelous that draw the visitor and that fuel the campaign to "save"; although this spectacularization is often formed around a landscape or species that conforms to specific aesthetic conventions ("charismatic megafauna"), the lure of the "last chance to see" is also significant. As Candace Slater (1995) notes, for example, the tropical rainforest has become a preservationist icon; apart from the very real possibility that the protection of the rainforest from humans will result in the forcible expulsion of those peoples who call it home rather than destination, there is also the fact that Amazonia has become inserted into and constructed by the global flow of nature images in a particular way. Amazon nature, as part of an Edenic narrative, not only masks its constructedness behind a thick wall of ecological science and biodiversity talk, but insists that its Edenic state is the primordial real that people should, if not visit themselves, then at least ensure will be around for others to visit in the future. Similarly, as Constance Russell and M. J. Ankenman (1996) note, ecotourism depreciates nature as it transforms it, via an aesthetic of the photogenic, into an object of consumption both in its image circulation before and after the nature experience, and during the event itself as the visit is organized around its (aesthetically conventional) visual preservation.

As a political project located in cultural globalization, wilderness preservation is grounded, at least in part, in a specific tourist aesthetic that demands differentiation among commodities. It is the natures that distinguish themselves in the constructed moral and aesthetic framework of spectacle and uniqueness that are marked as worth saving. Preservation thus appears to save from construction a nature that is actually already constructed in particular ways, and simultaneously participates in the illusion that real nature lies outside all construction. Even at its nineteenth-century origins, the movement for wilderness preservation began with this story of nature's near death; this story is not a rescuing but a keening over the grave of a nature that has already become something other than wild, is already dead in the impossible and colonial terms cast by wilderness discourse. Preserving wilderness is like walking out of Disneyland; our belief in the wilderness we enter masks the fact that the image exchange producing Disneyland produced wilderness in the same stroke, as simulacra.

Although the leap to Clayoquot can be made from here with little effort, I also want to point out that not all natures are equally subject to simulacral logic (which is where I am not Baudrillard). As Appadurai notes (1996, 3), global cultural flows are uneven and untotalized. Clearly, I believe that the idea of wilderness is thoroughly caught up in a global exchange of tourist image and spectacle; as a nature that never was but that preservationist politics insists is originary and exemplary, it is a simulacrum. But wilderness is not all of nature. As Cronon suggests, part of the ability of wilderness to pass as natural and originary derives from its foundational separation from human (productive) activity. *If* nature is understood and practiced differently, *if* a variety of activities that are not organized primarily according to the exchange of images can be practiced as natural, and *if* we understand that the uses toward which humans inevitably put nonhumans (and possibly vice versa) involve us all in a thoroughly unpristine series of conversations and interactions, then perhaps the simulacral logic of wilderness might be disrupted and exposed as the illusion that it has always been. A rupture is not an answer, a firm standpoint from which to see an underlying "truth," but it *may* be an opening to a less obviously problematic seeing.

Clayoquot Sound: Simulacra and Erasures

"Visit beautiful British Columbia. Picnic in the clearcut forests. Hike the eroded hillsides. See the dried-up salmon streams." So went a June 1995 Clayoquot campaign advertisement by the Rainforest Action Network in the (swank) magazine *Condé Nast Traveler*. The text makes clear the stakes of the struggle: "Ecotourism is a major industry here and it's growing. So is salmon fishing. But, if the presently planned clearcuts of Clayoquot Sound are completed, *there will be such devastation that you won't want to visit this place*" (emphasis in original).

There is no doubt in my mind that the self-conscious act of appealing to the aesthetic sensibilities and destination desires of a global tourist public played a crucial role in the struggle to save Clayoquot Sound from clearcut logging. Perhaps ironically, the struggle to preserve Clayoquot has constructed it more strongly according to the commodified logic of global tourism than it was before: How many more images of big trees were circulated? How many more visitors organized their experiences of nature to take those photographs? How many more paths were broken (not to mention "witness" trails built) in the forests by activists, tourists, and other visitors that were not there before? How many more forest workers found that their experiences of and practices in the forest landscape were not welcome in the sanitized nature sold to visitors? That this insertion occurred under the sign of saving Clayoquot from multinational capitalism highlights the simulacral qualities of this preservationist moment. In the belief that Clayoquot would be freed from construction by its preservation, wilderness activists evaded the fact that the rescue of the rainforest from clearcut logging is as much a globalized construction of nature as is timber production.

Perhaps especially in Clayoquot, what disturbs me is the logic that suggests that nature needs to be saved from culture when the nature that is being saved is not only a cultural product but a cultural product that, by definition, excludes almost all but one of the most commodified human relations to nonhuman nature. Perhaps even more problematic is the way in which wilderness serves as the only real nature against which other landscapes (both cultured and natured) are compared; this is simulacral politics at its most exemplary. Although part of my knowledge of—and caring about—the place exists and was generated because of the infrastructure of tourism (we did not get to Tofino until the road was paved), I see that it is in the long-term and iterative process of coming to know the land in the multiple forms by which it overflows the overdetermined Western Canada Wilderness Committee (WCWC) "big tree" posters that anything like sustainability might be approached (come to think of it, when I was a child I was far more interested in the "enigmatic microflora"[6] than in the trees, anyway). Resistances to simulacral politics—in which a very particular culture of nature acts to regulate and constrain human behavior without ever showing its face as a cultural artifact—lie in cultivating a healthy variety of human–nonhuman relationships, at least some of which must directly challenge the commodified logic by which real nature is understood as a site that excludes productive activities.

The struggles over Clayoquot Sound rode (and continue to ride) a knife-edge between succumbing to the globalized imperative of simulacral nature and resisting this imperative en route to a more varied, variable, and generally messy landscape. In order to approach the latter set of possibilities, the processes and forms in which wilderness stands for nature, and in which this model overwhelms the local and conflictual relations in which other natures may be negotiated, need to be made visible and thus (to some extent at least) negotiable. In Clayoquot, both surrounding and running directly through the politicized images of the landscape that have circulated globally, there is an active process of erasure that requires specific attention.

Overall, the nature that has been constructed as the essence of Clayoquot—in both global and local discourses of the region—is typical of the humanless, simulacral wilderness that Cronon and others have criticized. Although certain kinds of human presence are allowed as natural—a topic to which I will return—in general the nature that is considered to be under siege by logging interests in the region is one that does not include human activity. The act of working (on) the land in a "modern" fashion is, in this discourse, understood as antithetical to nature; thus, the dichotomy is (generally) between wilderness and work. Tourism, in this discourse, is not work; it is consumption. The act of building the infrastructure necessary to facilitate this consumption is, at best, considered a necessary evil for the full insertion of (preserved) Clayoquot into a tourist economy; at worst, tourism is not considered an intervention into nature at all, only a set of background practices to facilitate human appreciation of this real nature.

Nowhere is this contradictory series of erasures more explicit than in preservationist discourse;[7] although it is certainly the case that environmentalism did not create the idea of wilderness, it is also the case that this idea of nature permeates environmental discourse and, indeed, that environmentalism in North America has achieved some of its current import and shape from it.[8] In much of the environmental campaign literature from Clayoquot, there is a strong emphasis on saving the rainforest *from* multinational capital (MacMillan Bloedel and InterFor), *for* the enjoyment of future generations, *for* the aesthetic appreciation of kayakers and hikers, *for* a sustainable tourist economy for the Alberni-Clayoquot region, even *for* the Nuu-chah-nulth. This "saving" is never revealed as an act of construction, intervention, or management; tourism is understood either instrumentally, as a way of maintaining some degree of economic growth in the region while simultaneously preserving the forest, or as a sort of ecological service to the planet, in which the act of viewing (preserved) nature is to inspire other acts of ecological heroism. Nowhere is this more true than in the political tactic of witnessing. At the same time as witnessing is an active, constructed, and constructive gaze on nature—sometimes involving the creation of physical infrastructure such as the WCWC Clayoquot Witness Trail—its activity is completely erased in the construction of the human participant as simply an observer of a wilderness that goes on without her, a translator of natural truths. Wrote Betty Krawczyk of one witnessing action (in a passage that not only erases her own active presence but naturalizes that of aboriginal peoples):

> This particular section of forest remains undisturbed and unspoiled. Some of the trees attest to its antiquity, fat and full with age, soaring up into the bright sky. Our little party stops underneath a canopy of cedar trees. Among them are some very special trees, culturally modified trees. First Nation people knew how to strip bark and wood from a tree without felling or killing the tree. (Krawczyk 1997, 3)

From my limited perspective, there are at least five distinct elements involved in the erasure of the constructive gaze of tourism in Clayoquot Sound. As I have alluded, the first erasure lies in the move by which tourism never appears as an activity, as a specific series of practices from and around which the landscape is constructed, or as an active intervention into nonhuman nature based on particular (globalized) aesthetics and expectations. This erasure forms an interesting undercurrent in portions of the public workshops held under the rubric of the Clayoquot Sound Sustainable Development Strategy Steering Committee (CSSDSSC) in February and March of 1992. In many respects, workshop participants showed a considerable degree of awareness of the profoundly negative potential impact of large-scale tourism on the Clayoquot landscape. Many concerns were expressed there about the ways in which an influx of resorts and recreational vehicles would irrevocably alter the ecological and social character of the region. "Any industry," noted one kayak tour operator, "has the potential to destroy what nature we have here; I don't want to see little tourist lodges all over Clayoquot Sound." But what is not present in these discussions is any sense that the nature understood as under threat from industrial tourism (just like industrial logging) is *already* a product of a particular aesthetic expectation; the nature that is necessary for the continued success of small-scale "good" tourism is already a product of a particular desire for a particular nature. Thus, the act of saving Clayoquot's nature from "bad" tourism renders invisible the tourist practices that have already constructed the region in a particular, desired, threatened image. A few passages from the CSSDSSC discussion illustrate this construction:

> There's a great deal of wildlife to enjoy, and there is also the old-growth forest, which seems to be a neglected tourism asset.
>   The people I bring up here kayaking don't want to see clear cuts; they want to see nature. Islands like Flores, Meares and Vargas and the viewsheds along those inside passages are so central to the experience of wilderness, I don't think modification is possible.
>   As long as it's left beautiful there'll be tourists. If we blow it there won't be tourists. If people realistically sit back and take a look, tourism is one of the very few ways that we will be able to save Clayoquot Sound as we see fit to save it. (Clayoquot Sound Sustainable Development Strategy Steering Committee 1992, 6–7)

Look at the simulacral production: the nature that is saved is *already* an asset, a viewscape, a beautiful spectacle. This nature supposedly excludes production (clearcuts) but includes—and cloaks—the "modifications" that tourism has already wrought (the ones that allowed the kayakers to be there in the first place). Thus, the discourse dividing good tourism from bad tourism and industrial forestry serves to cover the tracks of nature's active cultural construction as (aesthetic) wilderness.

A related erasure occurs in the generally unproblematized linkage of the interests of small-scale tourist operators with environmental interests. I do not mean to suggest that the environmental concerns of Tofino residents can be reduced to narrow economic self-interest—they cannot—but the fact remains that in mass-mediated accounts of the Clayoquot conflict, and thus also in the on-the-ground local negotiation, the bifurcated production of the subject positions, "loggers" and "environmentalists," has tended to obscure the fact that many local environmentalists—especially many members of the Friends of Clayoquot Sound (FOCS)—had a strong, tourism-based economic interest in saving Clayoquot in a particular form. The logger/environmentalist dichotomy was effectively mapped onto an economic/noneconomic interest dichotomy in much public discourse. Although this construction is patently false (and although many FOCS members readily admit their concerns about livelihood in addition to their concerns about ecology), it ended up both polarizing the two sides in many understandings of the issue and effectively removing the stain of economic interest from the morally powerful preservationist discourses of many environmental groups involved.[9]

As already observed, wilderness is a construction of nature born of a tourist gaze and layered over with environmental discourse. In its political appearance, however, it seems as if this particular preservationist-environmental discourse emerges directly out of the needs of nature. Thus, the erasure here is that the environmentalist subject position claimed by tourist operators is seen to reside in the needs of nature, and not in the economically and culturally interested discourses of its profoundly human origin. The corollary erasure, of course, is that people whose economic interests in the region are *not* based on the preservation of this particular nature are, with the exception of aboriginal peoples, deemed to have no environmental interest whatsoever. At the same time as the tourist vision is equated with nature, other visions—notably those of forest workers—are branded with an antienvironmental label and understood as "only" economic (to be fair, a third option focused on selective logging and sustainable forestry was eventually included in some versions of environmentalist discourse).

Nowhere is this dynamic more present than in the bifurcation of Tofino from Ucluelet. A spread in the *Victoria Times-Colonist* on the region, including articles on the tourist boom in Tofino, the newly opened luxury Wickaninnish Inn on Chesterman Beach (Tofino), and the potential for a new year-round tourist market in storm watching, also includes a piece with the title "Working Town Ucluelet Resents Its Bad Guy Image" (Dutton 1997b). The stakes of the bifurcation are very clear: Tofino-the-beautiful (a k a "Whistler West" in Dutton 1997a) is concerned about the impact of bad tourism on the nature and hippie/village lifestyle that comprised the "old" Tofino, but is simultaneously reveling in its ability to show tourists nature (via whale-watching and adventure tours) in its supposedly pristine state (and, to some extent, its own history as an artifact in harmony with that nature). In contrast, Ucluelet "is a working town, a dirt-under-your-nails town where chainsaws vastly outnumber chain stores, and where an environmentalist is a guy who crushes his beer can before whipping it out the window of his pickup" (Dutton 1997b). The chains of signification are clear: tourism preserves where workers destroy. The intrinsic needs of nature appear to be spoken by small tourist operators, erasing all traces of economic interest or culturally located construction. Workers are not environmentalists, as their knowledges of and desires for nature are not consonant with the idea of wilderness.

In this move, it seems quite clear that the only knowledges of nature that are allowed to appear as environmental are those born from relations of consumption, even though the productive relations that support tourist consumption represent quite a considerable intervention and modification of nature, and even though tourists themselves have a considerable impact on the production of a particular, aesthetic nature. Here, then, is a third erasure: productive knowledges of nature do not count. In the chain by which forest workers appear only as beer-can-crushing environmental vandals, the practices by which workers know the land and the trees in their working lives are automatically deemed unacceptable and unenvironmental. In some respects, this erasure of working knowledges of nature from the spectrum of environmentalist possibilities is simply the flip side of the dichotomy in which the preservation of wilderness is so unproblematically tied to the tourist gaze. Perhaps more profoundly, environmental practices of preservation are grounded in a historical desire for a particular nature commodity with which particular kinds of visible modification are not consonant. The luxury Wickaninnish Inn is acceptable in a way that a clearcut is not, even though both have a large impact on nonhuman natures. The point is that a particular class-based aesthetic consumer desire is facilitated by the former, and interrupted by the latter. Whatever workers might think of the nature in which they work—and Dunk (1994) has shown convincingly that forest workers do not simply regard forests as dead resources for capitalist profit—these knowledges of nature do not appear within the nature that tourist operators claim to be their interest. Forest workers, despite their frequently long-term and intimate interactions with the forest ecosystem, do not count as knowing nature because the only apparently real knowledge of nature is a consumptive one.

It is, of course, important to consider the ways in which loggers' knowledges of nature are strongly influenced by an instrumental ("resourcist") logic heavily embedded in capitalist extractive practices and market desires. Loggers are workers, and that work is centrally concerned with the generation of profit for MacMillan Bloedel and InterFor shareholders. But what is interesting to note is that workers' knowledges were popularly represented throughout the Clayoquot controversy as wholly determined by the interests of the corporation;[10] the fact that loggers do have intimate knowledges of the forest that considerably overflow the narrow confines of commodity production from both productive and consumptive (recreational) activities was simply not part of the discussion. In contrast, tourist operators were able to claim a range of environmentalist desires apart from their clear economic interests.

As noted earlier, the understanding of wilderness as a natural place apart from human activity, as a place defined primarily by its subtraction of human presence, specifically excludes work. The erasure of the work of tourism in Clayoquot is thus part of the same process as the expulsion of production from the desired nature of the region. Logging is a reminder of a different view of nature. It does not take a great intellectual leap to realize that Clayoquot, as a *leisure* place (*not* a site of work) can be visited only in a world where *other* places (less spectacular, less like wilderness) are heavily logged, mined, and otherwise visibly worked in. Nonetheless, the presence of these productive sites is specifically erased in the places that get to count as nature. Spectacular wilderness sites are only spectacular because other places are not; the fantasy of pristine nature is only sustainable when the productive labor that makes the consumption of nature possible is largely conducted elsewhere. The act of working in nature interrupts this fantasy in a way that consumption does not. The invisibility of consumption and the banishment of production are necessary to the perpetuation of the fantasy that wilderness is not part of the global economy but a bastion apart from it, not a product of a particular, class-based desire but nature, pure and simple.

Of course, it is equally crucial to note that aesthetics are not the only rationale for the preservation of Clayoquot Sound. "Saving Clayoquot for Future Generations" should certainly be read as a text embodying the desire for an ongoing visual "resource," but it is also threaded through with environmentalist desires and concerns that cannot be reduced to questions of economic self-interest or consumerist desires present and future. Scientific knowledges of nature, as others discuss more fully elsewhere in this volume, have a strong impact in defining what counts as the nature of the region. In the context of my argument, what is crucial to note is that science, although always conducted within the frame of particular human relationships to nonhuman natures, appears as a relatively objective means by which the truths and needs of nature can be made visible and tangible. Although it is a distinct form of knowledge (perhaps more accurately, a distinct collection of knowledges) embodying particular desires and speaking from particular experiences and codes of conduct, it is also a resource used by various parties to the Clayoquot conflict to justify and legitimate views of nature.

This may seem an obvious point (although it never hurts to point out that concepts such as biodiversity and sustainability are umbrellas sheltering a whole host of relationships that include human uses as much as they do the needs of other species). What may be a bit less obvious are the ways in which the legitimating presence of science signals another form of erasure. If science holds the "truth" of nature, and if that truth needs to appear as a discourse *from nature* rather than as an interested human construct, then the particularity of the actors making use of the science cannot appear as part of scientific discourse itself. Insofar as the framing nature discourse of the Clayoquot controversy is wilderness, then only that science consonant with a wilderness view—a science that observes a separate nature and does not significantly interact with it—is able to appear as *from nature*, as true. Scientific knowledges that show their location—I am thinking here both of forestry science and indigenous science—are deemed particular, and not as truthful as those that are able to appear appropriately distant, objective, and universal. Scientific knowledges that might be generated from or validate long-term human interactions with nature are, at best, understood as a compromise. MacMillan Bloedel clearly realizes this, as evidenced by its invocation of objective scientific expertise in its justifications for the continued practice of clearcut logging: nature regenerates itself. Greenpeace also clearly realizes this, in its condemnation of precisely the same practice: nature does not regenerate itself exactly. Both positions rely on their supposed ability to know what nature would do if humans were not there; both positions erase their interested gaze on nature and their desires for the continuation of a particular kind of activity. And Greenpeace won this battle: MacMillan Bloedel was not able to cover the situatedness of its science partly because its view of nature was recognized as economically interested and unpopularly linked with production.

The point here is not to condemn science or Greenpeace's invocation of it in support of its desires for the region. The point, rather, is to suggest that the strategic use of a particular kind of science—objective, distant, truthful—erased the particularity of the construction of nature in which it was located. If the truth of nature is the ultimate truth of the region, and if that nature is already understood as the absence of human interest and presence, then only those interests that can erase their traces in the use of science will be seen as consonant with truth. And a human interest based on the perpetuation of a particular, class-based consumer relation to nature is far less jarring and far more invisible than is one based on productive work. Workers' knowledges of nature, even if often heavily informed by science, are irrevocably partial in a way that kayakers'—however "unscientific"—are not.

The final erasure concerns the ways in which First Nations' concerns appeared in the construction of nature and wilderness. As with scientific discourses, questions of aboriginal title and knowledge are far more complex than I can relate here, and I refer the reader to other works in this volume for a fuller exploration. It is the case, however, that the simulacral operation of wilderness has a particular set of relations to First Nations knowledges and concerns. As Bruce Willems-Braun notes:

> Native peoples on Canada's west coast have good reason to be wary of the representational practices of the environmental movement, for whom 'nature' is often understood in radically different ways than it is by Native groups. Certainly many perceived benefits have resulted from cooperation with environmental groups . . . , and many individuals and groups in the environmental movement are strongly committed to anti-colonial politics. Yet it is not immediately clear that the environmental movement's concerns for *preservation* can be mapped onto native *land claims* or, for that matter, onto the social and economic ambitions linked to these claims. (Willems-Braun 1996, 25–26; emphasis in original)

If I might put the matter somewhat crudely, there is a profound tension between a preservationist view of wilderness that has at its core a subtraction of human activity, and a particularly situated aboriginal view of the land as not only a home-place or sacred site but a place of work, modification, and interaction with nonhuman nature both historically and in the present. In preservationist representations of nature, given that nature excludes production—the labor of the present—its ability to include any representations of First Nations activities rests on the distancing of aboriginal peoples from the contaminating presence of the present. Thus, as Willems-Braun notes, there is a chain of signification going on in many environmentalist discourses about *modernity,* First Nations, and nature on British Columbia's west coast. In Adrian Dorst's wilderness photography, for example, Native peoples only appear as aligned with nature insofar as they are engaging in (supposedly) "traditional" activities. Aboriginal history is thus calcified; nature includes a romanticized view of (premodern) traditional activities, which are held out as natural in their reflection of a site apart from modernity (see, for example, Dorst and Young 1990, 20–21). Wilderness erases production as part of an erasure of the modern; thus, aboriginal peoples are allowed into nature and environmentalism only insofar as they are able to be "not modern" and only insofar as their activities in the land conform to a preexisting preservationist aesthetic, a thoroughly colonialist assumption indeed.[11]

An interesting place where this erasure of the present of First Nations occurs is in the discourse of "culturally modified trees." These trees, as a *San Francisco Chronicle* article notes, "bear the signs of the old ways" of the Tla-o-qui-aht. In land-claims negotiations, these trees are strong marks of historical presence and activity; they cement a sense of continuity between First Nations' past modifications of nature and their rights to continue to live in and use nature in the present. In many respects, these trees mark the fact that Clayoquot is not and has never been a wilderness in the sense described earlier. The region is physically organized by a rich history of human–nonhuman interactions: productive, ritual, spiritual, sustaining, medicinal, even recreational. In popular environmentalist discourse, however—although some environmentalists clearly respect Nuu-chah-nulth land claims with fewer strings attached—*past* cultural modifications are coded as natural, and *present* cultural modifications must either conform to these traditions or risk being coded as destructive. Only uses of the land that are already approved in wilderness view are natural, and any person who crosses the line beyond this narrow notion of tradition—say, into employment with MacMillan Bloedel—is not acting like a "real Native" anymore. This tension places First Nations between a rock and a hard place in terms of political alliance: to what extent does the strategy of invoking tradition interfere with the ability of the Nuu-chah-nulth to appear as "modern" subjects in negotiations and discourses of sovereignty?

But the simulacral logic of tourism has also appropriated First Nations interests and identities in other ways. "Walk the Wild Side," an initiative begun in 1994 by a group of First Nations women from Ahousaht, is a nature-tourism venture that includes, according to its Web site, "the wild beauty of the open Pacific," "our First Nation Village, Ahousaht, [which] is a pleasant mix of modern and traditional," and "interpreted forest walks . . . through some of the largest Cedar, Fir and Culturally Modified Trees." Although it is important to recognize the significance of this economic initiative for the women involved in the venture, at the same time, its (apparently) seamless repetition of the discourse linking wilderness, First Nations tradition, environmental preservation, and tourist spectacle is cause for concern. If wilderness tourism is a simulacral extension of global colonialism—as I believe it to be—then the following invitation should underscore the need to question this repetition. "Come and visit," says the Web site; "ecotourism is simply a new name for what has always been the best way to travel Nuu-chah-nulth territories."

Conclusions

Nature, in Clayoquot, is a paradox. Wilderness, understood as the absence of humans, is a cultural construct that relies on its ability to appear as pre-cultural. The image of nature creates nature as a reflection of itself; it naturalizes a specific culture, and is then held up as a true, ideal, and universal nature to which other sites are compared and found wanting. In its uniqueness it is a commodity, and part of its uniqueness is in its ability to appear as uncommodified. This construct is born from a largely consumer desire to see nature as a space apart from human activity; as such, it is not only historically and culturally specific, but it is strongly located in a global tourist logic in which certain natures are desired and desirable destinations and must be preserved so they can be visited. This construct excludes particular kinds of human activity but not, it seems, others; the basis for exclusion rests on the distinction between production and consumption, in which the former appears as a clear intervention into nature where the latter does not. This construct embroils science in its logic; only those knowledges able to present themselves as speaking objectively and uninterestedly about nature are able to claim its truth. And this construct also produces First Nations in particular ways: as supposedly traditional subjects in and of nature, in opposition to modernity. In its ability to erase its constitutive traces, the construct ensures its continuance.

In some respects, one can understand MacMillan Bloedel's eventual decision to withdraw its logging interests in the region as a triumph (however partial and temporary) of this construct. Environmentalists argued persuasively that Clayoquot Sound was unique, and needed to be reserved from clearcut logging as a last bastion of a particular, spectacular ecosystem. The mass political mobilization around Clayoquot validated this claim: this place is a wonder, a very special place that must be saved for future generations; this place is a refuge for both human and nonhuman activities that cannot happen elsewhere; this is an exceptional place of history, heritage, sacred meaning. Following this logic, MacMillan Bloedel conceded the point; it turned to somewhere less obviously special: British Columbia's central coast, where the tourist presence is considerably less well established, where some First Nations support for forest-related employment could be secured,[12] and where political mobilization by environmentalists would be hampered by both geographical distance and the presence of strongly established resource-based communities. And, politically savvy environmentalists responded brilliantly. They realized that they would have to construct the uniqueness of the place somewhat differently than they had at Clayoquot, but still carry on the fundamental logic of demonstrating the central coast's "special" qualities. After survey research conducted in crucial European markets, the allied environmental groups involved in the struggle for the central coast dubbed the region "The Great Bear Rainforest," thus unifying it—and the multiple aboriginal and white cultures that have staked conflicting claims to the place for many years—under a wonderfully photogenic ursine banner. (To cut a long story short, in 2001 in the last days of the NDP government of Ujjal Dosanjh, the Great Bear was declared "saved." One wonders where the next special place will be.)

Thus, ultimately, the saving of Clayoquot did not fundamentally challenge the logic of global capitalism and the system of image exchange in which many environmentalists operate (this would, of course, be a tall order indeed, especially for a movement that finds part of its origin in consumer desires). This logic may be pervasive and influential, however, but it is neither completely determining nor all-encompassing in Clayoquot, the Great Bear, or elsewhere. Not all of environmentalism is about the preservation of a particular aesthetic commodity; some environmentalism is about community negotiations over the meanings of nature, in specific *opposition* to capitalist insertion and homogenization. This promise was amply revealed in Clayoquot in the many conversations that took place about selective logging, community control and support, economic regeneration, and the potential for alternative economic ventures that hold the potential to address the needs of a wide variety of communities. I can only gesture toward this complexity here.

In Clayoquot, the prolonged struggle that forced members of different communities to engage politically with one another in discussions about the future of the region showed that the "loggers versus environmentalists" dichotomy presented popularly was not an adequate representation of the diverse issues involved. Although it is clear that these local interactions were not able to banish the imperatives—and views of nature—attached to these bifurcated positions, it is equally clear that the process of negotiation allowed for the contestation and negotiation of multiple positions, interests, natures, and desires. If the struggles over Clayoquot did not overcome the global tourist gaze and the commodification of nature apparent in wilderness and preservationist constructs, they *did* point to some of the limits and contradictions inherent in the discourse. Cracks were opened. Environmentalists moved—quite quickly, if not unilaterally—from a position of "no logging" to a position of "no clearcutting," thus implicitly acknowledging that there could be a coexistence of *some* productive knowledges of nature with an environmentalist agenda. Forest workers publicly confronted the seamlessness of the relationship of tourism to nature, articulately challenging the idea that tourism is sustainable for either human or nonhuman communities and implicitly (and sometimes explicitly) demonstrating their rich attachments to the region. Tourist operators began to question the places where the practice of their livelihoods might not be consonant with the long-term viability of the region (although the distinction between good and bad tourism does not really challenge tourism, at least it allows for the possibility that tourism is a modification of nature). The Nuu-chah-nulth, despite intracommunity differences of opinion, asserted strongly that their knowledges of the land were at least as important to the constitution of its truth and health as were the scientific voices of objectivity; they also forced issues of colonialism and appropriation onto the political table. With difficulty, they effectively shifted aspects of the conversation to include the awareness that wilderness is a culturally specific understanding of nature, that nature includes human activity, and that the point is to figure out ways of working in and with nature that respect the lives and livelihoods of a variety of beings.

From my perspective, it was in the constitution of Clayoquot Sound as a *political* site that these shifts occurred. At the same time as I realize that the public, political contestation of relations to and meanings of "nature" in various communities does not guarantee a democratic outcome—or even a lasting or generalizable discussion—it was only when entrenched positions were held publicly accountable to a *multiplicity* of coexisting others that any reflection and movement occurred. This multiple accountability overflowed official channels (including deeply flawed processes of "multistakeholder negotiations") and mediagenic protests from all sides; it was (and is) also deeply painful in both its direct and indirect consequences precisely because politics was not easily contained (and political identities were not captured by bloodless and propertied notions of "stakeholding").

Although one might argue that part of the politicization of Clayoquot occurred because of the public challenge to timber extraction posed by (passionate) preservationist ideas of nature, it strikes me that the continual presence of positions that rejected *both* extractive *and* wilderness views was crucial in forcing a more nuanced and reflective stance (however ultimately strategic) from all participants in the conflict. In other words, spaces of discussion and rearticulation were opened by those actors—including some forest workers, some environmentalists, and some members of Nuu-chah-nulth communities—who disrupted the positions laid out in the tension between extractive and attractive possibility. From these "hybrid" positions, the politicization of Clayoquot revealed and produced multiplicity beyond an entrenched bifurcation laid out in capitalist language; in multiplicity lay the possibility of negotiated shifting that defied, or at least nudged, views of nature that were always already commodified and simulacral.

These negotiated shifts are fragile, but they are extremely important. At the same time as the global tourist gaze has been firmly established in Clayoquot—a gaze to which a variety of actors orient themselves in a variety of different ways—spaces *were* opened in the controversy for a more complex series of local *and* global possibilities. The dominance of a monolithic, simulacral nature was disrupted, and more subtle (even defiant) positions emerged out of the disruption. It remains to be seen if these shifts will have a lasting impact in Clayoquot, and if their promise might be taken up elsewhere.

Epilogue

> *Snapshot 5 (1997).* I am on the Rainforest Trail in Pacific Rim National Park, with my five-month-old daughter in a blue baby carrier on my chest. I am holding her tiny hand to the bark of an ancient cedar tree, hoping that she will touch it again on her own in the future. The ritual is a homecoming; it is also about being a tourist.

This essay neither represents nor solves Clayoquot's many tensions. It does not aim to do so. Rather, its purpose is to take up a hybrid reflective position "between" home and destination and to use it as a starting point from which to question a particular constellation of relations concerning tourism and environmentalism. The essay, though critical, is not a judgment. Tourism is here to stay in Clayoquot, for better or worse. Indeed, the kinds of nature that are preserved and created (at least in part) to develop a tourist economy are gaining currency in many parts of the world. But these consumable natures, however magnificent, are only possible on the condition that the tracks of their constitution are masked.

Thus, an observer might choose, as a move toward a more complex engagement with nature, simply to think publicly about the conditions and contradictions that have enabled (and will continue to enable) her presence. These public thoughts are, I think, the responsibility of those of us who visit.

Notes

My thanks to the members of my winter 1998 graduate seminar in the Faculty of Environmental Studies for their discussion of an earlier draft of this essay. Special thanks go to Warren Magnusson and Karena Shaw for their insights and constructive criticisms.

1. As Timothy Luke describes in his essay in this volume, it is also important to note a general movement from extractive to attractive development; Clayoquot is "remapped" on the capitalist globe as a result of this shift.

2. As William Chaloupka notes in his essay in this volume, this self-consciousness can be understood as a form of *double*-consciousness, containing at once "dignity" and "competence."

3. Some tourist destinations sell their hyperreality overtly and intentionally (Disney); others use the language of authenticity and exoticism to construct their specificity in the tourist market (wilderness tourism). Both situations conform to the logic of the tourist market, even if neither completely determines the place that is being sold (Disney included).

4. "Unnatural," here, is roughly equivalent to "domesticated"; Cronon uses the opposition of human and nature that lies at the heart of (most) wilderness discourse.

5. The relationship between pristine wilderness and national identity is a crucial one in the simulacral logic of nature, especially in terms of national parks. In essence, parks were (and are) places where a nation can see its origins naturalized, and, in both the United States and Canada, its acts of colonial appropriation erased. It is thus important to note—as a complement to Thom Kuehls's remarks in his essay in this volume—that the emparkment of nature has been a strategy to deprivilege First Nations sovereignty claims in many contexts, Gwaii Haanas being an interesting (if partial) exception.

6. I thank Valerie Langer for this memorable phrase. Whatever else I might say about the campaign, I think that FOCS has done a fantastic job of presenting the nature of the place in a way that magnificently overflows the "Hawaii of the North" postcards. Despite the "strategic essentialism" of ecotourism-friendly preservation, a much greater complexity of relations characterizes Tofino's (and in the "opposite" vein, Ucluelet's) nature relations.

7. I would be among the first to concede that different environmental groups involved in Clayoquot produce and utilize very different representations of nature. Where the WCWC is thoroughly committed to the sort of images of nature that tend to appear in coffee-table books and calendars, the FOCS is generally more attached

to scientific discourses on biodiversity and habitat. As I will suggest, however, these representations are, at their core, linked through an ideal of humanless (or at least human-minimal) nature.

8. Lash and Urry (1994) note that environmentalism can be understood in part as a response to (rather than a critique of) consumption. Not only is nature tourism a distinct market niche, but even more broadly, the desire for a clean and healthy nature is stimulated by a "heightened [consumerist] reflexivity about the places and environments, the goods and services that are consumed, literally, through a social encounter, or through visual consumption" (297).

9. One could also argue that many "outside" environmental groups began with a tourist desire toward the environment; WCWC and the Sierra Club, for example, are strongly oriented to preserving places where particular forms of outdoor recreation occur. But if the origin of political environmentalism in Clayoquot is seen to reside in the first meeting of FOCS (1979), then it is highly significant that the economic interests of local tourist operators are almost never mentioned. FOCS became, throughout the controversy, a local group saving nature for its own sake; although many members have relations to the region that far exceed the viability of their bed-and-breakfasts and kayaking operations, the significant fact is that these interests were almost always hidden beneath the rhetoric of intrinsic value.

10. One could also argue that the formation of "Share" groups was a very conscious attempt on the part of corporate actors to take advantage of this linkage and turn it on its head. Rather than have workers appear as the pawns of capital, capital could appear as the supporter of working-class communities in their so-called grassroots organizing efforts.

11. Again referring to Kuehls's essay, discourses of sovereignty both support and disrupt this articulation.

12. Clearly, not all First Nations of the central coast support logging; it does seem, however, that forest corporations effectively mobilized the support of some aboriginal leaders.

Works Cited

Appadurai, Arjun. 1996. *Modernity at Large: Cultural Dimensions of Globalization.* Minneapolis: University of Minnesota Press.

Baudrillard, Jean. 1983. *Simulations.* New York: Semiotext(e).

———. 1986. *America.* London: Verso.

Birch, Thomas. 1995. "The Incarceration of Wildness: Wilderness Areas as Prisons." In *Postmodern Environmental Ethics,* ed. Max Oelschlaeger. New York: State University of New York Press. 137–61.

Boorstin, Daniel. 1992. *The Image: A Guide to Pseudo-Events in America.* New York: Vintage Books.

Clayoquot Sound Sustainable Development Strategy Steering Committee. 1992. *The Clayoquot Strategy News #2* (May).

Cronon, William. 1995. "The Trouble with Wilderness; or, Getting Back to the Wrong Nature." In *Uncommon Ground: Rethinking the Human Place in Nature,* ed. William Cronon. New York: W. W. Norton. 69–90.

Dorst, Adrian, and Cameron Young. 1990. *Clayoquot: On the Wild Side.* Vancouver: Western Canada Wilderness Committee.

Dunk, Thomas. 1994. "Talking about Trees: Environment and Society in Forest Workers' Culture." *Canadian Review of Sociology and Anthropology* 31:1 (February): 14–34.

Dutton, Ian. 1997a. "Boom Times in Tofino." *Victoria Times-Colonist,* May 17.

———. 1997b. "Working Town Ucluelet Resents Its Bad Guy Image." *Victoria Times-Colonist,* May 17, E2.

Jasen, Patricia. 1995. *Wild Things: Nature, Culture and Tourism in Ontario 1790–1914.* Toronto: University of Toronto Press.

Krall, Florence R. 1994. *Ecotone: Wayfaring on the Margins.* Albany: State University of New York Press.

Krawczyk, Betty. 1997. "Catface Campout." *The Friends of Clayoquot Sound Newsletter* (fall).

Lash, Scott, and John Urry. 1994. *Economies of Signs and Space.* London: Sage Publications.

McKibben, Bill. 1989. *The End of Nature.* New York: Random House.

Russell, Constance, and M. J. Ankenman. 1996. "Orangutans as Photographic Collectibles: Ecotourism and the Commodification of Nature." *Tourism Recreation Research* 21:1: 71–78.

Slater, Candace. 1995. "Amazonia as Edenic Narrative." In *Uncommon Ground: Toward Reinventing Nature,* ed. William Cronon. New York: W. W. Norton. 114–31.

Urry, John. 1990. *The Tourist Gaze: Leisure and Travel in Contemporary Societies.* London: Sage Publications.

Willems-Braun, Bruce. 1996. "Colonial Vestiges: Representing Forest Landscapes in Canada's West Coast." *BC Studies* 112 (winter): 5–40.

Williams, Raymond. 1980. In *Problems in Materialism and Culture.* London: Verso.

Wilson, Alexander. 1991. *The Culture of Nature: North American Landscape from Disney to the Exxon Valdez.* Toronto: Between the Lines.

Clayoquot and the Cultures
of Nature

Sharon Zukin

I cannot write about Clayoquot with Sandilands's or M'Gonigle's passion about home. Neither can I see myself occupying a place in the imagined nation forests evoke—not in the American sublime of Catskills pine trees and California redwoods, nor in blood-drenched German myths of the woods. I am just an urban visitor to the forests, a sometime traveler to "natural wonders," tied to Clayoquot by the acts of consumption environmentalists deplore.

Walking home one day from the organic food store, my groceries in a brown paper bag, I notice the word *PAPER* printed near the bottom in big blue letters. Underneath the word *PAPER*, the bag says:

> Reuse this package for its many alternative uses in the home OR fill
> it with old newspapers to be recycled.

The printed command—"reuse or recycle"—puts responsibility for the forests on my shoulders instead of blaming humans, logging companies, or manufacturers. This homely brown paper bag—a primal container from my childhood, tangible reminder of trips to the supermarket with Mom—is my personal connection with the forests.

Cultures of Consumption

The biggest environmental issue where I live, in New York City, concerns the detritus of consumer civilization—where to dispose of the solid remains of the goods we use after local landfills have reached capacity. Because New Yorkers produce so much solid waste, we export it to poorer regions. No longer useful or salable, the final remains of our consumption are buried in Virginia and Pennsylvania, in spaces for which New York City pays "rent."

This is at the opposite end of the production chain from British Columbia's old-growth forests. Some of New York City's solid waste may, in fact, have come from those old trees. Until environmental activists convinced the telephone company and the *New York Times* to stop buying paper made from British Columbia pulp, the pages of my telephone directory and my newspaper connected me with Clayoquot.

All of us environmentally challenged urban consumers are connected with "natural resource–dependent" communities. The books, toilet paper, and plentiful photocopies we expect as proof of our modern standard of living denude the forests. Importing the grapes and strawberries we eat during the winter months pollutes the skies over Central America with jet fuel exhaust. Irrigated lettuce fields in California's Central Valley, golf courses in Las Vegas, and air conditioning in New York's art museums: the most radical, potentially democratic social construction of modernity—consumption—destroys existing reserves of clean air, trees, and water all over the planet. Yet we demand both jobs and pleasure, abundant food and information, and maximum sanitation and comfort. What we understand as the value of life itself—our urbane standard of living—seems to depend on making nature scarce.

But we also want to experience the forests in their "natural" state. More people go each year to public forest preserves. We drive our cars into the national parks, causing traffic jams in front of the most popular views and "attractions." We reserve hotel rooms and campsites up to a year in advance. Unlike many residents of British Columbia, we do not make our living from the woods. Most of us go to forests for an excursion or a vacation from our homes in the cities and suburbs, turning distant regions into "metropolitan nature" (Green 1990). Our detachment from the everyday life of the woods encourages us to romanticize and aestheticize them. In the process of developing forest lands for tourism, however, we reorganize them with a "second nature" of roads, motels, and souvenir shops. If forests do not have this second nature, most of us cannot visit them.[1]

The reorganization of forests for our consumption transforms Yosemite into Disneyland.[2] We choose which forests to visit on the basis of their highly rated attractions—the tallest trees, hardest climb, and most scenic campsite, or alternatively, the most accessible roads, comfortable hotels, and adventurous cuisine. Preferably, like Disneyland, the attractions combine both danger and comfort: our goal is to find a safe place surrounded by wilderness, "a carefully bounded space in which to feel unbounded" (Slater 1996, 118). Ecotourism first developed as a mode of urban consumption—a rustic escape from the city's crowds and human-made dirt, bringing affluent travelers to beautiful, geographically remote, and economically impoverished regions. In the eighteenth century, English poets "discovered" the Lake District; in the mid-ninteenth century, French artists "discovered" the countryside in Barbizon and Fontainebleau; and in the late nineteenth century, American naturalists "discovered" Yosemite. In each period, a different region—a little more distant, a little more "different"—becomes a themed escape from the dystopia of urban life.

The idea of nature as a theme park goes back to early modern times (Solnit 1994; Mukerji 1997). Kings, nobles, and monks designed gardens to represent both human domination over, and communion with, nature and the power of the government, upper class, and church. In this framework, nature is a performance: waterfalls throb dramatically, the woods are dark and wild, and meadows undulate in waves of green. Visitors follow a prearranged itinerary, pursuing the attractions on a special map. Without this guidance, we might wander aimlessly, lost in both nature's complexity and its monotony, not knowing where to look and how to see. "These aren't just trees," we say to ourselves in the Grove of the Patriarchs at Mount Rainier National Park. "These trees are a thousand years old! They're really tall!" The programmatic organization of visual attractions confers meaning on nature, enabling a specific grove, forest, or national park to become a status destination, different from and better than our backyard. The more sights and recreational uses a forest has, the higher its status in the guidebooks.[3]

Habituated to exotic climates by magazines, books, and IMAX movies, we ratchet up our expectations. Natural wonders must be "worth a journey." This sort of travel demands more than physical exertion. It is expensive, and it exposes us to real danger. Travelers' excursions to see the Central American rain forest, Uganda's "gorillas in the mist," and the summit of Mount Everest—all status destinations—have ended in deaths.

Sandilands says that contemporary cultures of nature create global inventories of images. On this basis, how can Clayoquot compete? Pacific Rim National Park is only a beginning. The tourist industry will have to compete with other nature-oriented seaside resorts from Maine to New Zealand, with other national parks in the Pacific Northwest, and with rainforests in both temperate and tropical zones. And if developers do not build the second nature of highways and tourist hotels, tourists will not come. Just look at Brazil, whose incomparable rain forest loses potential visitors to Costa Rica, where tourist facilities are more reliable. Yet competition between tourist regions can lead to overdevelopment and the building of "artificial" attractions inconsistent with, or even harmful to, the natural environment: motorized water sports, gambling casinos (now legalized in British Columbia), and unprecedented deposits of solid waste in rivers, oceans, and landfills.[4]

Local Cultures

One of the environmental movement's great successes is to have created a sense of belonging to a community that transcends traditional borders—a culture of global citizenship (McNaghten and Urry 1998, 152). This global culture is rooted in a universal sense of risk from environmental dangers (such as acid rain, radioactivity, and oil spills) and a growing perception of the scarcity and fragility of natural resources. It also reflects the "cultural work" of environmental activists, mainly outside the nation-state and often working in opposition to government policy. Thus, the Rainforest Action Network has connected Clayoquot to a transnational region of old-growth forests stretching through North and South America. Environmental and community activists such as Michael M'Gonigle have substituted the trans-local region of the watershed for the fragmented localities of Tofino, Ucluelet, and Port Alberni. Advocates of local farmland in the United States have suggested the idea of regional foodsheds. Such revisions come slowly, however, for local landscapes of power, dominated by large employers, labor unions, banks, and the state, repress alternative representations of community (Zukin 1991).

Since the 1980s, the environmental movement has both changed local culture in Clayoquot and adapted to it. Just as many mainstream Euro-Canadians gradually accepted First Nations' continuing sovereignty (and rights of ownership in relation to the land), so did environmentalists. Environmentalists also accepted First Nations' traditional rhetoric of nature, a rhetoric that contradicts the Enlightenment rhetoric of science, progress, and instrumentality in which civil society and civic activism were born. For their part, the First Nations acknowledged that men and women do not have to be born on the land to identify with it. Although First Nations traditionally believe that community is inherent in territory and lineage, they saw that the desire to protect and preserve the natural environment could bond new members to an old community.

There have also been tensions over local cultures of decision making. Who speaks with authority for the First Nations? Males, elders, and elective band councils have overlapping spheres of influence. To speak on a world stage requires them to share power with other members of the community—with younger women and men, environmental activists, and others from outside the First Nations. At times, some leaders may have preferred to deal directly with the provincial government, rather than to block roads in protest. Environmental activists, who are generally used to public disputes over tactics and strategy, may not have seemed the most congenial bedfellows.

We do not know how their traditional values will affect First Nations' decisions about how to use the forests from this point. The Nuu-chah-nulth name "Clayoquot" (or "Tla-o-qui-aht") means "people who come from an-other place," but that migration occurred a long time ago. Thinking in terms of a long history on the land may encourage preservation of the forests be-cause of the First Nations' sense of what environmental writers call "glacial time." Or, their need for education, jobs, and health care, and the province's financial troubles, may turn them away from preservation and toward con-servation. They might try to combine logging, tourism, and preservation of the forests in a strategy of "wise use." Is it possible to choose, as M'Gonigle and other writers suggest, an environmentally sensitive growth strategy under democratic, local control? Another North American Indian nation, the Mashantucket Pequot Tribal Nation, which owns the wildly successful Foxwoods Resort Casino in Connecticut, advertises the gambling casino with the ecotourist slogan "Experience the wonder of the Connecticut woods." The casino's profits pay for college scholarships for tribal members, for the operation of the local public school system, and for redevelopment of local shipyards. To take M'Gonigle's argument seriously, local control over land use and tourist development—even if the community decides to build a gambling casino—may actually improve the value of nature.[5]

All this goes to say that we cannot predict which culture of nature is truly "local," or which local culture is best for "nature." But we can surely predict that increasing interest in consuming nature will increase local ten-sions. The culture of Clayoquot will continue to change as tourism replaces men's highly paid logging jobs with low-wage jobs for women, as First Na-tions combine sovereignty over the land with shared authority within the local community, and as outside investors build a second nature of hotels and casinos. "Cascadia rising," announces the cover of *blue* (October 1998), a new "adventure and lifestyle" magazine published in New York. "Loggers, activists, adventurers, everyone wants a piece of the Pacific Northwest."

Primal Cultures

Regardless of how important the forests are to Clayoquot, they are not the primary concern of most men and women around the world. Researchers conducting a focus group in the north of England found that people there think much less about what they called "higher-order," more abstract, envi-ronmental issues such as deforestation than about environmental issues that affect them immediately in their everyday lives—water pollution that makes their dog sick when it swims in the ocean, air pollution that causes their children to cough (McNaghten and Urry 1998, 239). If the rest of the world learns anything from Clayoquot, we will learn to bring all of nature into our primal culture. We will bring the forests home.

There is no more primal culture than that of "home"—whether this refers to the spiritual homeland defended by ethnic cleansing and mass murder or the territorial Fatherland (or Motherland) defended in war. Home resonates, more favorably, with the emotional attachment and sense of uniqueness that are so devalued by the standardization of places throughout modern times. Yet the stability of home is continually threatened by the desire of powerful groups to "improve" and control the land, leading to the commodification of raw materials and labor that can plunge a community into cycles of development, uprooting, and abandonment (Polanyi 1957, cited in Zukin 1991, chap. 1).

Reacting against these processes of moral and physical devaluation, today's environmental rhetoric plays on contrasting images of home. Home suggests both dwelling and nurturing, both stewardship and mutual responsibility, and unconditional attachment. When North American environmentalists talk about home, they mean both a dwelling and a working landscape—an active, dynamically changing place that may include both cultivation and use of natural resources—both first and second natures. In contrast to a simplistic view of nature that would exclude human production from our understanding of community, the environmentalist's rhetoric acknowledges all the cultures and technologies that create a sense of place. Like contemporary ideas about cultural difference, which are usually associated with a defense of urban life, the rhetoric of home accepts the variety, contradictions, and unexpectedness of place.

Such a rhetoric is both emotional and pragmatic. It suggests that Clayoquot belongs to both consumers and producers, to both lumberjacks and First Nations, as well as to environmentalists. That there is such widespread concern about the fate of this place shows us how much wealth and power are at stake.

Indeed, the forces of "markets" are always arrayed against "place." When MacMillan Bloedel, whose fortunes (people thought) were yoked to those of British Columbia, made an effort to respond to the decline of demand for its products in Asian markets, the company weighed shutting down the paper mill in Port Alberni against closing a mill in New Zealand, Chile, or Austria. It kept the Port Alberni mill open, after a labor strike, only because the workers assumed responsibility for increasing productivity. But less than a year later, MacMillan Bloedel was itself bought by Weyerhauser. Big companies have no moral tie to the communities in which they operate. Their moral obligation is to raise the value of their shares in the stock market. They reshape the social and spatial arrangements of place to keep up with changing markets.

Clayoquot has been both a victim and a beneficiary of this process. Both fishing and forestry were considered to be beneficial because they created jobs and hopes of economic self-sufficiency. But they also brought cyclical gaps in employment and dependence on capital investment from outside. Moreoever, in the last few years, people's desire to eat more fish has encouraged the industrialization of commercial fishing, with the result that giant trawlers scooped up too many fish and destroyed breeding grounds. Today, artificial fish breeding, or aquaculture, alters the genetic makeup of fish species and introduces diseases to which fish in the wild are not immune. Fish farming carries the risk of destroying the native stock. Like fishing, forestry also depletes natural resources. Old trees are cut down before new growth reaches its prime. Although these industries have created a second nature in Clayoquot Sound, they also diminish the resource base on which the local community depends.

It is apparent that a "third nature" of solid-waste disposal exerts a similar power of creative destruction. Waste is no longer just a problem of too much production and conspicuous consumption. Waste-removal and recycling firms have commodified and redistributed the unusable by-products of both production and consumption. Markets for waste have brought new income into impoverished rural communities from Virginia to Cambodia, along with toxic pollution and diseases. An emerging landscape of third nature confirms the inequality between rich and poor nations, between those that tolerate citizens' expression of their demands for a "clean" environment and those that are undemocratically condemned to serve as landfills.[6]

Just as second nature creates opportunities for business monopolies and collusion, so third nature also brings the same consolidation of large, transnational corporations that work together with the state. Nowhere are the results of this collaboration more tragic than in the disposal of radioactive waste. Whether they are buried deep in the earth or exploded into the atmosphere, the dispersion and disposal of radioactive materials confront us with "the fate of place" in a brutally immediate way. But this ending now is part of our primal culture of nature.

So, my brown paper bag is an ambiguous symbol. It is a commodity, after all. Not surprisingly, it is a symbol of international economic competition. Just below the command to reuse or recycle I read these words:

DISCOVER THE *PAPER* ADVANTAGE.
MADE IN THE USA.

The brown paper bag does not create the same culture of nature for everyone. Just as the bag's manufacturer competes with other paper companies, so it wants me to feel I am competing with the people of Clayoquot. The paper industry wants me to choose the "natural" material—paper—over artificial plastic.

But what are good environmental values? Among environmentalists we find, on the one hand, a "cult of the natural" that encourages demand for organically grown food, animal-rights movements, and avoidance of chemical products, and, on the other hand, an embrace of the "frankly fake" that is interested in aluminum Christmas trees, recycled paper, and parkas made of synthetic fleece. Even Marge Simpson, the usually sensible center of a television series about an animated cartoon family, rejoices when she can load thirty-two brown paper bags of groceries into her new sports utility vehicle—Marge Simpson, the dominatrix of nature.

Clearly, there are times when a paper bag is not just a paper bag.

Notes

1. In his study of Chicago and the Middle West in the nineteenth century, Cronon (1991) borrows the concept of "second nature" from Hegel and Marx to refer to the human-made or built environment, including the development of both cities and countryside by roads, railroads, architecture, agriculture, and other social and technological systems. Using a different term—the "culture of nature"—Wilson (1992) describes the making of second nature in North America in the twentieth century by highways, motels, souvenir shops, national parks, and theme parks, as well as by school curriculums, nature films, and the mass media.

2. This comparison was suggested by the students in my seminar on environmental sociology at the City University Graduate School. In fact, we can find the same type of visual ordering of nature in the late 1830s, when the publication of the first guidebooks to the forest at Fontainebleau identified trees and rocks in terms of visual themes, and laid out paths among these attractions (Green 1990, 175).

3. Some contemporary environmental writers (e.g., Pollan 1991; Cronon 1996) criticize the dichotomous view of nature that contrasts "untouched" wilderness with "cultivated" garden, preferring to see all spaces of nature on a continuum of human intervention. What we see when we look at nature, however, always depends on our point of view, and city dwellers since the early nineteenth century have been attracted to views that interpret trees and rocks as visual tropes (e.g., tall trees that look like "patriarchs" or like the French king Henri IV).

4. Royal Caribbean cruise ships are a flagrant example of ocean pollution and solid-waste disposal. These "floating cities" have regularly violated U.S. environmental laws even though they incur huge financial penalties for doing so.

5. The "fit" between gambling, the natural environment, and the social community has become a serious subject of discussion in Native American communities in the United States, from the pueblos of Arizona and New Mexico to the woods of Connecticut, especially because these communities have historically been excluded from the mainstream economy.

6. In the Cambodian countryside, residents of a village suffered from an outbreak of diseases soon after a Taiwanese company dumped toxic waste nearby. The company said it could not dispose of it in Taiwan without risking public protests.

Works Cited

Cronon, William. 1991. *Nature's Metropolis: Chicago and the Great West.* New York: W. W. Norton.

———. 1996. "The Trouble with Wilderness; or, Getting Back to the Wrong Nature." In *Uncommon Ground: Rethinking the Human Place in Nature,* ed. William Cronon. New York: W. W. Norton. 69–90.

Green, Nicholas. 1990. *The Spectacle of Nature.* Manchester: Manchester University Press.

McNaghten, Phil, and John Urry. 1998. *Contested Natures.* London: Sage.

Mukerji, Chandra. 1997. *Territorial Ambitions and the Gardens of Versailles.* Cambridge and New York: Cambridge University Press.

Polanyi, Karl. 1957 [1994]. *The Great Transformation.* Boston: Beacon Press.

Pollan, Michael. 1991. *Second Nature: A Gardener's Education.* New York: Atlantic Monthly Press.

Slater, Candace. 1996. "Amazonia as Edenic Narrative." In *Uncommon Ground: Rethinking the Human Place in Nature,* ed. William Cronon. New York: W. W. Norton. 114–31.

Solnit, Rebecca. 1994. *Savage Dreams.* New York: Vintage and Sierra Club Books.

Wilson, Alexander. 1992. *The Culture of Nature: North American Landscape from Disney to the Exxon Valdez.* Oxford and Cambridge, Mass.: Blackwell.

Zukin, Sharon. 1991. *Landscapes of Power: From Detroit to Disney World.* Berkeley and Los Angeles: University of California Press.

The Environment of Sovereignty

Thom Kuehls

On April 21, 1984, the Clayoquot Band Council and the Hereditary Chiefs of the Clayoquot Band declared Meares Island a "tribal park," claiming "title" to the land, insisting that visitors "adhere to the Laws of our Forefathers; which were always there" (CD II/A/1). The Tla-o-qui-aht[1] issued this tribal park declaration in response to plans by MacMillan Bloedel (MB) to log more than 4,500 hectares of the island. According to the Tla-o-qui-aht, it was necessary to preserve Meares Island in order to ensure "the survival of our Native way of life." Meares Island was to be preserved, "as the island is an economic base of our people to harvest natural unspoiled Native foods." Among the economic activities listed by the Tla-o-qui-aht in this declaration were harvesting seafood and shellfish, hunting deer and waterfowl, and gathering medicines and cedar wood for canoes.

About six months after the Tla-o-qui-aht issued their tribal park declaration, MB issued briefing notes on Meares Island titled "Meares Island in Perspective" (CD II/A/3). In this document MB asserted not just its "legal right to harvest the trees that it owns but also its contractual obligation to the B.C. government to manage the TFL [Tree Farm Licence]" that it had purchased. The BC government had created TFLs, MB wrote, "to insure that the province's forests are well-managed." Regarding the Tla-o-qui-aht's declaration of Meares Island as a tribal park, MB maintained "this to be unrealistic," adding "that any and all negotiations over land claims must be handled by the Provincial and Federal Governments."

These two documents offer an entry into what I argue in this essay are the environmental circumstances of sovereignty. MB's briefing notes contain an implicit assertion of British Columbian and Canadian sovereignty over the island. The implication of sovereignty in MB's briefing notes is very matter-of-fact. It is in the language of legal rights, property ownership, contractual obligations, forest management, and the authority to handle land-claims negotiations. Against MB's appeal to property ownership, contracts, and forest management, the Tla-o-qui-aht talk of adhering to "the Laws of our Forefathers" and ensuring "the survival of our Native way of life," which includes, among other things, harvesting shellfish, hunting deer, and gathering wood and medicines. The Tla-o-qui-aht's declaration operates as a challenge to the discourse of sovereignty articulated in MB's briefing notes, not by disputing MB's claims of legal rights, property ownership, and so on, but by (implicitly) challenging the circumstances of the sovereignty on which MB's claims rest.

Although no wars of conquest were fought and no treaties were signed that transferred Meares Island to the sovereignty of Canada / British Columbia, the language of sovereignty works for MB when it makes its claim to the trees on Meares Island. The language of sovereignty does not work for the Tla-o-qui-aht in their declaration of Meares Island as a tribal park. As I argue in this essay, the discourse of sovereignty works for MB and not for the Tla-o-qui-aht band owing to the environmental circumstances of sovereignty. Claims to sovereignty are not simply rooted in the presence of a power sufficient to keep the peace among a population within a specific territory and keep "foreigners" out. Claims to sovereignty, and in turn claims to the absence of sovereignty, are based in part *on the orientation a people has to the land on which they live.* MB's assertion of its "legal right" to "harvest the trees that it owns" contains the seeds of the environmental circumstances of sovereignty that I attempt to draw out. The Tla-o-qui-aht's declaration of Meares Island as a tribal park describes an orientation to the land that does not coincide with the circumstances of sovereignty. As such, it mounts a challenge to sovereignty, revealing its circumstantial character.

For students of the concept of sovereignty, my argument that sovereignty has environmental circumstances might appear strange.[2] After all, the environment on which sovereignty is exercised or proclaimed is typically considered to be tangential to the issue of sovereignty itself. Sovereignty has long been thought in terms of simple power—the power necessary to assert rule over a people and a territory. But sovereignty does not simply exist on this level. As F. H. Hinsley has argued in his work on the history of sovereignty, "Authority and power are facts . . . sovereignty is not a fact. It is a concept which men in certain circumstances have applied—a quality which they have attributed or a claim they have counterposed—to the political power which they or other men are exercising" (Hinsley 1986, 1). Hinsley's argument is not that sovereignty is simply absent in some societies, or that it could easily be put in place where it is missing. His argument goes deeper. He is claiming that in order for sovereignty to exist, certain circumstances must be present. In other words, not all peoples or lands are readily available for sovereignty. This is not a claim based on the superiority or inferiority of peoples or lands. It is a claim based on the specificity of the circumstances necessary for sovereignty. One set of those circumstances, I argue, can be described as *environmental.* The politics of Clayoquot Sound reveals this circumstance of sovereignty. Through a reading of its documents, alongside some classic works in modern political thought, I argue that sovereignty is bound up with a particular orientation to environment, an orientation that requires the land to be used in particular ways.

There is a political importance here that should not be overlooked, and that I attempt to develop in the final part of this essay. To the extent that thought about sovereignty continues as though sovereignty has no environmental circumstances, a significant political issue is concealed—that how land is used not only contributes to the existence of sovereignty, but also helps shape the parameters of political possibility. The great myth of modernity is that life is not possible without sovereignty. Sovereignty is cast in universalist terms in this myth, concealing what Judith Butler has called "the alterity within the norm" (Butler 1996, 51). Uncovering the environmental circumstances of sovereignty brings us face-to-face with this alterity and the violence implicit in the norm.[3] It can also teach us that life under the circumstances of sovereignty is only one possibility of political existence.

Early European colonization of the Americas was grounded largely in religious notions of sovereignty. When John Cabot set sail for "the New World" in 1497, he embarked with instructions from Henry VII to "occupy and possess all [non-Christian] towns, cities, castles, and lands . . . getting unto [England] the rule, title, and jurisdiction of the same" (quoted in Williams 1992, 121).[4] The implications of Henry's instructions are perhaps obvious. Christian peoples (the already-present Spanish colonizers, for instance) are bearers of sovereignty; non-Christians are not. More than five hundred years later, such a justification for sovereignty would sound foreign. Straightforward religious difference hardly resonates today as an appropriate justification for why one people may claim sovereignty and another not. As a justification for sovereignty, this purely religious and medieval argument lost its currency in Europe in the sixteenth and seventeenth centuries. A new justification for sovereignty, not completely divorced from certain theological underpinnings, would emerge in those centuries along with a new political entity (the state) and a new argument for appropriate land use.

As the modern era took shape, English colonizers began to rely less and less on their Christianity as a justification for settling on lands in North America. Increasingly, the justification for colonizing America was not simply that the continent was inhabited by "heathens" who could claim no sovereignty by nature of their religious error, but that the continent was "vacant" and "wild," and hence belonged to no one. These modern English colonists clearly recognized that people were living on these "vacant" lands. But the simple presence of people on the land was not sufficient to justify an already existing sovereignty. John Winthrop, the founder of the Massachusetts Bay Colony, addressed this issue in 1629 in his "General Considerations for the Plantation in New-England." "What warrant have we to take that land, which is and hath been of long time possessed of others the sons of Adam?" Winthrop asked himself. He answered: "That which is common to all is proper to none. This savage people ruleth over many lands without title or property; for they enclose no ground, neither have they cattle to maintain it, but remove their dwellings as they have occasion" (quoted in Segal and Stineback 1977, 50). In order for sovereignty over a land to exist, Winthrop implied, there must first be property in the land. And in order for property to exist, the land has to be used in specific ways. For Winthrop, that meant enclosing ground, maintaining said ground with domesticated cattle, and establishing permanent dwellings.

Sixty years later, John Locke would publish "An Essay concerning the True, Original and End of Civil Government" laying out a systematic argument for a conception of property that is rooted to a specific type of land use. Locke's essay contains one of the clearest articulations of the modern theory of a natural right to property. More important, at least with respect to my argument here, Locke's discussion of property provides an entry into the environmental circumstances of sovereignty. As James Tully has persuasively argued (Tully 1993, 137–76), Locke's works provided a systematic justification for the dispossession of "Amerindians" from their "traditional" lands. Specifically, the theory of property articulated in chapter 5 of Locke's essay functions "in such a way that Amerindian customary land use is not a legitimate type of property" (ibid., 139). Tully argues that the delegitimization of Amerindian methods of land use subjected Amerindian notions of property to European notions of property. I want to take Tully's interpretation of Locke's argument further. The delegitimization of Amerindian methods of land use also subjected Amerindian societies to the European concept of sovereignty (something I am not sure that Tully recognizes).[5]

Locke begins his discussion of the natural right to property with the claim that something becomes property through human labor. This general sense of property as the result of labor applies to what Locke calls the "Fruits of the Earth and the Beasts that subsist on it" (Locke 1963, 332). Property of the "Earth it self," however, requires an additional discussion. This is the discussion that is most relevant to my argument. Locke describes the type of labor necessary to establish property in the land in the following way: "*As much land* as a Man Tills, Plants, Improves, Cultivates, and can use the Product of, so much is his *Property*" (ibid.). In order for land to become property, it must be labored on in a specific way. The converse, of course, is that land that has not been labored on *in this particular way* belongs to no one. The particularity of how land becomes property is a key element of the environmental circumstances of sovereignty.

The colonial implications of Locke's argument are perhaps clear (although, as Tully has pointed out, in the vast majority of commentaries on Locke's "Second Treatise" there is little or no discussion of these implications [Tully 1993, 139]): where persons living in a specific area have not tilled, planted, improved, cultivated, and made use of the products of the land, there is no injustice in my moving in and doing so. The land actually belongs to no one until these things have been done to it. Property is based in a particular mode of land use. And property, in Locke's theory, serves as one of the circumstances of sovereignty.

Thomas Flanagan, in an essay on the role of this "agricultural argument" in the colonization of Indian lands, argues that "the real issue [in colonization] was not private ownership but public sovereignty; for sovereignty carried the underlying title to the soil that allowed the sovereign to convert common resources into private property" (Flanagan 1989, 602). For Flanagan, Locke's "agricultural argument" exists independently of the broader issue of sovereignty. The "agricultural argument" is blameless with respect to any injustice in European colonization of Indian lands, he asserts, because it is "formally consistent with the premises of natural rights philosophy" (591). The problem again, as Flanagan sees it, lies with sovereignty. But Flanagan does not see the extent to which Locke's "agricultural argument" actually frames the issue of sovereignty, establishing certain environmental circumstances of sovereignty. Property and sovereignty are not politically isolated. The manner in which land comes to be property in the "agricultural argument" of Locke and others helps set the parameters of sovereignty. If the individuals in a community have no claim to the land, then the community as a whole has no claim. Sovereignty only exists for those who use the land in certain ways.

Locke maintains that members of a sovereign political society may agree to leave certain lands "in common," or "unused," and not lose control over these lands (Locke 1963, 334). Sovereignty is extended over these "unused" lands by virtue of the "use" of the lands surrounding them. But where a people does not till, plant, improve, cultivate, and make use of the products of the land, leaving aside certain lands to be "unused" makes no sense. The whole of the land is "unused," hence no sovereignty can exist. In short, cultivation is necessary for property, and property for sovereignty.[6]

Flanagan's failure to recognize the link between the "agricultural argument" and the environmental circumstances of sovereignty is highlighted by the fact that he discusses Emer de Vattel's use of this argument. In *The Law of Nations,* published in 1758, Vattel directly connected the Lockean argument for a natural right to property to a natural law for international relations. "Every Nation," wrote Vattel, "is therefore bound by natural law to cultivate the land which has fallen to its share" (quoted in Flanagan 1989, 595). Speaking specifically of the situation of those "nations" in America that do not adhere to this natural law, Vattel added:

> these tribes can not take to themselves more land than they have need of or can inhabit and cultivate. Their uncertain occupancy of these vast regions can not be held as a real and lawful taking of possession; and when the Nations of Europe ... come upon lands which the savages have no special need of and are making no present and continuous use of, they may lawfully take possession of them and establish colonies in them. (Quoted in ibid., 596)

Vattel's work makes clear the link between property and sovereignty. The tribal peoples of America do not possess sovereignty owing to the fact that they do not "inhabit and cultivate" the land. European nations may "lawfully take possession" of these lands, establishing their sovereignty over them, through their (legitimate) interaction with the land. The Indians of America do not lack sovereignty simply because they are unable to repel the invading Europeans with force of arms: they lack sovereignty because they do not use the land on which they live in accordance with "natural" law.

Focusing more specifically on Vancouver Island and hence Clayoquot Sound, we can see the politics of Locke and Vattel in operation. In the midnineteenth century, the Hudson's Bay Company (HBC) was granted title to Vancouver Island by the British Crown. Under the terms of this grant the HBC was required to promote the colonization of the island. Addressing the issue of the already-present inhabitants of the island, Archibald Barclay, the secretary of the HBC, wrote: "uncivilized inhabitants of any country have ... a right of occupancy only, and ... until they establish among themselves a settled form of government and subjugate the ground to their own uses by the cultivation of it . . . they have not any individual property in it" (quoted in Foster 1992, 40). For Barclay, the issue at hand was specifically Indian *title* to the land, not sovereignty—the sovereignty of the Crown being presumed owing to a simple assertion of sovereignty rooted in the original assertion by King Henry VII in 1497. Still, the environmental circumstances of sovereignty are evident in Barclay's argument. The absence of cultivation signals an absence of property. And without property, no sovereignty can exist. The Indians of Vancouver Island did have a right to places they had "occupied by cultivation, or had houses built on," Barclay added (a very meager amount of land given the Indians' general orientation to the land), but all other land was "waste," open for settlement (quoted in ibid., 40–41). Recalling Locke, certain lands can be set aside to be held in common, unused, and not open to settlement, but only by a political community that has established its possession of the surrounding lands. The Indians had not established a broader possession, so they could not claim these unused lands off-limits to settlement. In short, they held no sovereignty in these lands.

For many of us who read the history of colonization with modern eyes, the circumstantial character of sovereignty is perhaps difficult to perceive. The problem of colonization often appears to rest, as Flanagan might put it, on a failure to apply the "natural right of property" consistently. In "Letting Go the Bone: The Idea of Indian Title in British Columbia, 1849–1927," Hamar Foster develops this position. Foster speaks of the need for the rule of law to "appear to be just," working not just *for* the powerful, but against them as well (Foster 1992, 67). At the start of his essay, Foster asserts that "the British had neither conquered the Aboriginal peoples of British Columbia, nor (with some minor exceptions) made treaties with them, [hence] the Crown did not enjoy clear title to the province's public lands" (ibid., 28). At the conclusion of the essay, Foster paraphrases and endorses the words of Peter Kelly, a spokesperson for the Allied Tribes of British Columbia in the 1920s, arguing the case for Indian rights: "If white men had property rights, so did Indians, and their rights had, in [Kelly's] view, been recognized by British law for hundreds of years. It was simply a matter of getting the white man to act in conformity with his own principles" (ibid., 67). The strategy seems simple enough: whites should recognize Indian property. But this strategy seems to posit a universality to property that simply does not exist. Property in the land, as I have been arguing, requires particular interactions with the land. Attempts to demonstrate the existence of Indian property bear this out.

In the "Cultural Heritage Background Study: Clayoquot Sound," prepared for the Clayoquot Sound Sustainable Development Strategy Steering

Committee by Ian Wilson, one such attempt is articulated. In this study the assertion is made that the "Westcoast Indians of Vancouver Island" have traditionally operated with a highly developed and diverse system of property rights (CD II/E/6). For instance, animals that are killed within certain territories fall within a chief's "hạhuulhi" (pronounced ha-hoah-thlee), or "economic privileges." What this means in part is that the chief is owed a portion of the killed animal. "Property rights" are also argued to cover specific plants, or areas where these plants grew. According to this study, boundaries were established among the Indians to divide patches of plants such as the Pacific cinquefoil. Moreover, with respect to the Pacific cinquefoil plant, "the people 'cultivated' these plants by placing the ends of the roots back in the ground so that they would grow the following year."

According to Foster, presumably, if the first English colonizers had acted "in conformity with [their] own principles" they would have recognized the property of the Indians described here. Unfortunately for the Tla-o-qui-aht, the colonizers *did* act in conformity with their principles: the *natural* right to property they were operating with was based on specific types of land use, types of land use not present here. Foster wants to believe that the law is blind, that it works equally in favor of whites and Indians, that it is neutral. If it is, then if whites are presented with evidence of Indian property, the law will force them to recognize Indian rights. But the law is not neutral; as a product of sovereignty, it is framed by the same environmental circumstances that frame sovereignty. The property it recognizes is culturally specific.

Both of these examples of "property rights" exist outside the parameters of Locke's *natural* right to property. The animals claimed by a chief as his hạhuulhi because they are roaming within the range of his "economic privileges" still exist within the state of nature from a Lockean perspective. As such, they may become the *private* property of anyone who puts her or his labor to them through the act of hunting. Not having labored over these animals, not to mention the land on which they roam, the chief has no legitimate claim to a portion of an animal killed by another person in these lands, nor does he have a legitimate claim to the land on which these animals roam.[7] Similarly, claims to patches of Pacific cinquefoil have no standing within Locke's presentation of property rights. The act of placing the roots back in the ground, described in quotation marks as cultivation in the "Cultural Heritage Background Study," would not meet the requirements of tilling, planting, improving, or cultivating that Locke lists as necessary for establishing property in the land. Yes, the plants that are picked belong to those who do the picking, but within Locke's theory of property, the pickers have no claim *to the land* on which these plants grow. With no property in the land, no sovereignty could exist. To argue that Locke and his fellow English colonizers should have recognized the property rights and the sovereignty of the Vancouver Island Indians ignores the specific environmental circumstances of sovereignty.[8]

Recognizing the cultural specificity implicit in such concepts as property, sovereignty, and agriculture is not always easy. But, as Frieda Knobloch has argued, those who "wish that white settlers had been able to extend their definition of agriculture to include, say, wild rice gathering" miss an opportunity "to understand language as having a history that belies the 'obviousness' of ordinary words like agriculture" (Knobloch 1996, 4). In *The Culture of Wilderness* Knobloch draws out this history, and with it the environmental circumstances of sovereignty. Knobloch informs us that the words *colonize, cultivate,* and *agriculture* all became a part of the English language in the early to mid-1600s (ibid.).[9] Moreover, she maintains that an important connection exists among these seventeenth-century additions to the English language:

> The word "colony" ... was derived specifically from the Latin word for farmer, at a time when European landowners were colonizing their own backcountry, enforcing their ownership by bringing new lands into cultivation, changing the land-use practices of peasants, and forcing many of them off the land. ... The two words [*colonization* and *agriculture*] work together: colonization is about enforcing land ownership through a new agricultural occupation of lands once used differently. Colonization is a good thing, according to its supporters ... [because] it brings about the "improvement" of land under cultivation—it brings culture to a wilderness. (Ibid., 4–5)

Put simply, "[c]olonization is an agricultural act" (ibid., 1). Colonization is not just the acquiring of lands that are geographically distant. And "agriculture as such has never simply been about raising food crops" (ibid., 2). Agriculture is a particular method of raising food that requires a particular utilization of the land, and, as Knobloch argues extensively throughout her work, a particular social formation. Colonization, then, can be understood as the act of bringing "culture" to a wilderness, even if that wilderness lies in one's own backyard. Knobloch's discussion of the origins of agriculture as a specific practice designed to domesticate the wilderness is crucial for understanding the environmental circumstances of sovereignty. In order to exercise sovereignty over a territory, one needs to colonize it—whether that territory is an ocean away or just outside the door.

Knobloch's discussion also brings out a certain spatial dimension to sovereignty that is bound up with its environmental circumstances. Bringing culture to a wilderness removes a spatial indeterminacy that confounds sovereignty. Wilderness defies geographic boundaries; sovereignty, on the other hand, requires fixed lines of demarcation. Part of the reason why "the weed" occupies the profound place that it does in the discourse of agriculture, Knobloch argues, is that the weed is "perpetually getting away" (ibid., 144). The weed's reluctance to stay out of specific areas disrupts the spatiality of agriculture/colonization. In this regard, the weed represents wilderness. Agriculture, as an enemy of wilderness and a circumstance of sovereignty, establishes set boundaries. Not only does agriculture provide the preconditions for having property in land, it also operates to bring culture and order to the wilderness. The absence of agriculture, however, leaves geographic boundaries indeterminate, if not unrecognizable.

People who do not practice agriculture (and remember, agriculture is not simply about raising food crops, it requires a particular utilization of the land and a particular social formation) live on lands with indeterminate boundaries, at least as far as determinacy is understood within the discourse of sovereignty. As Gilles Deleuze and Félix Guattari put it in *A Thousand Plateaus*, a spatial difference exists between what they call the "state trajectory" and the "nomadic trajectory." The state trajectory "*parcels out a closed space to people,* assigning each person a share and regulating the communication between shares, the nomadic trajectory . . . *distributes people (or animals) in an open space,* one that is indefinite and noncommunicating" (Deleuze and Guattari 1987, 386). The difference between these two "trajectories" is not determined by the movement of one and the absence of movement in the other. The "nomad" is nomadic in the eyes of the state not because it is in constant movement, but because of its orientation to the land. From the perspective of the state, the nomad lives in the wilderness. Sovereignty cannot exist in the wilderness; it requires a space that is well defined, ordered: a space that comes into existence through certain interactions with the land.

If we return to the two documents involving Meares Island that I began with (CD II/A/3), we can perhaps see how the environmental circumstances of sovereignty frame the debate between the Tla-o-qui-aht and MacMillan Bloedel. From the perspective of sovereignty, the Tla-o-qui-aht's determination to preserve Meares Island in order to ensure the "survival of our Native way of life" is problematic. It is problematic because of the types of activities put forth as the "economic base" of this way of life. The Tla-o-qui-aht do not speak in terms of property. They do not speak of making use

of the products of the land by way of tilling, planting, improving, and cultivating. They speak of preserving the island so that they may continue to
harvest seafood and shellfish, hunt deer and waterfowl, gather wood and
medicines. Theirs is not the language of agriculture; as such it is not the language of sovereignty. From the perspective of sovereignty, the Tla-o-qui-aht
speak from the wilderness.

That the activities described by the Tla-o-qui-aht in this document
did not establish either a property or a sovereignty in the land in the eyes of
their English colonizers more than 150 years ago has much to do with why
the Tla-o-qui-aht had to issue their declaration in 1984. It was not that
the English colonists chose not to respect Tla-o-qui-aht property rights and
sovereignty. Rather, the "Native way of life" of the Tla-o-qui-aht took and
takes place outside the environmental circumstances of sovereignty. In this
regard, the tribal park declaration is destabilizing. It draws out the circumstantial character of sovereignty. The tribal park declaration brings the environmental circumstances of sovereignty to the fore. Rather than viewing
sovereignty as a fact of all political societies, the declaration confronts us
with the circumstances of sovereignty. Rather than viewing sovereignty as a
universal concept, we can see it as a specific practice emerging out of specific conditions.

The responses issued by MB to the tribal park declaration also bring
to light the environmental circumstances of sovereignty. The extent to which
MB's 1984 briefing notes on Meares Island are based in the environmentally circumstantial character of sovereignty should be evident. MB not only
asserted its "legal right to harvest the trees that it owns," it couched this "harvest" in terms of ensuring "that the province's forests are well-managed."
In terms of the discourse of sovereignty, "well-managed" forests are "tree
farms." The discourse of agriculture helps establish the sovereignty that
supports MB's case. From the perspective of MB, the Tla-o-qui-aht were not
seeking to manage "the province's forests" well. Moreover, the Tla-o-qui-aht
were attempting to bar MB from exercising its legal right to harvest the trees
it owns. MB therefore saw the Tla-o-qui-aht's declaration as "unrealistic."

A decade later, an observer of the ongoing exchanges between the
Tla-o-qui-aht and MB might think MB had shifted its position on the issue
of land claims. Rather than simply declaring these claims as "unrealistic,"
MB now spoke of its desire to "increase First Nations' participation in our
business and their share of its economic benefits," through "joint venture
operations" (CD IV/8). According to MB, the establishment of such an operation "would signal an increased control by the aboriginal community
over resource use in their traditional territory." This would seem to be a

move toward recognizing aboriginal sovereignty. But we need to keep in mind the environmental circumstances of sovereignty. The increased control over resource use that MB was promising is severely restrained by those circumstances. The extent to which aboriginal peoples would actually have control over resource use would be tempered by the "*obligations* that currently flow from the right to harvest and manage publicly-owned timber" (ibid., emphasis added). The use called for in the Tla-o-qui-aht's 1984 tribal park declaration would not satisfy the obligations of managing publicly owned timber. In order for the Tla-o-qui-aht to have "increased control over resource use in their traditional territory," first that use must be a part of "participation" with MB in a "joint-venture operation," and second it must coincide with the obligations of properly managing a provincial tree farm. In other words, Tla-o-qui-aht control of resource use in their traditional territory will be determined by the environmental circumstances of sovereignty.

There might appear to be a certain level of irony to the use of the language of "tree farm" here. Historically, the practice of "managing" TFLs bore little resemblance to traditional methods of agriculture, although it has taken on a greater agricultural character of late. Trees were simply cut down, and all of the undergrowth cleared away in the process. After the trees were removed, the logging company moved on. Any regeneration of the forest was usually left up to natural processes. This type of logging, while it arguably created a property in the trees that are logged, did little to create a property in the land. There was no tilling, planting, improving, or cultivating going on there. It could therefore be argued that this type of logging did little to establish sovereignty in the land. This practice of logging created no more signs of use than the slash-and-burn techniques of many nonmodern, non-European peoples, who historically have not been granted either property or sovereignty in the land by Europeans.

The shift in the terms of discourse employed by the various logging companies operating in British Columbia in the face of environmental campaigns by groups such as the Friends of Clayoquot Sound and land claims by various First Nations is quite interesting in this light. In the face of these challenges to its logging practices, the industry began using explicit agricultural imagery to describe its operations. In other words, its discourse began to coincide much more clearly with the environmental circumstances of sovereignty. In an advertisement in an issue of *Paper Europe* that was devoted to the conflict in Clayoquot Sound, Weyerhaeuser Canada described its activity in the following terms: "harvested lands are reforested quickly" (CD IV/9). In a separate ad from the same publication, Avenor (formerly

Canadian Pacific Forest Products) emphasized the presence of new trees "just born but already standing tall" on lands recently logged. The land has been colonized and cultivated. These lands now show signs of (continued) use. Anyone taking a drive on Highway 4 across Vancouver Island can see these signs, literally. Travelers on this road are informed of the dates of the last cut, replanting, thinning, and future harvest. Moreover, they ought also to be able to see the signs of use in the straight rows of even-aged trees and the minimal amount of undergrowth. This is not the forest primeval; it has indeed become a tree farm.

These examples suggest the extent to which the parameters of contemporary politics are still shaped by the environmental circumstances of sovereignty. The tree farm asserts the mastery of the colonist over the wilderness. The tree farm signifies the presence of sovereignty. In the face of land claims by various Indian tribes, the logging industry's agricultural shift more firmly establishes Canadian sovereignty.

The logging industry has not been alone in asserting Canadian sovereignty in response to land claims by the First Nations of Canada. On December 11, 1997, the Supreme Court of Canada released its decision from *Delgamuukw v. British Columbia* (1997), wherein it sought to clarify the meaning of "aboriginal title" under Canadian law. The *Delgamuukw* case originated from a claim to ownership of and jurisdiction over fifty-eight thousand square kilometers in the province of British Columbia by the "houses" of the Gitksan and Wet'suwet'en peoples. This claim was denied outright by the trial court in British Columbia. On appeal before the Supreme Court of Canada, the claim was altered to one of "aboriginal title" (Persky, 1998, 26).

At trial in British Columbia, Chief Justice Allan McEachern ruled: "It is the law that aboriginal rights exist at the 'pleasure of the Crown,' and they may be extinguished whenever the intention of the Crown to do so is plain and clear" (quoted in ibid., 8). The Supreme Court of Canada did assert that something called "aboriginal title" does exist within Canadian law, but it did not deviate all that far from McEachern's ruling, arguing that "aboriginal title" only exists within the realm of "Crown sovereignty": "[W]hereas the time for identification of aboriginal rights is the time of first contact, the time for the identification of aboriginal title is the time at which *the Crown asserted sovereignty over the land*" (ibid., 31–32; emphasis added). The Court offered no discussion of the grounds for this medieval *assertion* by the Crown of its sovereignty over the land that would be Canada. However, when the Court attempted to lay out what aboriginal title actually means, the terms of its discourse shifted from simple Crown assertion to land use.

Aboriginal peoples, the Court argued, may retain "title" (not sovereignty) over lands they occupied "pre-sovereignty."[10] Aboriginal title involves a "general claim to occupy and possess vast tracts of territory [and] the right to use land for a variety of activities related to the aboriginal society's habits and mode of life" (ibid., 34). Hence, aboriginal chiefs may apparently still claim their "<u>ha</u>huulhi" over deer killed within their "titled" lands. Aboriginal peoples may still pick Pacific cinquefoil. They may still make canoes by "culturally modifying" cedar trees. In this respect, the Tla-o-qui-aht's tribal park declaration (CD II/A/1) seems to fit comfortably within the Court's notion of the circumstances that give rise to, or sustain, "aboriginal title." The Tla-o-qui-aht declared Meares Island a tribal park to ensure the survival of their "Native way of life." They sought to protect their "right" to "harvest natural unspoiled Native foods" through the acts of catching seafood and shellfish, hunting deer and waterfowl, and gathering wood and medicines. As long as the Tla-o-qui-aht pursue only these kinds of activities, they might (on the Court's reasoning) retain their title to the Island.[11]

But, should aboriginal peoples seek to use these lands in ways not related to their society's "habits and mode of life"—or, as the Court puts it, their "traditional way of life" (ibid.)—would they then forfeit their title to these lands? This question remains somewhat open. Chief Justice Lamer emphasizes that the "inherent limit" on aboriginal title does not *restrict* "the use of land to those activities that have traditionally been carried out on it" (95). The holders of land may use the land "for a variety of purposes, which need not be aspects of those aboriginal practices, customs and traditions which are integral to distinctive aboriginal cultures" (88). On the other hand, there is a "general limitation" implicit in "aboriginal title" that "arises from the particular physical and cultural relationship that a group may have with the land" (ibid.). Uses of the land that might—in the Court's judgment—jeopardize the nature of the group's attachment to the land would not be permitted: "uses of the land that would threaten that future relationship are, by their very nature, excluded from the content of aboriginal title" (93). This is—in part, at least—an allusion to the "environmental circumstances" of aboriginal peoples.

Although the Court provides some latitude in how the land might be used, it remains very definite about one thing: the Court itself will arbitrate; it will decide how aboriginal title may be used, and when the circumstances for it may have disappeared. Aboriginal title, after all, only exists within the context of Crown sovereignty. It is a specific form of land use granted by a sovereign community. The granting or "recognition" of aboriginal title is comparable to a decision by the political community to set certain lands aside for limited kinds of uses, rather than a decision to grant aboriginal peoples sovereignty, or access to the range of land uses consistent with the environmental circumstances of sovereignty. An attempt by aboriginal peoples to "use" these lands in a manner befitting a sovereign state might thus exceed the purpose of "title." It would amount to a counterassertion of sovereignty—something the Canadian state (or any state, arguably) might not tolerate. Such an assertion would require the aboriginal group to relinquish their title, and thus the protection of their special relationship to the land, in order to hold the land in *fee simple,* as "ordinary" property owners would: "If aboriginal peoples wish to use their lands in a way that aboriginal title does not permit, then they must surrender those lands and convert them into non-title lands to do so" (94–95).

This is not the only way that "aboriginal title" is constrained by the environmental circumstances of sovereignty. The Court also ruled that "aboriginal title" can be "infringed by the federal and provincial governments if the infringement (1) furthers a compelling and substantial legislative objective and (2) is consistent with the special fiduciary relationship between the Crown and the aboriginal peoples" (35). The Court lists several activities it claims might be consistent with these two purposes, specifically, "the development of agriculture, forestry, mining and hydroelectric power" (ibid.). Land uses that coincide with the environmental circumstances of sovereignty might thus, under some circumstances, take precedence over Indian title. Under the terms of the Court's ruling, should the provincial government of British Columbia decide that logging must commence on Meares Island to contribute, for example, to the general economic development of British Columbia, the rights of the Tla-o-qui-aht could be compromised. The language of MB in its 1984 briefing notes on Meares Island is still the language of sovereignty—managing the province's forests supersedes the survival of the Tla-o-qui-aht's native way of life. In this sense, one could argue, using the language of British Columbia Supreme Court Justice McEachern quoted earlier, "aboriginal title" exists at the "pleasure of the Crown." Put another way, "aboriginal title" not only exists within and is constrained by an abstract concept of sovereignty, it is specifically limited by the *environmental circumstances* of sovereignty.

Despite the Crown's simple assertion of sovereignty at some time in the past, what differentiates "title" from "sovereignty" in the Court's ruling is basically land use. It is not just that sovereign states are permitted to engage in agriculture, forestry, mining, and hydroelectric power, whereas the limits of aboriginal title put these kinds of activities into question; the "habits and mode of life" of "traditional" aboriginal societies preclude their recognition as sovereign. Sovereignty is not the simple exercise of power. To quote F. H. Hinsley again, sovereignty "is a concept which men in certain circumstances have applied—a quality they have attributed or a claim they have counterposed—to the political power which they or other men were exercising" (Hinsley 1986, 1).

By coming to terms with the circumstantial nature of sovereignty, a political opportunity may emerge. As Judith Butler has argued in an essay on universality in culture, the attempt to translate universals (like property rights or sovereignty) into different cultural contexts "exposes the alterity within the norm (an alterity without which the norm would not assume its borders and 'know' its limits)" (Butler 1996, 51). By seriously asking why the "universal" concept of sovereignty did not (and does not) apply to the Tla-o-qui-aht, we can begin to expose the "alterity within the norm"; we can begin to see the circumstantial nature of sovereignty; we can begin to see the connection between a specific form of land use and claims of sovereignty. The move to pass politically pertinent terms off as neutral or universal seeks to covertly frame the possibilities of political discourse. By exposing the circumstantial character of supposedly universal terms, we can open political thought to new political possibilities.

Here is where I take issue with Tully's argument regarding "aboriginal sovereignty." Tully's reading of Locke's concept of property within the context of British colonization of North America is employed with the hope of loosening the hold of Locke's theoretical arguments (in this arena) on political thought today. I wholeheartedly endorse this project. However, Tully seems to operate with a notion of sovereignty that is far from contextual. In his "Submission to the Select Committee on Aboriginal Issues," he argues that "During the nineteenth century a different relationship was imposed over the Aboriginal peoples without their consent and despite their active resistance. Their status as equal, co-existing and self-governing nations was denied" (Tully 1997, 4). Tully's claim is that prior to the nineteenth century "the universal criteria of the inherent right of self government," embodied in international law, were being applied in Europe–aboriginal relations (12). Siba N'Zatioula Grovogui has convincingly argued that the claim that European powers acted in accordance with the universal principles of international law throughout the sixteenth, seventeenth, and eighteenth centuries, only to deviate from these principles in the nineteenth century, is a "mendacious fiction" (Grovogui 1996, 12). The force of this "fiction," Grovogui argues, legitimizes the colonization of non-European lands in the centuries prior to the nineteenth. Moreover, it legitimizes a certain notion of sovereignty and certain principles of international law as universal and hence neutral.

Tully tends to do this when he appeals to the principles of international law, the arguments of former Chief Justice of the U.S. Supreme Court John Marshall, the positions of the British Crown, and so on, as examples of appropriate interaction with Amerindian peoples (Tully 1993, 175). His argument, in part, is that these sources drew on a universal and mutually consented to understanding of sovereignty in their interactions with Amerindians. Insofar as he appeals to such universals, Tully does the opposite of what he intends, and lends support to a discourse that potentially legitimizes English colonization in America and conceals the circumstantial character of sovereignty.

Opening the terms of political discourse is crucial to ongoing negotiations between colonial powers and colonized peoples. Political discourse in these negotiations must take place in terms other than those put forth by the colonial powers as universal. By drawing out the environmental circumstances of sovereignty, sovereignty (once again) becomes a contested term of political discourse. By examining the specificity of these circumstances, hopefully, the assumption that these terms are universal, neutral, and benign will fade. When the colonizer gives up his pretensions to speak in a universal language, then, and perhaps only then, real dialogue can begin to take place. Moreover, by making sovereignty a contested term of political discourse, we can perhaps unsettle the modern myth that politics, or even life itself, is not possible without sovereignty.

Notes

1. "Clayoquot" is the Anglicized spelling, and the one used on the tribal park declaration. More recently, Tla-o-qui-aht has become the dominant spelling. I will use Tla-o-qui-aht throughout the rest of this essay.

2. Throughout this essay, my use of the term *sovereignty* should be understood as referring to its particular modern variant.

3. As an American of European heritage, my use of "us" in this sentence, and elsewhere in this essay, should be read quite specifically. I do not believe that the peoples who have been colonized by European nations in the past five hundred years need to recognize the alterity within the norm. Many of them have lived their lives as the alterity.

4. Henry's instructions to Cabot fit within the general framework of a papacy-endorsed "doctrine of discovery." For more on the generation of this doctrine, as well as the development of counterjustifications for colonialism in the sixteenth, seventeenth, eighteenth, and nineteenth centuries, see Williams (1992).

5. I return to Tully's position on sovereignty later in this essay.

6. Where Locke's theory of property can no doubt be read as protocapitalist, it

is not my contention that the environmental circumstances of sovereignty operate only within capitalist circumstances. My argument is broader than that. Both Locke and Karl Marx see uncultivated land as waste. Locke writes that "Land that is left wholly to nature, that hath no improvement of Pasturage, Tillage, or Planting, is called, as indeed it is, waste" (Locke 1963, 339). In *The Manifesto of the Communist Party,* Marx and Friedrich Engels call for "the bringing into cultivation of waste-lands" (Tucker 1978, 490). As such, I would argue that Marx would agree with Locke when he maintains that "the increase of lands and the right imploying of them is the great art of government" (Locke 1963, 340). For both Locke and Marx, "waste-land" is an economic term. The issue is not whether people are living on these lands, but to what extent these lands contribute to the general economy of the state, whether through private or collective enterprise. The actions of both the United States and the Union of Soviet Socialist Republics in "bringing into cultivation of waste-lands," and hence displacing indigenous peoples, suggests the extent to which the environmental circumstances of sovereignty were operational despite the two countries' economic differences. For more on the similarities between the United States and the U.S.S.R. on this issue, see James C. Scott's *Seeing like a State* (1998) and Russell Means's "Same Old Song," in *Marxism and Native Americans* (1983). I explore the link between sovereignty and the practice of government in "Between Sovereignty and Environment: A Reading of the Discourse of Government," in *The Greening of Sovereignty in World Politics,* edited by Karen Liftin (1998).

7. In this sense, the kings and lords of Europe also can make no claim to animals hunted on "their lands." In another report prepared for the Clayoquot Sound Sustainable Development Strategy Steering Committee titled "The Nuu-Chah-Nulth Sustainable Development Interest in Clayoquot Sound," the "hahoothle" of the chief is compared directly to Crown title within the British legal system (CD II/E/7). I would argue that the notion of property that helps frame the environmental circumstances of sovereignty challenges Crown property in many of its manifestations.

8. I am not attempting to excuse the colonizers with this argument, but rather to demonstrate the circumstantial character of sovereignty, the contemporary political importance of which I hope will be made clear in later in this essay.

9. Note that in Thomas Hobbes's famous formulation of life in the state of nature, written in 1651, he remarks that there would be no "Culture of the Earth," not that there would be no "agriculture" (Hobbes 1980, 186).

10. The Court's use of the term *pre-sovereignty* has an interesting effect. The intent of this term, as I understand it, is to indicate time prior to the Crown's assertion of sovereignty. But the term also suggests a time prior to the very existence of sovereignty in these lands, which corresponds to a time prior to the Crown's assertion of sovereignty. In other words, prior to that assertion, sovereignty did not exist across what is now Canada.

11. If, of course, their title were acknowledged in the first place. By recognizing in the abstract that aboriginal title exists, the Supreme Court of Canada did not necessarily recognize any given First Nation's claim to title. Each nation will presumably have to pursue a court case to have its title recognized. Such recognition will rest significantly on an evaluation of their practices of land use at the time of the assertion of British sovereignty.

Works Cited

Butler, Judith. 1996. "Universality in Culture." In *For Love of Country: Debating the Limits of Patriotism.* Boston: Beacon Press.

CD [*The Clayoquot Documents.* 1997. Ed. Karena Shaw and Warren Magnusson, Clayoquot Project, University of Victoria.]

Deleuze, Gilles, and Félix Guattari. 1987. *A Thousand Plateaus: Capitalism and Schizophrenia.* Trans. Brian Massumi. Minneapolis: University of Minnesota Press.

Flanagan, Thomas. 1989. "The Agricultural Argument and Original Appropriation: Indian Lands and Political Philosophy." *Canadian Journal of Political Science* 22:3 (September): 589–602.

Foster, Hamar. 1992. "Letting Go the Bone: The Idea of Indian Title in British Columbia, 1849–1927." In *Law for the Elephant, Law for the Beaver: Essays in the Legal History of the North American West,* ed. John McLaren, Hamar Foster, and Chet Orloff. Regina, Saskatchewan: Canadian Plains Research Institute, University of Regina.

Grovogui, Siba N'Zatioula. 1996. *Sovereigns, Quasi Sovereigns, and Africans: Race and Self-Determination in International Law.* Minneapolis: University of Minnesota Press.

Hinsley, F. H. 1986. *Sovereignty.* New York: Cambridge University Press.

Hobbes, Thomas. 1980 [1651]. *Leviathan.* Ed. C. B. Macpherson. London: Penguin.

Knobloch, Frieda. 1996. *The Culture of Wilderness: Agriculture as Colonization in the American West.* Chapel Hill: University of North Carolina Press.

Kuehls, Thom. 1998. "Between Sovereignty and Environment: A Reading of the Discourse of Government." In *The Greening of Sovereignty in World Politics,* ed. Karen Liftin. Cambridge: MIT Press.

Locke, John. 1963 [1698]. "Two Treatises of Government." In *Two Treatises of Government,* ed. Peter Laslett. Cambridge: Cambridge University Press.

Means, Russell. 1983. *Marxism and Native Americans.* Boston: South End Press.

Persky, Stan, ed. 1998. *Delgamuukw: The Supreme Court of Canada Decision on Aboriginal Title.* Vancouver: Grey Stone Books.

Scott, James C. 1998. *Seeing like a State: How Certain Schemes to Improve the Human Condition Have Failed.* New Haven: Yale University Press.

Segal, C., and D. Stineback. 1977. *Puritans, Indians, and Manifest Destiny.* New York: G. P. Putnam's Sons.

Tucker, Robert C., ed. 1978. *The Marx-Engels Reader.* New York: W. W. Norton.

Tully, James. 1993. *An Approach to Political Philosophy: Locke in Contexts.* New York: Cambridge University Press.

———. 1997. "Submission to the Select Committee on Aboriginal Issues."

Williams, Robert A., Jr. 1992. *The American Indian in Western Legal Thought: The Discourses of Conquest.* New York: Oxford University Press.

Commentary

Discourses in and about Clayoquot Sound

A First Nations Perspective

Umeek of Ahousaht (E. Richard Atleo)

Among traditionally oriented Nuu-chah-nulth, discourses about begin-nings and about the nature of all relationships are heard from the time of a person's birth. These discourses explain, among other things, the origins of, and relationships between, the diversity of life-forms found in Clayoquot Sound.

The following is one such story told in the house of Keesta. Keesta was born eighty years after fur trading began and forty years before colo-nial settlement (circa 1900) in Clayoquot Sound. He was my great-great-grandfather, who survived into the 1950s, a full decade after my own birth.

A person is busy fashioning two knives in preparation to resist change. The prophetic word has it that someone is coming to change everyone's life. The knife maker is unaware that the person who approaches and begins a friendly conversation is the one who, in English, may be referred to as the Transformer. The Trans-former speaks first.

"What are you making?"

"Knives."

"Oh! For what purpose?"

"They say someone's coming to change us but nobody's going to change me!" (This is said with great conviction and resolve.)

"They are beautiful!!! Let me have a look at those!!!" (The knives are handed over to the Transformer.)

"Here" (placing the two knives on each side of the person's head), "from now on these shall be your two ears and you will make the forest your new home."

And that's how deer came to be.

This story is set in mythical time, and it offers a non-Darwinian account of the origin of one of Clayoquot's many species. The "origin of species" is in, and from, the first people. Other species, like the deer, are produced from the first people, but they themselves remain essentially like the first people throughout the ages. Creation is already complete at the beginning of historical time—people already exist—but changes, transformations are accepted and expected. This historical process is neither evolutionary nor developmental in the linear sense. Changes are not from simple to complex, as a more modern worldview would have it, but from complex to complex, from equal to equal, from one life-form to another. Biodiversity is produced from common origins; all life-forms are from the same family. In this discourse, which remained unchanged for millennia, Nuu-chah-nulth were encouraged to see other species, as well as other peoples, as equals. More than this, all life-forms, so to speak, sat equally at the same negotiating table as the Nuu-chah-nulth, and from this table came the protocols such as the ceremony to acknowledge the first salmon of the season, or the ceremony to take down a great cedar for a great canoe. It was a time of egalitarian discourse.

Then came the discourse of colonization. The nature of this discourse is unilateral, evolutionary, linear, hierarchical, and presumptuous. It completely overshadowed and ignored the first discourse. Consider the following story that records a conversation between humans only—a Nuu-chah-nulth chief and an Englishman. One of these men will presume to be able to improve upon the original creation through the contradictions of dispossession and enforced assimilation. The first speaker is Shewish, a Tseshaht chief. The second speaker is Gilbert M. Sproat, an Englishman, who records the conversation. This exchange takes place in Tseshaht territory, up the Alberni inlet, in August 1860, around the time of Keesta's birth. The political rumor is that the King George men are coming to dispossess and change everyone's way of life.

> "They say that more King George men will soon be here, and will take our land, our firewood, our fishing grounds; that we shall be placed on a little spot, and shall have to do everything according to the fancies of the King George men."
>
> "Do you believe all this?" I asked.
>
> "We want your information," said the speaker.
>
> "Then," answered I, "it is true that more King George men (as they call the English) are coming: they will soon be here: but your land will be bought at a fair price."
>
> "We do not wish to sell our land nor our water; let your friends stay in their own country."

"To which I rejoined: My great chief, the high chief of the King George men, seeing that you do not work your land, orders that you shall sell it. It is of no use to you. The trees you do not need: you will fish and hunt as you do now, and collect firewood, planks for your houses, and cedar for your canoes. The white man will give you work, and buy your fish oil."

"Ah, but we don't care to do as the white men wish."

"Whether or not," said I, "the white men will come. All your people know that they are your superiors; they make the things which you value. You cannot make muskets, blankets, or bread. The white men will teach your children to read printing, and to be like themselves."

"We do not want the white man. He steals what we have. We wish to live as we are." (Sproat 1868, 4–5)

This sort of story is also familiar to the Nuu-chah-nulth. It is not meant to affirm their right to exist or to encourage mutual respect between peoples. It leaves other species out of account completely. It suggests that an alien way of life is to be imposed on Clayoquot, regardless of what is right.

This second discourse, which brought massive changes, is being challenged now, even by some of the descendants of the colonists, as the presumption of colonial superiority is called into question. Postmodern notions of plurality that emphasize egalitarianism have striking similarities to Nuu-chah-nulth conceptions of the relation between life-forms. In fact, a new postcolonial discourse is foreshadowed by the Supreme Court of Canada in its Delgamuukw decision (1997). Although the decision is not directly about Clayoquot Sound, its impact is universal in Canada because of the original Crown–First Nations relationship. In the province of British Columbia, where Delgamuukw is situated, the traditional territories have never been ceded or sold by the original First Nations owners. Neither have these indigenous territories been conquered, as happened frequently south of the border. The Delgamuukw decision, which recognizes aboriginal title, dramatically alters the colonial agenda.

Situating Sproat, the Nuu-chah-nulth chief, and their descendants in relation to one another may be one approach to a discussion of the politics of Clayoquot Sound. Much of the misunderstanding about one another, which is apparent in the second story, continues to the present day. This essay presents my own perspective on the politics of Clayoquot Sound in an effort to clarify some of the misconceptions about aboriginals held by early European thinkers such as John Locke. Locke's work not only influenced colonists such as Sproat, but continues to influence people down to the present day, as Thom Kuehls's essay in this volume indicates. I want to highlight important cultural strands, which will help to situate the Nuu-chah-nulth chief (and his descendants) as a protagonist in a different story: a story like the first, in which the Transformer—not the white man—appears as a supernatural or divine being.

Let us think through that first discourse (in which the story told here is but one of many). In the beginning was the unity of creation. This unity is exemplified in the Nuu-chah-nulth phrase "hishuk-ish t'sawalk" meaning "everything is one." At that moment of creation everyone was a *quuʔas* (a person). Everyone was recognizably people—that is, until the Transformer came and created a great variety of life-forms, among which was *muuwatch*, the deer. Here, biodiversity is by divine design and origin. It situates contemporary people in a particular relationship to all life-forms. Among the Nuu-chah-nulth, this would be sufficient information to explain the necessary protocols developed between humans and animals, between humans and all life-forms. Perhaps others require more explanation.

Creation presupposes Creator whose essence of, and in, the spirit defines the origin and source of everything temporal and physical. Underlying all relationships on earth is the unifying source and demands of the Creator. One of these demands is not to be disrespectful toward any part of creation, because all, in the beginning, were people: *quuʔas*. One of the ways to influence the maintenance of the integrity and unity of this creation while engaged in the necessary act of resource extraction is to note the model presented by the Transformer in the first story.

From an empirical, scientific perspective it would appear that the creation of beautiful deer happened at the expense of a person. However, this appearance is misleading. The *quuʔas* who became a deer did not die but was transformed by the shedding of one "cloak" or "covering" for another. The shedding of a cloak, giving of flesh, is therefore a divine act of transformation, moving in endless cycles from life to life, giving to giving, transformation to transformation, creation to creation, mutual recognition to mutual respect, mutual responsibility to mutual accountability. In the temporal, physical, and empirical sense, it would be said that the salmon gives its life for the life of others, the cedar gives its life for the life of others, the deer gives its life for the life of others. But for the traditional Nuu-chah-nulth, the salmon does not give its life, but rather, in an act of transformation, is prepared to give and share its "cloak" in endless cycles, provided the necessary protocols are observed (such as the ceremony with the first salmon caught of the season), which indicate mutual recognition, mutual respect, mutual responsibility, and mutual accountability. For the Nuu-chah-nulth, the salmon and deer are brothers, and each is a brother's keeper; each is in a relationship of trust and honor. It is natural, among and within fallible humans, as evidenced in the first story, to experience tension between trust and distrust, honor and dishonor. The *quuʔas* who changes into Deer is at first preparing to resist this transformation, and this we recognize as a very human response to proposed change. It is an act of free will that is subsumed by divine will, an acknowledged superior order of design. This worldview is in marked contrast to the worldview brought by Sproat.

In the second story, Gilbert Sproat forecasts coming changes to the Nuu-chah-nulth. Where the first story ushered in the awesome wonders, beauties, and bountifulness of biodiversity, the second story ushers in modernity, which meant, for the Nuu-chah-nulth, oppression, dispossession, inequality, poverty, strange sicknesses, decimation, and enforced conformity to European ways of life. A typical and prevailing notion about aboriginals is expressed by a Jesuit missionary in 1632, who wrote the following in his journal:

> Their education must consist not merely of the training of the mind, but of weaning them from the habits and feelings of their ancestors, and the acquirements of the language, arts and customs of civilized life. (Cited in Vallery 1942, 114)

As an Englishman once said: "Ah, there's the rub!" The rub is in the assumption that civilization was absent in the aboriginal, and therefore this void had to be filled with the European version of "language, arts and customs of civilized life." Sproat is more pragmatic about what it means to be civilized. He equates it with technology. If you can make and use a cell phone, you are civilized. There are other assumptions of civility such as honesty, virtue, humility, kindness, responsibility, discipline, and so on. What has it meant, then, to bring the cruder, Sproatian version of civilization to the "wilderness"? If the proof of the pudding is in the eating, as Don Quixote says, then one only has to observe the current outcome of the colonizers' agenda. Rather than the expected "good" that colonizers claimed to be bringing to the world, we see instead a threatened state of the earth's environment. Civilization has been brought to the "wilderness" with destructive force. How did the earth come to its current state? What kind of ideas drove the colonizers of the world to bring such ruin to the earth?

Locke, like his contemporaries and subsequent thinkers, thought to contribute to bringing order and good government to an otherwise disordered (read wild, instinctive, savage, barbaric, inferior, without laws and morals) world. His base of observation was a comparatively young European culture just emerging from its own "dark ages." Europe was supposedly to be rescued by science, but the science at hand was both ethnocentric and disrespectful of the property and sovereignty rights of other peoples of the world. In Locke's *Second Treatise* we read:

> Thus we see, that the Kings of the Indians in America, which is still a Pattern of the first Ages in Asia and Europe, whilst the Inhabitants were too few for the Country, and want of People and Money gave Men no Temptation to enlarge their Possessions of Land, or contest for wider extent of Ground, are little more than Generals of their Armies; and though they command absolutely in War, yet at home and in time of Peace they exercise very little Dominion, and have but a very moderate Sovereignty, the Resolutions of Peace and War, being ordinarily either in the People, or in a Council. Though the war it self, which admits not of Plurality of Governors, naturally devolves the Command into the King's sole Authority. (Locke 1988, 339–40)

When Locke, together with other influential thinkers such as Rousseau, Hobbes, and Defoe, speculated about aboriginal existence, he did so, not from empirical evidence, but from the peculiar circumstances of his own cultural experience. Therefore, writing under such ignorant and biased circumstances, Locke could not help but write sheer nonsense about the nature of the aboriginals of America. Without firsthand evidence Locke is able to say that the Indians of the Americas represent the "Pattern of the first Ages," and the meaning of this phrase can be understood from the context of not only his writings, but also the writings of his contemporaries. The "Pattern of the first Ages" is synonymous with the notion of humans in an early evolutionary phase who lack all the European acquirements of civilized life. Again, without any hard evidence, Locke is able, in one phrase, to dehumanize a continent of people, by speculating that they have "no Temptation to enlarge their Possessions of Land." It is this kind of nonsense that contributed to the creation of such enduring myths as the "noble savage." How nonhuman, how unlike the civilized European, must an aboriginal be, who is not tempted in the same way that Europeans are tempted? Yet, beyond all doubt, it is influential thinkers such as Locke who contributed to the politics of Clayoquot Sound. Their misinformed ideas and speculations about aboriginals became the basis for the Indian Act, whose premise is consonant with the notion of the "Pattern of the first Ages." In this act, the Indians of Canada are wards of the state, in the same way that actual children can become wards of the state. The "Pattern of the first Ages" meant that aboriginals were like children who appear early on the evolutionary scale: innocent, instinctive, undisciplined, wild, without laws and morals. In this imagined state of nature, where there were no notions of property and no lands properly "striated," property and sovereignty were created by the labor of European hands. Until recently, that has been the colonizers' perspective.

However, change seems to be an ongoing characteristic of reality—of which the scenes in the first and second stories are examples. December 11, 1997, marks another change, a legal milestone, away from the dark ages. Only this time it is not the aboriginals who are being forced to change. The Supreme Court of Canada's Delgamuukw decision recognizing aboriginal title finally begins to break the colonial stranglehold on aboriginal ways of life first perpetrated (albeit in ignorance—but ignorance of rights is no excuse for violations of them) by the speculations of European thinkers such as Locke and his ideological offspring.

The decision on Delgamuukw expands the narrow confines of early European thinking to include another point of view, another perspective. Rather than limiting the notion of property to a particular and peculiar "striation" of land, the Supreme Court discovers that property can also be sui generis (*Delgamuukw v. British Columbia*, 1997, para. 82, 112, 126) and is also more than a fungible commodity (ibid., para. 129). Title to land is no longer described entirely from Locke's perspective. Aboriginal perspectives are now included. This decision is a triumph of legal, linear, logic.

This legal, linear, scientific logic has its problems, however, especially when it is founded in false premises. The colonizers, once having set themselves up as protectors of childlike aboriginals (a false premise), are now legally bound to carry on this bit of historical fiction created by Locke and others. A complement to this historical fiction is the "honour of the Crown." From a First Nations perspective, the activities on behalf of the Crown have been anything but honorable, and yet the phrase carries on, to good and bad effect. A major part of the historical fiction about aboriginals found its way into Canada's constitution and became the reality, first in the form of the Indian Act, and subsequently as section 35(1) of Constitution Act 1982. The irony is that it is these historical fictions (about the nature of the aboriginal) that later became legal realities. These realities, in turn, enabled the contemporary Nuu-chah-nulth to take an aboriginal rights stand on Meares Island, to which the court responded on its own terms. Environmentalists rejoiced and Clayoquot Sound was "saved" for the moment, but the outcome was not to stop the industrial practices in general. The forest companies simply began to focus their "barbaric and savage" attacks on the environment in other places around the world. This is the current situation of the politics of Clayoquot Sound from a First Nations perspective. Delgamuukw has changed, and perhaps strengthened, the negotiating position of First Nations, but the ultimate outcome remains to be seen.

In the final paragraph of the Delgamuukw judgment are found these words:

> So, in the end, the legal rights of the Indian people will have to be accommodated within our total society by political compromises and accommodations based in the first instance on negotiation and agreement and ultimately in accordance with the sovereign will of the community as a whole. The legal rights of the Gitksan and Wet'suwet'en peoples, to which this law suit is confined, and which allow no room for any approach other than the application of the law itself, and the legal rights of all aboriginal peoples throughout British Columbia, form only one factor in the ultimate determination of what kind of community we are going to have in British Columbia and throughout Canada in the years ahead.

The final paragraph of the Delgamuukw decision sets the ground rules for yet another discourse, and this may prove a comforting conclusion for the descendants of the colonizers. The Crown has imposed its sovereignty over the land; made some treaty promises (largely unkept) along the way; dispossessed a continent of people of their land, resources, and ways of life; grown to be the wealthiest on the face of the earth while depleting the once vast resources; grown overwhelmingly in population and political power, and it now says, from the vantage point of ascendancy, "the sovereign will of the community as a whole" will now determine our collective futures. From a First Nations perspective the future appears bleak. The "sovereign will of the community as a whole," in practice, has been the major source of Earth's problems with respect to the environment and with respect to the rights of aboriginals. The colonizers and their descendants have still not shown, for the most part, that they are capable of being, and behaving, in a civilized manner with respect to their relationship to the environment and their relationship to aboriginal people.

In addition to the Delgamuukw decision, the current treaty process in British Columbia is setting the stage for scene 4 of an ongoing drama. Scene 1 set the original state of Clayoquot Sound, the resources of which were ably managed for millennia under ha-huulhi;[1] scene 2 ushered in modernity and the subsequent devastations, and scene 3 (made possible by the Delgamuukw decision) might be said to usher in a postmodernity that espouses plurality. The discourses of scene 4 will emerge from Delgamuukw and the treaty process.

Civilization, among traditional aboriginals, requires mutual recognition, mutual respect, mutual responsibility, and mutual accountability. The references are not to humans only but to all life-forms, for it is believed that we all have the same source, our lives are bound up together inextricably, making us all relations, "hishuk ish t'sawalk," everything is one. In this view, a concept such as that held by modernity, of an "Other," is a self-destructive concept in practice because it is rooted in the malicious fiction created by early European thinkers about the place of the aboriginal. Postmodernity's notion of plurality is more hopeful because it mirrors the best of the ancient notions held, from the beginning of time, by traditional Nuu-chah-nulth, which is that the treatment of all life should be with respect because we all have the same origins.

Nevertheless, the "honour of the Crown" today has become the honor of postmodernity, the honor of the community at large. The question remains, is the community at large capable of exercising, or allowing, plurality? The question will not be easy to answer because the exercise of plurality will be to admit that the original inhabitants of Clayoquot Sound, and of the Americas, were not the "Pattern of the first Ages" but in fact had ways of life, the best of which, when practiced, could balance individual with group rights without violating the rights of either. The aboriginal genius for the balancing of rights is overshadowed by the current imbalance of the focus on individual rights, which has always resulted, since the onset of modernity, in enormous wealth for some and abject poverty for others. Listen, then, in conclusion, to a voice unheard, or disregarded, by the colonizer, spoken between 1615 and 1625. Sagard, a Recollet French missionary, observed and recorded in his journal the following:

> [T]hose of their Nation . . . offer reciprocal Hospitality, and help each other so much that they provide for the needs of all so that there is no poor beggar at all in their towns, bourgs and villages, as I said elsewhere, so that they found it very bad hearing that there were in France a great number of needy and beggars, and thought that it was due to a lack of charity, and blamed us greatly saying that if we had some intelligence we would set some order in the matter, the remedies being simple. (Cited in Jaenen 1974, 282)

The human relationships described here are not a function of a small population, as some have argued in defense of their own lifeways, but of values situated in a particular worldview. Plurality situated in an evolutionary worldview is not necessarily impossible in theory, but it has proven to be a contradiction in practice, whereas plurality situated in a worldview that permits respect for all life-forms allows the possibility to resolve the paradox of balancing individual with group rights.

Note

1. Ha-huulhi is the Nuu-chah-nulth word that, from a resource management perspective, describes a relationship of people to the environment and its resources. It refers to outright ownership of sovereign territory by the *ha-wiih* (chiefs) and commonly known specific rights held by subchiefs. Resource extraction was conducted through strict observance of sacred protocols that were designed to display recognition and respect in order to ensure sustainability.

Works Cited

Delgamuukw v. British Columbia. 1997. *3 S. C. R. [Supreme Court of Canada Reports] 1010.* Http://www.droit.umontreal.ca/doc/csc-scc/en/rec/text/delgamuu.en.txt.

Jaenen, C. J. 1974. "Amerindian Views of French Culture in the Seventeenth Century." *Canadian Historical Review* 55 (September): 261–91.

———. 1986. "Education for Francization: The Case of New France in the Seventeenth Century." In *Indian Education in Canada,* vol 1., *The Legacy,* ed. Jean Barman, Y. M. Hebert, and D. McCaskill. Vancouver: University of British Columbia Press. 45–63.

Locke, John. 1988 [1698]. *Two Treatises of Government.* Ed. Peter Laslett. Cambridge: Cambridge University Press.

Sproat, Gilbert. 1868. *Scenes and Studies of Savage Life.* London: Smith, Elder.

Vallery, H. J. 1942. "A History of Indian Education in Canada." Unpublished M.A. thesis, Queen's University, Kingston, Ontario.

Clearcut Identities

Tracking Shape-shifters in Clayoquot Sound

Gary C. Shaw

Clayoquot provides access to many of the dynamics—historical, cultural, epistemological, symbolic—of global transformation. As Umeek suggests, these dynamics—the "shape-shifting" that he identifies with the Transformer—have been profoundly affected by the practices of colonialism. This is nowhere more apparent than in the domain of science.

From the days of John Locke and Gilbert Sproat onward, science has represented Native people in particularly misleading ways. It has also represented places like Clayoquot in ways that may be equally misleading. As I shall argue (following on from Ashis Nandy, Donna Haraway, and others), the dominant forms of science are centrist (in the ways that R. Michael M'Gonigle describes in his essay in this volume), patriarchal, racist, and quite simply "domineering." These forms of science have, of course, been disputed, partly on scientific grounds. Clayoquot has been the site of some especially significant challenges, as well as some equally significant efforts to contain those challenges. Local environmentalists have developed their own scientific assessments of the effects of logging, aquaculture, whale watching, and other activities, and these assessments have been used to dispute the scientific claims of government and industry. Some of the environmentalists' studies put standard scientific methodology into question. In general, they dispute the possibility of assessing local environments within analytic frameworks that represent the world in standardized terms. To the extent that "local knowledge" has been used to develop alternative environmental assessments, the so-called traditional ecological knowledge (TEK) of the Nuu-chah-nulth has been especially important, politically and otherwise.

What I want to explore in this essay is a series of "shape-shifts" that are related to one another in complicated ways. In the first place, there has been a shift from the logging road and other sites of overt public dispute to private venues, where a scientifically informed consensus is supposed to emerge and to control conflict. Second, there has been a shift from a form of science that puts local or traditional knowledge aside, to one that formally honors such knowledge while nevertheless setting it within a standardized analytic frame and hierarchical relations of scientific practice. And, third, there has been a shift from a conception of Clayoquot as a place to be governed from a distance, to one that is to be organized through various forms of local participation. Whether colonialism or colonialist science has been displaced in these shapeshifts is doubtful.

Let me illustrate this with an anecdote that relates to my own experience with the now-defunct Clayoquot Biosphere Project (CBP), a small nonprofit organization that initiated locally managed scientific studies in Clayoquot Sound in the early 1990s. The lead scientist in the CBP was Dr. James Darling, an internationally recognized authority on whales. Darling lives in Tofino, and is not affiliated with a university. He runs his own whale-research center, and he has been fairly prominent in the local community as a critic of industrial forestry, aquaculture, and other activities that may have adverse environmental effects. In 1995, Darling learned that the Centre for Applied Conservation Biology at the University of British Columbia (UBC), led by Dr. Fred Bunnell (then cochair of the Scientific Panel for Sustainable Forest Practices) had secured sizable commitments from the newly created, locally based (federally financed), Long Beach Model Forest Society to fund the ecological inventories mandated by the Scientific Panel Report.

The Scientific Panel's mandate had been to develop standards for sustainable forestry; the government hoped that these would be acceptable all round: to the environmentalists, the Nuu-chah-nulth, the forest workers, local businesses, and the companies with logging interests in the region. To most people's surprise, the government of British Columbia had accepted all of the Panel's recommendations. The new procedures for approving logging operations theoretically gave the Nuu-chah-nulth coequal authority with the province for resource management, instituting a form of scientific assessment that would include local knowledge (and in particular Nuu-chah-nulth knowledge) in resource planning. Darling thought that the Clayoquot Biosphere Project could play an important part in the community-based inventorying and monitoring that the Panel identified as essential for sustainable forestry. Of course, this capacity required an appropriate share of the resources the government was providing for this purpose. Darling called

Ken Matthews, the Ministry of Forests official responsible for implementing the Scientific Panel's recommendations, and put his case to Matthews. He also used his contacts with local politicians, including the recently created Central Region Board, to raise questions about the wisdom and propriety of using outside organizations (such as Bunnell's Centre at UBC) to do scientific work that could be done through local bodies, such as the CBP.

Bunnell, having learned of Darling's intervention, sent an E-mail to Matthews on October 16, 1995. He began by saying that Darling's intrusion into the Scientific Panel processes in Clayoquot Sound could be a "very large step backwards." In fact, the specter was so frightening that it required an immediate, coordinated response. "It seems to me that somehow we have to create something like the God squad or Gang of four to streamline this . . . and show something happening at the community." He suggested creating a steering committee, "1 NCN [Nuu-chah-nulth], 1 CRB [Central Region Board], 1 ex-Panel [Scientific Panel], 1 NGO, 1 Union—gang of four, five . . . ?" Matthews would be there, but ex officio. "These guys take the heat for how the structure shapes up; others get on with the structure. Has to happen quickly. Daring approach because of who it leaves out, but would make an important statement. Some dollars [required] asap to charge someone with building a community approach." He ends by saying that "unless something like this happens, it is going to get tougher and tougher for government or anyone else to move" (Bunnell 1995).

Like Sproat, Bunnell wanted to move things along in a certain direction. Apparently, this direction did not include science of the type that Darling represented, science that was managed by local institutions rather than by distant universities. Bunnell's E-mail is a containment initiative: "we," the center, must maneuver the local community; "we" must do this or risk losing control. Bunnell is overtly soliciting the participation of the government in this conspiracy.

Perhaps he need not have worried. Within a year, UBC had received a $9.5 million endowment from the government for its Faculty of Forestry. UBC itself enriched the endowment with another $4 million from the President's Opportunity Fund (CD VI/16, v.2, 283). Bunnell received an endowed chair. Meanwhile, the Clayoquot Biosphere Project, which had never had funding of more than about two hundred thousand dollars a year, was gradually starved out of existence. Forest Renewal B.C., the government agency responsible for funding all research and monitoring initiatives in Clayoquot Sound, refused to fund any proposals from the Clayoquot Biosphere Project, even though several of these proposals were cosponsored by prominent researchers from prestigious universities in Canada.

In taking literally the text of the Scientific Panel, including its commitments to equality of methodologies and enfranchisement of the periphery in management decisions, Darling had inadvertently triggered the subtext of the Panel's report. Regardless of the rhetoric about alternative forms of science, community participation in scientific assessments, and a commitment to sustainable forestry, people in the central institutions (including the institutions of science) intended to maintain control over the way things were done. That impulse has been apparent in all the shape-shifts at Clayoquot, as I shall attempt to show. I do not want to suggest that recent developments at Clayoquot have been devoid of local benefit, but I do want to draw attention to the ways in which the changing of "cloaks" can conceal continuities in colonial relations.

From the Logging Road to the Ivory Tower

When the government of British Columbia created its "Clayoquot Compromise" in April 1993, it created the stimulus for a summer of blockades and arrests, and the impetus for an aggressive international campaign to repudiate the BC forestry industry. After a prolonged, expensive, and futile public-relations campaign to defend this "compromise," the government adopted a different strategy—the resolution of conflicting claims about logging by "knowledge" rather than by "politics." In first creating the Scientific Panel and later—in June 1995—adopting all of the recommendations in its report, the government changed the venue and the players in the Clayoquot confrontation (Scientific Panel for Sustainable Forestry Practices Standards in Clayoquot Sound [hereafter, Scientific Panel] 1995c).

The report is premised upon the integration of two epistemologies (science and traditional knowledge), an integration promoted as the foundation for developing logging practices that will not compromise ecosystem integrity. And the report contains a pluralist strategy of inclusion for ending the "War in the Woods." Of course, there is nothing new about a report or claim for "environmentally sensitive" resource extraction. What makes the report compelling is that it presumes to create an innovative authority to resolve environmental disputes, an authority that embraces the knowledge claims of both science and traditional ecological knowledge (TEK). The Scientific Panel included both highly regarded scientists and respected First Nations elders and scholars. Its sponsors and supporters hoped that the combined authorities of science and First Nations could end the shouting matches between proponents and critics of industrial forestry.

Government methodology for accomplishing this goal was "to put the task in the hands of an impartial panel of experts," Premier Mike Harcourt explained when the Scientific Panel was introduced in October 1993. "Through the work of this panel, British Columbians can be assured of the most current and effective forest standards for Clayoquot Sound" (CD III/C/14, v.1, 265). Creation of the Scientific Panel shifted the Clayoquot conflict from the tumultuous arena of social democracy, which the center no longer controlled, to the dispassionate, calming environs of the ivory tower, now culturally modified by a First Nations presence. The social-democratic question of what should happen in Clayoquot Sound became superseded by the technical question of what, scientifically, *could* happen in Clayoquot.

Premier Harcourt was in desperate straits when he created the "impartial panel of experts" to resolve the Clayoquot controversy. The previous, high-profile failures—the Task Force on Sustainable Development (1990–91) and the Clayoquot Sound Sustainable Development Strategy Steering Committee (1991–93)—were processes centrally created to negotiate a stakeholder consensus from self-interested positions. Harcourt's Clayoquot Sound Land Use Decision (the April 1993 "Clayoquot Compromise") was conjured from the ruins of the failed Steering Committee. Environmentalists were outraged by the Land Use Decision, believing that it was a betrayal of the consensus process created by the government.[1] This decision, together with the BC government's economic investment in MacMillan Bloedel shortly before the "compromise" was announced,[2] convinced environmentalists and their supporters that the government of British Columbia was simply another self-interested stakeholder in the conflict.

The crisis of political legitimacy which resulted from this investment and land-use decision forced Harcourt to create an impartial mediator; the bold and innovative method he developed was responsive to First Nations' demands, for Harcourt now was conducting a war on two fronts. His strategies for fighting the War in the Woods against environmentalists had become complicated by a First Nations threat to seek an injunction to halt all logging in Clayoquot Sound, pending the outcome of the newly inaugurated treaty processes (CD III/C/11, v.1, 253). It was this threat that forced the government to negotiate the Interim Measures Agreement in March 1994, with the Nuu-chah-nulth Central Region Tribes. This agreement, which created the Central Region Board, gave the Central Region Tribes "joint management of resource and land use in Clayoquot Sound until the completion of treaty negotiations" (CD IV/3, v.2, 25). The Scientific Panel report became its governing methodology with regard to forest planning and logging.

At the conclusion of these political maneuverings, confused and confusing as they were, was a new process and a new vision. On the Scientific

Panel, First Nations were integrated with equal status, epistemological as well as symbolic, into a significant, high-profile research and policy-recommending process. When the government endorsed all the Panel's recommendations, First Nations representatives, who comprise half of the members of the Clayoquot Sound Central Region Board, were given shared management responsibility for resource decisions in Clayoquot Sound. First Nations knowledge, values, and community health were officially on the table in the Clayoquot political arena as legitimate decision-making criteria. It appeared that Clayoquot contradictions would be resolved by the complete enfranchisement of First Nations. This was an outcome nobody could have predicted.

Playing the Science Card in the Colonial Shell Game

Government decision makers clearly were seeking political legitimacy in adopting the Interim Measures Agreement and the Scientific Panel report. But the price of bringing peace to Victoria was the recontextualization of political dynamics in Clayoquot Sound. The knowledge, power, identity, epistemology, hierarchy, and values of colonists, the invaders of the New World, and the peoples who were here when they arrived, the First Nations, all were problematized—this by placing in the same space (the Central Region Board), with equal authority, colonial decision makers, steeped in scientific epistemology, and First Nations decision makers, with their traditional ecological knowledge. This space is the site of our investigation, which will consider what kinds of knowledges and practices are emerging as this science/TEK hybrid is interpreted, discussed, and employed in planning processes.

Our inquiry initially will focus on three attributes of colonialism. First, we will consider the dynamics of science and colonialism; second, the relation of "self" to "Other" in scientific epistemology and liberal human relations and institutions; and, third, the positioning of First Nations peoples in processes associated with liberalism and colonization. These considerations will help us unpack the context for the Scientific Panel, thus revealing its potentialities and limitations.

The dynamism of modernity emerged from a traditional, conservative culture that, the discourse of modernity explains, was dogmatic, authoritarian, orderly, and unchanging. In a word, human behavior was "contained." Science was instrumental in the "freeings"—of peoples, resources, technology, energy, and military power—that made colonization possible. This has been true from the voyages of Columbus to the subsequent conquests of the Americas, Africa, and Asia and to contemporary resource and monetary flows.

The ideology of modernity, which began in Europe and now is global, is the secular worldview underpinning capitalist economic and social transformations; it received its intellectual impetus, its epistemology, its moral authority, and its compelling utopian vision—growth without limits—from science. Knowledge is limitless; there are no boundaries to human knowledge and, thus, to human potential. And there are no limits to economic growth. Ashis Nandy, a Fellow at the Centre for the Study of Developing Societies in Delhi, believes that this lack of a sense of limits pervades all the processes of late modernity (Nandy 1995–96, 23).

In the historical transformations accompanying colonialism, the scientist initially was revolutionary and critic, struggling against all the stultifying rigidity of traditional, agricultural societies. Galileo and Descartes are heroes of modernity. But the scientist was also a source of power; scientists were responsible for the innovations and technologies employed by ambitious monarchs and capitalists alike, as they "liberated" humans and resources from community and religious control by destroying the bonds of traditional societies, including their relationships with nature.

We can see this scientist, here participant in historical processes, as containing two modern identities: first, scientist as rebel, the neutral skeptic laboring in a hostile world of superstition, mysticism, and prejudice, confident in scientific methodology and committed to progress and the transforming power of knowledge; second, scientist as participant in and beneficiary of the material, intellectual, and cultural conquests that progress entails. Thus the scientist is a key player in both "liberating" processes. But, Nandy argues, as a social institution science has developed an essentially conservative social power, quite apart from the identity of any individual scientist:

> The earlier creativity of modern science, which came from the role of science as a mode of dissent and a means of demystification, was actually a negative force. It paradoxically depended upon the philosophical pull and the political power of traditions. Once this power collapsed due to the onslaught of modern science itself, modern science was bound to become . . . a new orthodoxy. . . . The moral that emerges is that modern science can no longer be an ally *against* authoritarianism. Today it has an in-built tendency to be an ally *of* authoritarianism. We must now look elsewhere in the society to find support for democratic values. (Nandy 1987, 110)

Distinguishing the persona of the individual scientist from science as a social institution is essential for our analysis. Scientists on the Panel were selected because of their individual expertise; their disciplinary contributions were woven, together with First Nations contributions, into the analysis and recommendations of the report. What the report will come to mean, however, is far more complex than the details of its creation. This meaning will involve negotiations on several levels, from the periphery to the center (the liberal state) to the dynamics of global economics.

In this political context, Nandy argues that science has become a new orthodoxy, allied with the liberal, authoritarian state. That these concepts— "liberal" and "authoritarian"—should coalesce in the same descriptive phrase is puzzling in itself, for they seem contradictory. But these are the contradictions we must sort out; which is to say, we must remember the forces and ideas that brought us to the Clayoquot Summer of 1993. Science is complicit in these forces and ideas. As such, its capacity to play a liberating role, as in liberating society from the dynamics that led to the Clayoquot impasse, by employing its putative neutrality, is problematic. "We have granted science the role of a fetish, an object human beings make only to forget their role in creating it, no longer responsive to the dialectical interplay of human beings with the surrounding world in the satisfaction of human needs" (Haraway 1991, 8).

A second aspect of colonialism, of particular importance to science politics in Clayoquot Sound, is the presumed relationship between self and Other in the foundation of scientific epistemology. This epistemology assumes that there is a self, and that the self is separate from all other selves. Moreover, it assumes that in a human, this self resides in the mind, and that the mind (civilization) is separate from and should rule the body (nature). These two separations—that of subject from object and that of mind from body—are what make the scientific gaze, objectivity, possible.

Knowledge is the coinage of science, and it is created when the potentially knowing side, the subject side in this dualist relationship, acquires knowledge/mastery over the Other, the object of one's gaze and manipulation. The gaze and the manipulation are one. There is hierarchy here as well; to know is to acquire status, power, and control. To be the object of knowing is to be passive, incomplete, and weak. Nandy believes these relationships to be at the heart of science: "I do not think it an overstatement to say that the culture of normal science, as we know it, will collapse if it gives up the division between the observer and the observed or the hierarchy between the scientists and the laity" (Nandy 1987, 117).

Western science also breaks down complex organisms and relationships to their simplest forms. This provides scientists with understanding sufficient for reconfiguring the elements in a mechanical way, so as to "improve" their functioning. Implicit in this analysis and subsequent control is progress: the objective world increasingly becomes subject to scientific improvement, to scientific domination:

> The degree to which the principle of domination is deeply embedded in our natural sciences, especially in those disciplines that seek to explain social groups and behaviour, must not be underestimated. In evading the importance of dominance as a part of the theory and practice of contemporary sciences, we bypass the crucial and difficult examination on the *content* as well as the social function of science. (Haraway 1991, 8)

Two important characteristics of science as practiced in the Clayoquot context flow from these relationships between subject and object. First, like other management relations in modernity, science activity tends to be hierarchically organized and vertically compartmentalized. Managers are distinct from workers and authority is centralized, flowing from the top down. The environment is reduced to conceptually discrete components that are managed separately. Second, science is based mostly on synchronic data; these are time-specific data collections over a large geographical area (Johnson 1992, 8).

Scientific research currently under way in Clayoquot Sound is consistent with these attributes. For the most part it is organized by scientists in the center; the scientists who do come here conduct their fieldwork in moments convenient for them to capture discrete bits of information. Organic processes and functionings are difficult to understand in these superficial encounters: interactions between the scientist and nature are brief and choreographed. "Science" happens not in nature but in the laboratory, in creating the research design, and in the subsequent manipulation of data. For the scientist, nature is raw material, as it is for the capitalist.

As we proceed to the third attribute of colonization, the positioning of First Nations, we must keep in mind the previous two: the context within which science attained its social power, and the relationship between subject and object inherent in scientific epistemology. These play compelling roles in colonial–First Nations relations.

Nandy identifies three legacies of Europe's encounter with "Indians" (First Nations) in the Americas. The first is to replace traditional modes of thinking and behaving with European modes. In Clayoquot Sound, one form of this was the residential school, where two or sometimes three generations

of Native children were taken from their homes and placed in boarding
schools run by churches. The intent was overt; Native children "had to be
engineered to produce institutions and personalities that would be familiar
to Europe and thus predictable and controllable" (Nandy, Davies, and Sardar 1993, 83). The content of this was described in a BC report as follows:
"The education philosophy was based on a three-pronged approach involving a justification for removing children from their parents in order to
be 'civilized', for 'resocializing' the children 'to kill the Indian in the child'
and for preparing them to fit into the non-aboriginal world. . . . Ottawa's
program for assimilation also required the destruction of aboriginal languages and culture" (Matas 1997).

Nandy attributes deeply rooted European anxieties about nature,
childhood, and the feminine as the stimulus for this cultural genocide:

> In the process colonialism reactivated the fear of liminality which
> women and children invoked in the European culture by being
> at the margin between human beings and nature. Previously this
> fear had accompanied some fear of the power of nature and of the
> sacredness and magicality associated with nature. These set limits
> on objectification. Under colonialism, as under industrialism, the
> secular, modern worldview removed these limits. There was now
> fear of being feminine but no fear of the feminine and certainly no
> fear of falling foul of the feminine principle in the cosmos. (Nandy
> 1987, 143)

It is important to recognize that all Others in patriarchal European thinking[3] were assigned similar identities and attributes: they were sensual, unpredictable, childlike, powerless, available—in need of remediation, education, and discipline. The Other is naturally very disruptive. The Other was
close to, or was, nature; the Other constitutes the border, the wild.

The psychology of this construction of Otherness is transparent, but
as a device for manipulating identity for political and physical domination
its coherence (all Others are essentially the same), its simple construction
(the logic and the metaphors), and its self-reference (the Other is what I fear
in myself) make it compelling, readily available, and malleable. Of course,
the consequences of manipulating identities to facilitate control flow both
ways, distorting both parties. The fears and anxieties toward the Other, both
within and without, are real; the resulting judgments of normal and abnormal become mirrors, and the "knowing" distorts not only the object (Other)
but also the subject (self) (Memmi 1967; Nandy 1983).

The second European legacy was that First Nations peoples were denied existence in their own historical space and time. Europeans identified themselves as the present and the future; Natives were the past. By extension, Europe's past was represented as the present for the indigenous community; that is, indigenous communities were living the childhood of Europe. By this logic, First Nations peoples were positioned as children and, like children, rendered incapable of participating in the management of their lives and resources—that is, not until they became rational and mature: European. First Nations were encouraged to see their future in the lives of their conquerors, not in their own past or present. In the present, like children, they were perceived as wards of the state. Their lands were reduced to one-half of 1 percent of their original territories; their traditional forms of livelihood were despoiled by overharvesting of resources to benefit the larger, colonial community. Simultaneously, First Nations economic relationships, including *potlatch* and *ha hoolthe* (private ownership), were outlawed or rendered impossible.

Finally, colonization gradually closed down avenues of dissent. To demur from the imperatives of rationality and progress is to reveal oneself as uncontrollable, disorganized, and childish. The crushing logic of scientific rationality, allied with the free-market economy, provides only one outcome: annihilation for any culture that organizes itself otherwise, particularly those that define themselves by organic relations with nature. Modern colonial practices contain a war on nature, including human nature; this is a price of modernity, "progress" is the reward. It is very difficult for First Nations to dissent from this logic because all their attempts to engage the colonialists are mediated by the prevailing discourse:

> The real achievement of the blinded gaze of *oculus mundi* is that
> even today all negotiation with Western civilization must be car-
> ried out through the West's convention. To secure amendment or
> concession, real people have to act either as if they were the Other
> invented by Europe or as if they have become part of the West. So
> seemingly complete is this triumph that today the Other too nego-
> tiates with its real self through the conventions of Western civiliza-
> tion. (Nandy, Davies, and Sardar 1993, 90)

Moreover, while participating in this discourse, First Nations not only have to talk the talk as colonized subjects, within colonial relations, they also must walk the walk; that is, they must wear the "First Nations" identity created for them in colonialism. However, colonists have shape-shifted out of their complicity in this relationship. Colonists get to be citizens—stakeholders, scientists, corporate executives, environmentalists, loggers, bureaucrats. "First Nations" is a colonial identity; it is a relationship with those who came later, and who stole the inheritance of those who were "first." But in these discourses the theft vanishes; the thief shape-shifts from colonizer to citizen. This is a drama in which the identity of half the cast is mystified continually, while the other half is contained within an identity and associated relationships that constrain it, but that it must embrace in order to achieve a seat at the table. Some have shape-shifted out of this foundational relationship, but others must remain within it.

After examining the complexity, rigidity, and mystification of colonial relations, it appears that First Nations participation and knowledge in Clayoquot planning processes will be problematic, particularly if one focuses on power and equality conventionally defined. But if one looks beyond these definitions it is clear that the relationships extant prior to the Clayoquot Summer and the enfranchisement of First Nations have been severely undermined, and that the political and economic agenda for Clayoquot Sound has become very ambiguous. Symbolically, First Nations have won significant victories, and these resonate throughout planning processes and public discussions. So, while formally discourses and practices of colonialism remain, their content is being subverted.

These local evolutions are complemented with emerging discourses that provide sites for resistance to the dominant discourse and relations. Feminist scholars, along with others, have contributed significantly to demystifying science and the arbitrary power undergirding colonialism and gender relations; these critical investigations challenge orthodoxy. Within science the ecology movement is integrating knowledges and cosmologies of traditional societies with Western scientific understanding:

> Over the past 20 years, the fundamental tenets of Western science—rational analytical thinking, objectivity, reductionism and the Judeo-Christian ethic of human domination over nature—have been challenged for being ethnocentric, antiecological, and ignorant of the cultural dimension of technological development. As a result, Western science is becoming increasingly interdisciplinary in response to today's globally interconnected world, in which biological, psychological, and social phenomena are recognized as belonging to interdependent systems. (Johnson 1992, 9)

The Scientific Panel report reveals that the Panel was informed by and responsive to these perspectives. But how responsive to these new sensibilities are elected officials, government bureaucrats, and stakeholders? Are these people willing to engage the multicultural epistemology and economic principles contained in the report? Or will they simply reiterate the old discourse in new planning frameworks and sound bites? These questions will be discussed as we investigate the conceptual and political maneuverings around the "marriage" envisioned by the Scientific Panel.

The Bride: Traditional Ecological Knowledge (TEK)

Creation of the Scientific Panel was an event in the evolution of colonial relations; "marriage" is a useful metaphor to use in discussing this event. We chose to identify TEK as the "bride" in this marriage because, as noted earlier, traditional peoples were feminized in colonial discourse; like women, they supposedly are controlled by, grounded in, nature and their natural instincts. Traditional knowledge is perceived as intuitive, soft, spiritual, unpredictable, parochial—feminine. But how is traditional knowledge understood by those who live it?

First Nations' Perspectives relating to Forest Practices Standards in Clayoquot Sound (Scientific Panel 1995a) contains the Nuu-chah-nulth concepts and philosophies relevant to the work of the Scientific Panel. Nuu-chah-nulth Panel members write that their beliefs are governed by three principles. The first is a commitment to what might be called the politics of inclusion. One of the first tasks confronting the Scientific Panel was that of creating a protocol within which members would conduct their deliberations. This was contributed by the Nuu-chah-nulth:

> The protocol is characterized by a demonstrable and inclusive re-
> spect for one another, for different values, and for data founded
> both in science and traditional knowledge. It calls for each Panel
> member to exercise patience, flexibility, tolerance, endurance, and
> faith in a process and task that are surrounded by conflict and tur-
> moil. (Ibid., 5)

The second principle of the Nuu-chah-nulth is sacredness and respect for all things. The Nuu-chah-nulth phrase for this is "hishuk ish ts' awalk" (everything is one). Panel member Roy Haiyupis explains this respect:

> Nothing is isolated from other aspects of life surrounding it and
> within it. This concept is the basis for the respect for nature that
> our people live with, and also contributed to the value system that
> promoted the need to be thrifty, not to be wasteful, and to be total-
> ly conscious of your actual needs in the search for foods. The idea
> and practices of over-exploitation are deplorable to our people.
> The practice is outside our realm of values. (Ibid., 6)

Respect is the core of Nuu-chah-nulth traditions, culture, and existence. It is embodied in the concept of stewardship, which contains economic, ecological, and spiritual dimensions. Nuu-chah-nulth elders are very critical of industrial forestry and industrial fisheries because neither has assumed a stewardship or spiritual responsibility for the land and resources that were taken from First Nations and given to them.

The third principle of the Nuu-chah-nulth is *ha hoolthe* (private ownership), which is their system of ownership, control, and resource use. The whole of their territory was delineated according to land and sea use sites. The sites were owned by chiefs, and their ownership was known to all members, being formally recounted and reinforced in oral presentations during feasts and other cultural gatherings:

> *Ha hoolthe* . . . indicates . . . that the hereditary chiefs have the responsibility to take care of the forests, the land and the sea within his *ha hoolthe* and a responsibility to take care of his *mus chum* or tribal members. . . . Embedded within the *ha hoolthe* initiated from his (the chief's) rights to, and ownership of tribal territories, lies the key to the social and cultural practices, tribal membership and property ownership, economical, environmental and resources controls to promote effective enhancement levels to sustain life for the tribe today and for generations to come. (Ibid., 9)

The first four principles adopted by the Scientific Panel incorporate Nuu-chah-nulth philosophy: the world is interconnected at all levels; human activities must respect all life; long-term ecological and economic sustainability are essential to long-term harmony; the cultural, spiritual, social, and economic well-being of indigenous people is a necessary part of that harmony (ibid., 3, 6). Of course, these principles and perspectives are not unique to the Nuu-chah-nulth, as the following description of traditional ecological knowledge reveals:

- TEK is recorded and transmitted through oral cultures.
- TEK is learned through observation and hands-on experience.
- TEK is based on the understanding that the four elements (earth, air, water, and fire) have a life force.
- TEK does not view human life as superior to other animate or inanimate elements; all life-forms are interdependent.
- TEK is holistic.
- TEK is intuitive in its mode of thinking; intuitive thought emphasizes emotional involvement and subjective certainty of understanding.

- TEK is mainly qualitative; detailed qualitative knowledge is gained through intimate knowledge of the resource.
- TEK is based on data generated by resource users; as such it is inclusive.
- TEK is based on diachronic data (long-time series of information in one locality).
- TEK is rooted in a social context that sees the world in terms of social and spiritual (stewardship) relations between all life-forms. (Johnson 1992, 7–8)

At the conceptual level, it seems that TEK and science are mirror opposites of each other. Indeed, Johnson contrasts the scientific posture for each of the items in this list and the two seem not only fundamentally different but irreconcilable. However, one also could argue that TEK occupies precisely those spaces—meanings and relationships—abandoned by science and capitalism. This perspective, which pervades the report of the Scientific Panel, provides a new set of possibilities. We must unravel more of the fabric of Clayoquot to observe the interplay of these alternatives. In doing so, we immediately encounter another thread—gender.

Father Science and Mother TEK

Science, in theory and in practice, is essentially masculine; so is colonization and so are the institutions of modernity, including the liberal state. The epistemological assumptions and cognitive practices undergirding all these processes have gender connotations. These are the conclusions of a significant body of literature (Haraway 1991; Mies 1987; MacKinnon 1989; Williams 1991; Takaki 1979; Memmi 1967; Harding 1986; Nandy 1983, 1987; Nandy, Davies, and Sardar 1993). This is not to argue that the behaviors associated with science, colonialism, and modernity are genetically mandated—that men behave as they do because of genetic programming. Rather, these are forms of social behavior, and within modern historical processes this is what the gender "male" has come to mean, in theory and in practice.

Nandy believes these behaviors might be contrary to nature, but compelling nonetheless:

> We choose sudden options for ourselves, which seem to go against basic human nature; and yet we pursue that alternative because we have come to believe that it will lead us to a new secular utopia, give us secular salvation, and the very fact that one is flouting the tenets of nature means that certain kinds of psychological processes are released within one's personalities. (1995–96, 54).

In the dramatic and stress-filled transforming processes in colonization, behaviors that were privileged in social relations may be marginalized, and behaviors that were at the margins may become empowered. Societies, like individuals, contain a range of potential behaviors; which of these is dominant at any moment may have less to do with human nature and more to do with the human context. When colonization upsets and redefines social relations, it also upsets and redefines individual moral and cognitive choices (Nandy 1983, 1987; Nandy, Davies, and Sardar 1993; Memmi, 1967).

Modern colonizing processes included subordination of European women as well as non-European indigenous peoples. Takaki (1979) argues that the first colonial movement occurred within the colonist, when the mind was privileged over and assumed management responsibility for the body; his metaphor for this is an "iron cage." The resulting war, the cognitive dissonance, between reason and desire in oneself extended to one's immediate family, then into the social arena, and finally into foreign lands. There the strange inhabitants had projected onto them attributes of Otherness from Greek, Christian, and pagan mythologies. Thus, what was marginalized in European anxieties and fears was identified as the heart of the Other (Nandy, Davies, and Sardar 1993). The attributes of Otherness that the colonized received were projected onto European women as well:

> I think the real decline in woman's power in English society more or less coincided with the full-blown theories of the colonized subjects being effeminate. I'm not only speaking about the historical correlation: I'm speaking of psychological colonization to that build-up of the entire edifice of effeminacy and masculinity that forced entire cultures into that framework. It is a formidable exercise: you have to do something to yourself, something to the women in your society: you have to begin to look at them differently. There also you pay the cost. I'm referring to that particular psychological process which has a reflection of course in the cognitive map which comes to arrange societies and communities in a certain point of time. But behind the cognitive map lie certain very deep emotional issues which you arrange in certain ways: you have to reconfigure your innocence in certain ways to arrive at that cognitive map. (Nandy 1995–96, 55)

The social dimensions of colonialism in Clayoquot Sound include gender. This was revealed during the environmental campaign. On the one side was the Ministry of Forests, the International Woodworkers of America, MacMillan Bloedel, Share B.C., the provincial government. Mostly guys. On the other side were the environmentalists. Although many important leaders and participants in the Clayoquot controversy were male, most of the leading environmental voices in the controversy since 1992 have been fe- male: Valerie Langer, Friends of Clayoquot Sound; Tzeporah Berman, Green- peace; Karen Mahon, Greenpeace; Adriane Carr, Western Canada Wilder- ness Committee;[4] Vicki Husband, Sierra Club of Western Canada. These were the people who defined the issues, addressed the media, and negoti- ated with government, labor, and management.

On the logging side, talk was about jobs, forest families, forest commu- nities; it was about science, industry, the Forest Practices Code. It was about continuing the resource relationship that made British Columbia prosper. It was about guys, and the things guys do. These evoked powerful, masculine images. Human, to be sure, willing to admit shortcomings; not afraid to show anger, pain, fear, hurt feelings. The world of logging clearly was mas- culine: men's jobs, men's families, men's pride, men's way of doing things.

And the women? They organized the "Ecofeminist Peace Camp." The Clayoquot Summer became an ecofeminist event; the protests and the camp were organized according to nonviolent principles—open meetings, con- sensus decision making, respect for all opinions and people, accountabili- ty, egalitarian relations, the rejection of all forms of violence—buttressed by conscious gender politics. Although men participated in the protests, composing most of the staff in the camp kitchen, for example, women con- trolled the campaign, represented the campaign in the media, organized the blockades, and were most often arrested:

> Definitions of eco-feminism differ among the dozens of people
> who have drifted here. . . . But they all agree on the basic philoso-
> phy: it is male-dominated, patriarchal society that has brought the
> planet to the brink of environmental disaster, and it is women who
> will lead the way to a better world. (CD III/C/3)

Ecofeminists were quick to define the controversy in gender terms, arguing that the cognitive styles and behaviors present in modernity have strong gender connotations. The War in the Woods is an extension of a gender war, the war of the fathers against the mothers. The media were reluctant to dis- cuss the conflict in these terms, however, as was the government-corporate- labor alliance.

But this does not mean that they were unaware of this construction. One revealing document to emerge during these controversies is an in- ternal memorandum, "The land use controversy: how did we get into this mess?" written by a woman, Nancy Scott, working in corporate communi- cations for MacMillan Bloedel (CD II/C/2). Summarizing the last century of industrialization, Scott writes that "typical values admired during this peri-od have been aggression, domination, vigorous action, decisiveness, mea-surable efficiency, individual achievement, acquisition of material goods. As a society we have acclaimed growth and progress as our goals." She sug-gests that men have been honored for what they achieved, not for how they achieved it. "Forestry can be characterized as representing the ultimate re-alization of the pro-development period."

Scott goes on to say that industry jargon is laden with terms such as *extraction, liquidation, exploitation,* and *denudation*; "we speak of a re-source, not a forest, of fibre, not trees." But times have changed; the old em-pires based on domination and colonization (Britain, the United States, China, Russia) have fallen. The new values fashionable in our societies are those of sustainability, conservation, nurturing, caring, slow or no growth, consensus, equal opportunity:

> If we can view the forest industry as being culturally at one far end
> of the patriarchal/masculine spectrum it may help explain why we
> are peculiarly ill-equipped to deal with an attack from the opposite
> far end of the matriarchal/feminine spectrum. . . . We stand ac-
> cused of 'raping and pillaging'. Our activities are described as
> 'skinning the earth alive' (a masculine hunting metaphor) result-
> ing in 'an environmental holocaust' (war is a classic masculine
> metaphor). Clearcutting and slashburning are viewed as acts of
> war against helpless Mother Earth. (CD II/C/2, v.1, 31)

Scott sees these conflicts of masculine versus feminine values as facing the BC forest industry daily. "We are losing the battle for people's minds be-cause we have trouble even recognizing the validity of their values." What to do? Shape-shift. Change the spin! Scott points out that there is a "bright side" to all of this; all the attributes and values MacMillan Bloedel needs to adopt to deal with these bad public relations are present in the discourse of the Other. The forest industry is perceived as masculine; it needs to add the feminine to its identity. As man it is incomplete; it needs a . . . what? woman? wife? partner? an ecofeminist perhaps? (CD II/C/2). In fact, when MacMillan Bloedel finally decided that the Clayoquot situation required a public-relations person, the job description specified a preference for fe-male applicants.[5]

Scott's memo was written on July 20, 1989; on August 4, 1989, the provincial government announced the creation of the Task Force on Sus-tainable Development. Included in the news release are words such as "community-based sustainable development," "environmental sensibility," "integrity of the environment," "social concerns," "aesthetics." The government clearly addressed many of the concerns raised by environmentalists, and by Scott, creating a consensus-based decision-making process to attempt resolution. But the imperative of industrial forestry was unchanged. When feminists, environmentalists, and First Nations entered the "consensus-based decision-making process," first of the Task Force and later of the Steering Committee, they were back in the logic of modernity. Environmentalists, including environmental representative Darling, soon walked out of the Steering Committee. The failure of these processes led to the Clayoquot Sound Land Use Decision, the Clayoquot Summer, the Scientific Panel, and the Interim Measures Agreement, which created the Central Region Board.

The Scientific Panel and the Interim Measures Agreement officially enfranchised First Nations and traditional knowledge. Women and the entire environmental community active in the controversy were left out of these processes.[6] What of the "feminine" values Scott referred to? What of consensus? nurturing? sharing? emotions? sustainable? status quo? preservation? These are presented by Scott as matriarchal/feminine values.

If we review TEK, we find these values present. This is not surprising because the identity of Native people and of women as Others is much the same. As Nandy notes, First Nations were "feminized" by colonial logic. Or rather, in this case their knowledge was feminized, shifted into a shape easily devalued.

With this recognition in mind, let's examine what happens in the dynamics of representation in formal settings when the feminized Other, now sitting at the table with equal status, is male. All of the First Nations representatives on the Central Region Chiefs (the First Nations governance body for the Clayoquot region) and the Central Region Board are male. All the chief councillors for the five Central Region Bands are male. In the drama of colonization, their roles are androgynous. How are they performing in the current act?

Application of Scientific Panel guidelines in Clayoquot Sound has almost stopped logging; the only locations where logging is occurring are previously logged watersheds whose productive life is nearly over. The fertile jewels of Clayoquot are six sizable, intact watersheds, some of which may be available for logging following inventory and planning processes required by the Panel. On the environmental front, drama in Clayoquot Sound currently revolves around the intact watersheds.

The metaphors environmentalists employ in describing these watersheds connote virginity: pristine, intact, helpless. The perfidious Land Use

Decision makes them available—for penetration, for ravaging, for plunder. These watersheds are the remaining "daughters" of Clayoquot Sound. Environmentalists are entirely unconvinced that the "constraints" of the Scientific Panel will "protect" them from Father.

Nor do they trust Father's new "wife," traditional knowledge, at least not so long as its only carriers are male. In some highly charged contexts, when the strategic positions of environmentalists and First Nations differed considerably, female environmentalists encountered all too familiar paternal behaviors. Environmental activists voiced two suspicions. First, are First Nations really protectors of Mother Earth? Are they really "female"? Second, are First Nations powerful enough to protect Mother Earth?

The environmental organizations that organized the Clayoquot Summer remain outside the formal processes, but the international campaign they mounted against MacMillan Bloedel and BC forest products gives them increasing leverage in negotiations. And this leverage put them in a quandary when it became clear that they likely could save some Clayoquot "daughters" if they were willing to negotiate the virginity of one or two of the others.

First Nations identities are experienced in a universe of meaning substantially different from that of nonaboriginal identities. Aboriginal people have lived in Clayoquot for thousands of years; there are no "pristine" or "virginal" watersheds as far as they are concerned. They have entered these watersheds, harvested from them, picked berries in them, lived in them. "Pristine" is an identity conjured up by environmentalists for their purposes. This is not to say that First Nations are any less concerned about the intentions of the white Father than are environmentalists. But, unlike the environmentalists, First Nations presumably have an equal status for negotiation; they are part of "the process." But in what role?

Ironically, it appears that their TEK responsibility, which is the knowledge that hopefully would liberate them from colonial identities, symbolically positions First Nations people back into those identities. First of all, TEK is identified with the elders, with knowledge from their past, of the past. A local First Nations chief councillor expresses frustration because when researchers come to his territory to seek out the TEK, as they now are required to do, they only want to speak with elders. Young men and women who are active in research and inventory in their own territory, now spending far more time in the woods than their elders, are identified *out* of TEK. Scientists, researchers, and bureaucrats cannot see them.

Second, First Nations peoples are sought out because they might have information that is essential for inventories; they are not sought out for their wisdom. Again, this is consistent with their colonial identity; they are people with sharp eyes for details—hunters and gatherers—but they do not possess reputable ecological knowledge. Information is sought, but not the cosmology that makes this information meaningful or important for First Nations. Ontology is European. "Information" and "knowledge" shape-shift *upon* First Nations; they do not get to choose the shape in which their wisdom is publicly presented.

Finally, the responsibilities that have been devolved to First Nations in planning processes essentially are domestic matters—spirituality, health, respect, the environment—but not knowledge, research, science. In these dimensions, First Nations are never trusted; specialists, consultants, and researchers from outside must verify First Nations' substantive knowledge claims.

The identities of the past are so important symbolically that they overpower the potentials in the present. People still are positioned in stereotypical roles. Rewards and instruments of power, including knowledge, remain closely guarded at the center. And there is little evidence to suggest that the center has any intention of relinquishing them. But people are talking, and they are meeting, and they are negotiating. What are they doing? Changing?

Science and Traditional Knowledge in the Planning Process

The articulation of positions in the Clayoquot controversy reveals a reluctance to recognize traditional knowledge as a cosmology, as an *economy*. Aside from the information that First Nations peoples have acquired from centuries of intimate relations with their environment is the larger question of how this information is used practically. Traditional knowledge is the knowledge a culture requires to live in the world, in a particular place, for generation after generation. It is a practical cosmology.

But not everybody sees it this way. In a heated discussion in Clayoquot Sound about the relationship between science and TEK it became clear that many scientists have quite different beliefs about TEK. For these scientists, TEK simply is bits of information, some of which might be useful, that intelligent people acquire as they go about living in the world. Indeed, all people who have lived in an environment for an extended period of time will possess some "traditional knowledge." What distinguishes the scientists who come to Clayoquot Sound from First Nations who live there is experience, that is all. And, the implication goes, the experiences of all intelligent people in the wilderness are pretty much the same (CD V/A/9, v.2, 162). Scientists, and indeed government bureaucrats, do not see TEK as a cosmology, a cosmology that includes an economy.

This understanding is revealed in the methodologies proposed by researchers in response to the requirement that they include TEK in their inventories. In their budgets is money to hire First Nations people to accompany them in their research and inventory projects, pointing out flora and fauna that researchers might otherwise miss. This, together with hiring First Nations elders to identify sacred sites or culturally modified trees or medicinal plants before logging begins—bits of information that loggers do not know or might overlook—pretty much sums up the way TEK has become an "equal" partner with science in Clayoquot Sound.

Another example of applied TEK occurred during a meeting (October 1997) of the Clayoquot Sound Planning Committee, the body that coordinates all logging in Clayoquot Sound. The body is composed of the Central Region Board plus four government representatives who are members of, and serve as staff for, the committee. These representatives compose the planning documents, thus controlling the agenda, and they control access to funding. No resources are provided for local participants in this process.

One of the government representatives introduced a model for watershed-level planning; under Scientific Panel guidelines, logging plans will focus on discrete watersheds and will include comprehensive inventories before logging can begin. The model began with the most simple information, valley contours with feeder streams, and then added layer after layer of pertinent information, including inventory and coordinating guidelines, in a series of planning stages. A First Nations member of the Central Region Board asked where the human communities fit into the model. The answer: at the very end of the process, to "Review and adjust plan to reflect local knowledge and local conditions." Shouldn't the planning process begin with community? the First Nations representative inquired. Isn't the goal of planning to produce healthy communities and ecosystems? For the First Nations representative, the issue contained an economic dimension.

The room was very quiet. Clearly, the government had not intended for the planning processes to be driven by community priorities, even though the Scientific Panel report provides space for them:

> In this report, frequent reference is made to ecosystem "health" and to ecosystem "integrity." These terms are meant to signify functioning, self-sustaining systems undergoing no systematic changes as the result of unnatural (i.e., human-induced) manipulation. These are not strictly scientific terms. They are . . . concepts which connect a scientific concept about the state or properties of a system with a social value about the normative or desired state. (Scientific Panel 1995c, 4)

This sounds like:

> Nothing is isolated from other aspects of life surrounding it and
> within it. This concept is the basis for the respect for nature that
> our [Native] people live with, and also contributed to the value sys-
> tem that promoted the need to be thrifty, not to be wasteful, and to
> be totally conscious of your actual needs in the search for foods.
> The idea and practices of over-exploitation are deplorable to our
> people. The practice is outside our realm of values. (Ibid., 1995a, 6)

Human communities are participants within these "self-sustaining systems." First Nations communities, Nuu-chah-nulth Scientific Panel members assert, recognize this and understand their relationship as being organic. This holistic relationship within an ecosystem, including all animate
and inanimate beings, is the "spirituality," the economy, if you will, of traditional knowledge. To split the economy of life from the relations of life,
to dichotomize relations in this way, is to rend the organic relationships
undergirding the traditional economy. Traditional knowledge requires one
to begin and end with the human community as an organic component of
the ecosystem. Does the Scientific Panel report also require this? Well, no:

> Managing forests (or any other aspect of the natural environment)
> entails the recognition and incorporation of human objectives for
> the system, even when a conscious attempt is made to ground
> management firmly in scientific principles. Used with care, bridg-
> ing concepts such as "ecosystem health" and "ecosystem integri-
> ty"... can enrich scientific thought with the values and judgments
> that make science a human endeavor. (Ibid., 1995c, 4)

Scientific thought and scientific management are to be enriched by their
marriage with traditional knowledge. Does this sound familiar? Although
"ecosystem health" and "ecosystem integrity" might indeed enrich science,
as the $13.5 million gift to the Faculty of Forestry at UBC reveals, the evi-
dence is fairly persuasive that the scientific establishment, when allied with
centrally driven economic institutions, willingly participates in impover-
ishing human communities within the ecosystem.

Silence in the room following the question of the First Nations representative is *the* silence of the Scientific Panel. Economics, by government
design, is entirely absent from the document. In fact, the government em-
braced the report without doing any "scientific" analysis about its economic
implications. And multi-national corporations went along. This is curious.

One can argue that the conflict in Clayoquot Sound is between two "spiritualities," two economies, that of liberalism—here conceptualized as the Father—and that of the Other. The spirituality, the economy, of liberalism requires no elaboration and no defense—not even a "scientific" analysis. Its ends are mystical, unlike its means.

Evidence of this is the "Clayoquot Sound Planning Committee Terms of Reference." This document, which organizes planning for all future logging in Clayoquot Sound, makes no reference to goals, values, or motive. Indeed, reading it gives no clue as to why it exists, why planning is being done, or what the ends of the process are. It is the epitome of rational decision making: action without purpose. Planning documents assert that "[n]o harvesting will occur in the undeveloped watersheds until comprehensive ecological assessments have been carried out and Watershed Plans are completed by the Planning Committee," but the documents entirely remove the human communities as organic participants in this ecology.

The documents also are inconsistent with the planning requirements—and in a very predictable way. In the report, the first objective of watershed-level planning is as follows: "to identify and describe the environmental resources [inventories]; natural processes [ecology]; and cultural, scenic and recreational values in the planning unit [local values]" (ibid., 167). The first objective, inventories, and the third, local values, are considered in the planning processes; the second, ecology, is conspicuously absent. Why is this? This is the knowledge and understanding that comes with time and with presence; it is traditional ecological knowledge. And it is locally sited.

But the planning process proposed by the Scientific Panel is a hierarchy:

> A consequence of this organization [of the report] is that planning—
> an activity that should embrace and precede all others—is ad-
> dressed near the end of the report. It has been assigned that posi-
> tion so that readers will appreciate the need for a new planning
> hierarchy in light of the significant changes that the Panel recom-
> mends. . . . A planning hierarchy wherein a higher-level committee
> coordinates any lower-level committees is essential to carry out
> the common planning goals defined in this report. (Ibid., 3, 187)

And what, exactly, are those "common planning goals"? Certainly, they cannot include ecosystem integrity; this is a means, not a goal—a means for sustainable development. But who is developing? And for what purpose? Why are we engaged in this at all? Shouldn't these questions be the foundation, the premise, that stimulates the sensitive planning processes of the Scientific Panel?

Volume 5 of the Scientific Panel really gives two incompatible answers. One can read this volume as providing a methodology for maximizing logging in a sustainable fashion, a process centrally driven to compete for profits in the global economy. For the center, ecology is conceptualized as a means. This is clear in the quotes above about TEK "enriching science," the epistemology of the liberal state. Ecosystem integrity is of economic value to the center, which has no other relationship with any specific, geographically removed ecosystem.

Alternatively, one can read volume 5 as a paradigm shift, as ushering in a postmodern, inclusive, community-based economy. Ecology in this place is lived; science and TEK combine to facilitate ecosystem integrity, including the integrity of human communities within the ecosystem. The community and the ecosystem share the same geography; the relationship is organic, not parasitic. This interpretation requires that economic priorities and relations be formally on the table, and that the ensuing conversation flow in many directions.

Which of these alternatives is selected is not a choice that the knowledge industry will make. The science establishment only answers the questions it is paid to answer—in case of the Scientific Panel, paid by the government. That question was how to log more effectively in Clayoquot Sound. Government did not ask whether logging should be terminated or whether another vision of economic development should have priority. That these questions are being posed with such determination by people in Clayoquot Sound, and amplified by people all around the world, reflects the crumbling consensus of modernity's goals, values, and processes. The center is no longer holding. What, now, is the role of science?

In discussing this loss of coherence in institutions of modernity, Clark Binkley, Dean of Forestry at the University of British Columbia, writes that "[w]ithout the bright beacon of science, forest management wanders in a fog of social constructions." But even with the "bright beacon of science" an ambiguity persists that science cannot resolve. "As a consequence, managers and policy makers must necessarily choose one social construction of nature in preference to another. Enforcing such a choice is inconsistent with the liberal notions underlying western democracies. This, I think is a central conundrum of contemporary resource management" (CD VI/ 16, v.2, 282). And, one wonders, which "social construction of nature" will "managers and policy makers . . . necessarily choose"? A few years ago an answer would have been readily available for this question, but not now. The clarity of modernist visions and institutions is disintegrating.

What is not a conundrum at the moment for central resource managers is who should control the knowledge necessary to manage resources—

and where the control should be located. Government and corporations continue to pour dollars into university forestry faculties for Scientific Panel research and inventories, and contracts are being awarded to private urban research companies for inventories in Clayoquot Sound. But no money is being provided to local communities, including First Nations communities, by government or corporations to create capacities for the local participation in management, a participation that the Scientific Panel describes as essential. And there is no money in the planning processes for community involvement. Thus, whereas the Scientific Panel report recognizes two possible futures for Clayoquot Sound, as did the discussion of the dynamics between science and TEK, the center continues to see only one.

Conclusion

The "center" has been a useful organizing metaphor for creating coherence among processes, actors, and ideologies in the Clayoquot controversies. As recently as the early 1980s, it made sense to speak of "the center," as the site for not only resolving resource issues, but also as the site of political legitimacy, of ideological and epistemological certainty. A review of media presentations and discussions about the first Clayoquot resistance, the Meares Island blockades of 1984, reveals a coherent discourse that marginalized, in every dimension, public resistance to provincially approved logging plans for Meares Island. Resistance to these plans, it was generally agreed, was both indefensible and futile. It also was unimaginable. Such was the level of certainty.

This kind of center is no longer imaginable. In every dimension— political, economic, social, ideological, and epistemological—the center appears to be under attack or crumbling, its authority dissipating. But, as our discussion reveals, centrist cohesion continues to resonate within people and processes. There is no longer an easily identifiable center of authority, but centralizing forms of authority continue to characterize the workings of politics, the structures and practices through which events at Clayoquot have been mediated.

Of course, the "center" always was diffuse; but our attention and allegiance, our metaphors (sovereignty, for example), required a centralized representation. However, Clayoquot politics has revealed that we are no longer willing to grant this exclusive legitimacy, this centralized representation. We have come to see this "center" with new eyes, to recognize it as particular, not universal, and this recognition has given us an illusion, an illusion of choice: this, then, and a bit of that and some of the other. But not that old discredited stuff. We will take the Scientific Panel report, and put an end to ecosystem degradation. No more clearcutting. Shape-shifters all.

This is not to denigrate shape-shifting, however. The energies that flowed into resisting centrist dynamics and institutions had remarkable political consequences. The "Clayoquot Summer," the Scientific Panel report, the Nuu-chah-nulth initiatives, the Interim Measures Agreement, the international campaign against BC forest products, the Central Region Board, the protocol agreement between Weyerhauser and environmental groups—these are significant activities and accomplishments. It is not at all clear what they will mean in the long term, but in their flowering they contained coherence and promise.

One generally hopes that, after an extensive examination of processes, players, and events, one has a sharper understanding of the "what is going on." That much has been going on in Clayoquot Sound is clear. Some things seem to have been resolved, if only temporarily. And perhaps that is the rub. We hope for some assurance of continuity, that the picture we have created about the processes in Clayoquot Sound not only is persuasive in detail, but also will remain so for some period of time. I fear not. Everything continually is subject to negotiation and areas of uncertainty are increasing. Even the clarity of the struggle between Bunnell and Darling, detailed at the outset of this essay, seems archaic now. The players and the stakes present in the "Clayoquot Summer" remain, but it has become difficult, if not impossible, to "see" them with any confidence. Multiple sites of engagement, complex, nuanced dynamics, shifting identities, and loss of coherence for authority undermine any static representation. Our challenge now is to recognize these "losses of coherence" as fields of opportunity, not for the reconstituting of centrist cohesion but for the creating and the "seeing" of new political relationships, forms, and strategies.

Notes

The author would like to acknowledge and thank Donna Haraway and Ross McMillan for their important contributions to this essay.

1. Environmentalists considered it a betrayal because the Steering Committee was created as a consensus process. Otherwise, environmentalists and representatives from Tofino would not have participated because the committee was heavily weighted in industry's favor. Harcourt described the Clayoquot Sound Land Use Decision as a solution acceptable to the majority of stakeholders at the table, implying that it had been arrived at through extensive negotiations. Thus, to create a favorable spin the government manipulated the consensus process into a majority process, revealing to environmentalists its political agenda and lack of integrity.

2. This investment, estimated at $50 million, made the government of British Columbia one of the largest shareholders in MacMillan Bloedel.

3. This included everybody identified with nature—literally, anybody who was not a European male sharing the beliefs and values of, initially, Christian and, later, scientific consciousness.

4. Carr is now leader of the BC Green Party.

5. The woman hired for this job was Linda Coady; she played an important role in all subsequent deliberations about forestry in British Columbia, first for MacMillan Bloedel and then for Weyerhauser.

6. In 1998, there was one woman on the Clayoquot Sound Central Region Board (which has twelve members), two on the Clayoquot Sound Planning Committee (which has sixteen members), and one on the subregional Planning Committees (which have twelve members).

Works Cited

Bunnell, Fred. 1995. "Research/Monitoring." E-mail. Clayoquot Archives, University of Victoria.

CD [*The Clayoquot Documents*. 1997. Ed. Karena Shaw and Warren Magnusson, Clayoquot Project, University of Victoria.]

Haraway, Donna. 1991. *Simians, Cyborgs, and Women: The Reinvention of Nature*. New York: Routledge.

Harding, Sandra. 1986. *The Science Question in Feminism*. Ithaca, N.Y.: Cornell University Press.

Johnson, Martha, ed. 1992. *LORE: Capturing Traditional Environmental Knowledge*. Hay River, Northwest Territories: Dene Cultural Institute.

MacKinnon, Catherine. 1989. *Toward a Feminist Theory of the State*. Cambridge: Harvard University Press.

Matas, Robert. 1997. "Telling Tales out of School." *Globe and Mail,* December 11, A10.

Memmi, Albert. 1967. *The Colonizer and the Colonized*. New York: Beacon Press.

Mies, Maria. 1987. *Capitalist Accumulation on a World Scale*. London: Zed Press.

Nandy, Ashis. 1983. *The Intimate Enemy: Loss and Recovery of Self under Colonialism*. Delhi: Oxford University Press.

———. 1987. *Traditions, Tyranny, and Utopias: Essays in the Politics of Awareness*. Delhi: Oxford University Press.

———. 1995–96. "Plural Worlds, Multiple Selves: Ashis Nandy and the Post-Columbian Future." *Emergences* 7–8: 1–242.

Nandy, Ashis, Merryl Wyn Davies, and Ziauddin Sardar. 1993. *Barbaric Others: A Manifesto on Western Racism*. London: Pluto Press.

Scientific Panel for Sustainable Forestry Practices in Clayoquot Sound. 1994a. *Report of the Scientific Panel for Sustainable Forest Practices in Clayoquot Sound*. Report 1 of 5. Victoria, B.C.: Cortex Consultants.

———. 1994b. *Progress Report 2: Review of Current Forest Practice Standards in Clayoquot Sound*. Report 2 of 5. Victoria, B.C.: Cortex Consultants.

———. 1995a. *First Nations' Perspectives relating to Forest Practices Standards in Clayoquot Sound*. Report 3 of 5. Victoria, B.C.: Cortex Consultants.

———. 1995b. *A Vision and its Context: Global Context of Forest Practices in Clayquot Sound*. Report 4 of 5. Victoria, B.C.: Cortex Consultants.

———. 1995c. *Sustainable Ecosystem Management in Clayoquot Sound: Planning and Practices*. Report 5 of 5. Victoria, B.C.: Cortex Consultants.

Takaki, Ronald T. 1979. *Iron Cages: Race and Culture in Nineteenth-Century America*. New York: Alfred A. Knopf.

Williams, Patricia. 1991. *The Alchemy of Race and Rights*. Cambridge: Harvard University Press.

They Seek It Here, They Seek It There

Locating the Political in Clayoquot Sound

R. B. J. Walker

There are many ways of making sense of events articulated in relation to a site identified as Clayoquot Sound, many ways of interpreting the multiple struggles and contentions centered on the logging practices rapidly erasing one of the world's last remaining temperate rainforests. These events have provoked considerable commentary and analysis; so much so, in fact, that it is not all that easy to see what else might be said. Still, even now there is much about these events that is difficult to characterize, and even more that is difficult to evaluate, even though there are many familiar characterizations and evaluations that have been, and continue to be deployed to keep things simple.

There is also much to be said for keeping things simple. Some people judge simplicity to be a good in itself. Many of those engaged in environmental movements, for example, strive for forms of simplicity understood by contrast with the supposed complexities of modern urban and industrial life. Scholars often invoke the principle of Occam's razor, the epistemological virtues of economy and minimalist elegance, when judging among competing explanations and theorizations. Many political actors prefer to tell the same old story over and over again so as to keep the journalists and social scientists happy, or to tidy up the messy narratives and jurisdictions so as to keep everyone from thinking too much about the clichés and caricatures that keep public debate on manageable terms. It may be that many events in Clayoquot Sound can be understood in relatively simple terms, perhaps even productively so. Nevertheless, there is also no doubt that these events provoke difficult interpretive puzzles. In this essay, I want to suggest that they ultimately raise far more questions—very interesting questions—than they provide illustrations of familiar narratives and comfortable theorizations.

They especially provoke questions about judgment: questions about the conditions under which we judge political practices to be important or unimportant, successful or unsuccessful, or even political or nonpolitical, as well as about who gets to decide what counts as good judgment, and how they get away with their decisions.

Most obviously, as with all social and political phenomena, the empirical data available for interpretation elude any single theorization. As sites of political contestation, the many theoretical traditions that have been deployed to interpret and explain these struggles in Clayoquot Sound attract readings and explanations that respond to different interests, identities, and authorities. These readings and interpretations, however, are not infinite. They can be articulated only within certain limits of intelligibility. The literature shows traces from rich and often provocative intellectual traditions. Not least, it is possible to draw upon theories of corporate capital, state structures, bureaucratic competition, public policy formation, democratic representations, the "new," "environmentalist," or "green" social movements, as well as relations between federal and provincial governments or between centers and peripheries of globally organized economic systems.

As with all other attempts to understand social and political phenomena, such theorizations are highly selective in their choice of data and their interpretations of competing narratives. Moreover, these theorizations have fed back into and helped shape the practices that they have sought to understand and explain. Whether through attempts by actors to understand what they are doing and what might still be done, or attempts to privilege and legitimize some possibilities rather than others, competing understandings of how we might—perhaps even must—understand the events articulated in relation to a site identified as Clayoquot Sound are part of the complexities that ought to undermine any claim that these events are fully susceptible to any simple analysis. To speak of Clayoquot Sound is to identify a contested interpretive field, one in which the difficulties of discriminating among interpretations mesh with very specific struggles over the discriminations and judgments that are at play in everyday practices of politicization and depoliticization. As several earlier essays have suggested, this is perhaps most obvious in relation to the competing conceptions of legitimate knowledge, of "science" and "tradition" that have been so prominent in this context. Political life hinges on questions of legitimacy, on what counts as a legitimate claim to authority in, say, the legislature, the courtroom, the evening news, or the faculties of forestry. Whether in terms of the underdetermination of theory by data, the convergences and divergences of competing theoretical traditions, or the slippery slope from scholarly categories to ideologies and legitimation strategies and back again, there are both scholarly and political reasons to resist the narratives—not least about small if heroic environmental social movements acting in marginal locations—that affirm and reproduce the common sense of modern politics.

But there is another, related sense in which the most common readings of these events are highly problematic, one that has struck me both as I have watched these specific events unfold and as I have been able to think about these events in relation to a range of other seemingly small and parochial sites of political action in various parts of the world. This sense is driven by three broad observations, each of which informs the analysis I want to develop in this essay.

First, I have been impressed not only by the difficulty of keeping track of the empirical complexity of events in and around—a long way around, and never entirely in—Clayoquot Sound, but also of identifying the grounds on which we might most usefully make judgments about what these events were and how important they might be. It is not clear to me what criteria of evaluation one ought to be applying to various attempts to explain what has been going on. Nor is it clear that even those very few scholarly texts that have to be taken seriously in this context have said very much about such grounds for judgment.[1]

Second, I have been impressed by the enormous capacity of the prevailing analytic categories to insist on an authority to make judgments about the character and significance of events despite what seems to be a troubling absence of clear grounds for judgment. On the whole, I find the presumed authority of the prevailing analytic categories to be more troubling than my sense of the absence of clear grounds for judgment, especially insofar as the most authoritative categories of analysis have been framed in relation to something identified as "Canadian politics" or the "politics of British Columbia." It may be heresy to many people who find that these labels apply quite well to something that seems consequential to their daily life, but I find them to be singularly unhelpful: the tips of large icebergs, perhaps, or toes identified as elephants, though neither metaphor quite captures the political practices involved in applying blandly homogenizing names to complex political sites.

Here I am influenced not only by a long-standing bemusement at the kind of ("comparative") political analysis that has been mobilized by such labels applied to apparently discrete (though structurally interrelated) places, but by the way in which the many claims to "realism" and "common sense" in political life that trade on such labels so often work as a normative insistence on what *must* be. Such claims effectively dissuade people from asking questions about the conditions under which the claim might be plausible as something more than a normative ideal. Indeed, the normative, and paradigmatically nationalist, claim of the modern sovereign state to be the be-all and end-all of political life seems to be just about the last ground from which to make claims about contemporary political realities while still retaining some scholarly or political credibility. Perhaps this is a consequence of my living too long in what seems to be a peripheral part of a highly decentralized state failing to resist the effects of an American empire and obviously subject to the effects of internationalizing and globalizing economic practices. I suspect, however, that it is because this place is far more typical of most of the world than the idealized self-images that count for reality in parts of Europe and the United States, the twin sources of our most authoritative political categories.[2] In any case, as I have thought more and more about the ways in which various scholarly traditions have been deployed in relation to Clayoquot Sound, I have been much more impressed by their normative commitments to a very specific account of what and where political life *must* be than by their capacity to capture political practices that only partly conform to these normative commitments. They are interesting mainly as an indication of the tremendous energy that goes into insisting that the ideal is indeed what is to be found in the world, and thus of the practices with which one has to engage in order to act in the world.[3]

Third, many of the events in and around Clayoquot Sound are interesting precisely because they express a practical necessity to challenge, evade, or even ignore the normative commitments that constitute both our prevailing sense of political realism and the authoritative grounds for judgment assumed by most of our traditions of political analysis. Not least, they challenge a deeply rooted connection between claims about what politics is and claims about where politics is. Much of the difficulty of interpreting these events, and much of what is so suggestive in thinking about the relationship between what has been happening in this specific place and in many other specific places, is that politics has not always played out where it is supposed to play out.

In working through this sense that events in Clayoquot Sound significantly exceed the plausibility of prevailing analytic categories, I do not wish to be read as saying that this is the only way of reading these events or even that prevailing analytic categories are irrelevant. On the contrary, precisely because prevailing scholarly categories express established accounts of what and where politics must be, they will both have access to structures and actions that affirm these accounts and play an important role in shaping the events they seek to explain. In political life there are many complex reciprocities between the authority of theoretical discourses and the authority of sites, practices, and actions that claim authority over political identities, communities, and obligations. There is a politics to the ways in which various authorities tell us what and where politics must be. In Clayoquot Sound, the politics of authorizing politics has a lot to do with proper orientation, with claims about where it is. My own response to both the place and the events articulated in relation to this place has been primarily one of disorientation. Clayoquot Sound can indeed be identified as a specific place, but it is not entirely obvious where this place ought to be placed in relation to what we claim to know about contemporary forms of power, authority, obligation, identity, or community.

Much of the politics in Clayoquot Sound has not occurred where it is supposed to occur, to the point at which we have to question the notion that we need to examine events *in* Clayoquot Sound, or treat this place as a mere locale in a bigger—national, global—space. Much of the politics associated with events in Clayoquot Sound has involved intense struggles over precisely where politics there should and must occur. It is wise to be aware that theoretical traditions that take the location of politics for granted are likely to misread and minimize the significance of certain kinds of events, to make judgments that work primarily to affirm prior normative and ideological commitments. This suggests that we should start asking questions about what it means to have a politics that does not occur where it is supposed to occur.

The events centered on Clayoquot Sound in the early 1990s involved not only a complex set of challenges to the exploitation of natural resources, but also challenges to the naturalization of political resources enabled by historically and culturally specific accounts of nature, accounts that are ultimately "grounded" in abstract naturalizations of where Clayoquot Sound is in modern political space. These events are interesting not because they can be claimed as models of success or failure judged according to established criteria of success or failure in political life, but because they suggest that such criteria hardly begin to get at the degree to which these events involved suggestive renegotiations of what is meant by political life and of success or failure in it.

Authority/Space

The struggles to exploit environmental resources in and around Clayoquot Sound, or to resist such exploitation in the name of ecological integrity, sustainable development, community control, and so on, seem to fall quite easily, and naturally, under the rubric of "politics." These events may have been framed as somehow "different," as somewhat peculiar variations on a form of politics as usual: as confirmation that politics in British Columbia is somewhat aberrant even in its most ordinary moments; or as evidence that environmental struggles in British Columbia manifest interesting signs of innovation and creativity. For the most part, however, they have been read as if politics is simply politics, whatever politics is presumed to be. The authentic norm or the sensible conventions may be locatable elsewhere, and British Columbia in general and environmentalists and logging companies in particular may be read as often spectacular deviations from them, but it is difficult to resist the assumption that there is indeed some norm or sensible and natural convention against which these events can be explained and understood. It is especially difficult because some of the most persuasive discourses about British Columbia and its resource industries affirm narratives of marginality, of a resource-dependent periphery, for example, or a remote outpost of the Canadian federation, or even of a Canadian empire centered somewhere between Ottawa, Toronto, and Quebec City and still demanding tribute from its far-flung subjects. Politics in British Columbia is supposed to be somewhat off the wall, close to the edge, and it can certainly be a disconcerting place, though the grounds on which it is judged to be more disconcerting than, say, Ontario or Ohio, are not entirely clear.

These narratives in turn affirm a broad range of conventions about who we are, where we are, and where we are going as inhabitants of a place called British Columbia, of what we consider to be the natural and necessary conditions under which we may engage in political action, especially action that is concerned with struggles over that which is taken to be somehow natural. After all, modern politics was established in relation to a specific set of understandings of political subjects as somehow—once upon a time, or potentially at some future time, or all the time by virtue of our reason, our science, our maturity—natural. It is unlikely that struggles around environments and ecologies will attain any long-term significance without these understandings coming into serious contestation.

In this context, it is possible to mobilize various narratives about the range of perspectives about what ought to be done in Clayoquot Sound and the various interests they express, whether in relation to governments, environmentalists, aboriginal groups, logging companies, corporate business, workers, emerging forms of tourism, and so on. At best, these narratives stress the incompleteness of events, an incompleteness that is especially difficult to appreciate given the extent to which so much of the discourse about these events has been framed by a grand metaphor of a game with clear winners and losers among a well-known cast of competing interests.

The temptation to ask when the game will be over so that someone can post the score has sometimes been overwhelming. This temptation has been reinforced both by the broad influence on modern political thought and practice of the kind of utilitarian analysis exemplified by theories of rational choice and liberal microeconomics, and by a long history of thinking about electoral politics in British Columbia, as in so many other places, as little more than a spectator sport.

Still, this is a metaphor that can be and has been pushed in ways that disrupt the familiar story of competing interests, as well as the corollary assumption that it might be possible to say who has come out ahead in Clayoquot Sound. It is possible especially to provoke questions about who is doing the refereeing, in which league, and at whose behest, for in political life it is just as important to keep one's eye on how the rules are set and maintained as on the ball that is in play according to a specific set of rules. Hence, the enormous consequences of disrupting basic constitutional principles, or basic concepts of sovereignty, security, and citizenship that most people would prefer to consign either to dusty libraries or to the unquestioned bedrock of common sense. In this context, narratives about competing interests are much less interesting than conflicts about appropriate sources of authority, especially in relation to ways these conflicts seem to exceed, undermine, and reconstitute the authority of the official authorities.

I think here, for example, of the conflict between the Nuu-chah-nulth and the provincial government and the crucial intervention over land claims that led to the creation of the Central Regional Board; or the struggles to maintain legitimacy through diverse media campaigns; or the sophisticated debates about knowledge that were expressed in relation to the constitution of the Scientific Panel; or the many microdecisions over what counts as research procedure, as expertise, as economy, as value, or as culture; or the succession of attempts by the provincial government to impose various decision-making entities on the situation and subsequent attempts to reconstitute these entities by various actors, not least by insisting on the legitimacy of local authorizations and agencies beyond the territorial jurisdiction of the provincial government. It is in such contexts that the fluidity and open-endedness of politics in Clayoquot Sound are most resistant to the prevailing narratives of victory and defeat, of episodic struggles on the same old playing field. The narratives of a politics as usual, even of a marginal politics as usual, are dangerously overdetermining. They work as expressions of a hegemonic common sense, or a sovereigntist disciplining of appropriate spaces for political action. But many of the events they seek to explain and discipline can also be interpreted precisely as challenges to the natural necessity of those narratives about norms and conventions of a politics as usual.

Hence the significance of the many different spatial contexts in which it is necessary to understand various attempts to challenge, reconstitute, and create sites of authority in Clayoquot Sound. Thinking about the rapaciousness of the forestry industry, for example, one is immediately drawn to accounts of a globally organized capital, and of what has been done to New Zealand, Indonesia, Finland, and many other places. It is not so far from a primitive slash and burn to sophisticated corporate strategies of "talk and log" (Wilson 1998) and "the living forest."[4] Thinking about a province dominated by Vancouver and the Lower Mainland, one thinks about the kinds of networks that link the populations of the so-called global cities, and the ways in which they disrupt our distinctions between urban and rural, or center and hinterland, or even big and small. As Magnusson, especially, has insisted elsewhere (Magnusson 1996; see also Isin 2000), it is not difficult to think of Clayoquot Sound as an urban space, as a neighborhood of a global urban community, even, judging from recent architectural trends in Tofino, as a kind of global garden suburb. Indeed, perhaps the previous event of most significance in BC politics was the mobilization of a coalition against the Social Credit regime in the early 1980s, one that faltered on a classic deal between a corporate union (the International Woodworkers of America [IWA]) and the provincial state, thereby ensuring the reproduction of crudely corporatist and populist forms of party politics for several more decades (Magnusson et al. 1984). In this context, Clayoquot Sound appeared on the horizon as an event more in touch with the progressive urban agendas found in Vancouver, Victoria, Seattle, and Portland than with the colonial and class politics that had come to seem the norm. Thinking about the ways in which many people talk about this part of the world as a region, one tries to understand the forms of community and authority that are being constituted under vague labels such as the Pacific Northwest, or Cascadia, or the Vancouver-Seattle-Portland Corridor. Perhaps most instructively, thinking about the specific place identified as Clayoquot Sound, one wonders about the stereotypes that equate locale and place either with a sense of community or with something small and weak.

One might also think about some of the central motifs at play in the media campaigns, which often imply spatial framings available for rhetorical deployment: the spaces of culture and nature, the spaces of industry, and the spaces of romanticism. Then one might start thinking about how various writers have drawn attention to the multiplicity and historical construction of lived spaces, to the phenomenologies, poetics, and productions of spaces examined by Gaston Bachelard, Yi-Fu Tuan, Clarence Glacken, Michel Foucault, David Harvey, Edward Soja, Henri Lefebvre, and many other scholars in many contexts (e.g., Bachelard 1965; Tuan 1977; Glacken 1967; Harvey 2000; Lefebvre 1991; Friedland and Boden 1994; Adams, Hoelscher, and Till 2001). One might especially meditate, like James Clifford (1997) thinking about the extraordinary historical geography/anthropology of a small site like the Russian settlement of Fort Ross on the central California coast, about the many peoples, cultures, directions, and histories that have played out in this specific place.

There is a simple cure for all such speculation, all such sensitivities to historical and cultural difference, all such engagements with urban spaces, global spaces, regional spaces, cultural spaces, all such wonder about where we are. It is the simple cure that is invariably mobilized by the apparently simple question: Where is Clayoquot Sound? It is, no doubt, a reasonable question. Most people already find it hard enough to distinguish between the city of Vancouver and Vancouver Island (though it is an island about the size of a small country such as The Netherlands, and with a population about the size of Cyprus), let alone locate a couple of small towns at the end of an often tricky road from the other coast, or the even smaller and mainly aboriginal communities accessible only by boat or floatplane.

I have been aware of the existence of a place called Clayoquot Sound for more than three decades, though for about two of them I had not the slightest clue even how the name was pronounced. I came in close proximity to it in the early 1970s, having traveled to Western Canada soon after escaping the damp depression of Harold Wilson's Britain to study in Ontario. But I drove south instead, wandering slowly down the coast to trendy San Francisco, and Clayoquot remained a vague outer limit of my experience. It might as well have been Alaska or the Queen Charlotte Islands, some vague beyond of cold seas, warm dragons, and colonial memories. It came no closer to my experience even when I moved to Vancouver Island to teach at the University of Victoria in 1980. Tellingly, the first time I began to link Clayoquot with the kinds of social movements that I had begun to notice in other parts of the world was when I saw an impressive poster of old-growth trees in an academic office in Frankfurt in mid-1986. Far away, in a modern urban office block, trying to get a sense of the broader significance of the emerging German green movement/party, I recognized a scrap of what had begun to be my "home." Since then I have watched events, mainly from a distance, though with enough contacts through students, friends, and family to read between the lines of the local reportage. I now know how to negotiate most of the bends in the road. I can at least find my way there. An

archetypal imaginary of wilds beyond has shifted to a place of familiar experience. As usual, of course, experience is incomplete and insufficient.

The most authoritative answers to questions about the location of
Clayoquot Sound invoke the skills of the official cartographer, or at least of
those cartographers who work from the established conventions for carv-
ing up geographical space. Thus, to identify a coordinate of about 126 degrees West and just over 49 degrees North will get us to more or less the right
spot. A long way west of Greenwich. A picturesque strait and a few mountain passes west of Vancouver. Just over halfway between the equator and
the North Pole. Out on the West Coast, *out* on the periphery of a spatial entity addressed, as the peculiar but instructive hierarchization of political
space would have it, c/o British Columbia, Canada, North America, the
World, the Universe. For curiously, but significantly, the coordinates of the
compass tell us not only about the mappings of space in a horizontal plane
but also guide our understandings of what is above and below. To speak of
events *in* Clayoquot Sound is to invoke a powerful metaphorical field in
which claims that we can distinguish what is in and what is out trigger a
now almost automatic geopolitics of scale, a translation of claims about
specific places into a common sense of big and small, local and global. The
concrete specificities of place are turned into abstractions, enabling normative claims to be solidified into repeated assertions about what it means to
be realistic.

Even more curiously, these abstract, mathematical answers have the
distinct advantage of affirming everyday experiential realities. Drivers, sailors, pilots, and trekkers all get a sense from these coordinates of where
they are and where they are supposed to go. Global positioning satellites
will tell us where we are to the nearest few meters. In an era in which so
many have lamented the collapse of all intellectual and moral foundations,
it turns out that no one needs to be lost, not even in the remotest wilderness. Just tune in to the satellites parked in orbit; and all for less than a few
hundred dollars.

Even so, the very precision of these coordinates already betrays a sense
of arbitrariness, a sense of history, a sense of disorientation. We specify west
of Greenwich because of the historical experiences of maritime empires.
Notions of East and West retain their connection with doctrinal distinctions
between socialists and capitalists, Orientals and Occidentals, and the forty-
year geopolitical freeze that turned to dirty slush in 1989. The parallels of
latitude and longitude have been used to carve up entire continents in
ways that have little to do with a nature understood as topography, or geo-
morphology, or ecology, and everything to do with nature as a phenome-

non described by a mathematical science of straight lines and angles adding up to 360 degrees. Moreover, it is not entirely irrelevant that these coordinates can be constructed so as to privilege accuracy of, say, directionality, area, or scale. Map projections are not all created equal.

The most interesting thing about the way we use modern cartographic coordinates to answer questions about where Clayoquot may be is that we are enabled to reconcile our most persuasive accounts of the most concrete realities of the world in which we live—the supposedly hard ground of territory, place and rock, the material experience of planet Earth—with a highly formalized, abstract, and nominal account of what those realities must be. It is an inherently unstable reconciliation. The map, we know, is not the territory. The experience of place, as most geographers are now primed to tell us, must not be confused with abstract Euclidean conceptions of space.

This reconciliation of map and territory—of nature as an apparently concrete and already existing world and nature as the representation of that supposed world in the categories of modern science and culture—is, of course, not simply a matter of improving the maps so as to better conform to the territory. The entire question of the relationship between map and territory, or between language and world, is constitutive of modern philosophical speculation—indeed, of modern culture in general. More important, this question has been central to the development of modern accounts of political authority and subjectivity. Here it is necessary to recall only four key moments in this development (recognizing that each of these moments has been treated to massive and contested elaborations in the literature): first, the rewriting of Aristotelian conceptions of place in terms of a modern (Euclidean, Galilean, Newtonian, Kantian) account of space (see, e.g., Casey 1997; Jammer 1954; Koyré 1957; Strikkers 1996; Kern 1983); second, the rewriting of "essentialist" (or in Platonist terms, "realist") accounts of nature as the "laws of nature" by nominalists such as Hobbes (1991); third, the further rewriting of the "laws of nature" into the legitimacy of private property in a world in which, as Locke put it (1988, chap. 5), God had given the earth to everyone in common: a problem to be solved by a labor theory of value and the accumulation of money; fourth, the massive elaboration, by Hobbes, Locke, and most of the other canonical figures of the modern traditions of political thought, of a theory of representation through which modern citizens could be reconciled with each other through their participation and representation in, and thus legitimation of, the sovereign authority of the modern state. This is a long and contentious story, with even more twists and turns than the road from Port Alberni to the Pacific Ocean.

But it does suggest that there are some very high stakes involved in the claim that Clayoquot Sound can be located, given its proper place, in the coordinates inscribed by the children of Euclid.

Contemporary philosophical debate arguably turns more on a sense that this question of the relation between map and territory or language and world is badly posed than on a sense that answers might soon be forthcoming. Even so, the philosophers have not persuaded very many people that language is more complex than a simple representation of the world. Contemporary political debate arguably also turns more on a sense that seventeenth-century European metaphysics, with its dualistic accounts of man and nature, language and world, the national citizen and the universal human, has come to seem inadequate to contemporary conditions; even so, the notion that nature, territory, and abstract space come in the same neat package is hard to shake.

It is thus no surprise to find that the easy answers to questions about the location of Clayoquot Sound that are framed in terms of the apparently natural authority of cartographic coordinates tend to encourage an account of the political practices in Clayoquot Sound in terms of the established forms of a politics of representation. To answer a question about location in these terms is already to answer questions about what politics must be as well. Thus, we find ourselves among the familiar routines of "policy" and "governance." An account of location framed in terms of an apparently incontrovertible claim about the hard realities of nature is also a way of framing an explicitly normative account of what must be treated as appropriate forms of political practice and of the criteria by which they may be judged. This, after all, is to work within the established limits of political authority.

To read the politics of Clayoquot Sound in these terms is to engage with a specifically modern account of place/space and the politics of representation. Place is interpreted in terms of a *prior* concept of space, just as "nature" enters into modern politics only on terms set by a prior law of nature; that is, modern politics is constituted on a ground of law, of a sovereign authority to define that which is legitimate/included and that which is illegitimate/excluded. It is constituted as an order of precedence: sovereignty before governance, law before nature, citizen before human.

This space expresses a familiar contradiction between extension across an area and the representation of that area at a single point, a contradiction that we have become used to calling the problem of democracy, though it is only one form of the problem of democracy, and a form that suggests that democracy is certainly a problem. On the one hand, the political space of British Columbia is in principle homogeneous. It offers a site from which modern individual subjects can be represented equally under a common law. The most important practice flowing from this requirement involves the construction of voting constituencies, the attempt to get as close as possible to a mechanism through which claims to equality translate into something recognizably close to equal representation in the provincial legislature. On the other hand, the political space of British Columbia is in principle centered in one place, the provincial legislature in Victoria (which also doubles as a kitsch palace of lights, a mock Taj Mahal, and certainly a mockery of something, presumably to amuse the tourists from Texas, Tokyo, and Tinseltown).

This contradiction is, of course, the standard contradiction expressed by all modern systems of political representation under sovereign authority. It is resolved, in principle, by the practices and institutions of democratic citizenship. The regulative principle at work here, as in all modern systems of representation under sovereign authority, is the claim that the popular sovereignty of all free and equal people can be reconciled with the legitimate authority of the sovereignty that both constitutes and is constituted by the sovereign people. This claim has always been highly problematic, not least with respect to the possibilities of reconciling principles of individual freedom with those of individual equality and the possibilities of ever drawing a clear and acceptable line between the spheres of popular and state sovereignty. Nevertheless, as a relationship between "the many" spread out in territorial/abstract space and "the one" centered authority representing these many, it affirms the priority of abstract space over territory, of the language of modern reason over the nature this reason claims to name.

This resolution in principle suggests a range of appropriate sites and strategies of political engagement. These include the practices of electoral and party politics, interest group articulation, the varying roles of executive, legislative, bureaucratic, and judicial dimensions of the state apparatus, and so on. The details of this resolution are complex, in British Columbia as elsewhere. They absorb most of the energies of most of those who seek to analyze what goes on in what is generally called politics in British Columbia, again as elsewhere.

Both the general formulation of appropriate practices and institutions of democratic representation and of the appropriate sites and strategies of political engagement are often widely contested. This contestation occurs within well-known limits, usually articulated as some sort of national consensus, as the realm of plausible electoral popularity among political parties, or as the possibility of erecting quasi-republican institutions or practices of civil society that can lend some form of stability to the essentially unstable tension between popular sovereignty and state sovereignty that lies at the heart of any modern politics of representation. As must be expected of a modern system of representation, however, attempts to cope with this tension or contradiction between the sovereign represener and the sovereign represented have two especially critical limits: those involving the "big" and those involving the "small"; or, alternatively, those involving the "local" and the "different" and those involving the "global," the "international," and the "human."

The fundamental reasons for this involve the peculiar character of the claim to spatial homogeneity, the claim that all territorial, ecological, cultural, or any other kinds of difference must be capable of equal representation within the space of a bounded political community, at least in principle. This claim is enshrined not least in Hobbes's account of the necessary relation between sovereign and subjects, Kant's account of the necessary, if only potential, relation between mature autonomous subjects and the universal moral law, and Swift's satire on the Newtonian world in which the only significant differences are those of scale. It is enshrined most effectively in the resolutions of space/time/identity reified in the principle/institution/practice of state sovereignty and sovereign subjectivity.

Given the need to reconcile space with place, to mediate between the abstract homogeneous space of freedom and equality under a sovereign law and the sensuous concrete differences that appear to be in tension with these abstractions everywhere, and given also the ontological necessity of homogeneous space, and the requirement of sovereign authority to constitute all judgments about authority within that space, as the condition under which judgments about sensuous concrete differences might be made, it is not surprising that the primary forms in which it has been possible to accommodate "difference" have involved a judicious return of hierarchical "levels" within the space of the modern state as a way of coping with the obvious incongruities between empirical tendencies and the normative claims of modern democratic states. For example, Hobbes may now be viewed as the paradigmatic subversion of theological hierarchies in favor of a horizontal account of subjects in the homogeneous space of the world-machine, or what was subsequently framed as the perfect market, but he simultaneously reintroduced the vertical dimension both as a series of constitutive distinctions between the sovereign and the people, the legal and the illegal, the political and the mere freedom under the law, and as a rather light-handed account of social (and, not least, gendered) inequalities. Similarly, contemporary attempts to "solve" the problems of representation, to save the appearances of a modern politics constituted through a reconciliation of territory and abstract spatiality on terms set by the priority of abstract space, tend to appeal to a rehierarchization of authority as the only possible alternative. This eternal return of the Great Chain of Being, the necessary counterpoint to a modern politics constituted on a ground of horizontal spatiality, continues to inform aspirations for the future.

It is in this context that one can read five major themes that have long been at play in the constitution and reconstitution of modern politics. These themes seem to me to be central to an understanding of the events in Clayoquot Sound in the 1990s. Moreover, these themes suggest that these events must be understood less as a slightly weird local aberration in a minor periphery than as an interesting exemplar of challenges to the possibility of reading the politics of a place from an extrapolation of a cartography that may be helpful for drivers, pilots, sailors, and hikers, but not for understanding contemporary rearticulations of power, authority, identity, or political practice.

First, the theme of the apparently "local." The Lilliputians may have been able to tie Gulliver to the ground through a majestic feat of collective action, but it remains the case that the local has absorbed all the resonances of an early-modern metaphysics of scale and size so that local implies small, weak, and parochial. By this measure, the little towns of Tofino or Ucluelet barely count as a speck of dust in the modern political calculus. A few villages and a hinterland of large trees does not quite measure up to something serious. Press the button and a thousand stories of David and Goliath go into automatic replay. Small men chop down large trees, and small groups of activists sometimes achieve great things, especially if they are capable of the tactical brilliance and collective intransigence that has somehow been sustained in this place. But David is the exception that proves the rule. For the most part, large corporations and states gobble up loggers and activists alike. But the same also applies, in principle at least, to Vancouver, Seattle, New York, and a variety of other merely urban centers, other merely local sites with mayors and street cleaners rather than presidents and ministers; which may suggest a slight problem with the laws of modern political calculus.

Two interesting questions emerge in this context. One concerns what it means to act "locally," not least in view of simple-minded injunctions to "think globally, act locally," injunctions that reproduce dualisms of both thought/action and local/global that affirm a very conventional account of where and what we are as political subjects.[5] Another concerns what it means to refer to political practices under the heading of "social movements," a heading that reinscribes political practices as both "small" and in some crucial senses apolitical.

Clayoquot Sound is, in the modern political imagination, simply a local site, but in many respects it is difficult to understand what goes on there simply as a form of local politics. Moreover, events in Clayoquot Sound have been articulated around claims about the appropriate politics of nature—about forests, environments, ecosystems, and the planet—but many of these claims challenge the ways in which accounts of nature have been written into the most basic accounts of space/time/identity that inform the primary categories of modern politics. They especially challenge the dualistic modern accounts of "man and nature," or "culture and nature," that are expressed by the framing of "territory" in the formal/legal/representational codes of an abstract homogeneous space—the space of the modern state that claims to resolve all contradictions between local and global within its sovereign jurisdiction. Clayoquot Sound is an interesting focus for contemporary political analysis precisely because it sometimes exceeds modern expectations of what it means to engage in a politics of the local, and sometimes exceeds modern expectations of how nature must be constituted in the practices of modern politics.

Second, this modern metaphysics of scale implies the necessity of nesting all locals under the hierarchical authority of the sovereign state, or at least under the provincial authority, which is in turn relatively weak in relation to the federal authority under whose authority the provincial authority must be nested. Events in Clayoquot Sound express distinctive accounts of political life in relation to the different communities and identities that have been involved: provincial and federal governments, indigenous peoples, loggers, multinational companies, environmentalists, town councils, officials of government departments, and so on. But these accounts are supposed to be orchestrated according to a common score, to invoke a metaphor of harmony rather than one of competitive games. Modern political life is founded on the assumption that, whatever the diversity of accounts of politics in a specific territory, they are all ultimately subordinate to one privileged account of politics, the account that constitutes a monopoly on legitimate authority over all that territory. All accounts of difference are ultimately subordinated to a single account of a common identity, community, territory, polity, obligation, law, and representation. The small and the weak must gather together under the hierarchical embrace of the spatially disaggregated sovereign state, just as Hobbes said we must.

Democracy is thus miraculously transferred away from local places to those institutions of state that can maximize their claims to legitimate representation while minimizing the damage from local participation. And states that find it difficult to reconcile their territoriality, or their cultural diversity, with the demands of the homogeneous space of modern sovereignty are driven to construct institutions of federalism. The characteristic forms of federal politics are then shaped by negotiations and compromises both across territorial space (whether between provinces or between two nations, in the Canadian case) and across hierarchically arrayed jurisdictions (whether federal or provincial). Whether it is now possible to sustain even such loosely articulated federations as the Canadian state, which might be read as operating very close to the limits in which it is possible to reconcile contradictions between territorial differentiation and the homogeneity of sovereign spatiality, is not clear.

This subordination is ultimately expressed in the principle of state sovereignty, a principle that is broadly considered to be in some trouble in many contemporary contexts. Clayoquot Sound is one of those contexts. It is a site at which political practices express not only competing conceptions of politics that ultimately can be contained within the tidy jurisdictions and subordinations of state sovereignty, but some often serious disruptions to the politics that constitutes the appropriate contours of modern politics.

Third, the apparent weakness of the "local," and the consequent need to construct elaborate forms of hierarchical subordination within what is in principle a homogeneous space, are specific manifestations of the difficulty of reconciling claims to difference of any kind with the sovereign claim to represent all differences across the space of political community in which all subjects are, in principle, equal. The history of modern politics can be told in terms of the various ways in which reconciliations have been attempted, or even partly achieved. It remains the case, however, that modern political life is still beset not only with claims about massive failures on the ground of "equality," but also on the ground of various kinds of "difference," especially differences in "culture" and "gender." It is not surprising, therefore, that so much contemporary political theory takes the form of implicit or explicit explorations of the potential contours of a political pluralism. It is not surprising, either, that most of these explorations either assume some common space of political community within which differences and pluralisms may be articulated or, in recognizing the somewhat unfortunate experience of liberal nationalisms in the twentieth century, have begun to think about what pluralisms and differences would look like without the ultimate arbiter of the sovereign state to decide what constitutes acceptable differences, or acceptable conversations/negotiations/ disputes among those differences.

Which brings us, fourth, to the so-called problem of "international relations," the problem that arises when claims about "difference" in relation to the homogeneous spaces within the modern sovereign state are also played out in the context of a "world" that is constituted as a system of such homogeneous spaces. Contrary to assumptions sustained by all the major traditions of modern political thought, it is necessary to insist that although modern states may claim sovereignty, a monopoly of legitimate authority within their territory, the very possibility of modern politics depends on the organization of the system of states. No states system, no sovereignty.

Many paradoxes, with crucial consequences, can be unpacked in this context, but for my present purposes it is necessary only to note that the problem of international relations sets the primary limit condition of modern politics. It is the point at which politics is always liable to turn into an appeal to the exception, to the state of emergency, the point at which the claims of citizenship clash most ominously with claims to humanity. Crudely, politics is supposed to occur in those spaces in which modern subjects can be represented, and the only way that it has traditionally been possible to be represented outside the space of the modern state is to move further up the hierarchy of subordination; at which point the modern political imagination has scant resources to even name all those strange phenomena that, in addition to the familiar logics of the states system, have also become conditions of the possibility of political life almost everywhere. Hence the paucity of credible accounts of what it means to speak about politics under conditions of "globalization."

Which is where, finally, and again not surprisingly, we begin to see the limits of the modern attempt to reconcile an account of nature as something concrete and primordial and an account of nature as the great law of reason, of science, that can also tell us how we, as humans and citizens radically split off from nature, can nevertheless reconcile ourselves with it. "Nature" may appear to us now as an existential and increasingly global problem, even a threat, but it is also becoming clear that the way in which "it" is coming to be seen as a "problem" is also a problem. Neither the great split between Aristotelian essences and modern nominalisms that allowed seventeenth-century thinkers to construct our accounts of modern political subjectivities, nor the great split between Enlightenment universalists and Romantic subjectivists, which articulates key aspects of the tension/contradiction between abstract universal space and concrete nature (to take only the two most obvious historical episodes that might be invoked in this respect), offer much help in thinking politically in this context. Put slightly differently, given that "nature" is already a constitutive aspect of the way in which modern political subjectivities have been constructed, there are obvious difficulties in now simply trying to add nature to the politics that have thereby been constituted. "Nature" is implicated not only in many of the most intractable political problems, but also in the problem of what we mean when we say that a problem is somehow political.

These five themes are being explored in a wide range of contemporary literatures and across many disciplines. To follow these literatures is to see not that the easy answer to the questions about the location of Clayoquot Sound is entirely wrong, but that it brings with it some enormous baggage as a consequence of the historical experiences through which the character of modern politics, and our identity as modern political subjects, is tightly interwoven, and indeed constituted by, accounts of a representational space. This representational space has always been problematic and inherently unstable, in ways that are familiar from many of the great controversies that have shaped the rearticulation of modern political principles over at least three centuries. Political life is increasingly characterized by practices that are even more difficult to accommodate either through forms of representation that rest ultimately on claims about the necessary convergence between territoriality and homogeneous spatial sovereignties or through the hierarchizations of identity, community and authority that have been constructed within such spatial sovereignties. Moreover, political life is increasingly characterized by other sorts of answers to questions about location. Events articulated in relation to a site identified as Clayoquot Sound are difficult to analyze as if they were happening *in* Clayoquot Sound, or *in* British Columbia, or *in* Canada. They are interesting both because the limits of the representational model are fairly obvious to almost all the important actors and because it is a site at which politics came to be articulated in large part specifically as struggles over very different answers to the question of where it is, and thus over what politics must be.

Clayoquot Sound as Political Space

There are other ways of responding to questions about the location of Clayoquot Sound that are perhaps just as obvious, just as much a part of contemporary forms of common sense, but that are usually framed as less important, less necessary, less real than the grids of representation on which we judge the victories and defeats of political life. These other responses conjure up somewhat different claims about political possibilities.

One might start with the usual conventions of radical alterity, or "otherness," as they play out in that part of the world and suggest that Clayoquot Sound ought to be understood as part of a place, or territory, or land associated with the Nuu-chah-nulth people. In this context, both an account of location by geometrical coordinates and an account of "nature," of land, or territory, or property dependent on a prior account of abstract homogeneous space are immediately suspect. The projections of early-modern accounts of subjectivity onto the "state of nature" in "the Americas" still have profound effects. However else one tries to understand the complexities and diversities of "indigenous peoples" or "First Nations," it is difficult to avoid the double concern with often very basic struggles for physical and collective survival and sophisticated readings of the need to engage with prevailing political authorities by resisting the rules of engagement. The long-standing struggles over "land claims" have been central here in relation to what it means to refer to "land" and what it means to stake a "claim." At which point, we encounter vast libraries on the politics of cultural imperialism/relativism/ethnocentrism, and the centrality of ongoing contestations about treaties (or their absence) and territorial jurisdictions grounded in competing accounts of the relationship between "nature" and political legitimacy.

Not surprisingly, this competition has generally been resolved on terms set by the authority of a sovereign representation in homogeneous space, by an abstract law that decides the possibility of all exceptions on terms set by itself. Hence the primarily legal procedures through which contestations are enabled, and the familiar option of affirming the rules of inclusion and scientific rationality, for example, or adopting the status of a radically other. Still, this alternative account of location, and the alternative accounts of the relationship between "nature" and political authority, have clearly been of tremendous importance in this context.

It has been important not least because the Nuu-chah-nulth are not alone. They express accounts of nature and legitimate authority that find resonance, although not necessarily complete agreement, among many other peoples, not least among other indigenous peoples elsewhere in British Columbia. Thus, on the one hand, to start thinking about where Clayoquot Sound is in terms of the Nuu-chah-nulth people is to remember other historical accounts of nature, place, land, ownership, tradition, and value; but, on the other, it is also to start thinking about largely unheralded connections through which various peoples in similar situations have sustained networks of information, exchange, and solidarity that do not quite mesh with any immediate experience of small villages out in the back of beyond.

Another line of analysis would suggest that Clayoquot Sound has to be understood as a specific site in the contemporary global circuits of capital. It is in this context that we see a focus on the forestry companies en-

gaged in stripping the forestry cover as internationally or globally organized practices, subject to globally organized commodity prices and mobi-
lizing globally organized capacities to discipline provincially organized
labor forces and institutions of political authority. Here nature comes to be
understood primarily in terms of a particular kind of abstract and homogeneous spatiality, namely, as property and as commodity amenable to exchange on a world market.

Given the historical experience of an industry rooted in nineteenth-
century forms of commodity extraction married to modern cutting techniques that can do to trees what the modern machinery of war did to sol-
diers in the Somme, a marriage organized primarily for the short term
profit of distant shareholders, it is easy to be persuaded of the invincibility
of Goliath. This is one of the reasons why it is so pointless to examine events
in Clayoquot Sound as some form of local or provincial politics, rather than
as a site of international relations or global politics. But although the imagery of Goliath encourages a monolithic and determinist reading of the
impact of the global on the local, the big on the small, it is also possible to
engage with a much more complex and more open field of contestation.

From one direction, for example, we can see attempts to construct an
alternative account of the potentials of Clayoquot Sound in relation to the
circuits of global capital as a site for a globally organized but "locally controlled" ecotourism. Even as a commodity, a tree, one might say, is not a
tree. As the old neo-Kantian philosophers would say, a tree can be viewed in
the categories of the physicist, the chemist, the painter, and the carpenter.
As the contemporary entrepreneur would say, there is more than one way
to boost the bottom line. In both cases, we are faced with conflicts over
which perspective, which source of value, has priority. These conflicts can
be read in terms of competing interests. Port Alberni might change its allegiance from pulp mill to retirees. The ecotourists and storm watchers will
berate the lunacy of towns that strip-mine their best views. But in the process, the meaning of "nature" will also be rescripted, the value of the commodity, or resource, will also be contested and revised.

Consequently, and from another direction, we can also identify some
of the key strategic decisions made by apparently small and weak forms of
activism, of social movements that by rights stood little chance of making
any kind of voice heard in the channels sanctioned by a politics of representation in Victoria or a global political economy of resource extraction. These
decisions were predicated on the simple observation that Clayoquot Sound
was in part to be found in the global markets in which its products were
being taken: hence the international campaign, as well as the development

of networks of relations among environmental activists in many other supposedly local places. Here "nature" becomes an extraordinarily mobile political resource, capable of tactical rearticulations, and always subject to counter-rearticulations, in the struggle to constitute trees as raw material, as tourist destination, as wilderness, as Mother Earth, as, indeed, natural.

References to globalization, of course, invoke claims not only about transformations in contemporary economic life, but also claims about the globe or the planet or the human species as somehow capable of being grasped as a single entity. Thus, a further alternative answer to questions about location would be to situate Clayoquot Sound as a specific site on the globe or planet or a specific part of some community that is envisaged as encompassing humanity as such.

At this point we run into some of the most stressful contradictions of modern political discourse; for there is no modern account of politics that might enable claims to be able to represent the globe or the planet or humanity as such, popular readings of the United Nations notwithstanding. Insofar as there is a political system on a planetary or global scale, it is a system of spatial fragmentations, of sovereign jurisdictions that might be able to sustain forms of cooperation and accommodation but ultimately privilege aspirations for autonomy over those for human or planetary or global solidarity. Hence all the usual complaints about the difficulty of responding to environmental and ecological problems in a world of divided jurisdictions.

Moreover, if it is the case, as it seems to be, that some forms of political community and governance are emerging so as to respond to, say, ecological disruptions that demand some kind of global/planetary/human response, the political character of these forms of community and governance is not entirely clear. We may refer to the emergence of international "regimes" on this and that, or refer to Greenpeace as a "transnational social movement," or speak of the development of something labeled a "global civil society" that is not always quite so civil, but it remains unclear how these phenomena fit into a conventional account of legitimate authority within sovereign states. Terms such as *regimes, transnational social movement,* and *global civil society* are aspects of a widespread fudging of political categories, a widespread sense that these terms refer to something important yet refer neither to a world of simple territorial sovereignties nor to a world that can be spoken of as in any way a political unity. It is clear, however, that the widespread sense that these terms refer to something important is at odds with the demands of a politics of representation strung between a clearly bounded and homogeneous space guaranteeing equality under the law and a single center of authority in Victoria. Contemporary forms of governance have far outstripped contemporary institutions of democratic representation.

Recent events in Clayoquot Sound have indeed been enabled and consciously articulated in relation to some or another version of this account of where Clayoquot is located. Much of the animating force of environmental protest comes from a deep sense of the ecological integrity of the planetary biosphere, of the need to privilege the long-term sustainability of a global habitat, of the dangers of political fragmentation in a world of ecological interdependences and fragilities. Many and often competing narratives converge here, often in ways that sustain cultural and spiritual attachments that mesh only at odd tangents with the rationalities of modern life, and certainly with accounts of nature and territory as representable in abstract homogeneous space. In any case, it is clear that Clayoquot Sound is indeed situated among networks of international regimes, transnational social movements, and global civil society, whatever such terms are taken to describe, though none of these terms really begins to get a grip on the puzzling phenomena they seek to name.

There are probably other answers to questions about location. It could also be said, for example, that Clayoquot Sound is situated everywhere and yet nowhere; that is, that what is most important about it is that it is merely one site among many similar sites and thus a place in which precedents can be established or challenged. It is not that any of these answers are in some way intrinsically correct. They all provide some degree of contextualization for specific events and contestations, but none has either the aesthetic clarity and elegance or the broad cultural legitimacy of the strange abstractions that sustain our primary accounts of big and small, global and local, here and there, real and ephemeral. In some ways, in fact, the very metaphor of a ground, of a foundation, expresses a radical instability. All these other accounts get at aspects of the ways in which Clayoquot Sound is situated in modern political discourse, and they do so by resisting the assumption that we can somehow go looking for politics in Clayoquot Sound. Moreover, all these other accounts carry with them different accounts of what and where Clayoquot Sound is to be situated in relation to, what one might mean by the "nature" that is at the center of political dispute, what political community or identity might be invoked as the source of legitimate authority, what kinds of judgment might be appropriate in any given situation, and so on. There is literally no ground, no homogeneous and neutral space, on which all practices can be judged from some sovereign center, although, of course, the claim that there is constitutes one of the primary practices at play in this context.

Given the plurality of answers to what can seem like a very simple, and indeed politically irrelevant, question, one would expect there to be a politics at play in the practices through which some answers to this question are privileged over others, and through which the very question is made to seem politically irrelevant. These contested accounts of location work to destabilize or restabilize accounts of the supposedly proper place of "the local"; the structures of hierarchical authority vested in sovereigntist and federalist mediations of the local and the global, or small and large; the necessary mediation of all claims to difference by an ultimately sovereign center; the proper articulation of all claims to community and identity within the spaces of sovereign citizenship; and the proper place of nature and territoriality in modern political life as that which can be described and represented through an abstract homogeneous space set among other such spaces in a horizontal system of sovereign jurisdictions. In this sense, Clayoquot Sound resembles many other places and sites of contemporary politics, but not because a David beat a Goliath, or because, despite a few minor setbacks, Goliath eventually clawed back all his old privileges, though both of these narratives too have their place. Clayoquot Sound is interesting because it is just an ordinary, and sometimes extraordinary, site at which it is impossible to act as if here is here and there is there, local is small and global is big, citizens are in and enemies are out. What this means for the multiple sites of legitimate authority that so clearly exceed the tidy jurisdictions preferred by those who prefer to keep their stories simple, their ministry of forests omnipotent, and our democratic options massively constrained is still to be negotiated. Such negotiations, and renegotiations, in many different places, constitute the most important political practices of our times.

Notes

1. The texts I have found most useful, even though my argument tends to run against the grain of the account of political life they express, have been less about Clayoquot Sound specifically than about attempts to read the broad historical-structural context of resource exploitation and forestry policy formation in British Columbia more generally; see especially Marchak 1983 and Wilson 1998.

2. For doubts about the European case, see Walker 2000, Jönsson, Tägil, and Törnqvist 2000, and Van Ham 2001. The notion that it is possible to understand the United States as just another containerized state in a system of equal and autonomous states is obviously absurd, though the assumption of this notion in the standard discourses about "American politics," "comparative politics," and debates about, say, "humanitarian intervention" or "national security" remains instructive.

3. This theme is developed in Walker 1993.

4. The corporate slogan designating tree plantations in which scarcely anything can live.

5. Hence the popular use of such concepts as "glocalization" (see Robertson

1995), but also the difficulty of making sense of claims about globalization in political terms.

Works Cited

Adams, Paul C., Steven Hoelscher, and Karen Till, eds. 2001. *Textures of Place: Exploring Humanist Geographies.* Minneapolis: University of Minnesota Press.

Bachelard, Gaston. 1965. *The Poetics of Space.* Boston: Beacon Press.

Casey, Edward S. 1997. *The Fate of Place: A Philosophical History.* Berkeley: University of California Press.

Clifford, James. 1997. "Fort Ross Meditations." In *Routes: Travel and Translation in the Late Twentieth Century.* Cambridge: Harvard University Press. 299–347.

Friedland, Roger, and Diedre Boden, eds. 1994. *NowHere: Space, Time and Modernity.* Berkeley: University of California Press.

Glacken, Clarence. 1967. *Traces on the Rhodian Shore: Nature and Culture in Western Thought from Ancient Times to the End of the Eighteenth Century.* Berkeley and Los Angeles: University of California Press.

Harvey, David. 2000. *Spaces of Hope.* Berkeley: University of California Press.

Hobbes, Thomas. 1991 [1651]. *Leviathan.* Ed. Richard Tuck. Cambridge: Cambridge University Press.

Isin, Engin, ed. 2000. *Democracy, Citizenship and the Global City.* London: Routledge.

Jammer, Max. 1954. *Concepts of Space: The History of Theories of Space in Physics.* Cambridge: Harvard University Press.

Jönsson, Christer, Sven Tägil, and Gunnar Törnqvist. 2000. *Organizing European Space.* London: Sage.

Kern, Stephen. 1983. *The Culture of Time and Space, 1880–1918.* Cambridge: Harvard University Press.

Koyré, Alexandre. 1957. *From the Closed World to the Infinite Universe.* Baltimore: Johns Hopkins University Press.

Lefebvre, Henri. 1991. *The Production of Space.* Oxford: Blackwell.

Locke, John. 1988 [1689]. *Second Treatise on Government.* Ed. Peter Laslett. Cambridge: Cambridge University Press.

Magnusson, Warren. 1996. *The Search for Political Space: Globalization, Social Movements, and the Urban Political Experience.* Toronto: University of Toronto Press.

Magnusson, Warren, William K. Carroll, Charles Doyle, Monika Langer, and R. B. J. Walker, eds. 1984. *The New Reality: The Politics of Restraint in British Columbia.* Vancouver: New Star Books.

Marchak, M. Patricia. 1983. *Green Gold: The Forestry Industry in British Columbia.* Vancouver: University of British Columbia Press.

Robertson, Roland. 1995. "Glocalization: Time—Space and Homogeneity—Heterogeneity." In *Global Modernities,* ed. Mike Featherstone, Scott Lash, and Roland Robertson. London: Sage. 25–44.

Strikkers, Kenneth W. 1996. "Ambivalences of Modernity: The Great Escape from Place into Space." *International Studies in Philosophy* 28:1: 87–101.

Tuan, Yi-Fu. 1977. *Space and Place: The Perspective of Experience.* Minneapolis: University of Minnesota Press.

Van Ham, Peter. 2001. *European Integration and the Postmodern Condition: Governance, Democracy, Identity.* London: Routledge.

Walker, R. B. J. 1988. *One World, Many Worlds.* Boulder, Colo.: Lynne Rienner.

————. 1993. *Inside/Outside: International Relations as Political Theory.* Cambridge: Cambridge University Press.

————. 2000. "Europe Is Not Where It Is Supposed to Be." In *International Relations and the Politics of European Integration,* ed. Morten Kelstrup and Michael Williams. London: Routledge. 14–32.

Wilson, R. Jeremy. 1998. *Talk and Log: Wilderness Politics in British Columbia.* Vancouver: University of British Columbia Press.

Clayoquot and the Politics Beyond

Warren Magnusson and Karena Shaw

We began this book with a series of claims: that we could read the global *through* the local at Clayoquot, that such a reading would disrupt assumptions about the political, and that the method we have used could be applied productively to other sites. Have we proven any of these claims? Readers will judge.

In this Conclusion, we propose to do two things. The first is to tease out political conclusions from the ideas that run through our contributors' essays. Academics are often shy about saying what they mean politically. Not so Michael M'Gonigle, who brings an activist's sensibility to his academic work. We begin our discussion with his essay, because he comes closest to proffering a definite *solution* to the issues that have arisen at Clayoquot. Our other contributors take us further from the problem of solutions, in that they focus on the conditions of possibility for creative politics. This focus is not always explicit, but it is nonetheless at the center of everyone's thoughts. We move from Luke, Sandilands, Zukin, Kuehls, Umeek, and Shaw to Chaloupka and Walker, the latter two of whom give particular attention to the question of how to conceptualize or theorize the political. Most political analysis focuses on two questions: "How do we explain this?" and "What is the solution?" All of our contributors imply that there are other questions to be asked, but the language of politics seems to fail us when we try to put those questions clearly.

That dilemma, among others, forces the discussion back to us, the editors, and to you, the readers. In the second part of this Conclusion, we try to explain what we, the editors, think has been shown in this book and through the Clayoquot Project. Our conclusions are not definitive, nor could they be. We cannot say what Clayoquot is—still less, what the politics

of the present must be—without defeating our own purpose. The Clayoquot Project is open-ended, and the project itself is only one part of a larger
effort in which we and others are engaged. *The Clayoquot Documents* and
The Clayoquot Archive offer readers the means to carry their own investigations further. As readers who go to our Web site will see, the documents raise
many issues that have scarcely been discussed in this book. Clayoquot,
even its documentary form, is a protean site, and we do not pretend to have
exhausted it. Our intention has been to draw attention to this site, to smooth
the way for further investigations, and to suggest that others might identify
similarly interesting sites through which we all might investigate the politics of the present. Obviously, we must investigate the political through
many sites, and it would be wrong to become fixated on Clayoquot. Nevertheless, as we shall argue, Clayoquot is a better point of entry than most—
perhaps better than a center of government or a site of violence. Clayoquot
is one of those places where global politics appears in a way that enables
us to see new possibilities and new problems. We will try to explain how
that is.

We have presented this book as a work of political theory, but we acknowledged at the outset that few theorists would be prepared to accept it
as such. We are trying to situate ourselves on the ground and in the mode
that good political theory requires, but this is at some distance from the
place where most theorists are comfortable. Two recent books illustrate the
problem we are addressing. The first is Naomi Klein's *No Logo: Taking Aim
at the Brand Bullies* (2000) and the second is the discussion between Judith
Butler, Ernesto Laclau, and Slavoj Žižek under the title *Contingency, Hegemony, Universality* (2000). In a way, these books engage a similar problematic, but they do so in very different terms. Klein offers a young radical
journalist's account of the world as it now appears—a world literally
"branded" by corporate capital—and explains how a new politics has been
taking shape in response to it. Butler, Laclau, and Žižek, on the other
hand, attempt to make sense of the new politics theoretically: to give a post-
Marxist, post-Gramscian, post-Lacanian, post-"post" account that somehow redeems what is best in the progressive thought and practice of the
twentieth century and sets us up to think about the politics of the future.
Each of these books is valuable, taken on its own terms; however, if high
theory and practical observation fed off one another as they should, the
discussion between Butler, Laclau, and Žižek would have been illuminated
by observations from reporters such as Klein, and Klein herself would have
deployed insights from Butler, Laclau, and Žižek to make sense of what
she was seeing. Instead, there is a disjuncture. The theorists talk mainly

about each other's ideas, and rarely mention anything other than the most difficult theoretical texts. For her part, Klein disdains "postmodern" theory and relies mostly on the observations of other journalists to confirm her own readings of the world. This parting of the ways between theorists and others (both observers and activists) is more typical than not. Usually the theorists are blamed for failing to make themselves clear and also for failing to engage with the right issues, the issues of obvious practical importance. The theorists' response—that they are being as clear as they can be, given the difficulty of the matters they are trying to explain, and that the question of what is of practical importance is precisely the issue, and an immensely difficult one at that—never quite satisfies anyone but the theorists themselves. Is there no middle ground, no way of bringing "high theory" and practical observation into a productive relation?

The problem is not that intelligent journalists find the theory too difficult to read. They may complain about bad writing and obscure jargon, but the ultimate source of their impatience is different. What especially bothers them (and others) is that theorists seem to get most excited—seem to be most convinced of their own insight—when they focus on matters that other people think are trivial. The more trivial the matter, the grander the theory. Ironically, the theorists are following the example of journalists in this regard. The standard journalistic technique is to pick a person or an event or a situation and use it to exemplify a wider reality. Many theorists—especially the ones the journalists find obscure—do the same thing. Michel Foucault— arguably the most influential theorist of the late twentieth century—was a master of this technique. Although theorists have often focused on Foucault's general formulations, these formulations were secondary to his own scholarly work, which involved the accumulation of vivid examples that he read against the grain of standard historiography. The exemplars and the dissident readings were deployed against the established accounts of reality and more particularly against the established accounts of politics. To read Foucault sympathetically is to discover a range of problems and a range of practices that are obviously political, but that lie outside the established political domain. Similar discoveries await the readers of other poststructuralist theorists. The difficulty is that the discoveries are proliferative. Nothing in particular demands our attention, except the theory itself. Hence, theory for the sake of theory—and journalism for the sake of journalism.

Between theory and journalism is politics: politics as it has been taken to be and politics as we wish it were. The proliferation of examples in the writings of theorists and journalists is incited by dissatisfaction: in particular, by dissatisfaction with standard accounts of serious politics. The examples are meant to show that there is something serious *here,* in a site at the margins of serious politics. The implication is that a *more* serious politics would engage with this site (as well as with others), and generate new possibilities. Unfortunately, we have only one account of what a serious politics would look like, an account that presupposes the centricity of the modern territorial state. We all know that such an account is partial at best, but no one really understands how a different account might read. Hence, the squabblings that conceal a shared ignorance.

Our strategy here has been to start from a site that journalists and activists (or at least some journalists and activists: see, for example, Klein 2000, 152–56) think is important: a place where *they* think that the new politics is happening. Rather than abandon the site for our own speculations, we have tried to return to it again and again, in the hope of seeing the shape of the new/old politics and assessing its possibilities. The fact that the site is not one that we would have chosen if we had begun from the standard account of serious politics is an important advantage. As we shall argue in the last section, it is also helpful that the site is not in Europe, not in the United States, and not in the Third World. Clayoquot Sound is an oddly interesting place, a place from which we can think together productively about politics.

Solutions and Problems

A number of important challenges are implicit in the way that our contributors have approached the politics of Clayoquot. All the contributors reject the idea that Clayoquot is a place to be *managed,* by putting appropriate institutions and practices in place. The management focus of the environmental policy literature—and even of the environmental philosophy literature—is startling and disturbing. That the issue is not one of management or ethics ought to be clear to anyone who reads this book. Politics is the central problem, and politics can never be regulated by managerial routines and ethical maxims. Politics is what generates and hence inevitably exceeds both the routines and the maxims. Politics also exceeds and structures the *science* that is brought to bear in these situations. People normally link science to technique and hence to management, but our contributors make clear that science is always already politicized. At Clayoquot that politicization is more than usually apparent. So too is the politicization of *nature, economy,* and *culture.* These are not givens, not structures that are prior to politics. They are better understood as effects of political struggle. Our contributors help to make the character of that struggle apparent. They also show us that the *space and time* of the political is different from what is usually assumed: not confined to or even focused on the state as such, and certainly not bounded within territories designated by the state system. Nor is the *narrative* of modernity (in any of its guises) adequate to account for the political stakes at Clayoquot. The movements in and out of the site defy singular description, and the politics of the site is at least in part about the way it is to be represented. All this is indicated, more or less clearly, in our contributors' essays, and yet of course there are fruitful disagreements and differences of approach.

M'Gonigle poses the problem of Clayoquot with particular force:

> With so much at stake, it is easy to appreciate why the conflict at Clayoquot Sound, or other similar conflicts to date, remains un-solvable. The problems are structural in nature, and the solutions are transformative in design.

As he suggests, the whole system—political, cultural, economic, social—is at stake at Clayoquot. The Biosphere Agreement and the memorandum of understanding (MOU) may gesture—but only gesture—toward a few of the required changes. M'Gonigle describes the root problem in terms of a ten-sion between "centrist" and "territorialist" modes of organization. As he sees it, the existing system is overwhelmingly centrist. The system depends on unsustainable flows of natural and other resources. He calls for "de-veloping sustainability": that is, for a process of "social self-constitution" attuned to "ecosystem-based management." The idea is that people in par-ticular territories—territories conceived as ecosystems—should reclaim control over their own destinies. This is not just a matter of passing a few laws or adopting some new consumer practices. At stake is the very basis of social, cultural, economic, and political life. People have to reform things in the most fundamental way, so that they begin to live within the limits of their local ecosystem, and produce goods and services that do not depend on flows from elsewhere. This will only be possible if people regain control over their own territories, and they will not strive for this if they do not have a sense of local community and an understanding of their local environ-ment. Rootedness, in both the natural environment and the local commu-nity, is evidently essential for effective resistance to the centrist practices that now tend to constitute people in ways that alienate them not only from their natural environments, but also from their own local communities. From M'Gonigle's perspective, the centralized state and the globalized market economy are dimensions of the same thing: a system that must be counterbalanced, if not overcome, by territorially rooted communities.

M'Gonigle's framing of the problem, in terms of the tension between center and territory, resonates with many ideas in modern critical thought.

One is reminded of Rousseau's vision of popular sovereignty, Tocqueville's discussion of the American town meetings, and Mill's insistence on the need for local self-government. One thinks of the practices of the ancient Athenian democracy, the early Roman republic, the medieval Italian city-states, and the rural cantons of Switzerland. One remembers the Paris Commune and the soviets of revolutionary Petersburg. One recalls Kropotkin and the earlier utopian socialists who tried to create self-governing communities on new models. One thinks of the guild socialists and anarcho-syndicalists who developed visions of communal self-government that complemented their ideas about industrial democracy. One remembers Murray Bookchin and his lifelong advocacy of "municipalist" alternatives to centralized forms of government and economy. One even thinks of Marx, who spoke famously of a communist future that "makes it possible for me to do one thing today and another tomorrow, to hunt in the morning, fish in the afternoon, rear cattle in the evening, criticize after dinner, just as I have a mind, without ever becoming hunter, fisherman, cowherd, or critic" (McLellan 1977, 169). A vision of an egalitarian, democratic, self-governing, freedom-loving, *naturalistic* community runs through much of the critical commentary that has developed in concert with modernity. The economic practices of which M'Gonigle speaks—"diversifying the economy into non-consumptive uses of the environment (e.g., ecotourism), and developing new forest industries (in local woodlots, community-forestry initiatives, and value-added secondary manufacturing),"—seem highly sensible in terms of such a vision, as do ideas about ecosystem-based management, developing sustainability, community economic development, local self-government, participatory democracy, and so on.

The difficulty, as always, is one of agency. Who is to bring about these reforms, and how? M'Gonigle's own analysis turns on the claim that the system is so deeply entrenched that revolutionary change is required. Of course, he speaks of "transformation" rather than revolution, and he emphasizes that the changes must be gradual. (This is the twenty-first century, after all!) Nevertheless, he is talking about a process that Marxists in the 1970s called "revolutionary reformism": reforms that would generate their own momentum and ultimately produce the necessary social transformation in a sort of peaceful upheaval. (Of course, it was the neoconservatives and neoliberals who actually succeeded in effecting such a transformation in the 1980s—a change that went in the opposite direction from the one Marxist "revolutionary reformers" had hoped for.) M'Gonigle's vision is inspired by a different sensibility: communitarian, localist, democratic, environmentally sensitive. Communities are to be encouraged to "opt in" to a new system of ecosystem-based management. As the new system proves itself in particular areas, other communities will be encouraged to follow. But the problem is how to get things started. M'Gonigle refers to legislative changes that the defeated government of "the left" in the province was not willing to make. It is unlikely that the right-wing Liberals, who have succeeded the NDP in power, will be any more enthusiastic. So, how is the transformational process to start, if the means of initiation are denied to local communities, and those communities remain within the old "centrist" structures?

At present, as Timothy Luke points out, "each and every community must find a niche in one or many of the commodity chains linking localities, regions, and nations to every other marketplace around the world." Opting out—let alone challenging the whole economic system—is very difficult, if not impossible. Luke draws our attention to the ways in which environmentalism itself fits into strategies for global capitalist development. In the Clayoquot region, Native and environmental protests attracted attention to the area, and ultimately enhanced its allure as a tourist or retirement destination. This was consistent with a global/local shift from "extractive" to "attractive" modes of economic development. What had formerly been resources to be extracted—timber and salmon and shellfish—now appeared as parts of an attractive environment to be managed for sale to people wanting particular life experiences. On the new model, the greatest opportunities for profit were in providing simulacral experiences of nature for people who were doing well in the new global economy. The social effects of this are bound to be divisive:

> As Tofino, Ucluelet, and the surrounding countryside are gradually becoming gentrified by members of the new middle class (either as temporary leisure-seeking visitors or as permanent new environment-defending residents) and redeveloped as simulacral sites (whether it is for ecotourism, the nature experience, or other sorts of cultural consumption), one finds the working classes, the poor, or the First Nations being made less welcome, especially if they cling to older extractive types of work that degrade the environment.

Not surprisingly, the Clayoquot region is torn by divisions between those who are benefiting from the new economy and those who are not.

> Workers who held or still hold comparatively high-paying and high-status positions in extractive industry see themselves paying for deindustrializing environmental reforms with their old or existing

jobs. Whatever new jobs are made available in attractive industries are rarely as numerous, well paid, or high status as those tied to extractive industrial work. Historically, these sorts of service-sector jobs went to women, teenagers, First Nations workers, or older people. This psychocultural transition from logger, miner, or mill worker to hotel bartender, whale-watching guide, or ticket taker is a very uneasy economic and social process.

To put it mildly!

The social divisions that Luke mentions were not external to the local community in Clayoquot. They were part of the character of that community. The "actually existing" community does not stand outside the social relations that establish gender hierarchies, put particular nations on top, and make the majority of people into the employees of others. Thus, the problem of liberation is always a matter of changing relations within the community itself, as much as it is of freeing the community from external strictures. As Luke points out, environmentalists are part of a process that advantages some and disadvantages others within the Clayoquot region. It is easy for urban environmentalists to applaud the shift from extractive to attractive development, and to identify themselves with people such as Maureen Fraser and Valerie Langer. Some may notice an empowerment of women—or at least the disempowerment of certain sorts of men. On the other hand, the patterns of class identification between middle-class city dwellers and their peers in outlying regions are all too evident. So, too, is the romanticization of Natives and others who seem to "walk lightly on the earth." Luke's analysis reminds us not only that a progressive politics is bound to be difficult (because the external constraints are not just that: they are also internal divisions), but also that such a politics is always complicit in the structures and relations that it seeks to challenge. Contemporary environmentalism is as much a component of the contemporary economic system (and hence of the social divisions connected with that system) as it is a form of global resistance. Thus, the struggle—whether in M'Gonigle's terms or otherwise—is always compromised.

Catriona Sandilands emphasizes this fact. Sandilands, like M'Gonigle, poses the issues in poignantly personal terms. She focuses attention on the way that Clayoquot Sound has been produced—for her and the rest of us—as a "global tourist destination." Ostensibly anticapitalist struggles turn on representations that actually facilitate particular forms of capitalist economic usage:

> The problem is ... that this representation comes disguised as a liberation; one set of capitalist-embedded (consumer) construc-

tions of nature gets to pass as a freeing of the landscape where another, less romantic (productive) aesthetic is demonized as if it were the only representative of multinational capitalism around. The problem is, then, that the tourist aesthetic appears innocent, and that this innocence passes in many circles as ecocentrism or as environmentalist political success, as a genuinely long-term and sustainable solution for Clayoquot. Rendered innocent, Clayoquot's "success" becomes a foundation-less model to which other communities aspire.

Of course, the model to which she refers is not the same as the one that M'Gonigle is promoting. Rather, it is the model implicit in the "attractive development" strategy to which Luke refers. As Sandilands argues, such attractive development involves the transformation of Clayoquot into a simulacrum, "a copy of a copy that successfully poses as real":

> In tourism, the destination is modeled on a vision of reality that never really existed except in the minds and desires of tourists and promoters. The simulacral destination is not only a fake but, in its ability to pass as reality, covers up the fundamental absence of reality behind it. . . . Far from nature being the site from which simulation begins but at which it also ends, nature has become—especially in its creation as spectacular destination—precisely the simulacrum that hides the possibility of a nontotalized (and potentially democratic) reality in Clayoquot Sound.

If so, the democratic future to which M'Gonigle points is blocked not only by centralized state power and by globalized market relations, but also by the conceptions of nature on which we tend to rely.

According to Sandilands, such conceptions involve a series of erasures: of the work that is involved in constructing the "wilderness" we admire; of the immense, ecologically damaging infrastructure of globalized tourism; and of the hierarchies and exclusions that are involved in giving particular places and particular forms of activity "special status" within a globalized economy. She is particularly concerned about the way that forest workers and Native people are shunted to the side: devalued and even dehumanized by practices that set them outside the frame established by a conception of nature as "wilderness." Although, as she notes, the most sophisticated local activists have attempted to break out of this frame and repose the issues inclusively, there is little doubt that Clayoquot's image as a "pristine wilderness" was used by environmentalists to mobilize support outside the region. Insofar as environmental activism tended to set Clayoquot aside as a special place invested with cultural meanings derived from "nature" or "wilderness," it remained complicit in some of the practices that it sought to overcome.

Sharon Zukin draws our attention to the way in which these practices work at the other end of the commodity chain. New York City is one of the organizational centers of a globalized capitalism; if capitalism had a capital, it would have to be New York. It is here (and in places like it) that another aspect of the "wasting" of the wilderness becomes apparent. Mounds of unwanted material accumulate, and toxic chemicals leach into the air, water, and soil. As Zukin points out, ordinary people are most frightened by the pollution of the urban environment. For the typical inhabitant of the global city, forests are a distant reality to be appreciated on television or perhaps during an occasional holiday visit. The forests are not a daily presence. And yet, there are globalized "cultures of nature" that nonetheless shape forest usage in places such as Clayoquot, places where New Yorkers rarely go. The conflicts to which Sandilands and Luke point—most especially the ones between logging and ecotourism, but also between aquaculture and fishing, whaling and whale watching—are local variants of a global phenomenon, in which different cultures of nature collide. That these various cultures of nature are all mediated by capitalist economic relations seems obvious: the dominant cultures of nature are also cultures of capitalism. That there is more than one culture of nature, of capitalism, and of the global city is of great political significance, however. Environmentalists have been engaged in a global culture war, the object of which is to shift people's attitudes in a fundamental way: to get them to think of the whole earth as their home, to make them conscious of what they consume and what they do with their wastes, and to get them to think critically about the commodity chains on which they depend. Thus, the environmentalist campaign around Clayoquot and other forest sites has been designed to bring the forest home to urbanites. This has led to a subtle but important shift:

> Home suggests both dwelling and nurturing, both stewardship
> and mutual responsibility, and unconditional attachment. When
> North American environmentalists talk about home, they mean
> both a dwelling and a working landscape—an active, dynamically
> changing place that may include both cultivation and use of natu-
> ral resources—both first and second natures. In contrast to a sim-
> plistic view of nature that would exclude human production from
> our understanding of community, the environmentalists' rhetoric
> acknowledges all the cultures and technologies that create a place.
> Like contemporary ideas about cultural difference, which are usu-
> ally associated with a defense of urban life, the rhetoric of home
> accepts the variety, contradictions, and unexpectedness of place.

Efforts to sell Clayoquot to New Yorkers as a threatened wilderness have tended to domesticate the forest in the urban imagination. As such, they have opened the forest up to a different global imaginary, one that allows for normal human activities (such as resource attraction) and that acknowledges the fact that human cultures inevitably shape the places they inhabit (even if the inhabitation is only by wildlife photographers).

If Clayoquot Sound ever was a true wilderness, that was before the Nuu-chah-nulth came there. The Nuu-chah-nulth have lived in the area for thousands of years. Umeek of Ahousaht speaks with particular authority about the place. He is a hereditary chief of the Ahousaht, one of the five tribes of the Nuu-chah-nulth Central Region. Another of his names is E. Richard Atleo. Atleo River runs into Clayoquot Sound. Umeek's traditional rights in relation to that watershed have never been extinguished. Much of the area has been logged without his authority and without the authority of anyone in his family, clan, or tribe. To say that land has been stolen from him and others like him is not to put too fine a point on the matter. Nevertheless, Umeek is less inclined to talk about property rights than about the broader denial of Nuu-chah-nulth culture. As he says, a principle of universal and mutual respect is central to that culture. It is a more encompassing principle than the one that has informed Western humanism, for it extends beyond the merely human to encompass animals and the wider "natural" environment. Umeek illustrates the principle with one of his great-great-grandfather's stories: a story about the origins of the deer. In traditional Nuu-chah-nulth thinking, the deer (like all other animals) was supposed to have been human once. The deer's ancestor was transformed precisely because he resisted change. The story not only suggests that we have to be open to change; it also underscores the fact that all beings have a common origin—not in a cold, external nature, but rather in a common *humanity*:

> Underlying all relationships on earth is the unifying source and demands of the Creator. One of these demands is not to be disrespectful toward any part of creation, because all, in the beginning, were people: *quuʔas.* . . . From an empirical, scientific perspective it would appear that the creation of beautiful deer happened at the expense of a person. However, this appearance is misleading. The *quuʔas* who became a deer did not die but was transformed by the shedding of one "cloak" or "covering" for another. The shedding of a cloak, giving of flesh, is therefore a divine act of transformation, moving in endless cycles from life to life, giving to giving, transformation to transformation, creation to creation, mutual recognition to mutual respect, mutual responsibility to mutual accountability.

To understand one's place in this way is not to claim a special status—on the contrary. It is to suggest that people have to be understood as connected not only with one another, but also with the places where they live and with other beings who have assumed animal form. To dwell in a place is not to dominate it or to exclude everyone else from living in it. It is certainly not to denude the place. It is, however, to establish relations of mutual recognition, mutual respect, mutual responsibility, and mutual accountability— relations very different from the ones that "the King George men" and their successors have demanded.

The Canadian government, as successor to King George, claims sovereignty over the Clayoquot region. Limited aboriginal rights have been recognized within that framework. Recent decisions of the Supreme Court of Canada suggest that a more liberal understanding may be forthcoming, but the Court still refers to "the sovereign will of the community as a whole" as the ultimate arbiter of aboriginal rights. As Umeek remarks:

> The "sovereign will of the community as a whole," in practice, has been the major source of earth's problems with respect to the environment and with respect to the rights of aboriginals. The colonizers and their descendants have still not shown, for the most part, that they are capable of being, and behaving, in a civilized manner with respect to their relationship to the environment and their relationship to aboriginal people.

Thom Kuehls sheds light on this. He points out that the dominant ideology today, the ideology of sovereignty, was historically connected to practices of colonization, practices that were conceived in *agricultural* terms. On this conception, land belonged no one until it had been fenced and tilled in the European manner. Sovereign authority made fencing and tilling possible, and the fencing and tilling made sovereignty legitimate:

> Agriculture, as an enemy of wilderness and a circumstance of sovereignty, establishes set boundaries. Not only does agriculture provide the preconditions for having property in land, it also operates to bring culture and order to the wilderness. The absence of agriculture, however, leaves geographic boundaries indeterminate, if not unrecognizable.

Because the traditional Nuu-chah-nulth way of life did not fit the model of settled agriculture, the Nuu-chah-nulth themselves were regarded as aliens in their own land. They not only were denied sovereignty; they also were denied property. Their rights were regarded as inchoate and, in any case, subordinate to a sovereign authority dedicated to agricultural colonization.

The irony is that in this region (unlike many other parts of North America) the settlers themselves practiced little agriculture. Not only did they leave most of the land uncultivated, they scarcely used it all, except for hunting and fishing. The more recent tree cutting is certainly not "agriculture" in the traditional sense. It might be argued that, by John Locke's standards, most of the Clayoquot region is as little (or as much) anyone's property as it was three hundred years ago.

As Umeek would be quick to remind us, the Nuu-chah-nulth already had their own arrangements in relation to the land, one another, and other beings, long before any European visited the area. Whether these arrangements fit the modern European model of property and sovereignty should scarcely be the determining question. Where there are genuine differences—as there were between King George's men and the Nuu-chah-nulth—the expectations of the one party cannot determine the rights of the other. Even so, the Nuu-chah-nulth are now forced to articulate their understandings within the frame that "the other" has provided. Difficult as this is, it has at least one productive effect: It "bends" the dominant categories. Such bending is quite apparent in the reasoning of the Supreme Court of Canada. It is also apparent in the creative uses of words such as *rights* and *property* by aboriginal leaders. In an earlier draft of his essay, Kuehls noted the paradoxical character of the Nuu-chah-nulth's declaration of a "tribal park" on Meares Island in 1984. A park is normally a *reservation from* normal usage of a portion of the territory that is already under the jurisdiction of a sovereign government. In this case, the park was supposed to be a *reservation for* normal usage on behalf of a people who were contesting a sovereign government's jurisdiction. But, of course, the empire can strike back, not only in its own right, but also through the colonists that it fosters. As Kuehls notes in this volume, MacMillan Bloedel and the other logging companies have tried to buttress their own property claims by refiguring themselves as tree *farmers*. They and the government are pressing the Nuu-chah-nulth to move in the same direction by becoming partners in joint enterprises. Thus, nineteenth-century attempts to force Natives to become agriculturalists are being repeated in a new form.

Gary Shaw reviews the events that positioned the Nuu-chah-nulth as the region's future tree farmers. Crucial to these events was the Clayoquot Sound Scientific Panel, which ostensibly put the Nuu-chah-nulth and others in a relationship of equality. Traditional ecological knowledge and modern science were supposed to have equal status in the Panel's deliberations on matters of general policy and procedure. This parity was to be maintained in subsequent studies of particular issues. In turn, the findings were to guide the decisions of the Clayoquot Sound Central Region Board, which itself would be constituted on the principle of parity. MacMillan Bloedel also offered the Nuu-chah-nulth equal status in the joint venture agreement, an agreement that was designed to facilitate the resumption of logging. Thus, the Nuu-chah-nulth were positioned as "partners" in projects that continued the process of colonization. As Shaw remarks:

> First Nations not only have to talk the talk as colonized subjects, within colonial relations, they also must walk the walk; that is, they must wear the "First Nations" identity created for them in colonialism. However, colonists have shape-shifted out of their complicity in this relationship. Colonists get to be citizens—stakeholders, scientists, corporate executives, environmentalists, loggers, bureaucrats. . . . [Thus,] the theft vanishes; the thief shape-shifts from colonizer to citizen.

This is not to say that the colonizers were unbent. On the contrary, moves to grant "equal status" to traditional ecological knowledge or to First Nations representatives had a destabilizing effect on the authorities that made these concessions. The authorities were particularly fearful of any alliance between First Nations and scientists who might be open to their perspectives. The point was not to displace established ways of doing things, but rather to incorporate Nuu-chah-nulth understandings into those established ways. The process was inevitably unsettling.

It is not the traditionalism of the Nuu-chah-nulth that unsettles the colonial authorities. Traditionalism can be contained. It can be put on a reserve, and offered as a tourist spectacle. It need not interfere with larger operations. Much more threatening is the *modernity* of the Nuu-chah-nulth: the Nuu-chah-nulth's capacity to articulate a modern vision of their own place and their own lives that actually connects with other such visions, and so forms part of a global cultural imaginary. This is the danger or promise implicit in the thought that traditional ecological knowledge and modern science are actually complementary. Equally dangerous or promising is the idea that colonists can become Natives, rather than the other way around, or that the locality can actually be a community of nations, or that global connectedness is implicit in the specific character of any place. Shaw points us to the figure of James Darling, because Darling is a scientist who has "gone native": Darling has done so simply by embracing the idea that the science of a region should be based on long-term study of the area. From this perspective, general understanding necessarily depends on local knowledge, and local knowledge necessarily has its roots in what the Natives understand. To the extent that the Nuu-chah-nulth can be walled off and confined to their own little patch of land, the challenge implicit in their way of thinking can be contained. But, to the extent that their way of thinking connects with others locally and globally, the challenge that it poses is profound.

This is the challenge that William Chaloupka and Rob Walker consider, although in different terms. Chaloupka's focus is on the environmentalists who mounted the blockades in 1993. What intrigues him is the way that the Clayoquot campaign drew the environmentalists into a "strategic" space. In such a space—the space of politics proper?—the "grand gesture, wrapped in moral certainty, self-righteousness, and clarity of purpose," is never sufficient. Not only do conditions change; not only does "the enemy" respond by undercutting one's position and establishing a high ground of its own; but the issues at stake are always many-sided, always open to various interpretations, and always available to a compromise to be constructed. The challenge to the strategist is to structure the space available, and to make the best compromises possible. Mere moralism is self-defeating. As Chaloupka says, "moral power . . . is not 'possessed' or owned on the basis of righteous analysis. That authority has to be created in action." Protest politics always involves an effort to create new authority, but authority comes from action, not from statements of principle. To be effective, action must be strategic:

> When protesters talk to reporters, they are all values, justifications, and pious outrage. This is as it should be; not everyone knows their reasons as well as they do, and this is a way of reaching out. When they go back to camp, however, they talk little of those things, perhaps even instituting rituals so these lofty elements will not be entirely forgotten. In camp, there are strategic decisions to make, not to mention a thousand logistical details to be resolved. How fast to push? How much to demand? Which coalitions to nurture, and which to abandon? How to balance the need for international visibility with the sometimes conflicting need to build a local organization? Who cooks dinner, and who cleans up? What should we do about a disruptive camper? A strategist is unashamed to recognize that such questions lie at the very core of their activity. This is what "think globally, act locally" actually looks like, late at night before the next morning's dawn arrests.

If the Clayoquot protesters were more effective than their counterparts elsewhere, it was because they were less ashamed of the fact that their actions were *political* rather than simply moral. Chaloupka notes how the campaigners kept altering their tactics—here a blockade, there a negotiation, there another spectacle for the global media, here another compromise in a trailer—and kept opening themselves to possible compromises with the loggers, Native people, and the public authorities. This flexibility kept their campaign alive.

To put it otherwise: The leading environmentalists at Clayoquot were not fundamentalists. This made them more than usually dangerous, for they would not sit in their spot and spout righteous slogans. They kept moving, learning, and innovating. As Chaloupka sees it, American environmentalists have too often been locked into their own righteousness. They have been reluctant to recognize that their activity is political, and that politics is always a matter of strategy. By contrast, the Friends of Clayoquot Sound seem to have been prepared to strategize, and hence to accept the political character of their activity. Many local observers would be surprised to hear the Friends being characterized as "flexible": the Friends are supposed to be the fundamentalists. But, a look at recent events seems to confirm Chaloupka's reading. The Friends were not signatories to the 1999 memorandum of understanding between the environmentalists, the Natives, and the main logging company. On the other hand, they were involved in negotiating its terms. They did not sign the agreement because they could not bind their own members (more of an excuse than a reason) and because they wanted to retain their own freedom of action. Nonetheless, they offered enough informal assurances to give the other parties confidence that the agreement could be implemented without interference from the Friends. The Friends thus positioned themselves as a local watchdog, in relation to an agreement that went some way toward their own objectives. Was this not sensible strategically? And, did it not indicate a willingness to deal with the forces at hand?

> Although one might argue that part of the politicization of Clayoquot occurred because of the public challenge to timber extraction posed by (passionate) preservationist ideas of nature, it strikes me that the continual presence of positions that rejected *both* extractive *and* wilderness views was crucial in forcing a more nuanced and reflective stance (however ultimately strategic) from all participants in the conflict. In other words, spaces of discussion and rearticulation were opened by those actors—including some forest workers, some environmentalists, and some members of Nuu-chah-nulth communities—who disrupted the positions laid out in the tension between extractive and attractive possibility. From these "hybrid" positions, the politicization of Clayoquot revealed

and produced multiplicity beyond an entrenched bifurcation laid out in capitalist language; in multiplicity lay the possibility of negotiated shifting that defied, or at least nudged, views of nature that were always already commodified and simulacral.

Sandilands's words, but not much at odds with Chaloupka's.

Walker furthers this analysis by reminding us that the very *location* of Clayoquot is political. Extraordinary force is required to keep Clayoquot where it is supposed to be, in an unquestionably subordinate position within a sovereign state. Global relations—not least the ones implicit in the market economy—keep prying the place loose, and it has to be hammered back in. Local autonomists, environmentalists, Native activists, and dissident scientists all play a part in opening the place up and setting it in motion. The linkages of which Luke and Sandilands warn—ones that enable extractive or attractive development within the framework of a global market economy—are habitually mediated by states. Other ways of making the local global are less familiar and more threatening. This is the hybridity at which Sandilands points, and at which many of the other contributors gesture. As Walker observes,

> the events centered on Clayoquot Sound in the early 1990s involved not only a complex set of challenges to the exploitation of natural resources, but also challenges to the naturalization of political resources enabled by historically and culturally specific accounts of nature. . . . These events are interesting not because they can be claimed as models of success or failure judged according to established criteria of success or failure in political life, but because they suggest that such criteria hardly begin to get at the degree to which these events involved significant renegotiations of what is meant by political life and of success or failure in it.

Hence we are drawn to a strange place: a global locality and local globality, where we must confront the ethics of strategy and the strategy of ethics, the politics of culture and the culture of politics. That is the *there* there, where we posed the problem of agency.

To ask where Clayoquot is, is to ask where politics is. And, to say "where," we must also know when, why, how, and who. In their different ways, our contributors all suggest that to read Clayoquot as a *little* place far *outside* the centers of politics, economy, culture, and society is not only to misinterpret Clayoquot, but—more importantly—to misunderstand politics, economy, society, and culture. We need to approach space, time, and identity differently: to have a different political ontology.

Beyond Clayoquot

We have focused on Clayoquot precisely because it puts the contemporary ontology of the political at issue. That ontology presumes sovereign identities. It takes for granted that people are normally and naturally "individuals" and that "individuals" have to be reduced to order by sovereign authority. "Sovereignty thinking" has many variants, but in all its forms it presents sovereignty as both problem and solution: problem in the sense that sovereign individuals, sovereign states, and indeed sovereign desires are always at odds with one another, always in a form of strife that demands resolution; solution in the sense that sovereignty at some other level—of the individual over his or her desires, of the state over individuals, of global governance over states—appears as the only possible resolution. The problem/solution of sovereignty appears eternal, always there to haunt us. No amount of empirical evidence will make it go away, because this supposed "fact" about the world is not a fact at all: it is as presupposition, a presupposition that enables us to make sense of the world, to identify "facts," to order them in certain ways, to test them, and to orient ourselves accordingly. That the world is a world of sovereign identities is an assumption that we make before we go looking for "facts" or start developing theories that tell us which facts to look for and how to test them.

We have tried to tell the stories of Clayoquot in a way that puts sovereignty thinking at issue—that makes us doubt whether people have singular identities, places have singular locations, problems have singular dimensions, or politics has a singular guise. Clayoquot appeals to us as a site of analysis precisely because it eludes us. We cannot reduce its stories to one or represent "it" (what? the place, the story, the problem, the solution, the politics?) as a singularity. Clayoquot defies and disturbs our own recourse to sovereignty thinking.

One insistent question is, "Why Clayoquot? What's so special about *this* place or *this* set of problems or *this* sequence of events?" (Note the presumption of singularity.) When we try to answer this question, we can only do so by means that trouble the question itself. Let us illustrate this. Writing in a BC context, we are acutely aware that there have been many struggles about forestry in the province, struggles that have pitted environmentalists against logging companies, Natives with and against both, small towns against distant authorities, and so on. Among all these struggles, what makes Clayoquot stand out? Is the selection of Clayoquot purely arbitrary? The only answer that we can give to that question is that what had become a typical struggle in British Columbia (and indeed in other parts of the

Pacific Northwest) changed its dimensions at Clayoquot. Or, the "global" character of these struggles became manifest in ways that had not been so apparent before. That the struggle was in British Columbia, rather than Washington, Oregon, or California, was important, for British Columbia/Canada was too "small," both as a market and as a state to contain the struggle effectively. The environmentalists especially, but also other participants in the struggle, discovered that there was a *political* space other than the space of Canada/British Columbia. They could act (and indeed *had* to act) in that space. What that space was, whether in fact it was a single space or many, was to be discovered. It became clear all round that the political space of the global market (and of the various regions of that market, especially the United States and the European Union) and the political space of the global media (again, regionally articulated) were important—in some ways decisive. Not to be *there* politically was to risk defeat at the hands of one's opponents. Some of the surprise and interest of Clayoquot lies precisely in the apparent effectiveness of the environmentalists (and to a lesser extent Native activists) in operating in these spaces that are evidently "other" than the space of the nation-state. Clayoquot shows us something interesting about the way that these various spaces are configured in relation to one another.

Some would say that the most obvious feature of Clayoquot is that it is so comfortably situated in the First World. Many of the other struggles with superficially similar features (forests at issue, environmental activism, native land claims, etc.) are in what we used to (still?) call the Third World, and many of those struggles have featured a level of violence, environmental degradation, and abuse of human rights not seen at Clayoquot (or elsewhere in the world's richest countries). So, why focus on Clayoquot if we wish to see politics in new ways? Part of the rationale is this: when Westerners write about the Third World, they almost inevitably slide back into a series of familiar assumptions about the savagery and poverty of the world "out there" beyond the "civilized" corner of the world where they (and their readers) live. Conscious as we are of this problem, we are not at all confident that we, our contributors, or our readers are capable of avoiding it altogether. Our strategy has been to focus on a site close to "home" where issues of colonialism and colonial exploitation are nonetheless visible. Clayoquot is such a place, as was revealed by the effects that the colonial past had on the shape of its politics. Much as the struggles at Clayoquot politicized global markets and global media, forcing actors to engage on that terrain, the presence of colonialism politicized spaces of knowledge, history, identity, community, and science, forcing all actors—local residents, environmentalists, logging companies, the provincial government—to engage with the relations of power embedded in these sources of authority. We might have anticipated histories of colonialism to politicize these sources of authority in Africa, India, or other more widely recognized "postcolonial" political spaces. But Canada? The impact of its colonial past on events in Clayoquot surprised not only observers from far away, but the residents of the region itself. The struggles at Clayoquot politicized relationships in the region in ways that could not be understood without reference to and understanding of this past. The region was thus redefined in the minds of inhabitants (as well as observers) as a postcolonial political space. The future of the region will be developed in and through negotiations over what this means.

Moreover, Clayoquot is a place where other issues familiar to readers in the Western world are also apparent: issues arising from the shift toward a postindustrial economy, changes in the relation between urban and rural, changes in assumptions about gender roles and gender identities, challenges to standard scientific method, demands for democratization, and so on. Clayoquot is a little exotic for a reader in New York or London or Frankfurt, but not so exotic that it can be imagined as a place outside what for him or her is a familiar world. The problems and solutions are more or less familiar, the politics of a type that can be related to what is happening at "home." The *there* there is not something that can be so easily shoved aside as a problem for "them," those unfortunate people on the other side of the world who lack "our" advantages. Clayoquot is in Canada, after all, and (as the current prime minister, Jean Chrétien, never ceases to remind Canadian electors) Canada has usually rated first on the United Nations' Human Development Index. If there is any place where things should work out well, it is a place like Clayoquot.

We have tried to show that things have not worked out all that "well" at Clayoquot: that the apparent successes have concealed many failures, that the place remains deeply problematic, that the difficulty of responding well to its challenges is no less than it ever was. In doing so, we have been trying to expose the fact that there is no "sovereign solution" for Clayoquot, or indeed for anywhere else. To return briefly to the environmental campaign, it should be obvious that a shift in the locus of "sovereign resolution" from the Canadian state to the global market or to global public opinion is no victory in itself. Environmentalists and others are wise to recognize that they cannot succeed politically if they confine themselves to state-spaces, but they should be (and usually are) under no illusion that other spaces, such as the market, are configured democratically. If the new politics is a matter of begging at the door of shareholders' meetings or leafleting outside Home Depot or Wal-Mart, so be it; but this is no gain to be welcomed, only a reality to be negotiated. Precisely because Clayoquot is a hopeful sort of place, a place where the new politics (as frequently conceived) has been practiced for some time quite effectively, it may work as a reminder to us that the new politics (if that is what it is) is no easier than the old. If anything, that new politics is more difficult and less promising than what we have come to take for granted.

Since the struggles at Clayoquot hit the headlines in 1993, the forms of politics that Clayoquot seems to represent have become much more widely recognized. This recognition was most obviously expressed in reactions to the "battle in Seattle": the protests against the World Trade Organization (WTO) in December of 1999.[1] (It was something of a comfort to us, as editors, when we noticed how many of the Clayoquot activists were "there" in Seattle, carrying on their struggle in that forum, confirming by their presence a certain lineage between Seattle and Clayoquot, as there was between Clayoquot and the Redwood Summer or Greenham Common.) What was perhaps most notable in debates about the significance of "Seattle," though, was the reproduction of a familiar set of assumptions about the way events there should be understood politically. Either "Seattle" marked a turning point for politics (the emergence of a global civil society capable of contesting such institutions of global governance as the WTO), or it was a "flash in the pan" (only revealing the limitation of political space afforded by the mobile character of these institutions). Either it was a resounding defeat of the creeping authoritarianism of globalization, or it was irrelevant, in the sense that the failure of the WTO negotiations had much more to do with disagreements among governments than with anything that related to the protests in the streets. Either it marked the extension of democracy into the global arena, or it exposed the lack of democracy inherent in social movement activism. Either it revealed the potential of the Internet as a medium through which alliances of "unity without uniformity" might be formed, or it highlighted the long-term unsustainability of such alliances. Either institutions such as the WTO will now move toward greater democratization, or global governance will be only slightly troubled by the protests and retain all its present characteristics. In short, either "Seattle" is the dawn of "new" politics or a variation on the "old"; either the state continues to be the frame for democratic politics or we now have a "global" civil society; either nothing has changed or everything. Occasionally, of course, there have been those who have sought to avoid the absolutes: perhaps there is something new here, but it is at best a tenuous variation on the old, worthy of equal parts celebration and caution.[2]

The question that was rarely posed is the question we sought to raise in relation to Clayoquot: not, is this new politics or is it old, but what is the political here? What does this site—this particular configuration of events, actors, discourses, representations, strategies, identities—enable us to see about the political that we could not see at more familiar sites? What can we tease out from it that might enable us to disrupt the assumptions about the political (including those about novelty and political change) imposed by the ontology of sovereignty? What are the implications of the difference in our question? Consider, for example, how we would misunderstand the politics of Clayoquot if we were to attend to the blockades—their character, participants, "success" or "failure"—as the primary locus of the political in Clayoquot. We would miss the ways in which the struggles at Clayoquot, the very possibilities for its future, were configured not only—or even primarily—through democratic protest against a sovereign authority, but through the constitution of nonterritorial communities, the politicization of consumption, the recognition of complex identities, the development and effects of new economies, the politicization of science, the mobilization of ideologies and imaginaries, the creative deployment of images, the redefinition of political authority, the micropolitics of management discourse, and so on. In retrospect Clayoquot and Seattle may, or may not, come to seem like telling moments in the development of something significantly novel, but it is much more important to engage with them as sites that enable us to explore the complex political practices that shape our possibilities today. Engaged in this way, rather than fixed in assumptions about old and new, winners and losers, local and global, singular event and determinate structure, they might allow us to open up and renegotiate terrains of politics through which identities, communities, possibilities, natures, authorities, economies, "realities," are being produced, reproduced, and lived.

The contributors to this book have sought to produce narratives that disrupt, that politicize, our sense of the political. (Naomi Klein, Judith Butler, Ernesto Laclau, and Slavoj Žižek had similar ambitions.) The challenge we all face is to create and explore lines of connection among our politicizations, to provoke not only new explorations into the character of the political, but more effective engagement with the sites and practices of politics through which future possibilities are being shaped.

We began with a Clayoquot that caught our imagination: a small, dynamic, engaged community seeking to seize some control over its surroundings, its economy, its future. It seemed an ideal that fitted well within a certain democratic imaginary, one that should have found expression through familiar channels of democracy and governance. As we have tried to show, the events that followed were marked by complicated struggles, ones that far exceeded any such understanding of the political. The crucial point is not just that these struggles created a new set of political spaces—as we know, science, economies, communities, identities, representations are always potentially political—but that in these struggles such spaces were politicized, and became explicit terrains through which the communities' futures were negotiated. This conclusion does not sit comfortably with the democratic imaginary that inspired us. This is not necessarily cause for despair, or celebration, but it does highlight the many challenges—theoretical, practical, analytic, administrative—of rethinking the legacies of modern democracy. As seems to be the case in so many other places, responding to these challenges requires a more sustained engagement with the problem of the political.

Notes

1. For some of the grumpier reactions, see Friedman (1999), Melloan (1999), and Wolf (1999).

2. For thoughtful discussion along these lines, see Kaldor et al. (2000).

Works Cited

Butler, Judith, Ernesto Laclau, and Slavoj Žižek. 2000. *Contingency, Hegemony, Universality: Contemporary Dialogues on the Left.* London: Verso.
Friedman, Thomas L. 1999. "Senseless Battle in Seattle." *New York Times,* December 2.
Kaldor, Mary, Jann Aart Scholte, Fred Halliday, and Stephen Gill. 2000. "Seattle: December '99."*Millennium* 29:1: 105–140.
Klein, Naomi. 2000. *No Logo: Taking Aim at the Brand Bullies.* Toronto: Alfred A. Knopf Canada.
McLellan, David, ed. 1977. *Karl Marx: Selected Writings.* Oxford: Oxford University Press.
Melloan, George. 1999. "Welcome to the Seattle World's Fare, circa 1999." *Wall Street Journal,* November 30.
Wolf, Martin. 1999. "WTO: In Defense of Global Capitalism." *Financial Times,* December 8.

Research Guide

The Clayoquot Documents and the Clayoquot Project Web Site

Below are some resources to facilitate research into the events at Clayoquot Sound and beyond. *The Clayoquot Documents* were provided to all of those who attended the International Workshop on the Politics of Clayoquot Sound in May 1997, and thus contain virtually all of the primary documents contributors used to write the essays contained in this book. They are now available in full-text versions on-line at the Clayoquot Project Web site: web.uvic.ca/clayoquot. Volume 3 of *The Clayoquot Documents* (1997–2001) is also on-line there.

In the book, volumes 1 and 2 of the *The Clayoquot Documents* are cited by reference number (e.g., CD II/D/1). The document numbers refer to this Table of Contents. The relevant numbers are at the left-hand margin; so, for example, CD II/D/1 is the "Announcement and Terms of Reference for the Task Force." To read the actual document, please go to the Web site.

Following the Clayoquot Documents Table of Contents is a list of Web Site Addresses. Many of them are sites that we have referred to in the Introduction and in Karena Shaw's essay. There is a more extensive "Web Research Guide," including an annotated list of relevant Web sites, on the Project's Web site. The Guide also includes an index to *The Clayoquot Archive,* a larger collection of documents now in the care of the Clayoquot Biosphere Trust in Tofino, British Columbia.

Clayoquot Documents Table of Contents

Volume 1

I. Introduction
    A. Introduction i
    B. Reader's Guide ii

Web Site Addresses

These addresses were current as of May 25, 2001. Please consult the Clayo-quot Project Web site at web.uvic.ca/clayoquot for updates.

Aquaculture
BC Salmon Farmers' Association www.salmonfarmers.org/
BC Shellfish Growers' Association www.island.net/~bcsga/
Commissioner for Aquaculture Development
www.dfo-mpo.gc.ca/ocad-bcda/

Environmental Organizations
BC Wild www.helix.net/bcwild
Coastal Rainforest Coalition www.coastalrainforest.org
Ecotrust www.ecotrust.org
Forest Action Network www.fanweb.org
Friends of Clayoquot Sound www.ancientrainforest.org
Greenpeace Canada www.greenpeacecanada.org
Greenpeace International www.greenpeace.org/~forests/
Markets Initiative www.oldgrowthfree.com
Natural Resources Defense Council www.nrdc.org
Raincoast Conservation Society www.raincoast.org
Rainforest Action Network www.ran.org
Sierra Club of British Columbia www.sierraclub.ca/bc/
Western Canada Wilderness Committee www.wildernesscommittee.org

First Nations Organizations
Aboriginal Mapping Network www.nativemaps.org/
Assembly of First Nations www.afn.ca/
Central Region Board www.island.net/~crb/index.html
Nuu-chah-nulth Tribal Council www.nuuchahnulth.org/
Union of BC Indian Chiefs www.ubcic.bc.ca/

Forest Industry
Canada's Forest Network www.forest.ca/
Canadian Forest Service www.nrcan.gc.ca/cfs/
Council of Forest Industries www.cofi.org/
Forest Alliance of BC www.forest.org/
Forest Renewal BC www.forestrenewal.bc.ca/
Industrial, Wood and Allied Workers of Canada www.iwa.ca/
International Forest Products www.interfor.com/

Pacific Forestry Centre www.pfc.cfs.nrcan.gc.ca/
Weyerhaeuser www.weyerhaeuser.com/

Government of Canada
Department of Fisheries and Oceans www.dfo-mpo.gc.ca/
Department of Indian and Northern Affairs www.inac.gc.ca
Natural Resources Canada www.nrcan.gc.ca/

Municipal Government
Capital Regional District [Greater Victoria] www.crd.bc.ca/
City of Port Alberni www.city.port-alberni.bc.ca
City of Victoria www.city.victoria.bc.ca/
Coastal Communities Network www.coastalcommunity.bc.ca/
Tofino–Long Beach Chamber of Commerce www.island.net/~tofino/

Provincial Government (British Columbia)
BC Fisheries www.gov.bc.ca/fish/
BC Treaty Commission www.bctreaty.net/
BC Statistics www.bcstats.gov.bc.ca/
Elections BC www.elections.bc.ca/
Ministry of Aboriginal Affairs www.gov.bc.ca/aaf/
Ministry of Agriculture, Food and Fisheries www.gov.bc.ca/agf/
Ministry of Environment, Lands and Parks www.gov.bc.ca/elp/
Ministry of Forestry www.gov.bc.ca/for/
Ministry of Municipal Affairs and Housing www.gov.bc.ca/marh/

Tourism and Parks
Olympic National Park (United States) www.nps.gov/olym/home.htm
Pacific Rim National Park www.harbour.com/parkscan/pacrim/
Pacific Rim Tourist Association www.alberni.net/~pacrimtourist/
Strathcona Provincial Park www.strathconapark.com

Contributors

Umeek of Ahousaht (E. Richard Atleo) is an instructor in the First Nations Studies B.A. program at Malaspina University College, Nanaimo, British Columbia. He was cochair of the Clayoquot Sound Scientific Panel, and he is a hereditary chief of the Nuu-chah-nulth. He is completing a book tentatively titled *Tsawalk: An Indigenous Theory Founded in Nuu-chah-nulth Origin Stories.*

William Chaloupka is professor of political science at Colorado State University. His books include *Everybody Knows: Cynicism in America* and (coedited with Jane Bennett) *In the Nature of Things: Language, Politics, and the Environment,* both published by the University of Minnesota Press. He helped found and is currently coeditor of *Theory and Event,* an international journal of political and cultural theory published on-line by Project Muse and The Johns Hopkins University Press.

Thom Kuehls is associate professor of political science at Weber State University in Ogden, Utah. He is the author of *Beyond Sovereign Territory: The Space of Ecopolitics* (Minnesota, 1996).

Timothy W. Luke is University Distinguished Professor of Political Science at Virginia Polytechnic Institute and State University in Blacksburg, Virginia. He is the author of *Museum Politics: Power Plays at the Exhibition* (Minnesota, 2002), *Capitalism, Democracy, and Ecology: Departing from Marx,* and *Ecocritique: Contesting the Politics of Nature, Economy, and Culture* (Minnesota, 1997).

Warren Magnusson is professor and chair of political science at the University of Victoria in British Columbia. He is a specialist in urban politics and political theory, and his most recent book is *The Search for Political Space: Globalization, Social Movements, and the Urban Political Experience.*

R. Michael M'Gonigle holds the Eco-Research Chair of Environmental Law and Policy in the Faculty of Law and the School of Environmental Studies at the University of Victoria, where he also directs the POLIS project on ecological governance. He is the editor (with Fred Gale) of *Nature, Production, Power: Towards an Ecological Political Economy,* and he has written recently on related topics in journals such as *Ecological Economics* and *Conservation Biology.* A longtime environmental activist, he is a cofounder of Greenpeace International, a founding director of the Sierra Legal Defense Fund, a former chairperson of Greenpeace Canada, and a cofounder of Smart Growth B.C., Forest Futures, and the International Network of Forests and Communities.

Catriona (Cate) Sandilands is associate professor in the Faculty of Environmental Studies at York University in Toronto. Her work focuses on questions of identity, place, and democracy in environmental politics, ranging from lesbian separatist communities to national parks. She is the author of *The Good-Natured Feminist: Ecofeminism and the Quest for Democracy* (Minnesota, 1999).

Gary C. Shaw is professor emeritus of politics and public administration at California State University, Stanislaus. He has been immersed in politics and research in Clayoquot Sound for the past decade and now resides in Tofino, British Columbia.

Karena (Kara) Shaw teaches in the School of Politics, International Relations, and the Environment at Keele University in England. She has written in the areas of indigenous politics, feminist theory and politics, and political theory. She formerly taught at the University of Victoria.

R. B. J. (Rob) Walker has spent two decades at the University of Victoria, teaching political theory and writing about various challenges to the claims of the modern state and the practices of modern sovereignty and subjectivity. He is currently professor of international relations in the School of Politics, International Relations, and the Environment at Keele University in

England. He is also the long-term editor of the journal *Alternatives: Global, Local, Political.*

Sharon Zukin is Broeklundian Professor of Sociology at Brooklyn College and the City University of New York Graduate Center. She is the author of *Loft Living, Landscapes of Power: From Detroit to Disney World* (winner of the C. Wright Mills Award), and *The Cultures of Cities,* and the coeditor, with Michael Sorkin, of *After the World Trade Center: Rethinking New York City.* She often writes about urban changes, the built environment, and cultures of consumption.

Index